PUCCINI

PUCCINI

A Biography by

Howard Greenfeld

G.P. Putnam's Sons
New York

Copyright © 1980 by Howard Greenfeld

Library of Congress Cataloging in Publication Data

Greenfeld, Howard.
    Puccini.

    1. Puccini, Giacomo, 1858–1924.   2.   Composers—Italy—Biography.
ML410.P89G73   782.1′092′4 [B]   79-20455
ISBN 0-399-12551-5

PRINTED IN THE UNITED STATES OF AMERICA

Acknowledgments

Very many people have helped me in the preparation of this book, and I want to thank them all for their cooperation. Before naming individuals, however, I want to express my thanks to the librarians — especially those in Lucca, Florence, Paris, London, and New York — who made my task both easier and more enjoyable than I had anticipated.

Among those individuals in and around Lucca who shared their knowledge of Puccini with me and led me to sources I would have otherwise ignored, I am especially grateful to Professor Felice Del Beccaro, the Countess Maria Bianca Gaddi Pepoli, Francesca Pancaccini, the Count and Countess Minutoli-Tegrimi, Grayce Murabito, Yvonne Davidson, Anna Landi, Michele Wimer, and Dr. Alberto Amoretti. I was able to make use of the letters of Puccini to Alfredo Caselli through the kindness of the granddaughters of Professor Gabriele Briganti, to whom the letters had been given. Lia Pierotti Cei of Milan gave me access to the papers of her father, Gino Marinuzzi, whose biography she is preparing, and Ida Angelucci was of assistance in Rome.

In London, Dame Eva Turner provided me with valuable leads to possible sources for this biography, as did Arthur Boyars. Tamara Gold helped me through the labyrinth of libraries in Paris, and Stella Seidenman and Assia Werfel gave generously of their time in helping me document the composer's last weeks in Brussels. My thanks, too, to Constance Tolkan for obtaining for me material from the Library of Congress in Washington.

In New York, I spent many months at the Library for the Performing Arts, and I am grateful to Jean Bowen for her guidance and to other members of the staff of the Music Division for their assistance. In New York, too, Mrs. John DeWitt Peltz, of the Metropolitan Opera Archives, Barbara A. Bannon, Janet Stayton, and Walter Dusenbery deserve my gratitude. Without the initial encouragement of Claire M. Smith and William Targ, it is unlikely that I would have undertaken this project.

Finally, very special thanks are reserved for my wife, Paola: not only for her unfailing patience and support, but also for her skills as a researcher and translator.

For Paola, with love

Contents

Introduction

My initial interest in Puccini's life was the result of an enormous enthusiasm for his work. The first performance of a Puccini opera I attended was a Metropolitan Opera *Tosca* many years ago; the cast included Grace Moore, Jussi Bjoerling, and Lawrence Tibbett. It was a memorable evening for me. Since that time I have listened to the composer's operas whenever and wherever possible — in New York and Milan and London and Paris, and even in Mexico City and in Budapest — and I have never tired of them.

When, several years ago, I moved to a small village in Italy just a few miles from the city in which the composer was born and brought up (Lucca) and a few miles from the village he called his home (Torre del Lago), I decided to find out all I could about the man whose music had given me so much pleasure. It was a fascinating and ultimately rewarding task. Pieve di Camaiore, the village in which I lived, is in the heart of what might be called Puccini country. Each town has its memories of the composer, whether it be Celle, from which his ancestors came, or the slightly larger hill town of Bargecchia, where he traveled to study the sounds of the church bells which he would use in the *Te Deum* of *Tosca*.

What started as a personal search for the understanding of the man in relation to his music and his world soon became something far more serious. The more I observed, the more people I spoke to, the more interested I became in writing a biography of Puccini. And the more I studied the books that had already been written about the composer, the more I realized that there was a need for a new biography of one of the most popular of all composers.

Given his enormous popularity, during his lifetime and since his death, Giacomo Puccini has been the subject of surprisingly few serious biographies. One reason might be that he has always been more popular with the public than with scholars and musicologists, and it is the latter who write books. Another is that many vital sources for a biography have not come to light until fairly recently, most of them within the past decade.

The first books about Puccini appeared, in Italian, in the years following his death in 1924. These books by his friends Fraccaroli, Marotti, and Adami are little more than charming personal memoirs, colored more by affection than by a search for the truth. The first serious biography of the composer, written in English by George R. Marek, was published in 1951. It is a lively, readable book, important because it contains many previously unpublished letters by Puccini, but it is now out of date since it includes none of the vast amount of information which has been made available in the almost thirty years since its publication.

In 1958, with the celebration of the centenary of Puccini's birth, two important volumes were published. One was written in Italian by Claudio Sartori and has never been translated into English. It is an interesting and intelligent work, but it is a study of the composer from one well-informed man's point of view and does not pretend to be a complete biography. The other book, written in English, is Mosco Carner's *Puccini*, which, since its publication, has been considered the definitive biography of the composer. It is not that. Not as colorful or lively as Marek's book, it is nonetheless the result of serious research, but it is also dated since it includes none of the new material (in spite of a superficially revised version published in 1974) that has come to light since its publication. In addition, Dr. Carner's book contains a number of mistranslations from the Italian, and his excessively Freudian interpretation of the composer's life and work discolors his often impressive scholarship.

Since that time, a few biographies of Puccini have appeared, but none is worthy of serious consideration. The latest, by Claudio Casini, is an exhaustive life of the composer which is unfortunately distorted by many inaccuracies.

This book, then, is an attempt to bring Puccini scholarship up to date as well as to present a more complete portrait of the composer than has heretofore been possible; I have relied heavily on recently uncovered material. My major source has been the composer's letters. Puccini was a prolific letter writer, but his letters have not been brought together in a single collection. Many of them have been published in a number of books and periodicals; I have found others in libraries—in Lucca, Florence, London, Paris, New York, and Washington.

The first substantial volume of Puccini letters was that edited by his friend and librettist Giuseppe Adami and published in 1928. It is a useful though not completely reliable — many of the dates are inaccurate — selection of letters dealing mainly with the composer's creative process. Ten years later, Vincent Seligman, the son of Puccini's close friend and confidante Sybil Seligman, published a biography, *Puccini Among Friends,* containing a large number of interesting personal letters from the composer to Mrs. Seligman. These letters have never been published in the original Italian, so that a Puccini biographer is forced to rely on Vincent Seligman's own translations into English. Another drawback is that none of Mrs. Seligman's letters to the composer are included — they would have presented a more complete picture of this interesting relationship.

In 1958, a volume containing over nine hundred letters from, to, and concerning Puccini was published in Milan. Exhaustively annotated by Eugenio Gara, these letters cast invaluable light on the development of each Puccini opera and on his working relationship with his publisher and his librettists. Unfortunately, this collection is most carefully selected and edited, in order not to offend the memory of Puccini, and more especially, the House of Ricordi, Puccini's publisher and the publisher of this otherwise fascinating collection. For example, the name of Doria Manfredi, the central figure in a tragedy that almost destroyed the composer, is not even mentioned, and Sybil Seligman is almost ignored.

It was not until 1973, with the appearance of *Puccini com'era,* edited by Arnaldo Marchetti, that another, more personal and intimate, side of the composer could be examined. This collection of almost five hundred letters, which belonged to Albina Franceschini Del Panta, the composer's niece, portrays a more relaxed and uninhibited Puccini — the earthy Lucchese, the troubled family man. These letters show the human side of the composer as the earlier collections had not. The same can be said of another collection of 276 letters, edited by Giuseppe Pintorno, and published in 1974. These are not nearly as significant as the Marchetti letters, but they too add to a portrait of the composer.

There are many, many more letters, found in a number of newspapers and magazines, as well as a valuable collection of more than seventy letters sent by the composer to Maria Bianca Ginori-Lisci, daughter of the man to whom *La Bohème* was dedicated. These were recently published in a special issue of a provincial journal honoring the composer, and I was fortunate to be able to discuss the circumstances in which these letters were written with their recipient, now the Countess Gaddi-Pepoli. These letters add still another facet to a portrait of Puccini. Written to a very young woman, there is a tenderness and compassion in them lacking in his other correspondence.

Finally, and most unexpectedly, a footnote in a volume dedicated to the letters of Giovanni Pascoli led me to the source of more than two hundred unpublished and previously unexamined letters from the composer to his close friend Alfredo Caselli. These letters had been locked in a trunk found in a vacant apartment in Viareggio, and I was able to locate and consult them through the help of the editor of the volume of Pascoli's correspondence, the distinguished scholar Professor Felice Del Beccaro. They proved to be of inestimable help in my research, filling in gaps and providing me with further means of understanding the character of this far from uncomplicated composer.

I am certain that more of Puccini's letters remain to be discovered, but I am convinced that they would not substantially alter the portrait of the composer presented in this biography. (Puccini's letters to a friend, Riccardo Schnabl-Rossi, for example, will be published within the next year or so, but I have been assured by Simonetta Puccini, the composer's granddaughter, that they add nothing essential to what is already known.)

I must emphasize that this is a biography of Puccini and not a study of his operas. Though the creative development of each opera is clearly an important part of the artist's life, and has been treated as such, no attempt has been made to present a musical analysis of the operas. For that, I refer the reader to excellent studies by William Ashbrook, Ernest Newman, and Spike Hughes. I also admit that I have paid little attention to Puccini's nonoperatic works. The composer himself wrote to a friend, "God touched me with his little finger and said, 'Write for the theatre, only for the theatre,' " and on the basis of what I have heard, I would heartily agree with Puccini's own assessment of his talent.

While I have been working on this book, many people have confessed to me, with some embarrassment, a "weakness" for Puccini. I am convinced that the cause of his great success and the durability of his operas lies not in any weakness on the part of the listener, but rather in the composer's extraordinary melodic gifts, his understanding of the art of singing, and his sure sense of the theatre. I myself approached the subject of this biography with enthusiasm and not embarrassment, and in the course of writing it my enthusiasm has grown to a profound respect for Puccini, the man as well as the artist.

"Only a Musician, Only a Fool"

GIACOMO Antonio Domenico Michele Secondo Maria Puccini was born on December 22, 1858, in the small Tuscan city of Lucca. It has often been said that because he was the latest of many generations of musicians named Puccini, it was inevitable that he would become a musician himself. This, of course, is not true; many of his ancestors were not musicians, and his one and only son was not to become a musician. Nonetheless, music was an essential part of his natural inheritance, and during his formative years it was taken for granted that he would become a musician.

The first of the known Puccinis came from the mountain village of Celle, reached only by mule path, a part of the small town of Pescaglia in central Tuscany. Pescaglia, perched on the side of a mountain, is undistinguished except for its rich chestnut trees, its sprinkling of olives, and its scattered vineyards on the plains below. Celle, the community which gave birth to the first Puccinis, is on top of that mountain. Most of it is today still inaccessible to cars; virtually unchanged throughout the centuries, it remains a tiny labyrinth of narrow, winding stone-paved paths, overlooking spectacular views of the valley below. Undoubtedly, the isolated position of Celle and its harsh mountain climate account for the fact that its inhabitants are known as a sturdy, resourceful, and imaginative people.

Nothing is known of him—not even his first name—but early in the eighteenth century a man named Puccini came down the mountain to settle in the city of Lucca. He married there, and on January 26, 1712, his son, Giacomo, was born there. This Giacomo was to be the first in the long line of

15

musicians. Demonstrating his musical gifts at an early age, the young man was sent to study in Bologna, home of the famed Accademia Filarmonica and a center of Italian musical life since the early seventeenth century. There this first Giacomo came to know Padre Giambattista Martini, the well-known theoretician (who later encouraged the young Mozart when he came to Bologna), and in 1739 it was through the recommendation of Padre Martini that he obtained the post of Maestro of the Cappella Palatina of the Serenissima Repubblica of his hometown of Lucca. The eighteenth-century Giacomo Puccini distinguished himself both as a teacher and a musician. As organist and choirmaster at the imposing Cathedral of San Martino, he composed a vast number of masses, oratorios, cantatas, and instrumental works, all of which show his mastery of the techniques of the baroque style.

When he died on February 3, 1781, he was succeeded in his posts at San Martino by his son, Antonio Benedetto Maria, who had been born on July 31, 1747. Antonio had followed much the same path his father had, studying in Bologna, being received into the illustrious Accademia there, and then returning to Lucca as his father's assistant. His wife, Caterina Tesei, was also a musician — a teacher, composer, and organist — and their son Domenico Vincenzo, born in 1771, continued the family tradition by studying first with his father and then with the distinguished musicians in Bologna. After further studies in Naples, where he took lessons from Giovanni Paisiello (whose *Barber of Seville* preceded that of Rossini), Domenico returned to Lucca where he became his father's assistant at San Martino. He made himself known, too, as a composer, not only of church music and instrumental works, but also of opera. Upon his death in 1815 — a rather mysterious one, presumably after having taken a cup of poisoned sherbet at the home of a nobleman — he left a young widow, Angela Cerù, also of a musical family, and an infant son, Michele.

Michele faithfully carried on the family traditions. With no father to guide him, his musical education was supervised by his grandfather, who saw to it that he studied first in Bologna and then in Naples. In the latter city, he was a student of both Donizetti and Saverio Mercadante — the latter, much admired by Verdi, was director of the Naples Conservatory. After these studies were completed, Michele returned to Lucca, where he became organist and choirmaster at San Martino. As a composer, he wrote both secular and religious music; he was also the author of two textbooks on harmony and counterpoint and for many years director of Lucca's conservatory of music.

His premature death, at the age of fifty, on January 23, 1864, was deeply mourned throughout Lucca's musical community. And it was a tragic blow to his thirty-three-year-old widow, Albina Magi, six months pregnant at the time of her husband's death. Surviving, too, were six daughters; they all bore uniquely Tuscan names — Otilia, Tomaide, Iginia, Nitteti, Macrina, and

Ramelde Onfale Alleluia — names he had found in a list of martyrs and given to the girls to show his anger at having daughters instead of sons (in the case of Ramelde, his youngest child, it must have been sheer rage). However, Michele also left a son, the five-year-old Giacomo, and it was to Giacomo above all that the distinguished composer and teacher, and friend of Rossini, Giovanni Pacini, addressed Michele's eulogy, delivered in Lucca on February 18.

"You, dearly beloved brothers, to whom the meaning of Christian charity speaks so warmly to the heart," the maestro said after his Requiem Mass had been performed, "should turn your thoughts to the eighty-year-old mother of the deceased, to a desolate wife, to six tender young girls, and to a boy, sole survivor of and heir to that glory so justly deserved by his ancestors in the art of harmony, an art which he will perhaps be able to bring to life again one day."

The continuity, Pacini hoped, would be preserved, and to confirm it on that February 18, Albina Magi Puccini's brother, Fortunato Magi, was named Michele's successor at San Martino, on the condition that Magi "should and must turn over to Signor Giacomo, son of the aforementioned deceased maestro, the post of organist and choirmaster as soon as that Signor Giacomo is able to undertake such duties."

This did not come to pass, however. Signor Giacomo, then too young to understand the grave pronouncements concerning his future responsibilities, would indeed become a musician, the last and the greatest of the composing Puccinis, but he would reverse the process of his ancestors. He would not leave Lucca to study music and then return there to practice it; instead he would take all he could from his hometown and then leave it to broaden his horizons. The magnificent medieval wall of Lucca could not contain or limit him — he would want far more than the provincial capital had to offer.

Nonetheless, Lucca formed him. He had been born a Lucchese and would always be one, so Lucca would remain an important part of Giacomo Puccini, important enough so that a few words about this unique and beautiful city and its people help to explain Puccini the man and the artist.

Lucca is defined by the huge wall which encircles it, just as the character of the Lucchesi is profoundly influenced by this enclosure which in a way separates and protects them from the rest of the world. The wall, result of almost a century of work, was built as a bastion against a potential Florentine threat, but it was never needed as such. It was broad enough so that in Puccini's time horse-drawn carriages might be driven on top of it. Today it can handle the steady flow of automobile traffic which circles the city.

The wall is alive, too; the extraordinary humidity of the region keeps the grass which grows between the stones green all year round. Sections of the wall jut out into small parks, comfortable playgrounds for the young Lucchesi.

Lucca has expanded—in Puccini's time the population was 30,000 and today it is closer to 90,000—and spreads beyond the wall. Yet to be a pure and proud Lucchese, it is necessary to have been born within the wall.

Pride is one element which characterizes the pure Lucchesi, and this pride is in many ways justified. Rich in splendid architecture, it is also a city of affluence—at the time Puccini was born, it was the capital of what was then the richest province of all Tuscany. The Lucchesi work tirelessly and are noted for their ambition and seriousness. They are also known for their frugality, which is attributed to the fact that they work especially hard for their money and thus have an inordinate respect for it.

Lucca has all the drawbacks of a small town. It is a closed society, polite but not openly friendly to outsiders of whom the residents are suspicious. The family unit, even closer than that in most Italian communities, is very strong. There is a sense of loyalty to one's family, and then a sense of loyalty to other Lucchesi. Because of overpopulation, large numbers of Lucchesi emigrated, for the most part to North or South America. But unlike emigrants from other parts of Italy, they returned to their homes in Lucca once they had made their fortunes abroad. Gossip and narrowmindedness are also characteristic of life there, but this is not surprising for Lucca, in spite of its relative proximity to the worldly, sophisticated city of Florence, is essentially a small provincial capital.

The Puccinis were very much Lucchesi, and their home, well within the city wall, was located in the center of town, at 30 via di Poggio. This narrow, short and sunless street leads to the imposing twelfth-century Romanesque church of San Michele, noteworthy for its magnificent marble façade, topped by a statue of the Archangel Michael. In front of the church, which is less than a city block from the Puccini home, is a busy, crowded market, and across from it the powerful Renaissance Palazzo Pretorio and a huge municipal loggia. It was in this section of Lucca, the heart of the town, with its palaces, secret courtyards, graceful towers, and rows of quaint shops, that Giacomo Puccini grew up.

Life for Albina, still a young woman, was not easy after the death of her husband—there were the many daughters and Giacomo, and then a second son, Michele, born three months after her husband's death—but a generous pension allowed her to keep two maids, Carola and Assunta, and to maintain her modest yet comfortable apartment. However, there was no room for waste or luxury or frivolity. The girls had to be educated, which they were, and the infant Michele had to be cared for, which he was, but her husband's heir, and her hope, was Giacomo.

Giacomo was raised to carry on the family's distinguished musical tradition. He had few memories of his father, but he later recalled that Michele did introduce him to the world of sound. His father would place coins on the tops of the keys of the church organ, and the infant, Giacomo, in trying to grasp the shiny coins, would press down the keys and thus produce a tantalizing variety of sounds.

It was not a very significant beginning, but Albina was determined that the young boy be exposed to music. Not that a musical education was enough. Her husband had often told her, *"Puro musicista, puro asino"* ("Only a musician, only a fool") so she insisted that her son have as broad an education as possible. However, the young boy seemed to be without promise, either as a musician or as a scholar. He was a happy boy and a friendly one, but he was lazy and completely uninterested in school. He studied first at the seminary of San Michele, and then at that of San Martino, but his school reports were poor. He was a dutiful choirboy at both seminaries, but he did badly in his studies—he barely passed his courses in the humanities, he almost failed in rhetoric, and his grades in mathematics were not even passing. One teacher is said to have noted that the boy "comes to school only to wear out the seat of his trousers. He pays no attention to anything and keeps tapping on his desk as though it were a keyboard. He never reads a book . . ."

The young Puccini's pleasures were strictly extracurricular. He enjoyed the company of friends, enjoyed hunting birds in the fields near the river Serchio—hunting is a passion for the Lucchesi, and it would always be so for Puccini—and practical jokes were of far more interest to him than were his studies. He was charming and he was good-looking; tall, with a winning smile that lighted up his long sensitive face and his brown-green eyes as he savored the rough, earthy humor so popular, even now, among the young Lucchesi. As much as his mother might have asked of him, he did not seem burdened by the weight of a future that was relentlessly imposed upon him.

Nonetheless, music was a major part of his world, even if he did not take it quite as seriously as his family might have wanted. His first teacher was his uncle, Fortunato Magi. A short-tempered, strict disciplinarian, Magi taught his nephew singing and organ. Whenever the young boy sang a false note, his uncle would kick him on the shin—Puccini was later to attribute his own involuntary jerking of his knee whenever he heard a wrong note to this early training. Magi's serious, joyless approach to music was hardly an inspiration to Giacomo; he did not respond to it, and finally the exasperated Magi told his sister that her son was, in his opinion, hopelessly without talent.

Albina Magi Puccini was, however, a stubborn as well as a wise woman. She had no intention of giving up on her young son, and upon his graduation from the seminary—he repeated his last year there—she enrolled him at the Pacini Institute, the city's music conservatory. Though the contribution of Lucca to the history of music is minor, two forms of what might be called musical entertainment had developed there. One was related to Lucca's religious life and the other to its forms of government. The former was called the mottettone, a large-scale work for soloists, choruses, organs and large

orchestra—there were well over two hundred participants in these performances, which were held in the Cathedral as a climax to the annual procession
of the Holy Cross on September 13. The mottettoni were so theatrical that
they were banned by the Vatican as too profane and operatic in 1903.

The second musical entertainment unique to Lucca was called La Festa
delle Tasche (the holiday of the pockets). Local governments were elected by
a public vote every three (later 2½) years, and the ballots were placed in
pocketlike receptacles. These specially written, elaborate stage representa-
tions, that lasted for three days, were put on to celebrate each new government. A tradition that began in 1431, these musical spectacles were ended in
1799 with the termination by Napoleon of the freedom of the republic.

Thus, music—interestingly, in view of Puccini's future, of a rather theatrical nature—was a part of Lucca's history, and the Institute, though not on a
level with those of Milan, Venice, Bologna, or Naples, was a distinguished
one, which numbered among its pupils at one time or another, Boccherini,
Luporini, Catalani, as well as Puccini himself.

At the Institute, Puccini found the ideal teacher, Carlo Angeloni. Angeloni
had been a pupil of Giacomo's father and was a composer of operas and choral
works. He understood Giacomo and seemed to sense, intuitively, the boy's
potential. An avid hunter himself, he would ask the boy to join him while he
hunted and took the opportunity, while walking through the woods, of
instilling in Giacomo a genuine interest in music. He introduced his pupil to
the marvels of Verdi's scores—especially Rigoletto, La Traviata, and Il Trov-
atore—and Puccini's enthusiasm for opera can be dated from the period when
he began to study with Angeloni.

In spite of the enthusiasm engendered by his contact with Angeloni, it was
still far from certain that Giacomo would ever apply himself seriously to his
studies. There is little information about his early years, but stories, later
rather romantically told by his childhood friends, of his adolescent pranks
abound. These indicate that he was a cheerful young man, more interested in
defying authority, dancing the polka with a pretty girl, hunting birds, or
secretly smoking cigarettes than he was in doing his homework. Some of the
pranks are significant in that they are most complex and highly theatrical in
nature—especially one long story involving the feigned suicide of a friend of
his which ended in both the friend and Giacomo being arrested.

Nonetheless, Albina apparently made her son understand that, even while
young, he had to earn money to contribute to the support of his family. His
only way of doing this was through his music. As a result of Angeloni's
teaching, by the age of fourteen he was good enough to play the organ at
church services in Lucca and in the neighboring villages of Mutigliano,
Pescaglia, and Celle. He also occasionally played the organ for the nuns at the
cloister of the Servi, for which he was given sweets, which he appreciated
almost as much as he did cigarettes. Most of the money earned this way was

turned over to his mother, though at times he would take a small amount out of the pay envelope to buy his beloved cigarettes or small cigars. According to reminiscences of some of his friends, another way of getting cigarette money was by ordering his younger brother and friends who acted as organ blowers to steal the organ pipes, which were then sold for the price of the metal to junk dealers. This required considerable ingenuity on Giacomo's part, since he was forced to make appropriate changes in the music, avoiding the notes of the missing pipes so the theft would not soon be discovered.

In addition to playing the organ at church, Giacomo joined some friends in forming a small dance orchestra. Rehearsals — with Farnesi at the counter-bass, Picchi at the clarinet, Michelangeli playing the violin, and Puccini at the piano — were held at the Puccini apartment, and the boys became expert enough to perform in cafés and dance halls not only in Lucca but in the rather fashionable resorts of Bagni di Lucca and Lerici.

At about the age of sixteen, the young Puccini began to improvise his own music. He daringly introduced remembered pieces from operas and from Tuscan folk songs into the organ music he played for church services — much to the dismay of his sister Iginia, who was preparing to take the veil as a nun. Writing these improvisations down on paper, he demonstrated a genuine if undeveloped talent for light music. By September 1875, even his formal studies had improved to such an extent that he was given a certificate from the Pacini Institute stating that he had so distinguished himself in the study of the organ during the scholastic year that he was worthy of the first prize. This official document was signed by both the superintendent and the mayor of Lucca; it is proof that the young man was no longer the lazy and not very serious student of the past. Additional proof lies in the fact that a young man named Carlo Della Nina, from a neighboring village of Porcari, felt that Puccini was competent enough to be his teacher for four years, beginning in 1874, during which Della Nina, Giacomo's contemporary, came faithfully to the latter's home for weekly music lessons.

In early 1876, Puccini was introduced to the world of professional opera. The musical sensation of Italy for four years had been Verdi's *Aida;* it had had a hugely successful première in Cairo at the end of 1871 and had had an equally brilliant success at its La Scala début in February 1872. On March 11, 1876, it was to be given for the first time in Pisa. Puccini and two friends, Carlo Carignani and Giuseppe Papeschi, decided to attend the performance. Early in the morning, they began the long walk to Pisa, arriving at the Teatro Nuovo (today the Teatro Verdi) after seven hours — three hours before the performance. Without the money with which to buy tickets, they talked the stage doorman into letting them into the theatre, with the excuse that they had an urgent letter to deliver personally to the stage manager. They climbed to the 1100-seat theatre's top gallery of unreserved seats and hid until the public started filing into the theatre. Taking three seats in the front of the gallery, they sat enchanted through the entire performance. Years later, Puccini said, "When I heard *Aida* in Pisa, I felt that a musical window had opened for me." What he saw through that window was the immense potential and power of musical theatre; the drama, the spectacle, the ability of opera to move and involve the spectator. It is doubtful that this was Puccini's first opera—Lucca's Teatro del Giglio was active though at best a competent provincial theatre, and it is unlikely that a serious music student would not have attended at least one performance there—and we know that he was already familiar with some of Verdi's earlier scores. But a production of the spectacular *Aida* in a far larger theatre than the Giglio would certainly have been an experience of great importance to the young student.

Whatever the specific reason, if there was one, from that time on Puccini's goals broadened. He began composing more seriously and he came to realize that he would have to look beyond Lucca—to Milan—to further his studies.

Beginning in 1876, when he was eighteen, he started to compose not only organ works or clever improvisations, but more ambitious, complex pieces for voice and for orchestra. A *Preludio Sinfonico in A Major* of that year, which survives today and has even been recorded, is richly melodic, and sweepingly dramatic, though rather cloyingly sweet; another *Preludio Sinfonico*, also for large orchestra, is of the same period, but it has never been published, and the original score is in the possession of Natale Gallini in Milan.

In the following year, 1877, Puccini was sufficiently confident to enter a competition held in conjunction with a Treasures of Sacred Art exhibition in Lucca, for the best setting of a patriotic text, "*I Figli d'Italia Bella.*" Puccini's composition, however, did not win, and the piece was returned to him with the advice to study harder and acquire a more legible handwriting. (This was not the last time Puccini would lose a competition, and far from the last time there would be a complaint about the legibility of his scores.)

It was in 1878 that the young man's talent was first recognized beyond the confines of the Institute. As an essay for Angeloni's course in counterpoint, he composed a Motet for four voices in celebration of the feast of San Paolino, the patron saint of Lucca, who, according to legend, was the inventor of church bells. Upon hearing the work, Nicolao Cerù, a cousin of Puccini's father, was so impressed that he wrote an article praising the work in a local newspaper, *Il Moccolino*. In the article, Cerù noted that "*I figli dei gatti pigliano i topi*"—literally, "The children of cats catch the mice," or "Acorns don't fall far from the trees."

A month later, on July 12, this Motet, together with a Credo for soloists, chorus, and orchestra was performed in the Church of San Paolino. It was an unqualified success, and the following day *La Provincia di Lucca* reported that it seemed the work of a mature composer rather than that of a beginner.

In 1880, Puccini incorporated this Motet and Credo into a Mass, written as his graduation exercise from the Pacini Institute. This Mass for Four Voices and Orchestra runs to 202 pages and lasts for almost fifty minutes. The composer's first major work, it was first performed for the annual feast of San Paolino on July 12. It was greatly acclaimed, even by the highly critical Angeloni whose only reservation was that the Mass was somewhat too theatrical. The critic for Lucca's *Il Progresso*, in praising it, noted that "the distribution of the parts is well divided, the work as a whole is harmonious, the melodies rich and spontaneous, and the construction effective." This dramatic and theatrically effective work of the twenty-two-year-old composer was rediscovered in 1951 and later recorded under the title *Messa di Gloria*. There were other compositions of this period—a waltz for band of 1879, short choral pieces and a *Salve Regina* for soprano and piano—but it was in the large-scale Mass that Puccini began to emerge as a composer of more than ordinary promise.

Once his studies had been completed at the Institute, serious decisions had to be made. There were several possibilities for the young man. He was clearly qualified to take the post of choirmaster-organist at the Cathedral which had been promised him at the time of his father's death; he would also have no difficulty in finding a teaching position. Or, he could pursue his career as a composer. The first two possibilities were not, it seems, even considered. Giacomo's ambitions went far beyond Lucca as did Albina's ambitions for her son. But furthering his studies, with the goal of composing in mind, meant Milan and three years of study at the conservatory there. The conservatory was Italy's finest, and study there meant not only the opportunity to learn from the country's most capable teachers but also exposure to the rich musical life that the city could offer. However, the financial obstacles seemed insurmountable. Not only did the Puccinis lack the means to pay for three years of Giacomo's studies and his support, but his earnings in Lucca, small though they were, were important to Albina's tight budget.

Nonetheless, Albina was stubbornly determined to give her son every possible chance to fulfill what she knew were his immense possibilities. She first turned to the city of Lucca itself, requesting financial aid that had in the past been granted to the city's talented young musicians. Her request was rejected for unknown reasons—perhaps the provincial city officials did not want to help a student whom they felt would not return to Lucca to give his home the benefit of the city-subsidized education.

Undaunted, Albina sought other means to obtain money. At the suggestion of a certain Duchess Carafa, an acquaintance of hers, and with the aid of an old friend, the Marchesa Pallavicini, who was a lady in waiting to Queen Margherita di Savoia, Albina made application for a royal scholarship given to musicians of indigent families. The queen, wife of Umberto I, the first ruler after the Unification, was known as a lover of violets, pearl necklaces and music, and Albina wrote her directly.

MAJESTY!

You are the Queen and the mother of all the poor, and you are also the patroness of artists, while I am a poor widow with two young sons, whose ambition in life is to give them the best education. My children are students of music, and the older of them, Giacomo, shows great promise. For five generations, the Puccinis have formed a dynasty of musicians, and if the opportunity should arise, Giacomo will continue the glorious tradition. He has terminated his studies at Lucca; he desires to proceed to Milan, the capital of music. I cannot myself pay his expenses at the Conservatorio, for I have only a meager monthly pension of 75 lire allowed me by the City Council. The Duchessa Carafa, who knows me well, has encouraged me to write to Your Majesty. Will you therefore in your immense generosity come to the help of a poor mother and an ambitious boy.

Kissing your munificent hand, I am

ALBINA MAGI-PUCCINI

Albina's request was granted. However, the grant of 100 lire per month for one year was hardly enough to pay for Giacomo's studies and support him, and for further help, the proud and determined mother turned to her late husband's cousin, Nicolao Cerù, the man who had earlier called attention to Giacomo's talent in the local newspaper. Cerù, a bachelor doctor, was a legendary figure in Lucca. The white-bearded, rather nervous man was so tall that it was said that he lit his cigarettes from street gas lights. But he was also known for his kindness and generosity, and he was an unfailing source of help to his family. Because he cared for and understood Giacomo and believed that it would be best for him to go to Milan, he came to Albina's aid and promised to provide the additional money necessary to subsidize Giacomo's education.

Milan—The Early Years

Given his provincial training, it was a rather surprisingly self-confident Giacomo Puccini who arrived in Milan in the fall of 1880. Milan was, as it is today, the cultural center, the artistic heart of the country. The avant-garde, the theatre, and above all the musical life of Italy were centered in Milan. It was Verdi's Milan, the Milan of La Scala and of the great Conservatory. The extraordinary intellectual activity of the northern city should have intimidated the young man from Lucca, but it seems that he accepted it as a challenge, and one he could meet without too much difficulty.

In the very beginning, young Puccini still had to face the question of his admission to the Conservatory, which was complicated by the fact that he was almost twenty-two years old, past the limit for admission as stated by its bylaws. Yet, in November 1880, he was able to write a letter to his mother in Lucca, showing not only his realistic appraisal of his own worth, but confirming his ability to survive in a totally new environment.

DEAREST MAMMA,

So far I have no news concerning my admission to the Conservatory, since the council met Saturday to consider the candidates; that is, to see which of them can be admitted since there are very few openings. I expect to be admitted because I have the best grades, and I hope they will overlook the question of age. . . . The examination was ridiculously easy. . . .

In the evening, when I have money, I go to a café, but there are many evenings that I don't go because a punch costs fifty centesimi.

25

However, I go to bed early, because I get tired walking around the Galleria. I have a pretty little room, all clean, with a beautiful polished walnut desk, which is magnificent. In short, I am happy to be here. I am not starving; I fill up with minestrone or thick broth, etc. My stomach is satisfied. . . .

In the same letter, Puccini noted that he had heard two operas—Meyerbeer's *L'Étoile du Nord* and Auber's *Fra Diavolo*. For the former, he spent only a few cents for a seat in the gallery, and he paid nothing for *Fra Diavolo* since a ticket was given him by an old friend from Lucca. It was already clear that Milan was the ideal place for him to perfect his knowledge—through the experience of listening—of opera.

A few days later, he again wrote to his mother, giving his address as via Monforte 26; this time his message was squeezed on the back of a postage-paid reply card, furnished by Albina. All was going well, he reported, in spite of his financial problems. The results of the examination were, as he had expected, excellent; his grades were higher than those of all the other candidates. There remained the problem of his age, but he had been assured by the director of the Conservatory, Stefano Ronchetti Moteviti, that admission would be granted solely on the merits of the individual student—and since he had done so well in his examinations, there was no real doubt that he would be accepted. In his letter, too, he stated that he would call on Giovannina Lucca, a prominent music publisher, as soon as his rather shabby clothing was replaced by a new pair of trousers. An increasing number of invitations for meals, largely from Lucchesi in Milan, made him certain that he would soon be eating better, and the letter ended on a cheerful note: "How beautiful Milan is, and what youth!"

As expected, Puccini was admitted to the Conservatory, where he was extremely fortunate in being able to study with two of Italy's finest teachers of music, Antonio Bazzini and Amilcare Ponchielli. Bazzini (born in 1818) was a thoroughly trained musician, who in his youth had been a virtuoso violinist. A minor composer, he had written one opera, *Turanda*—the same subject matter served Puccini many years later—which had been produced at La Scala in 1867 with little success. Bazzini's fame rests on his successful academic career; he joined the faculty of the Milan Conservatory in 1873 and was named its director in 1882, upon the death of Moteviti. Bazzini was a strict disciplinarian, a severe taskmaster for Puccini, insisting that his student master the art of classical composition, demanding that he carefully study fugues and string quartets, forms Puccini would never excel in but which certainly aided him in the formation of his own musical language.

While Puccini respected Bazzini, theirs was a formal teacher-student relationship. On the other hand, Ponchielli was for the young Lucchese not only an inspiring teacher but a loyal, encouraging friend, the greatest influence on

Puccini during his years at the Conservatory. Ponchielli's passion was opera; his joy was in writing music for voice. He had started writing for the musical theatre while in his early twenties but achieved no success until 1872 when, at the age of thirty-eight, a new version of an early work, *I Promessi Sposi*, was produced in Cremona. This, however, was overshadowed by the huge success of his *La Gioconda* following its première at La Scala on April 8, 1876. Finally, critics agreed, a successor had been found to the aging Verdi, and Ponchielli's fame spread throughout the world. Ponchielli, however, never fulfilled that promise. Though three later operas of his met with some success, at the time of his premature death in 1886 he was remembered solely for *La Gioconda*. Today he might best be remembered not as the composer of the "Dance of the Hours" but as a vital influence in the life of Puccini, a student who far surpassed his teacher in musical accomplishment.

The kindly, young-spirited Ponchielli took an almost paternal interest in Puccini, introducing him to important figures in Milan's musical circles and even keeping Albina informed of the young man's progress. Not concerned with maintaining rigorous discipline in his classes, Ponchielli's lessons were marked by his good humor and contagious laughter. The bearded professor enjoyed teaching, and this enjoyment was communicated to his students. Puccini's classroom notebooks of the period are filled with witty caricatures of his teacher, testimony to the genuine warmth felt by the student for his professor.

Before he started studying with Ponchielli, however, Puccini was already working toward his goals and setting for himself a satisfactory routine. A letter to his mother, written on December 18, 1880, sums up his life those first few months at the Conservatory—a fruitful period, yet one inevitably marked by a degree of loneliness.

DEAREST MAMMA,

Yesterday I had my second class with Bazzini, and it's going very well. That is the only class I have now, but on Friday I begin aesthetics. I have made myself the following schedule. In the morning I get up at eight-thirty; when I have a class, I go to it; otherwise I study the piano a little. I don't need to do much, but I do have to practice a little. I am going to buy an excellent "Method" by Angeleri, the kind from which one can learn by himself. I go on until ten-thirty when I eat, and then I go out. At one, I go home and study for Bazzini for a couple of hours; then, from three to five, I go back to the piano and a little reading of classical music. I would like to take out a subscription for musical scores, but I haven't enough money. Right now, I am going through Boito's *Mefistofele*. . . . At five, I go to my frugal (very frugal) meal. I have minestrone alla Milanese, which, to tell the truth, is rather good. Then I light up a cigar and go off to the Galleria, walking up and down, as always. I stay there till nine and then come home, dead tired. Once home, I do a little counterpoint, but I don't play because it is not permitted at night. Afterwards I get into bed and read seven or eight pages of a novel. That's my life. . . .

I need one thing, but I'm afraid to tell you because I know that you too have no extra money. But listen, it's not much. Since I have a great longing for beans (they did make some for me one day here, but I couldn't eat them because of the oil which is made of sesame and linseed here), then, as I was saying, I could use a little oil, the new oil. Please send me just a little. Just a little is enough, I promised to let some friends here taste it too. Then, if my pleadings bear fruit, would you be kind enough to send me (how I grease you, speaking of oil) a little tin, which costs four lire from Eugenio Ottolini, who sent some to the tenor Papeschi as well. Here everyone is doing operas as quickly as possible, but I . . . nothing. I am biting my nails with rage.

Puccini's entire first year in Milan was characterized on the one hand by the stimulation which life in the great city offered to him; and on the other hand by a profound longing for his hometown, his family—and, above all, his mother. There was, too, the very real poverty that made the homesickness even more painful. For a while, he had difficulty in finding permanent, satisfactory lodgings. As early as February 1881, the young student had been talked into moving from his room on via Monforte to another one, at via Zecca Vecchia 10. "The place where I've been living up to now," he wrote to his sister Ramelde on February 3, "was not for me. The room was cold, and I paid 25 lire which was too much for that room. And they did nothing for me; they didn't clean my clothes or my shoes. You can imagine that for me . . . I, who am so sloppy . . ." And only two months later, on April 4, he again wrote to Ramelde that he would have to move, this time from via Zecca Vecchia to less expensive quarters.

All of his letters to Lucca during this period are filled with tales of his necessarily spartan way of life. There are frequent, if guiltridden, requests for money and regrets that his financial situation makes it impossible for him to go home for Easter; at the same time he shows sincere appreciation for all that his mother is doing for him as well as a desire to be able to help out his family as soon as possible. Puccini's attachment to his mother was clearly strong, as it was to his sister Ramelde, closest to him of all his sisters. She was a young woman of intelligence, wit, and charm who was temperamentally more attuned to Giacomo than were other members of the family.

Essentially alone in Milan, Puccini made no effort to hide his feelings and showed a keen interest in his friends back home, in news of their lives, and in local gossip, which always delighted him.

Nonetheless, there were pleasures away from Lucca: outings in the country with friends from the Conservatory, drinks and sometimes meals with friends from back home, and, above all, the satisfactions of his studies, which he thoroughly enjoyed—with the exception of his boring drama classes.

His determination to be a musician compensated for whatever difficulties life might have presented to him and if, as he wrote his mother, his existence was somewhat monotonous, it was still enormously stimulating to be in the musical center of Italy. Milan was preparing for a huge National Exposition, which was to open in May 1881 and last until the following winter, so that there was even more activity in the city than ever. There were parades and races and plays and ballets, but above all the city was for months alive with special performances of opera—not only at La Scala, but also at the Teatro Manzoni and the Teatro Dal Verme. Puccini wrote home excitedly of performances of *Ernani, Simon Boccanegra, La Forza del Destino, Der Freischütz, Mignon, Don Giovanni, Mefistofele, I Puritani, Faust, La Favorita, Guglielmo Tell, Semiramide. . . .* This excitement is all the more touching because it is doubtful that the young student was able to attend many (or any—he never mentioned them in his letters) of these performances. But these masterpieces of opera were certainly a vital part of Milanese life during that period, and as such a source of stimulation for the young man.

Puccini's studies were going well. A certificate, signed by Bazzini on July 10, 1881, confirms that his grades had been excellent. His highest marks were in composition, which he studied with Ponchielli, and in the history and philosophy of music. A worn copy, with notations in Puccini's handwriting, of an Italian translation of Berlioz's *Traité de l'instrumentation*, bears testimony to his seriousness. His grades were somewhat lower in piano and in poetic and dramatic literature (he studied epic poetry, Dante, Tasso, and Ariosto) but in an official paper dated November 6, 1881, it is noted that he was an honor student for that academic year.

The young man's personal life during his Conservatory years is poorly documented. Most of what is known comes from his letters home, and these letters tell very little about his friends, his entertainments, and his leisure time. Nonetheless, there is available an overabundance of anecdotes concerning these years, almost all of them found in the early biographies of the composer written by his friends. These stories make his student days in Milan resemble to an astounding degree the life led by the characters he so brilliantly portrayed in *La Bohème*. Many of them originate in an article written by Eugenio Checchi and published on December 1, 1897; all of them would be more convincing if they had been reported before the 1896 première of *La Bohème*, for they mirror a bit too closely the antics experienced by Puccini's comic-tragic Bohemians. They would today be considered clever publicity handouts. Nonetheless, some of these amusing tales were passed on by Pietro Mascagni, and Mascagni never had reason to act as Puccini's publicity manager so there must be an element of truth in some of them, if not in fact, at least in spirit.

During these years as a student in Milan, Puccini was reported to have shared his room with any number of other students—his brother Michele, a cousin, various friends from Lucca, and Mascagni himself. From the evidence of Michele's brief, sporadic stays in Milan, it seems unlikely that he ever shared a room with his brother—nor is there any indication of what cousin or exactly what friends lived with him. However, both Mascagni and Puccini reported that they had shared a room during Puccini's second year at the Conservatory. They were both students of Ponchielli, and they were both in financial straits. Mascagni, five years younger than Puccini, was born in Livorno, not far from Puccini's home. The son of a baker who discouraged him in his attempts to study music, he was brought up by an uncle who was in sympathy with the young man's goals. Temperamentally, the two aspiring composers were opposites. Guglielmo Marconi, who knew them both, was to comment that he liked the company of the often silent and pensive Puccini because it gave him time to think, and he enjoyed being with Mascagni because the expansive, talkative musician offered him the pleasures of listening. While Puccini pursued his studies with seriousness and with discipline, Mascagni was bored and unruly; after one year the composer from Livorno was expelled from the Conservatory for what was described as "a serious shortcoming."

According to Mascagni, when he and Puccini lived together, their financial situation was critical. Together they set up an itinerary of safety, making red marks on a map of Milan to show which squares, streets, and other places were to be avoided because of the danger of running into creditors. Their one extravagance was to share the costs of the purchase of the score of *Parsifal* which they both pored over enthusiastically.

There are many other stories concerning Puccini's Conservatory years. Presumably he kept as a souvenir an expense register for the year 1881; money, according to the register, was spent on coffee, wine, herring, rice, bread, tobacco, pipes, cigars, sugar, and cream. On November first, one herring was purchased, and that had to serve three young men. When there were no funds for tobacco of any kind, Puccini smoked cocoa leaves. Cooking was strictly forbidden in the room, so the noise of frying was covered up by the loud playing of a piano. There are tales of the young musician hiding in a closet to avoid creditors, and of Puccini pawning an overcoat in order to woo a pretty young girl, as a result of which he had to spend three cold winter months without a coat. There is a story of how the landlord, who worked in the post office, would open the envelope containing a small monthly sum Puccini received from a Roman charity organization and deduct his rent before turning it over to Puccini.

These stories are all too familiar to those familiar with *La Bohème*. Yet, in them there is most certainly a kernel of truth. Puccini worked hard, and he was undoubtedly homesick and poor. But, he enjoyed the good life—good food and wine and especially the company of pretty women—and in order to do so he had to resort to imaginative schemes and tricks, at which he had already proved expert in Lucca.

So there were good times and jokes and pranks, but for the most part life was difficult, so much so that shortly after he had started his third and final year at the Conservatory, on December 6, 1882, Puccini was forced to turn again to Dr. Cerù, his faithful benefactor, with a request for additional help:

> . . . My studies are going well and I work hard. The cold up here is extraordinary and worse than in the past years; therefore I have to ask you for a favor which I hope you find justified. I have to study and as you know I study for the most part at night—all through the night, and since my room is very cold I could use some fire. I have no money, for as you know the money that you send me serves for the basic necessities, so I would need money to buy one of those coal stoves that give off much heat.
>
> The expense for the stove itself is not very high, but what worries me is the coal which costs a lot and by the end of the month adds up to a considerable amount. I have written about this to my mother, too, so please see if between the two of you you can come up with some money since time is pressing and it is becoming colder. . . .

It is interesting to note that in this same letter, he first mentioned his search for a libretto—from a certain Medarse Cappelletti in Lucca.

A few months later, Puccini's studies at the Conservatory were coming to an end. In June of 1883, he was completely preoccupied with his final examinations; the last one took place on the twenty-fourth, and on the twenty-eighth he learned that the results had been more than satisfactory. But his financial situation was so desperate that he had no money for postage and was thus unable to communicate the good, if not unexpected, news to his mother until July 2 when he received a letter containing fifty lire from Dr. Cerù. Not that Albina was worried; Ponchielli had kept her informed of her son's progress, had assured her that he was one of his best students, and had promised her to help him in any way possible.

These examinations out of the way, Puccini was able to devote full time to his graduating composition, a piece of music required of all those who were completing their studies at the Conservatory. Puccini's was to be a symphonic work, a *Capriccio Sinfonico* which would be publicly performed by an orchestra that was made up largely of students but would be conducted by one of the country's most respected conductors, Franco Faccio. A graduate of the Conservatory, Faccio had made his name as a teacher and an operatic composer, and in 1871 had been appointed a conductor at La Scala where the following year he had conducted the Italian première of *Aida*. Under these auspices, Puccini's work would be heard by the discerning, sophisticated Milanese public as well as by some of Italy's most influential music critics. If the *Capriccio* were well received, he would have a calling card with which to present himself to Milan's powerful music publishers—Giovannina Lucca, whom he had already met, and Verdi's publisher, Giulio Ricordi, to whom Ponchielli had promised to introduce him.

Rehearsals of the new work began on July 10. Both Puccini and Ponchielli were skeptical about the capability of a largely amateur orchestra to play what they felt was a difficult work, but the first rehearsal went well. On July 12, a confident Puccini wrote to his mother:

> Today I had the second rehearsal. My piece will be successful; the performance might not be perfect, but (modesty aside) the material is very good. . . . Ponchielli, my beloved teacher, with a heart of gold, is really very happy. Tomorrow at two, the public rehearsal, and the performance is the following day. . . . A kiss. I am completely broke. If you could send me a little money by telegram . . . Thank you.

The *Capriccio Sinfonico* had its first public performance at the student concert on July 14, 1883. That same evening Ponchielli wrote to Albina of the work's enthusiastic reception, of her son's great future, and he mentioned that he had already spoken to Ricordi about him. And on the following day, one of the country's most influential critics wrote, in the newspaper *Perseveranza*, a review of the performance that more than fulfilled Puccini's and Ponchielli's hopes:

> In Puccini there is a decided and most unusual musical temperament, especially as a symphonist. Unity of style, personality, character, more of these than is generally found among more mature composers of orchestral music or concerti. This *Capriccio*, which is a fiery allegro in the midst of calm ruminations, has for me the great merit of spontaneity, of unity of style and of color. There are no uncertainties or hesitations, and the young composer, once he has taken off, does not lose sight of his ideas. His ideas are strong, clear, and most effective, sustained by variety and the boldness of his harmony, and the different movements are connected in a logical, clear and orderly fashion. The predominant color is strong, daring, almost harsh, but agreeable. . . .

A few days later, after the orchestra had performed the *Capriccio* for the third time (very badly, according to Ponchielli), Antonio Bazzini, then director of the Conservatory, handed Puccini his diploma in composition along with a bronze medal which the committee of professors had unanimously decided to give him in appreciation of his outstanding work at the Conservatory.

It was an exciting time for Puccini. He had graduated with the highest possible honors; his first publicly performed work in Milan had been recognized by the influential press. Even better, the great Faccio had promised to include this apprentice work in one of his regular, professional concerts. Elated, the young graduate wrote home to have the parts of the score quickly copied—twelve first violins, ten second violins, nine double basses; he need not have rushed, since Faccio did not program the *Capriccio* until the following year when he included it in one of his "pop" concerts in Turin. But Puccini's joy was such that he not only urged that the copying of the score be hurried, but that the original manuscript be returned as soon as possible so that he might show it to the publisher Lucca.

However, once the excitement of his first real success had subsided, Puccini had to face a serious turning point in his life: what next? His accomplishments in Milan had been considerable, but it was difficult to translate them into the making of a livelihood, a career, a future. There were, basically, two choices. He could return to Lucca and there make a living as an organist or as a teacher or, even, as a composer—but with little chance of recognition beyond the city's wall. Or he could remain in Milan and stubbornly make every effort to further his career as a composer. The former was out of the question. Apart from the humiliation of what would rightly be thought of as a step backward, Puccini remained confident that his talent would earn him a place in the world of opera. Never, in spite of his critical financial situation, did he even consider one other alternative, that of earning his living as a teacher while composing on the side as would have seemed natural at the time.

There was, however, the practical problem of gaining professional acceptance in Milan's musical world, and this could be done only through the patronage and aid of one of the city's great music publishers, who might well subsidize a promising young composer in the hopes that he or she might one day reach success and prove profitable to the firm. Chief among these were Giovannina Lucca, who had made Wagner's works known to the Italian public, and, most important of all, Giulio Ricordi, a towering figure in the world of music publishing whose firm had championed Verdi. Ponchielli had promised Puccini that he would present him to both of these publishers; he had responded compassionately to Albina's pleas of aid in light of the fact that she could no longer help her son financially. However, it was already July, Milan was emptying out, both Lucca and Ricordi were already installed in their summer homes away from the city, and there was little chance of making fruitful contacts until the fall.

In spite of this, Puccini refused to return home after his graduation from the Conservatory; he would not go back until every possibility had been exhausted. With this in mind, he eagerly accepted Ponchielli's invitation to spend time with him and his family at their summer home in Maggianico, near Lecco. Lecco was not too far from the Swiss village in which Giovannina Lucca spent her holidays (Puccini did not know at the time that Lucca was not at her home but at Bayreuth); thus it would be easy for Puccini to go to see her. In addition, Lecco was situated in the area between Lake Como and Bergamo, a summer retreat for many artists and intellectuals of Milan, which meant that many of Ponchielli's neighbors might be of help to the young composer. Specifically, Ponchielli's villa was near Caprino Bergamasco, the site of a pensione called Il Barco, run by Antonio Ghislanzoni, the librettist of *Aida*, and frequented by musicians and writers. Il Barco was always crowded because its owner rarely if ever presented his guests with a bill. That July among the guests was Ferdinando Fontana, a minor poet, dramatist, critic, and occasional writer of librettos, and a chance meeting with Fontana led to Puccini's first opera, and thereby justified his visit to Ponchielli.

The three men—impoverished poet, impoverished musician, and the bearded composer-professor—came together at the Lecco railroad station, and they rode the train together the short—four kilometer—distance to Caprino. In the course of this very short train ride, Ponchielli kept his promise to his desperate student. He found him a librettist and an exciting project on which to exercise his talents. The librettist was, of course, Fontana, and the project the men would work on would be a one-act opera, to be entered in a competition which had been announced in the magazine *Il Teatro Illustrato*, sponsored by the music-publishing house of Sonzogno, for the best one-act opera written by an Italian.

Ponchielli conscientiously followed up this verbal commitment at once, writing to Fontana on July 25:

> After what you told me in the train concerning young Maestro Puccini, and the libretto for the little opera in one act which you would be willing to write for him for a moderate price, I hereby ask you in his name just what amount you would ask. It is needless to repeat to you that Puccini is without means; I thus appeal to your well-known generosity.

Fontana's reply came quickly, and it did demonstrate his "well-known generosity":

> I should be very happy to be of use to Maestro Puccini, but you know how I am always sailing in shallow waters. I have managed to keep the wolf from my door even without resorting to the boring

task of writing librettos, and if I write one now I expect to make a profit at least. Therefore, I shall write no more librettos for less than 300 lire per act.

However, since I consider myself an intelligent and not unattractive young man, and you know that I am not intransigent and the fee I am quoting is the minimum within reason . . . writing a libretto is an appealing occupation and very amusing and more in keeping with my intellectual tastes. Therefore, I propose to follow your suggestion, and I ask 100 lire to be paid on the completion of the libretto with an additional 200 lire to be paid if Puccini wins the contest. Surely this is sufficiently reasonable!

An agreement was quickly reached. Fontana had already heard the *Capriccio* and had liked it. Though he had already started work on a libretto for another composer, he thought the subject so well suited to Puccini that he would write it for him. This subject for the opera at first known as *Le Willis* and later changed to *Le Villi* was based on a German or Slavonic legend of a girl who is abandoned by her fiancé, dies of grief, and returns to join other spirits, the Willis, in encircling her faithless lover with dance and laughter until he dies. The tale successfully served as the subject in 1841 for a ballet, *Giselle*, but it is hard to know why Fontana thought it suitable for Puccini; his stated reason was that after hearing the *Capriccio* "a fantastic subject seemed to me what the young composer needed."

On August 7, Puccini left Milan for Lucca, where he would work on his opera, protected from financial cares by his mother. Within a few days, Fontana sent him the first scene, and by the beginning of September, the entire libretto was in the composer's hands. There was no time to lose—the deadline for the competition was December 31—and Puccini immersed himself in work for the better part of four months.

Composer and librettist met only briefly during this period—Puccini spent a few days with Fontana in Milan in late September—and their work proceeded by correspondence. Working for the most part alone on his first opera, and under the pressure of an early deadline, it seems almost miraculous that Puccini was able to finish his work on time. Nonetheless, on December 31, the last possible day, the composer sent his one-act opera to Milan, there to be judged by the jurors of the competition. Puccini was forced to write out the score so hurriedly that it was hardly decipherable.

After a month's rest, Puccini returned to Milan, at the beginning of February, there to await the outcome of the competition which was to be announced at the end of February. He had written his first opera, he had hopes that it might win, but other than that life for him in the great city was much as it had been before. With Ponchielli's help, he managed to meet Ricordi, but he was not particularly encouraged by the meeting. Giovannina

Lucca, too, was of little help, though her firm was to publish a piano version of the *Capriccio Sinfonico*. All, it seemed, depended on the success or failure of that first opera.

While waiting, the composer's financial problems remained critical, so much so that it was necessary to sell some of his family's collection of rare books in Lucca in order to support his stay in Milan. No effort, however, was too great for Albina, whose faith was unswerving. Though her letters to her son during this period kept him informed of an illness which had afflicted her—a very serious one—she not only insisted that she would recover (so as not to worry him), but she offered her son an unending stream of suggestions as to how he might make his way in Milan, even suggesting that he might ask Ponchielli to persuade Ricordi to allow him to conduct a performance of one of Ponchielli's works at the opera house. This devotion was such that in spite of her health, in spite of the imminent marriage of her daughter Nitteti, her only real concern was the future of her beloved eldest son. "I cannot rest because I think of you," she wrote him in February.

Just as Albina's determination to help her son was remarkable, so was that son's stubborn need to further his career. His mother's illness, his sister's wedding . . . neither could persuade him to leave Milan at a time he felt that remaining in the city might be of professional importance to him.

By the end of February, when the decision of the jurors was to be announced, word spread throughout musical circles in the city that the winner of the Sonzogno prize was the author of a work dealing with magic and the fates, with witches and spirits. Puccini and Fontana were, prematurely, elated. A prize would radically alter the careers of these two young men (Fontana was only thirty-three at the time). Because of this they must have been profoundly dejected when the results were finally announced. In spite of their acquaintance and even friendship with the jurors—among them Faccio and Ponchielli—*Le Willis* was not even singled out for an honorable mention among the twenty-eight works submitted. Because of the poor condition and illegibility of the score, it seemed that their opera hadn't even been seriously considered. The prizes went instead to Guglielmo Zuelli for *La Fata del Nord* and Luigi Mapelli for *Anna e Gualberto*. As part of the prize, these two works were performed in Milan, at the Teatro Manzoni, on May 4. When he heard them, Puccini reportedly told a friend: "My God! Is it possible that I could have written anything less good that these?"

Even this failure, however, did not discourage Puccini, did not convince him to return to Lucca. He liked his one-act opera, and he could count on the persistence and enthusiasm of Fontana whose ego at this point could not easily accept defeat. The influential Ponchielli, too, believed in *Le Willis*; somehow it would be performed. . . .

Puccini was so certain that he would find a way of surviving in Milan that he urged his brother Michele to join him there. Michele, though clearly less talented than his older brother, wanted to follow in his footsteps and to be admitted to the Conservatory. However, Albina, her resources spent, could not help her young son as she had helped Giacomo, so that the latter was forced to assume responsibility for his brother. When Michele arrived in Milan at the end of March, Giacomo, though unable to provide him with lodgings, found him part-time work in a music store and did what he could to arrange for his admission to the Conservatory. The two brothers were close. They regularly met at a colorful neighborhood trattoria, *Aida*; the attraction of the Tuscan food served there combined with the owner's reluctance to force his patrons to pay their bills made it a popular eating place among those Tuscan musicians who had been transplanted to the North. This latter factor made it especially attractive to the two brothers, for whom mere survival was an everyday problem. How Giacomo managed is unknown, but a month after the disappointing news about the competition, Michele was able to send word home that his brother was well, though for the time being there was "nothing new."

Soon, however, there was something new; Puccini's stubborn determination was to pay off.

Fontana's enthusiasm for *Le Willis* had never flagged. Because of all the work he had put into the libretto, because of his feelings of friendship for Puccini, he refused to let the little opera die before it had a hearing. In early April, with the help of friends, he arranged for what amounted to a backers' audition for the opera. It was to be held at the home of a wealthy Milanese, Marco Sala, an eccentric patron of the arts who occasionally wrote music himself—some of it dance music that attained a certain fleeting popularity. Among those guests invited to Sala's salon that evening were Alfredo Catalani, Giovannina Lucca and, most important, Arrigo Boito. Boito, a poet, critic, and composer, a man of great sensitivity and refinement, was a leader of Milan's intellectual community. As a composer, his opera *Mefistofele*, after its initial failure in 1868, had met with great success in 1875. As a librettist, he was responsible for Ponchielli's *La Gioconda* and, at the time of Sala's evening for Puccini, he was at work on Verdi's *Otello*. A man of tremendous learning and knowledge, his opinion carried as much weight as that of any other person in Milan's musical circle. He was not only a close friend of Verdi's; he was a collaborator of Ricordi's. His presence that evening at Sala's added great prestige to the gathering, and his role, though unofficial, as representative of the House of Ricordi on that occasion, was clearly implied.

In the midst of this distinguished company, Puccini was ill at ease, by comparison with these illustrious figures, he was naïve and unworldly. Yet this was the opportunity he had waited for and, encouraged by their warm

greeting—he was, after all, not completely unknown, and he was a disciple of
Ponchielli's—he sat down at the piano to play (badly) and to sing (even
worse) excerpts from his opera. Sala and his friends were enthusiastic, and a
decision was taken. A performance of the opera would be arranged. Money
would be raised by subscription. Puccini's defeat in the Sonzogno competition
would be vindicated.

Within a short time, Boito had arranged for the use of the Teatro Dal
Verme for the première of Le Willis, and Ricordi had been convinced that it
would be a good investment to print the libretto of the opera at no charge.
Remarkable progress, too, was being made in raising the money to finance the
production. By the end of April, Fontana was able to write Puccini, who had
returned to Lucca:

> Today I received 60 lire from a friend, a stockbroker, Signor
> Vimercati, to whom I had turned for help, and who is joining in
> together with some of his friends. I will show you his kind letter. I
> expected at most 20 or 30 lire from this friend of mine. Instead, you
> see, it's double. That is cause for hope. But I already told you I was
> not worried about the money. In fact, here is the amount we can
> count on up to now: Vimercati, L.60, Marco Sala L.50, Arrigo Boito
> L.50, the Sala brothers L.20, the "Unknown Woman" of Marco Sala
> L.50. That makes 230 lire. Still to come are Duke Litta, Noseda,
> Count Sola and Biraghi. Let's say that among them they give at least
> 100 lire which would make 330 lire. And Melzi? That will make it
> 430. The expenses being L.450 (250 for costumes and 200 for copies),
> so you see that at most you will have to spend 20 lire. At the
> moment, I am putting the finishing touches on the libretto, and
> tomorrow morning I will send it to Ricordi with a good letter. I will
> arrange the intermezzo as you wish. Did you receive the sketches for
> the sets? Are they all right? You take care of your music and don't
> think about the rest. I say and I repeat that I will take responsibility
> for it all.

In spite of these assurances, Puccini continued to worry that something
would go wrong; he seemed overwhelmed by all these developments and
hardly able to believe that his chance had really come. His insecurity was
such that he even asked his librettist if they could get a contract, so that there
would be no question of a last-minute cancellation. Fontana assured him that
a contract would be useless and that the opera would unquestionably be
performed. To calm the anxious composer, he repeatedly wrote him that he
must worry only about the music and the details of the staging—that the rest
was in his hands. But Puccini was so uncertain that it wasn't until a little
more than two weeks before the scheduled performance that he even wrote
the good news to Albina, whose health was by that time rapidly deteriorat-
ing. That letter, written from Milan on May 13, read as follows:

As you must have heard, I am giving my little opera at the Dal Verme. I hadn't written to you sooner because I wasn't sure of this. Many people from here—among them people as important as A. Boito and Marco Sala—have joined together to present it, each one pledging to contribute a certain amount. I have written to relatives and to Cerù to help me for the copying, which will come to at least 200 lire, I'm still not sure, it could be even more. . . .

The official announcement of the event on May 31, 1884, was an unusual one—almost a challenge: "Tonight at the Teatro Dal Verme, the first performance of another of the operas submitted to the *Teatro Illustrato* competition, one of the works which received neither a prize nor an honorable mention, will be given."

The theatre was packed, and the public was enthusiastic from the start. Because of the unusual sponsorship of the production, the leading members of Milan's musical and intellectual circles were present, as were a large number of students from the Conservatory, there to cheer on their former fellow. Puccini himself appeared in a coffee-colored suit which he hoped the audience would mistake for the more appropriate black. At the end of the performance, with only forty centesimi in his pocket, he had to borrow money to send a jubilant telegram to his mother: CLAMOROUS SUCCESS. EIGHTEEN CURTAIN CALLS. FIRST FINALE REPEATED THREE TIMES. AM HAPPY.

The success of the evening was confirmed by the next day's newspapers. Filippo Filippi, writing in *Perseveranza*, reported: "Puccini to the stars! Enthusiasm for *Le Willis!* Applause from everyone, from the entire public, from start to finish. . . ." Marco Sala, not surprisingly, wrote in *Italia*, "Puccini's opera is, in our opinion, a small and precious masterpiece, from beginning to end." And Antonio Gramola, the critic of the influential *Corriere della Sera*, was equally enthusiastic. "Who could have imagined that among the operas entered in the competition and found unworthy by the jury not only of the first prize but even of a kind word there could have been found the best—and by far the best—of the works of our younger composers. . . . In the music of the young maestro from Lucca there is a freedom of imagination, there are phrases that touch the heart because they must have come from the heart, and there is such elegant and polished craftsmanship that from time to time we seem to have before us not a young student but a Bizet or a Massenet. . . ." Even Sonzogno's magazine, *Musica Popolare*—admitting implicitly the publishing house's error in not recognizing the worth of *Le Willis*—reported that never before at the Teatro Dal Verme had a beginning composer been as enthusiastically acclaimed as was Puccini that evening. This is all the more interesting since Sonzogno's weekly magazine had months before, in October 1883, published a song written by Puccini, "Storiella D'Amore," commenting that the young Lucchese was "already favorably known in the world of music," and that "art can expect much of his talent." (The text of that song, also set to music by Ponchielli, was written by Antonio Ghislanzoni.)

Le Willis was given again on the evenings of June 1 and 2. Again the public was wildy enthusiastic, delighted by the romantic, dramatic music and apparently oblivious of the shortcomings of the rather melodramatic libretto. At the close of the last performance, the composer was presented with a laurel wreath, a tribute to what the newspaper Il Secolo felt was his "talent and exceptional artistic worth."

On the morning of June 4, Puccini and Fontana were called to the offices of Ricordi. The head of the firm had not been at the première, but word had of course reached him of the opera's enormous success. Though the firm almost monopolized the world of Italian opera, its mainstay was the aging Verdi, and thought had to be given to the future. With this in mind, negotiations for Ricordi's purchase of Le Willis, as well as future works by its composer, began. Puccini was satisfied with Ricordi's terms, but the somewhat more self-important Fontana held out for a higher percentage of the earnings. They all met again the next day, and on June 8 the Gazzetta Musicale, published by Ricordi, made it official:

TITO DI GIOVANNI RICORDI
Music Publisher
In Milan, Rome, Naples, Florence, and Paris
announces that he has acquired the sole
copyright, including rights of translation and
production in all countries, of the Opera
LE WILLIS
Words by Ferdinando Fontana
Music by Giacomo Puccini
Produced with great success at the Teatro Dal Verme
in Milan
He has further commissioned Signor Puccini to compose a new
opera
with libretto by Ferdinando Fontana

It is not difficult to imagine Puccini's joy. On the one hand, he had been sure of himself, but he had also been filled with doubts—this pattern would not change throughout his extraordinarily successful career. In any case, his gamble had paid off. He had been right not to abandon Milan for a more secure future in Lucca. The terms of Ricordi's contract included not only a two-thousand-lire advance against future earnings (he used half of that to pay old debts to the astounded proprietor of the trattoria Aida), but a monthly sum of two hundred lire to keep him going while he wrote his newly commissioned opera. He and Fontana were fêted at a dinner at Ricordi's home, and with Ricordi's backing he was suddenly a composer to watch, not just a promising student. His new fame even reached the ears of the great Verdi, who referred to him in a letter of June 10, 1884, written to his friend Opprandino Arrivabene:

> I have heard good things of the musician Puccini. . . . He follows modern tendencies, which is natural, but he keeps strictly to melody which is neither modern nor ancient. It seems, however, that the symphonic element dominates in his work. All right, but it is necessary to be cautious. Opera is opera and symphony is symphony, and I don't think it is good to insert symphonic passages into an opera only for the pleasure of giving the orchestra a chance to cut loose. . . .

Unfortunately, Puccini's immense elation at his new prospects was diminished by bad news from Lucca: his mother's health had taken a turn for the worse. Even before the official announcement from Ricordi, he was called back home to be with Albina during what would surely be her last days.

The confusion of emotions when he returned home was exhausting. The joy of his own more-than-ever promising future and the still-fresh memory of his triumph in Milan were overwhelmed by his sadness at the serious illness of the woman who had stood by and encouraged him for so many years. As soon as he arrived home, Puccini dutifully took charge and arranged to have his mother examined by a well-known specialist in Pisa. The news was not good, but the doctor held out some hope. Upset as he was by his problems at home, Puccini found time to keep up with the continuing publicity he was receiving in the Italian press, all of which confirmed his newfound fame. He managed to order photos of himself and of Fontana and to work on revisions of the score of the *Capriccio Sinfonico*, which Faccio would finally be performing in Turin in early July. His hope was that his mother's condition might improve by the end of June so that he might leave for Turin to attend rehearsals as well as the first professional performance of his *Capriccio*.

When the time came, there was no sign of deterioration of Albina's condition, but Puccini left Lucca with a heavy heart. The trip to Turin was important for his career, as was a planned visit to Milan for conferences with Fontana and Ricordi, but the composer's mind was very much on his mother. Certainly his trip to Turin proved to be justified, and his stay in the Piemontese capital was most successful. He was entertained at the home of the influential music critic of the *Gazzetta Piemontese*, the rehearsals of his *Capriccio* pleased him—and, to make things better, he had word there that his mother's condition seemed to be improving. Because of this unexpected good news, he was able to enjoy fully the immense success of his work in its first professional performance, on the night of July 6. Not only was he personally acclaimed by the large and distinguished audience; his *Capriccio* had to be encored before the applause would stop.

After Turin, Puccini went on to Milan and to Belluno, where he spent time with Ricordi, who had asked ,the composer to expand *Le Willis* to two acts for future productions in Turin'and at La Scala. This was the first chance for these two men — an enormously talented beginner and a most successful and perceptive publisher — to spend time together. It was the start of a very close relationship that was to be vitally important for both of them.

Puccini, too, had a chance to visit Fontana's home in Caprino. The composer and librettist had become good friends. The latter felt a genuine affection for his rather nervous colleague and wrote of him in an 1884 issue of the *Gazzetta Musicale:* "He is happy and passionate, cordial and sweet, but also decisive and judicious. . . . A good-looking man who likes the simple life and dislikes salons. He thinks a good deal before he writes . . . but when he begins he goes on without interruption. He is," Fontana went on, "one of the most intelligent and one of the dearest young men I have had the pleasure to meet."

In the middle of his stay in the North, Puccini was called home. Albina had taken a turn for the worse, and on July 17, shortly after his arrival in Lucca, she died. Distraught, he lovingly placed the wreath given to him after the last Milanese performance of *Le Willis* on her deathbed. Her loss was a tremendous blow to her elder son. She had stubbornly believed in and had relentlessly struggled for him; she had been both mother and father from the time he was a small child. No sacrifice had been too great, and if sometimes she had seemed overly domineering, she had been so with the passion of a widow, both protecting and guiding her favorite son. There were the daughters, whom she loved and enjoyed, and there was Michele, another son but a troubled and moody boy, who had never shown that special flair and gift for music that Giacomo had. And Giacomo was always aware of his mother's special attachment to him; she never bothered to hide it. Her very presence, her reliability and faith had been the main source of his courage, and he felt her loss profoundly — a loss all the more bitter because it had come just when he was beginning to repay her confidence by fulfilling her expectations of him.

Friends and family rallied to give their support to the bereaved young man, and Fontana proved to be especially compassionate, urging Puccini to go ahead with his revisions of their opera, reminding him that "work is the only medicine that can relieve great sorrow," as he put it in a letter of July 31.

However, in August, when Puccini had returned to Milan, he was still obsessed with the death of his mother. "I am always thinking about her," he wrote to Ramelde, "and last night I saw her in my dreams. Today I am sadder than ever. Whatever triumph art can supply, I will always be unhappy because I will miss my mother. I hope you will find the peace that still eludes me. . . ."

Driven by the urgent need to finish the revisions of *Le Willis*, Puccini did his best to follow Fontana's advice by throwing himself into his work, but he was frustrated in the attempt, unable to visit his librettist in Caprino because a few cases of cholera, threatening an epidemic, had broken out in nearby Bergamo. And Fontana did not feel he could leave his wife and son alone to visit Puccini in Milan. So the two men collaborated on the changes by correspondence, with Puccini comforted only by the knowledge that the opera would be performed in Turin in December and at La Scala in January of the following year.

No matter how smoothly his professional career was progressing, the distracted young man was unable to recover from the death of his mother. He felt lost in Milan, while in Lucca under the supervision of Dr. Cerù, the family home and furnishings were being sold. His feelings about this were mixed; he desperately needed the money that would result from the sale — this would be divided equally among all the children — but he also regretted the loss of objects which had played such an important part in the history of his family. He insisted that the house itself be sold only on the condition that it might — if his fortunes improved — be redeemed one day. He worried, too, about Michele, who seemed to be drifting without purpose between Milan and Lucca. There was too much on his mind to enjoy his newfound success and on September 3 he wrote a sad and lonely letter from Milan to Dr. Cerù. "I am leading a retired life," he commented. "I go out only to eat and by seven I am back home. I work, I smoke, I read. I go to the window to see who passes by. In short, my life is restricted to the house, the house, and the house."

In spite of this, work on the expanded version of *Le Willis* continued, and composer and librettist were in agreement concerning the needed changes. Most important, Ricordi was pleased with their efforts, so much so that he began urging Puccini and Fontana to begin thinking of their next opera. Their immediate concern, however, was the forthcoming production of their first opera at Turin's Teatro Regio, and what they found when they arrived for rehearsals did not please them at all. They complained to Ricordi about the singers, the chorus, the orchestra, the staging, the ballet company — and even the acoustics in the distinguished theatre. Their only hope was that the performance at La Scala in January would be better.

Their fears concerning the Turin production were not founded. *Le Villi* (this was its new title), in its two-act version, was performed on the night of December 26 to a large and enthusiastic audience, and the composer was called before the curtain four times.

The opera's première at La Scala, on the other hand, was a disappointment.

The public on the night of January 24, 1885, was reserved and cool. In spite of this, Le Villi was performed thirteen times at Italy's leading opera house that season — a more than auspicious beginning for the first work of a young composer. Even more important, during those Scala performances Puccini showed the first signs of asserting himself and obeying his own instincts for the theatre. Among the spectators at one performance was Puccini's mentor, Ponchielli. Though the kindly professor was enthusiastic, he advised his former pupil to cut out one of the scenes of the opera. Puccini gave it serious thought and then summoned Fontana and informed him that the scene which Ponchielli wanted eliminated would have to be, instead, expanded. The result was one of the opera's most successful arias. This small act of defiance toward a man who was not only his teacher but the composer of one of the most successful musical dramas of the time was evidence that Puccini knew what he wanted and felt sure enough of himself to impose his will. He would impose that will and show his unfailing theatrical instinct many times in the future.

The House of Ricordi

More than four years passed between the La Scala première of *Le Villi* and the first performance, also at La Scala, of Puccini's next opera. They were difficult years, not very productive musically, and yet they were of great importance, for during this period Puccini developed profound relationships with two people who would play major roles in his life.

The first of these was Giulio Ricordi, whose distinguished music publishing house gave the young composer his first chance and, with one exception, was to publish and manage the productions of every opera he wrote. Founded in 1808 by a musician named Giovanni Ricordi, the firm had risen to such eminence that it practically held a monopoly on Italian opera during the nineteenth century. Giovanni was succeeded as head of the firm by his son Tito, who was then succeeded by his son, Giulio. By the time Giulio had taken over as director, the firm had acquired rights to the works of Rossini, Bellini, Donizetti, and Verdi. Without the operas written by these composers, there would be no Italian opera. The power of the House of Ricordi was staggering. When an opera house wanted to perform the work of any of these composers, it could do so only with the consent of Ricordi. Ricordi set the fee, the place of performance, the time of performance. . . . . The firm had a voice, and a powerful one, in matters of casting and of staging. In addition, Ricordi published the scores which, of necessity, had to be bought by whoever performed their works. The power of the firm was also self-perpetuating. If they decided to take a gamble on a new composer — as they did with Ponchielli and Boito, among others — they could withhold permission to produce an opera of Rossini or Verdi unless the opera house would join them in taking a chance on the new composer.

Giulio Ricordi was a worthy successor to his grandfather and father. Distinguished-looking with a slightly turned-up mustache and a greying beard, he was a shrewd businessman and an intelligent musician. A man of broad culture and impeccable taste, he was especially well versed in literature—he knew his Dante and Shakespeare, just as he knew the writings of his contemporaries. With a background in Latin, he spoke French perfectly and could manage well in German and English—very important for the growth of his internationally important firm. He was a passionate lover of the theatre, he wrote poetry, and, under the pseudonym of J. Burgmein, he even wrote music, some of which was performed professionally. He was therefore in a good position to give useful creative advice to his composers. He was not infallible—he rejected Leoncavallo and Bizet and Mascagni's *Cavalleria Rusticana* ("I do not believe in this opera," he said), but he was very often right.

He was, of course, right when it came to Puccini. From a practical point of view, the firm badly needed a successor to Verdi, who was Giulio's idol and whose imposing portrait dominated the wall of his somber, drab office and almost overwhelmed the publisher's immense desk. Verdi, already in his seventies, was still remarkably active, but even the energetic, powerful giant of Italian opera was not immortal. Giulio Ricordi's conservatism was well known; it was reflected in the costume he inevitably wore—a grey suit with a white shirt and a high stiff collar and a discreet single-pearl tie pin. Yet the time had come for the cautious, self-confident publisher to take a chance, and his instincts told him that the future of his firm would be dependent on the young man from Lucca. From the time they concluded their agreement on *Le Villi*, Giulio Ricordi and Giacomo Puccini became trusted colleagues and friends. Ricordi never let Puccini down, seeking new librettos for him, advising him sympathetically and intelligently, and offering him his friendship to such a degree that by 1889 Puccini was to write his sponsor and friend that he was "the only person who inspires me with trust and to whom I can confide all that is going through my mind." It might be, as most earlier biographers have said, that Ricordi, eighteen years older than Puccini, played the role of father in the composer's life, but it is indisputable that Ricordi needed Puccini—he was staking the future of his publishing house on the younger man's success—as much as the composer needed his publisher, that the two men were temperamentally well suited to one another, and that their relationship was a mutually beneficial one in every way.

The same cannot be said of Puccini's relationship with the other person whom he met during this period and who was to play a vital role in his life, the woman who was to become his companion and, later, his wife. Her name was Elvira Bonturi Gemignani, and they met toward the end of 1884, when

Puccini was temporarily back in Lucca. Elvira was tall, classically beautiful, statuesque, and dignified. She was also married—to a merchant named Narciso Gemignani. According to some sources, Gemignani had been a friend of Puccini's long before either one knew Elvira, and it was Gemignani who brought the two together, urging his musician friend to give the modestly talented young woman voice lessons. However they met, Elvira and Puccini fell in love and took full advantage of Gemignani's frequent business trips to demonstrate their affection for one another. By the middle of 1886, Elvira left Lucca, unable any longer to hide the fact that she was pregnant. Her friends and relatives were told that she was going to Palermo; the truth was that she left for Milan, to be with Giacomo Puccini. The two remained in Milan for a while and then moved to Monza where, on December 23, their son Antonio was born.

In later years, Elvira would become cold, sullen and possessive. Her flight from Lucca with Puccini, however, showed her to be a woman of considerable courage, a woman clearly motivated by passion and by love for the young composer, a strong-willed and determined woman prepared to defy the closed, provincial society in which she had been raised. Not only was Elvira married to a respected member of that society, she was also the mother of two children, a six-year-old girl, Fosca, and Renato, a three-year-old boy. When she left Gemignani, she took Fosca with her, leaving young Renato with his father.

The proper Lucchesi were scandalized; and Puccini's rather straitlaced sisters were horrified, blaming the young woman for seducing their brother. Neither Puccini nor Elvira could ever live in Lucca again—nor is there any indication that they wanted to, even after the uproar had died down.

For the next few years, however, after the birth of their son, the couple could not live anywhere together for a long period of time. The monthly payment from Ricordi was far too little to support the composer, Elvira, Fosca, and the newborn infant, so Elvira and the children spent most of their time in Florence—at her mother's home or her sister's—while Puccini stayed in or near Milan. It was difficult for the composer to work for many reasons: the turmoil of his own personal life, complicated by worries over the future of his aimless brother who had become his concern after the death of Albina, and by endless, nagging financial worries. Fortunately, Ricordi proved to be understanding, and Puccini's monthly allowance from the publisher was extended beyond its original date of June 1886. Nonetheless, the composer was not permitted that peace of mind which would have made the writing of his second opera somewhat easier for him.

Another problem that most likely slowed the composer down was Fontana's choice of subject for this second collaboration. This was Alfred de Musset's *La Coupe et les lèvres*, a confusing, turgid drama even Musset felt was not suitable for theatrical performance. If the libretto for *Le Villi* was ill suited to Puccini, Fontana's *Edgar* was even more so. In adapting this literary "closet" drama for use as a libretto, Fontana robbed the work of its poetry—its only merit—and transformed it into an absurd opera. That Puccini, who would prove to be extraordinarily demanding of his librettists in the future, accepted Fontana's libretto could be explained by either his personal fatigue or a kind of euphoria based on the success of their first opera; but how Fontana convinced the wise and experienced Ricordi to allow the newest and most promising composer of his distinguished publishing house to waste his time on such an ill-conceived project remains a mystery.

Progress on *Edgar* was slow. Puccini began work on it in Milan in May 1884. He continued work in Lucca—Fontana visiting there for a short time—and the finished libretto arrived in late May 1885. Not until May of 1886, shortly before Puccini was forced to leave Lucca because of Elvira's pregnancy, did he feel that the end was in sight. But the opera was not finally to be completed until October 1887, after extended stays in Monza and at Caprino Bergamasco.

During this time, Puccini visited Lucca several times, but because of the continuing effects of the scandal, he was able to stay but a short time and did not make his presence widely known. Also during this period, in February of 1887, the revised version of *Le Villi* was again performed, this time at Trieste. The production was a huge success, and at the end of the performance the composer was given a crown—a show of appreciation by all those involved in the production. Slightly less than a year later, however, Puccini suffered his first real failure with his first opera. It happened in Naples, where the composer traveled to supervise the production, confident that it would again be greeted with enthusiasm. Instead, a noisy, unruly audience reacted angrily to the young Lucchese's work. His friend Mascagni was there to console him, but the composer was baffled and hurt by the audience's reaction. As soon as possible, he returned to Milan; a large banquet to celebrate the Neapolitan success of *Le Villi* had been planned. The banquet was not canceled, but it was instead turned into a good-natured protest at the opera's failure in the South.

If Puccini and his friends took this failure with good humor, such would not be the case with the reaction to the first performance, at La Scala, of *Edgar*, a few months later. Three weeks before this world première—a première that had been much delayed by the opera house's scheduling difficulties—Ricordi's *Gazzetta Musicale* warned that serious problems faced the production of Puccini's second opera. The most serious was that Novelli, the soprano who was to sing the exceptionally difficult role of Tigrana, had taken sick and would not be able to perform. Romilda Pantaleoni, Verdi's first Desdemona, who had also sung in *Le Villi*, agreed to undertake the role, and to show their appreciation, Puccini and Fontana had written a new scene in

Act Three for the prima donna. According to Nardi, in his biography of Boito, it was Verdi, at Boito's urging, who talked Pantaleoni into undertaking the role at what was almost the last minute.

All problems seem to have been satisfactorily solved, however, because a few days before the première, Puccini's good friend Pericle Pieri wrote to the composer's family in Lucca that a great success was expected, and that Verdi, then in Milan, was supposed to attend the première. In neither case was Pieri's prediction correct. There is no evidence that Verdi, though in the city at the time, attended the opening . . . and *Edgar* was hardly the success expected.

The world première took place on Easter Sunday, April 21, 1889, with Franco Faccio conducting. The reception to the eagerly awaited opera was polite but unenthusiastic. The opera, with its sporadically interesting score and its unbelievable libretto, simply did not rouse the public. The review by Antonio Gramola in the *Corriere della Sera* is worth quoting in part — it goes on at great length — because it describes the reaction of the audience and is also a fine example of a critic trying to praise a work but, in the end, absolutely unable to do so.

> Maestro Puccini must have been flattered by the demonstration of affection and esteem which the Milanese public showed him by coming to the theatre in such numbers on Easter Sunday and punctually so as not to miss a bar of *Edgar*. The fears of some concerning the mood of the spectators who were forced to shut themselves in a theatre immediately after their Easter dinner were absolutely without foundation. Rarely has there been in our greatest theatre an atmosphere of goodwill as there was last night. Goodwill, however, that was always accompanied by a calmness, an impartiality of judgment which was a credit to the public of La Scala. The attention of the audience didn't waver for a moment, and the applause afforded the composer and the performers was characterized by a most dignified spontaneity.

Ricordi's own magazine, of course, tried to make the best of it. The April 28 issue of the *Gazzetta Musicale* found *Edgar* to be a work of genius. While admitting that the critics had their reservations, the writer for the *Gazzetta* reported that the public was more than enthusiastic. This in spite of the production problems: the illness of several members of the chorus, of the chorus director himself, and the fact that the première was scheduled at the very last moment. In any case, the severity of the critics was aimed, above all, according to Ricordi's publication, at the libretto, and thus the fault was entirely Fontana's. Certainly, according to the publisher's magazine, there was no reason for Puccini to be discouraged; after all, long and serious articles were not devoted to criticisms of mediocre operas, further proof that *Edgar* was a substantial and worthwhile work of art. In addition, even those critics who found fault with the opera expressed a desire to hear it again. . . .

Another review, in the authoritative weekly *Illustrazione Italiana*, was mildly encouraging. "This young man from Lucca," according to the April 28 issue of the magazine, "can be pleased with his success. *Edgar* is something more than *Le Villi*, and at the same time something less. It is no longer a brief effort; it is opera, a full-fledged work. However, after *Le Villi*, in which one admired a vigorous burst of inspiration, we expected a more inspired and stronger *Edgar*. However, the beauties of the new score, even if they don't demonstrate the full measure of Puccini's talent, are certainly enough to confirm his status as a master. . . ."

Another futile attempt to mask the failure of the new opera is found in Puccini's gracious letter to Faccio on April 25, acknowledging the conductor's important role in the "cordial reception I had from the Milanese public." Nonetheless, *Edgar* was not a success. It was withdrawn after two more performances at La Scala, and its future — as well as that of its composer — was very much in doubt.

In a postmortem session, Ricordi was attacked by his board of directors. A large sum of money had been invested in Puccini with, so far, highly unsatisfactory results. Certainly there seemed no chance of ever recovering the eighteen thousand lire in advance payments that the firm had already given to the composer. Ricordi, the board felt, had made a mistake in backing the young man from Lucca. It would be better to withdraw the firm's support of Puccini at once before more money was lost.

Ricordi, however, was firm in upholding his protégé, unyielding in his belief in Puccini's future. Since he controlled the publishing house both financially and artistically, the publisher, of course, had his way. He even told his directors that he would personally repay any loss that his support of Puccini might cost the firm.

Nonetheless, it was clear that something had to be done. Six days after the première, Ricordi summoned Puccini and Fontana to his home. There were many questions to be resolved, among them whether or not a revised version of *Edgar* could be ready for production at La Scala within a few weeks. The following morning, Ricordi had a long letter delivered to Puccini:

Dearest Maestro:

The long discussion of last night has troubled me much. Because of it I was unable to pass a tranquil night. . . . Concerning the modifications which were proposed, except those which are absolutely necessary and which you yourself could make, you have let yourself be carried away by your natural and exuberant musical instinct. . . . I doubt that these modifications can be made in time so *Edgar* might again be given in May on two or three evenings. The theatre will open from the tenth to the fourteenth and will be closed from the twenty-fourth on. I am wondering how all the changes can be made in so short a time, how the score can be corrected, the parts, the choruses, etc., etc. What is the impresario going to say, who will ask himself all these questions? If the opera will not be ready — then trouble . . . protests! — and then it will not be given again.

It is a question here of rapid and feverish labor. I understand that that could cost you a great deal, after the fatigue and the emotions of the rehearsal. But in God's name, one is not Puccini for nothing. One is not in the flower of life if one fears these problems and problems even more grave. Certainly you have full liberty to do what you want. I can only talk as a practical man who has known people and business for many years. I can only state the facts with that frankness which I derive from the affection and esteem in which I hold you.

Remember, Puccini, that you are in one of the critical and difficult moments of your artistic life. I say this not because of the idiocies given forth by our famous music critics, but because now we must open a breach, scale it with courage and perseverance, and there plant a victorious flag. I, who am neither a writer nor an artist nor an opera composer, yet sense the worth of this *Edgar*. I read in it clearly all your gifts, all the hopes for the future. But to realize these hopes it is necessary to follow one motto: Excelsior!

That interminable discussion of almost five hours!! Yesterday it frightened me. Your good Fontana has shown himself to be an eloquent orator but a caviling one. More of a philosopher-lawyer than a poet: the subtleties of his reasoning are admirable but they do not convince, they do not persuade. He holds to the same ideas as before . . . I honor him. Yet, after all, it is the imagination and the personality of the musician which are everything. It is the musician who colors the work, who presents it to the public. Without him it is a zero. Please understand, dear Puccini, that I am not in agreement with the systematic belittlers of the libretto of *Edgar*. There are two effective acts; that is something. But it also contains much obscurity, many fallacies which derive from the theories of Fontana, who assumes that everybody thinks with his head. What impressed me all the more during the long discourses yesterday is that he will never benefit, not now, not later, from the experience of these days. Let us admit all the exaggerations, all the malice that the cruel critics have expended on the libretto; nonetheless there is some truth in what they say and we must reckon with it.

The conclusion of my long letter is this: that before you lay your hands on *Edgar* in order to retouch it, it is necessary that I talk to you alone. It is also necessary that aside from the artistic part of the work the material part be stabilized if we are not to make a hole in the water and find ourselves at the opportune moment with empty hands!! . . . It is necessary that we decide absolutely if the opera can or cannot be given again within a few days. . . . Therefore I ask you to come to my house this very day at twelve o'clock noon precisely, because afterwards I shall have to leave. It is urgent that I talk to you once again of all that I have just written.

There is no record of what happened at that private meeting between Ricordi and Puccini. Fontana had obviously been adamant that no major changes be made in his libretto, and Ricordi was more than ever anxious to put the blame for the opera's failure on the librettist. It is more than likely that Ricordi strongly urged Puccini to find himself a new librettist. In the meantime, one decision was made. On May 4, Puccini wrote to Raffaello Franceschini, Ramelde's husband, that there would be no more performances of *Edgar* at La Scala that year. He gave as reason the inferior performances of the work and stated that it would be the opening opera of La Scala's 1889–1890 season.

This was not to be the case. *Edgar* was revised and later produced with some success in Lucca, Madrid and Buenos Aires, but even the composer realized that its defects were serious and irremediable. Years later, he gave his close friend Sybil Seligman a vocal score of the opera with some of his own scathing marginal comments. The title page read as follows:

E Dio ti GuARdi da quest'opera

(May God protect you from this opera)

Alongside the finale of the second act, the composer wrote—"the most horrible thing ever written." In Act Three, after Edgar shouts out "Edgar lives," Puccini writes, "A lie!" And at the very end of the opera, when the chorus cries, "Horror," the composer notes, "How right they are."

In a more serious critical vein, years later, Puccini told his friend and biographer Fraccaroli that *Edgar* could never succeed because it was a thea-trically defective organism. "The basis of an opera is the subject and its treatment. The libretto of *Edgar*, with all respect to the memory of my friend Fontana, is a blunder which I accepted. . . . The fault is more mine than his."

Manon Lescaut

Though deeply disappointed by the cool reception to his second opera and worn out by the long and often painful discussions with Ricordi, Puccini made a remarkably fast recovery, as he had before and as he would again in the face of temporary setbacks. Obviously, his publisher's stubborn faith in him was of utmost importance — as was his own faith in himself — and only a few weeks after *Edgar's* première, the young composer was already searching for a libretto for his next opera. In a letter of May 7, 1889, he implored Ricordi to do all he could to obtain the rights to what was then one of Europe's most successful plays — Victorien Sardou's *La Tosca*. A vehicle for Sarah Bernhardt, who first performed it in Paris on November 24, 1887, Sardou's melodrama was enjoying a triumphant tour throughout Europe in the spring of 1889. The idea of turning it into an opera seems to have originated with Fontana, though it is entirely possible that Puccini saw and was impressed by Bernhardt as Tosca that year at the Teatro Filodrammatici in Milan. In any case, he wrote Ricordi that "in this *Tosca* I see the opera I need, one not of excessive proportions either as a decorative spectacle or as a work which calls for the usual overabundance of music." Ricordi did what he could, but he was unable to obtain Sardou's permission at that time; the French dramatist most probably did not want to give the rights to his hugely successful work to a relatively unknown composer — to whom, when he was far from unknown ten years later, he would eagerly grant those rights.

Sometime in the spring of 1889, Puccini read the Abbé Prévost's short novel, *L'Histoire de Manon Lescaut et du Chevalier des Grieux.* He was deeply moved by this passionate and dramatic love story, which had served as the basis for Jules Massenet's opera, first produced in Paris in 1884. Puccini was well aware of the enormous success of the Frenchman's opera — during its first ten years, it had been sung two hundred times at the Opéra-Comique — but he saw no reason not to go ahead with his own version of the novel. "Massenet feels it as a Frenchman with the powder and the minuets; I shall feel it as an Italian, with desperate passion," he stated. The beautiful Manon was such an extraordinary woman, he believed, that she could have two lovers, and he wrote to Ricordi that he had found the perfect subject. "Manon is a heroine I believe in, and therefore it cannot fail to win the hearts of the public." This time, however, he would be more careful in his choice of a librettist. "No idiotic librettist," he wrote, "must be allowed to ruin the story — I shall certainly put my hand to the making of the libretto."

The composer did indeed put his hand to every libretto he came across in the years that followed, but he was a musician and not a writer, so to write the libretto, Ricordi turned to a talented young man who was still wavering between a literary and a musical career. This was Ruggero Leoncavallo, Puccini's contemporary, then unknown; not until 1892 would he win fame with his I Pagliacci, his one and only masterpiece. Leoncavallo was to be but the first of many of Manon Lescaut's librettists.

While Leoncavallo worked on Manon Lescaut, Ricordi pursued other ideas for his composer, and on June 15, 1889, Puccini wrote to Enrico Del Carlo in Lucca that he had reached an agreement with Giuseppe Giacosa for a new libretto. This was excellent news, for Giacosa was already well established as one of the most important and respected playwrights of his time. Only two years before, his play Tristi Amori, which he had written for Eleanora Duse, had been a sensation throughout Europe. That this eminent dramatist was willing to write a libretto for Puccini — undoubtedly at Ricordi's urging — was a great compliment to the young and still little-known composer.

The story proposed by Giacosa was set in Russia and on July 19, Puccini apologetically wrote Ricordi of his disillusionment with the project.

> I am tortured by doubt concerning Giacosa's libretto. I fear that the subject is not suitable for me. I am afraid that I shall not succeed in writing the kind of music it should have. I wonder if you could find a way of suggesting to Giacosa, without hurting him, that he should leave it alone for the present? On my return from Germany, I should go and spend a week or so with him, and we could then come to an understanding about it. We should look for, and certainly find, something more poetic, more pleasing, and less gloomy, with a little more nobility of conception.
>
> That Russia of his frightens me, and, to tell the truth, does not convince me. I am sure that what I am writing will displease you

very much, but—supposing I had to compose an opera which I did not *entirely feel?* I would be damaging you as well as myself. The contract with Giacosa could still stand. We could just change the clause about delivery by November and postpone it to January or February. I have plenty to do. I will have *Manon* in August. . . .

The trip to Germany mentioned by Puccini was a significant one for the composer, a sign of Ricordi's considerable respect for his musicianship and theatrical gifts. The firm of Ricordi, having bought out its former rival publishing house Lucca upon the death of Signora Lucca, had acquired the Italian rights to the operas of Wagner. *Die Meistersinger* was to be performed at La Scala the following season, but Ricordi—no great admirer of the German composer—felt that its length would not be acceptable to the Italian public and believed that the opera had to be made "slender and effective." To suggest possible cuts in the score and to study the Festspielhaus production of Wagner's masterpiece, Ricordi sent Puccini, together with Franco Faccio and the set designer Adolfo Hohenstein, to Bayreuth in mid-July. The trip was an exciting experience for Puccini, who was most enthusiastic about the opera itself and entranced by the brilliant production, conducted by Hans Richter.

More than that, Ricordi's enlisting the young composer's help in so important a task was proof that Puccini remained in the publisher's favor, still the one and only hope of the House of Ricordi. Alfredo Catalani bitterly took note of this in a letter to a friend in which he stated that "not all of us have the luck to travel at the expense of the publisher, as Puccini has, furnished with a good pair of scissors and commissioned by the publisher to make the cuts necessary in the score of *Meistersinger* so that it might fit the shoulders of the good Milanesi like a suit. . . . I don't hide the fact that I feel bitterness in my soul on seeing what is happening and am frightened at the idea of what my future can be now that there is only one publisher, and that publisher doesn't want to hear a word about anyone but Puccini. . . . All this seems absurd, but instead it's absolutely right, because now there are dynasties in art, too, and I know that Puccini *must* be Verdi's successor. . . ."

Upon his return from this exhilarating trip to Germany, in late July, Puccini went to Vacallo, a small Swiss village above the Italian border town of Chiasso, where he spent a few more months working on revisions for *Edgar* and on *Le Villi*, which was again to be performed at the Teatro Dal Verme in November. While there, he received the promised version of *Manon Lescaut* from Leoncavallo. It proved to be disappointing; as a result he would have to look elsewhere for the right librettist for his new project. His next idea was to approach Marco Praga, an old acquaintance and at the time a very successful playwright, author of *La Moglie Ideale* which had also been written for

Eleonora Duse. Praga's version of his dealings with Puccini were reported by
Giuseppe Adami in his biography of the composer:

> One evening soon after the production of my play, *La Moglie
> Ideale*, I had gone, as usual, to Savini's for a game when Puccini
> entered and asked to speak to me. We went out together and took a
> turn around the Galleria. Suddenly, without any warning, he said,
> "You must write me a libretto." I confess that the unexpected
> proposal took my breath away; the friendship and admiration I felt
> for Puccini made my resistance rather weak. I had never written a
> libretto; I had never even thought of writing one. "That doesn't
> matter," said Puccini, "especially as you don't even need to be
> concerned about the choice of a subject: it is *Manon Lescaut*. You
> have a sure theatrical instinct, you know how to construct. If you
> refuse to write the verses" — I had it made plain from the start that,
> though the son of a poet, I could not do this — "you may choose your
> own collaborator."
>
> . . . A few days later, I had a second conversation with the
> composer and explained to him briefly how I would divide the
> acts. . . . Puccini was delighted. I wrote the plot. I submitted it to
> Puccini and to Giulio Ricordi, who approved it. Domenico Oli-
> va . . . agreed to collaborate, lost no time in writing the verses, and
> the libretto was soon complete. In the summer, I went with Puccini
> and Oliva to Cernobbio, where the Ricordi family was spending the
> summer, and we read the poem. Paolo Tosti was present at the
> reading, which was completely successful. . . .
>
> Back in Milan, we concluded our agreement and Puccini departed
> with his, or rather our, manuscript. Things could not have been
> better. But such a pleasant state of affairs was of short duration. A
> few months later, the composer was no longer satisfied with the
> plotting or with the division of the acts. He no longer felt that it was
> an *opéra comique*. He wished to eliminate the second act, substitut-
> ing the third for it, and for the third he wanted to find a striking and
> dramatic situation. As a dramatist, I did not approve of the change.
> Neither did I, from my own point of view, feel like changing the
> structure of the libretto. I declined the task and turned over the
> whole matter to Domenico Oliva, with complete freedom to change
> it as he saw fit. Oliva adopted Puccini's ideas and completely recast
> the work. . . .

By the end of March 1890, Oliva had finished the first two acts; Puccini
seemed delighted with them, and, encouraged, the poet went on with his
work. Within a few months, however, the composer had his doubts and
complained bitterly to his sister Tomaide that it was impossible to find a poet
who could do a decent job. Thus, it is surprising that Puccini again expressed
his satisfaction when Oliva presented him with the first part of the third act.

Given the composer's vacillations, it is not surprising, however, that by September he was again unhappy — an unhappiness expressed in a letter written to Ricordi from Vacallo:

I have thought it advisable to send you Oliva's manuscript, so that you may read it and get an exact idea of the defects and distortions which it contains. There are some good things in it, but the quartet, to take one example, is ugly. I don't understand why Oliva has departed here from the original outline which was so clear . . . the fact remains that I am not at all satisfied, and I believe you will agree with me. The departure from the outline has, in some respects, been an improvement, but in many other respects it has been for the worse.

I shall write to Oliva that the manuscript, with my notes, is in your hands. I beg and beseech you to see him and explain the contents of this letter and say anything else you think on your own account.

The writer of this letter was a new Puccini — a man with a sure sense of the theatre and certain of what he wanted; he was also willing to make demands to see that he was given just what he felt was needed. Oliva was, of course, discouraged, and in a letter to Ricordi in October he complained that when he began he had had no idea of the difficulties involved in writing a libretto. He was now merely awaiting his turn to be slapped down once and for all.

But Puccini was far from predictable, and on November 15, 1890, he wrote a letter from Vacallo to Ricordi indicating that all was well — a cheerful, even playful letter in which he referred to himself as the Doge of Vacallo, a term Ricordi often used to describe the young composer because of his dignified bearing and aristocratic reserve. "My favorite Manon is growing and seems to me in good health," he wrote. "No word from my prime minister Oliva. Am awaiting the fourth act and the second. . . ."

Before too long, however, the prime minister was forced to offer his resignation. It became obvious to Puccini as well as to Ricordi that another collaborator had to be found.

As work progressed slowly, very often coming to a complete halt, on *Manon Lescaut*, Puccini was losing heart. As early as January 1890, he had written to his brother Michele, who had settled in Argentina, that he would consider joining him in South America. He was gaining some recognition, there were projected performances of his two early operas, and a short string quartet *Crisantemi*, written in memory of the Duca d'Aosta, was to be performed in Milan in February, but there was no money and, it often seemed, little hope. In addition, he was no longer a carefree student. There was Elvira, and there were the children, responsibilities which frequently seemed a burden.

There was bad news from Lucca, too; his sister Nitteti's husband, Alberto Marsili, had died, leaving his widow penniless—and Puccini was in no position to help out. In addition, all efforts to buy back the family home on via di Poggio, so full of meaning to the composer, were failing. Finally, in April of that year, the kindly and generous Dr. Cerù, known to be annoyed at Puccini because of his elopement with Elvira, suddenly demanded all the money he had given him for his studies—with interest! In an angry note, he accused Puccini of being ungrateful and told him that he could now pay him back, for he must have earned at least forty thousand lire from Le Villi. The composer answered him briefly, explaining that it was impossible to repay the debt and enclosing a statement from Ricordi showing that his total earnings had been a mere sixty-five hundred lire.

Weary, he wrote a desperate letter, dated April 30, to Michele in Buenos Aires. "The pharmacist keeps bothering me, and I will have to pay your bill of 25 lire. I am terribly broke. I don't know how I can go on. The monthly 300 lire from Ricordi—an increase over the original amount—keeps coming but that's an advance. It's not enough, and debts keep accumulating. . . . If I could only find a way to earn a living, I would even come to where you are. Is there anything for me to do there? I'd give up everything here and leave . . . I'm ready; if you write me to come, I'll come and we'll invent something. However, I warn you that I need money for the trip!"

Puccini did not join his brother in South America—fortunately, his moods of despair were offset by his passion for his work, no matter how great the difficulties involved. Nor, however, was he ever to see his brother again, for in April 1891 the composer received word of Michele's tragic death. The composer was stunned, and his profound grief at the death of his twenty-seven-year-old brother, sincere though it was, was undoubtedly deepened by a sense of guilt. Since the death of Albina, Michele had been his responsibility. The young man had drifted from job to job, between Lucca and Milan, always in the shadow of his older brother and often acting as little more than an errand boy for him. He had seemed unable to find a proper outlet for whatever talents he might have had. His stay at the Milan Conservatory, interrupted by military service, had ended in failure in his third year. He had no money, and he had no home in Lucca or elsewhere. It was impossible for him to live with his sisters, and though he stayed with him at various times, it was impossible to remain long with his brother in the latter's already overcrowded home. Thus, South America, to which so many Italians emigrated, must have seemed the perfect solution. There were many people he knew from back home, among them Elvira's father, and apparently more possibilities of finding work there than in Italy.

Because of this, Michele had embarked for Buenos Aires in October 1889. Upon his arrival, he was helped above all by Ulderigo Tabarracci, who had sailed with him, and by Edoardo Aromatari, a fellow Lucchese. He felt at ease in the Argentinian city. "I hear more Italian spoken than I do Spanish," he wrote home—and he was optimistic about the possibilities the city, dominated by Italian culture, offered to him. Nonetheless, in spite of a few teaching jobs, he found life in Buenos Aires difficult and expensive and, after six months, was more than pleased to accept an invitation to teach in the provincial capital of Jujuy, 800 miles from Buenos Aires, at the foothills of the East Andes. He was an "important" man in this smaller city, where he worked in the music school teaching voice and piano, as well as Italian, and where he also did secretarial work for the Italian consul. He seemed to have found a solution to his problems.

However, after a short time, tragedy struck when he fell in love with one of his pupils, who also happened to be the wife of Senator Perez, one of the most powerful and influential men in town. After eight months, the clandestine romance was discovered by the senator, who challenged Michele to a duel. Perez was injured in the duel, and Michele, pursued by the police, had to be rushed out of town. With the aid of Italian friends, he was back in Buenos Aires by early January 1891, but Perez's influence reached as far as the capital, and it soon became clear that the young Puccini's life was in danger as long as he remained in Argentina. Because of this, he embarked for Rio de Janeiro, where he took refuge with his old friend Tabarracci, who had moved there from Argentina. But Michele's bad luck had followed him. He arrived in the Brazilian capital at the time the city was ravaged by an epidemic of yellow fever. In a matter of weeks, he himself became a victim of the disease, and he died on March 12, 1891.

Puccini took the news badly; it seemed the final straw in a period marked not only by poverty but also by difficulties in putting in order his new position as a family man—he was still unable to settle down with Elvira and the children in a permanent home of their own. He wrote to Ramelde: "I am almost a dead man. I could say that I didn't even feel such deep pain at the death of our mother, and yet that was trememdous. What a tragedy! I cannot wait to die myself; what am I doing in this world now? Poor Michele. Whatever happens to me, honors, glory, satisfactions—all will be meaningless for me now. . . ."

His one consolation was to be found in his work, but with Oliva's dismissal, progress on the libretto was faltering. Ricordi, however, remained determined to find still another librettist for Puccini; and for this he addressed himself to Giacosa, trying to involve the experienced playwright by asking his advice as to who might complete the often-revised libretto, while hoping that Giacosa himself might undertake the assignment. Giacosa, however, was not interested; while making himself available for guidance and advice whenever needed, he recommended a journalist, playwright, and occasional poet named Luigi Illica for the actual job.

The decision to ask Illica to work on the libretto was a good one. He was a fast worker, sharp-witted, resourceful, and generous in giving of himself and his time. He was also impulsive and quick-tempered—his temper once led to a duel in the course of which he lost half an ear.

His anger was quickly forgotten, however, and in the words of Renato Simoni, himself later to be one of Puccini's librettists, "he was amazed that the men he had offended didn't immediately forget having been offended as he quickly forgot having offended them." This ability to recover was to serve him well in his often stormy dealings with Puccini, just as his great knowledge of the theatre was of immeasurable value to the composer.

Initially, Illica was reluctant to take on the task of revising the libretto; he did not want in any way to offend his colleagues, Praga and Oliva, and not until he had a formal authorization from those two men was he willing to sign an agreement with Puccini and Ricordi. With this in hand, he enthusiastically set to work.

Puccini, from the start in the spring of 1891, made his wishes known to his new collaborator. Sending him a copy of the Praga-Oliva libretto for what was then a three-act opera, he wrote Illica that he wanted a new act, to be the second act, "full of love, spring, youth . . . the background a garden filled with trees in bloom . . . and a floor of green grass." He required an air of freshness and of romance as a setting for Manon and Des Grieux, then happy and passionate lovers. The composer saw the ending of the act as the major problem. Anything similar to Massenet's version was to be avoided at all costs, and something different had to be done. An abduction at the end of this second act was impossible, since the first act ended with something very close to an abduction. "There," he wrote, "is where Illica has to find a solution. . . . All I know is that we need something—an ending for the act that is effective, convincing, and most of all an original stage effect, since it would be useless to add an act if this act were not greatly advantageous and effective. . . ."

The two men worked well together, and for the most part their collaboration—the first of many—was a successful one—though Illica often believed that he was being treated as a subject of the Doge rather than a collaborator, with rights of his own. Certainly the composer was stubborn, demanding and, at the same time, given to sudden changes of heart, and the librettist was not always willing to accommodate without a struggle. While the work on *Manon Lescaut* went forward, there were a large number of disagreements, and to settle and arbitrate these, both men leaned heavily on the wisdom and judgment of Giulio Ricordi, whose role in the creation of the libretto was so important that he could be justly considered a full collaborator in the enterprise. Ricordi not only gave advice and settled arguments; he even contributed several verses of his own to the finished work.

Excerpts from his letters to Puccini attest to his close involvement with the actual creation of his protégé's new opera, especially when the work was coming to an end. On July 22, 1892, Ricordi wrote: "I observe that you want eight verses for the tenor . . . at the end of the second act [this was to become the third act]! What you need is not eight verses, but eight words: that might do. Consider that the whole dramatic action is in a state of suspense. The less the tenor declaims, the better, while the orchestra indicates the movement of the condemned toward the vessel. You must cut the thing short, short, short. And find just the *right* effect to bring down the curtain. . . ." Enclosed with this letter were four verses written by Ricordi himself.

The publisher's suggestions are even more explicit in a letter written shortly afterward, on August 2:

> . . . There are still two or three points which do not satisfy me and certain words which positively need to be changed because they are either too audacious or they smack of operetta. The end of the second act still does not persuade me! But we will manage that. The libretto, taken all in all, seems to me interesting, although in certain parts a little too puffed up and in other parts overloaded with episodes and with dramatic incidents: the music will solve many of these defects.
>
> There is a quantity of characters who are episodic and useless. Merely annoying supernumeraries destined to frighten impresarios and nothing else. Oh, how I cursed, seeing every so often one of these characters spring forth. Away, away! What need is there for a postmaster? The host of the inn is quite capable of receiving Geronte's orders. And that official who says three words in the second act? And then the officer who says two and a half? *Mamma mia!* To hell with all this uselessness!
>
> . . . For pity's sake, dear Puccini, don't make me suffer more agony on account of your excessive length; your music is altogether beautiful, too beautiful. Don't let yourself be led astray by musical philosophy or by the libretto. Forward, forward and quickly!

Two days later, Ricordi expressed concern about another detail. "I think we overlooked one thing. In the first act while Lescaut and Geronte gossip and the students joke and laugh with the girls, there is in the libretto a little part for Edmondo. I don't believe you set that part to music, and if not, so much the better. The scene will go just as well. Let's eliminate those verses. . . ."

On the following day, Ricordi wrote still another letter, with more suggestions. It is clear that the success of the new opera was as important to the publisher and the future of his publishing house as it was to Puccini.

> As I wrote you, the whole of the libretto doesn't seem bad to me. . . . The corrections made by you are good, and I am pleased

that in general you have approved the edition as I envisaged it. As far as I'm concerned, in the finale of Havre I am little pleased with that embrace. It doesn't ring true to life. How can a young man be permitted to kiss a condemned woman, and in front of the commander, the soldiers, and the entire populace? This offends common sense. How about this: Manon marches slowly with the others while Des Grieux begs her: "I have obtained permission"; then, half crying, half speaking: "Manon, Manon, I will follow you!" Manon turns, she falls to her knees, she lifts her arms to heaven in a gesture of joy and gratitude. Des Grieux runs toward Manon, and the curtain falls. It's not so wonderful. No! But it's more believable. Consider it. . . .

Throughout the month of August, Puccini was working at full speed, busily sending off material to Ricordi as it was ready, both men concerning themselves with each and every detail. The composer even turned again to Leoncavallo, then enjoying the huge success of *I Pagliacci*, asking him to redo a few verses of *Manon Lescaut*. Ricordi was appreciative of his protégé's efforts and optimistic at the results of these efforts. "Don't tear your hair if from time to time I am a great, a very great nuisance," he wrote him on August 24. "When I make observations, I do so unwillingly. I do not want to belittle your music. I understand how painful it is to touch a beautiful statue. But when that statue is too colossal for the public to grasp, it is necessary to make concessions and to chisel off a little. . . ." And a few days later: "Life is hard, but when one makes one's way without shameless charlatanism, one comes out ahead and with a clear conscience. With all my heart I hope that you will now begin to climb and climb, for your moral satisfaction — and material. That last is not so contemptible either. The one who will always pull the cart like an ox, that will be I."

Ricordi had pulled the cart valiantly, settling with great tact the many differences that had arisen between Puccini and Illica, up to the completion of the libretto. He believed in the collaboration between the two men and felt strongly that they should continue to work together. In September, he told Puccini that Illica had found another subject which was both "formidable and commercial," and in December, when *Manon Lescaut* was completed, he reminded the composer that Illica had found a "beautiful" plot that could serve as their next work.

Illica, however, felt that there should be further clarification of his role in any dealings with Puccini, that the next project should be a collaboration in the full sense of the word. Quite simply, he had found it difficult to cope with the composer's demands and vacillations, and he expressed his anger and frustrations to Ricordi a few weeks before the première of *Manon Lescaut*:

Puccini has acted with me in a way I don't care to define. Petty gossip has nothing to do with art, but permit me to tell you that artistically both you and I are very mistaken to wrack our brains to look for or invent plots for Puccini.

Puccini has confided to a friend that he can do very well without my librettos . . . that no one can understand him because he longs for something . . . something . . . that!

You must understand that this *something*, explained in this way, is rather difficult to interpret. Do I have to grope in the darkness in search of the *something* that Puccini longs for, only to hear him say, as always, "I don't like it," with the risk of ending up with a libretto that will be set to music by Puccini in the same way *Manon* was, with macaronic verses? . . .

Allow me to tell you that I don't feel like going back to paraphrasing music—and let me tell you I don't think well of this method. . . .

For everybody's sake, and especially for Puccini's, Puccini should make clear in advance what he wants because from the way he expresses himself one might suspect that he himself doesn't know what he wants . . .

Let him bring an idea, a situation, a character, something of this something, and we will write a libretto for him—well thought out by you and me—which will be presented to him complete and, for God's sake, Puccini will have to put the music to the words of the libretto, with the feelings which these words inspire and with the nature of the characters of the libretto in mind. . . .

Excuse my letting off steam, but Giulio Ricordi, as a good publisher-father, should love his musician-children and librettist-children.

Illica's letter to Ricordi served to put his feelings on record, for future reference. Before any serious consideration could be given to the next opera, however, all concerned had to await the outcome of the première of *Manon Lescaut*, which was to take place on February 1, 1893. The verdict of the public and the press, Puccini knew, would be crucial to his future, and he had confided to Giulio Gatti-Casazza, at the time of the first performance of the three-act version of *Edgar* in Ferrara in January 1892 (Gatti's father was director of the Ferrara opera house), that if *Manon Lescaut* were not a success he would be forced to change his profession.

Certainly neither of his previous operas had caught on, in spite of Ricordi's efforts. *Le Villi* had been produced successfully in Venice in March of 1892, and *Edgar*, in additon to the performances in Ferrara, had been presented in Brescia, Turin, and in Lucca. The production of the latter at his hometown's Teatro del Giglio was in a sense a homecoming for the composer, an answer to those who had ostracized him after his elopement with Elvira. The night of its first performance there, September 5, 1891, was a triumph for the composer. In spite of the presence in the theatre of certain hostile groups— friends of Catalani's and of Elvira's husband—*Edgar* was ecstatically received. There were seven encores, and Puccini was called before the curtain more than forty times. After the first performance, he was given a hero's acclamation, festively escorted with music and lighted torches to the Hotel Universo, where he was staying. After the second performance, which was an even greater success, the composer was showered with gifts and given a sumptuous banquet at the restaurant Rebecchino, at which Ricordi toasted him as "the living hope of the Italian musical theatre."

Nonetheless, neither *Le Villi* nor *Edgar* had become part of the repertory of any Italian opera house in the years preceding *Manon Lescaut* (nor, incidentally, would they in the future). More important to Puccini during those difficult years were the first foreign productions of his two early operas; they would be a sign of international recognition.

Since late 1890, both Puccini and Ricordi had been trying to arrange for a production of *Edgar* at Madrid's Teatro Reale; this seemed a good choice because the theatre's musical director was Ricordi's friend Luigi Mancinelli, who had conducted *Le Villi* in Bologna in 1885. By early 1892, definite plans were finally made, but two months before the often-delayed première, the tenor Eugenio Durot, who was to sing the title role, broke his contract with the theatre. Puccini was frantic and in desperation turned to one of the great tenors of the time, Francesco Tamagno, who had created the role of Otello in Verdi's opera. Tamagno and Puccini had become friends during the latter's student days in Milan, and the composer had Tamagno in mind when *Edgar* was first done at La Scala. The tenor, however, was unavailable at the time. Now, upon learning that Tamagno was about to go to Madrid to sing other roles at the Reale, Puccini again turned to his old friend, appealing for his help in what he described as a period of moral and material need. "If I could only have this good fortune after all the sorrow I have had to endure," he wrote to Tamagno in a letter he called a "request-prayer."

Tamagno was not immediately persuaded, but after several letters and telegrams from the composer and from Ricordi who wrote, "If you, with your talent and your kindness, will accept, then you will have given immense encouragement to a young man who really deserves it," he agreed to undertake the role.

Puccini's trip to Madrid in March 1892 marked the first time he had visited a foreign city to participate in the preparations for one of his operas. Understandably, he was apprehensive upon his arrival in the Spanish capital, and even more so when he found, after a few rehearsals, that neither the orchestra nor the chorus lived up to his expectations. He feared that *Edgar* would be poorly received, too, because an influential newspaper, *La Correspondencia*, had printed an article warning the public of the inadequacies of the libretto and because he had heard that a Spanish composer was "waging a fierce crusade" against him. In addition, he felt lonely in a strange city, and he wrote to Elvira, "I'd give ten years of my life to have you here."

His fears were not founded. The première of *Edgar*, with Tamagno, Eva Tetrazzini (sister of Luisa), and Giuseppina Pasqua, and conducted by Mancinelli, was a rousing success. The composer was cheered by the Spanish public at each curtain call, and he was summoned to the royal box after the second act and there congratulated by members of the royal family and invited to pay an official visit to the queen of Spain the following day. With the exception of an 1886 production of *Le Villi* in Buenos Aires, it was the first production of a Puccini opera outside of Italy, and the composer had every reason to be pleased with his first taste of international acclaim. The success was short-lived, however, and *Edgar*, did not become a part of the repertory. Puccini's moral needs were partially fulfilled but not his material ones.

If this Spanish production of his opera actually solved none of his problems, it did serve to encourage him to seek further foreign productions of his works.

His dream was to have *Le Villi* performed in Vienna's Imperial Theatre, and he enlisted the aid of Adriano Bastiani, mayor of Bagni di Lucca and a distinguished physician who had studied in the Austrian capital, in an attempt to have the opera performed there. This effort failed, however, but a performance of his first opera was arranged for Hamburg's Stadttheater; this would be the first foreign-language production of any of his operas. Puccini traveled to Germany for the occasion, and on November 29, 1892, *Le Villi*, conducted by thirty-two-year-old Gustav Mahler, was enthusiastically received by both the public and the press. The composer was particularly pleased that many critics, upon hearing Puccini's 1884 opera for the first time, felt that Mascagni's enormously successful *Cavalleria Rusticana* of 1890 owed a great deal to its predecessor. "Mascagni," commented the reviewer for the *Hamburger Nachrichten*, "can consider himself lucky that he was performed in Germany before Puccini," so that the public had not had a chance to see how much he had taken from the latter's opera.

Once again, however, the success of his opera served to raise the composer's spirits and little more; *Le Villi* did not take hold with the German public. By early 1893, it was clear that Puccini's future depended on the success or failure of *Manon Lescaut*. Puccini knew this, as did Ricordi, who had placed all of his hopes, and a good part of his firm's prestige and financial resources, on the young Lucchese as the successor to Verdi. Significantly, only eight days after the première of *Manon Lescaut*, Verdi's *Falstaff* was to have its première at La Scala. This would almost certainly be the last work by the much-beloved composer, who was nearing his eightieth birthday. There was more and more talk in operatic circles about a successor to this giant of Italian opera, and it was far from clear that Puccini would qualify for that role. In 1889, Mascagni's *Cavalleria Rusticana* had won the Sonzogno competition and had had great success at its début at the Teatro Costanzi in Rome on May 17, 1890. (The first congratulatory telegram the desperately poor young composer had received had been sent by his old friend Puccini, who had suggested the subject of the opera to Mascagni.) Two years later, Catalani's *La Wally* had triumphed at its première at La Scala, and in that same year of 1892, Leoncavallo's *I Pagliacci* (conducted by Toscanini as *La Wally* had been) was enthusiastically acclaimed at Milan's Teatro Dal Verme. Thus, Mascagni, Catalani, and Leoncavallo were all strong contenders for Verdi's crown.

Puccini, nonetheless, was confident when, in January 1893, he left for Turin and the rehearsals of his new opera. As these rehearsals progressed, he was concerned with the production, which he felt would be "wretched because the voices can hardly be heard," yet he wrote to Elvira, "Let them say what they want — this time I have a feeling that I have done a successful piece of work."

The composer's optimism was not completely shared by Illica, who felt that the libretto had serious weaknesses. Above all, he disapproved of the opera's ending — later he confided to Sir Thomas Beecham that the whole idea for that ending was Puccini's, that the composer had written the music for it and was determined that it be used — even at the expense of the opera's dramatic action. In addition to the decidedly anticlimactic last act, too much of the opera's action takes place between the acts rather than during them. All of these faults can be explained by the conscious effort to avoid duplicating what Massenet had done, and, even more, by the fact that too many authors had worked on the libretto. This last fact had become a rather touchy issue by the time the opera was ready for its first performance, with Praga, Oliva, and Illica all claiming at least partial authorship of the libretto. With the diplomatic aid of Giacosa, this matter was somehow settled, and it was decided to give credit — or blame — to no one for the libretto of *Manon Lescaut*. To do justice to all, the program would have had to read: "Libretto by Leoncavallo, Praga, Oliva, Giacosa, Illica, Ricordi, and Puccini."

The première of *Manon Lescaut* took place on the evening of February 1, 1893. The conductor was Alessandro Pomé. Cesira Ferrani sang Manon, and Giuseppe Cremonini sang the role of Des Grieux. Whatever faults the libretto might have had were obscured by Puccini's richly melodic score, so aptly described by Beniamino Gigli as "a supreme musical expression of youthful passion and ardor." That evening marked a decisive turning point in the life — personal as well as artistic — of the composer. In the course of a few hours, he was able to put aside his past, the anxieties over money, the artistic struggles, the tragic deaths of his mother and his brother, and the emotional turmoil caused by his elopement with Elvira; and he was able to enjoy fully what was to be the only unqualified triumph of his life.

At the start of the evening, however, there were doubts, normal ones under the circumstances. Turin's operagoers were known for their restraint, their sophistication, and their cynicism; how they would react to a new work by a little-known composer was uncertain. In addition, the opera's première was scheduled for the same night as was an elegant ball given at the palace of the Duchess of Genoa—there were fears that the ball might attract the cream of Torinese society, thereby robbing the new opera's première of some of its glamour. In spite of this, however, a distinguished, bejeweled audience filled the Teatro Regio to hear Puccini's new work. Music lovers from Turin as well as the rest of Italy, especially nearby Milan, were present, as were members of the press from every part of the country. There was an air of expectancy, of electricity, heightened by the presence in the royal box of Italy's Princess Letizia.

When the curtain rose, the public proved to be suspicious and wary, but in a short time, after Des Grieux had sung his first aria, all reserve was abandoned; the cheers were such that even the composer was forced to take a bow on the stage. At the end of that first act, it was clear that the audience had been completely won over as Puccini and the cast were repeatedly called before the curtain. Throughout the second act, there were several encores, and at the end of the act, even louder ovations for the principals and the composer. At the conclusion of the third act, the most dramatic of the opera, the public seemed to roar its approval, with bravos filling the theatre. The princess was so moved that she invited Puccini to her box so that she might personally express her gratitude and admiration. By the end of Act Four, the last act, this habitually reserved audience was almost out of control; near-hysterical ovations were showered upon Puccini, the cast, and the conductor. During the performance, the composer had been called to the stage an estimated twenty-five times; at the conclusion of the opera, he had to take almost forty bows.

After the performance, Puccini was radiant as he greeted his many admirers. Among those present to congratulate him was Giulio Gatti-Casazza, to whom he confided, according to Gatti's memoirs, "Now I think I have hit the mark. I believe I have an understanding of the operatic stage. I am confident now that I will succeed in the end."

The newspapers the following morning confirmed Puccini's extraordinary triumph. Giuseppe Depanis, of the *Gazzetta Piemontese*, concluded his lengthy, minutely detailed review of the opera by stating his satisfaction at the "agreement between the critics and the public in celebrating and acclaiming the vigorous opera of a young Italian maestro, a maestro who honors his name and that of his country. Art has no boundaries, it's true, but among all sentiments national pride is legitimate and sacred; and last evening was a beautiful one for art and for Italy." The reviewer for *Perseveranza* agreed: "I have rarely been present at so important an evening as last night's and to note, at the appearance of the opera of a young composer, so firm a conviction of public judgment, in complete harmony with the impression the opera made on the critics."

There was further praise in the *Gazzetta del Popolo*: "Puccini reveals himself in this *Manon* for what he is: one of the strongest if not the strongest of the young Italian operatic composers. What in his previous operas was merely promise in *Manon* becomes an affirmation, a reality. . . . His music is always original . . . for the most part he is himself, nobody but himself." The evening for this reviewer could be summed up in one word— "Triumph."

In another long and serious review, Giovanni Pozza, writing in Milan's influential *Corriere della Sera*, said: "Although the expectations had been high, the opera surprised us by its great artistic value, its powerful musical conception, its theatricality. . . . Puccini is really an Italian genius. His song is that of our paganism, of our artistic sensualism; it caresses us and penetrates us. . . . *Manon Lescaut* is a work of talent, conscious of its own power, master of its art, a creator and perfector of it."

His many years of material and artistic uncertainties were at an end. Puccini was a hero, and on February 7 he was named Cavaliere dell'Ordine della Corona d'Italia, an impressive honor. The following evening, at the end of *Manon Lescaut's* seventh performance before packed houses, the city of Turin offered a banquet in the composer's honor. Held at Turin's most elegant hotel, the Hotel d'Europe et Grand Hotel on the piazza Castello, it was a gala occasion—the menu included a "soupe Des Grieux" and a "tarte Manon." Realizing that he would be called upon to make a speech, the shy, reticent composer enlisted the aid of his Lucchese friend Alfredo Caselli, who wrote the speech and went over it word for word with the composer, even promising to be at his side during the dinner. Though stubbornly maintaining that he was no speechmaker and was capable of writing music and nothing else, the composer dutifully memorized the formal discourse. However, when his time came to respond to the pronouncement of Melchiorre Voli, the mayor of Turin, which concluded with the words, "Your great glory commences this evening," Puccini rose to his feet, acknowledged the ovation and, tongue-tied, barely managed to mumble "I thank everyone," compounding his embarrassment by knocking over the glass of Champagne which rested on the table in front of him. The reporter from the *Gazzetta* noted appropriately that the response might have been an excellent one if only the composer had had an orchestra and some singers at his disposal. There was, indeed, no doubt that the newest star in Italy's operatic world could best express himself through his music and not his words.

International Fame

The première of *Manon Lescaut* proved to be the turning point in Giacomo Puccini's life, and the period that followed it and preceded the completion of his next opera was marked by one triumph after another. He was no longer a struggling, promising composer; his promise had been brilliantly fulfilled.

His name quickly became known throughout all of Italy, and, soon, throughout the world. In 1893 alone, the new opera was performed in Trent, Udine, Brescia, Lucca, Bologna, Rome, Ascoli Piceno, Messina, Novara, Ferrara, Genoa, and Verona; outside of Italy, there were performances in Hamburg, Madrid, Buenos Aires, Rio de Janeiro, and St. Petersburg. Wherever he went, his presence was noted. In February, he was much commented upon at a reception for Verdi, given in Milan shortly after the première of *Falstaff*. The following month, he was himself guest of honor at a banquet offered by Count Porro Schiaffinati and attended by the leaders of Milan's artistic world. In that same month, in the course of what he hoped would be an unnoticed visit to Lucca where he planned to rest and go hunting, he was besieged by admirers and forced to participate in a series of banquets in his honor, in spite of his protestations. Hoping to leave town quietly, he was instead accompanied to the train by crowds shouting, "Viva Puccini, the author of *Manon Lescaut.*"

Whenever possible, he traveled to attend new productions of his opera; when his presence at a new production was impossible, his spirits were buoyed by the glowing accounts of his opera's reception, wherever it had been produced. On June 10, he attended the first performance in Trent; it was a huge success, with standing ovations for the composer who was called to the curtain twenty-four times. At the end of the month, he returned there for the final performance of his opera, this time called before the curtain no less than fifty times and fêted at a large banquet in his honor.

In early June, without his personal participation, *Manon Lescaut* had its first foreign production, in Buenos Aires where, according to *El Mundo del Arte*, it achieved "a colossal success." In Italy, in late August, the new opera was acclaimed in Brescia; following the second performance, on August 26, Puccini was practically drowned in gifts from his adoring public.

Shortly afterward, the new work was performed for the first time in Lucca, and before the première the composer was wary of the reception the opera might receive in a town which was the home of many of his enemies and rivals. He need not have worried. At the first performance, attended by Mascagni, he was called to the stage forty-seven times; when the performance came to an end he was escorted to his hotel by two bands which serenaded him following his triumph. *Manon Lescaut* was performed eleven times in the small provincial capital, and the composer was showered with gifts, among them the inevitable laurel crowns, a gold ring and, appropriately, a gun. In that same month, word reached Italy of the opera's huge success in Brazil.

At the end of October, Puccini again visited Hamburg, this time to supervise the première of *Manon Lescaut*. Because of the indisposition of one of the principals, the composer was forced to leave Germany before the opening performance — he had a commitment to supervise the production of his opera in Bologna — but word reached him in Italy of his work's success in Hamburg — "He breathes the same fervent breath as Wagner but maintains gifts of absolute originality," wrote the critic for the *Berliner Börse Courier*.

Two important Italian productions followed. The first took place at Bologna's Teatro Comunale, where the opera's success was so great that it was performed for a total of eighteen times in the course of that season. Even more important was the first performance in Rome, which took place on the night of November 9 and was the first production of any Puccini opera in the Italian capital. Once again, *Manon Lescaut* triumphed, this time in the presence of a most distinguished audience which included representatives of the Triple Alliance and the Grand Duchess Catherine of Russia (the queen of Italy attended a later performance). Puccini was called to the stage twenty-eight times on opening night; he had conquered Rome as he had the rest of Italy.

That same month, the opera enjoyed great success in Madrid, as well as in several smaller Italian cities — among them Ascoli Piceno and Novara, where a slightly revised ending of the first act was first tried out.

The following year, 1894, was no less triumphant for the by now widely acclaimed composer. In January he traveled to Naples. Anxious to vindicate himself in the city where his *Le Villi* had failed so miserably, he threw himself into his work with unusual energy. "Puccini works furiously," a local newspaper reported. "He shouts, he gesticulates, he extends himself to the point of losing his voice." This extra effort was apparently worthwhile, and the opera, first performed at San Carlo on the evening of January 21, was a resounding success. The following day the newspaper *Roma* reported: "Naples, the city which had been so hostile (perhaps unjustly) to the author of *Le Villi*, wanted to make honorable amends to that severe judgment, demonstrating not only faith in his merits but also wanting to reconfirm the triumph achieved by a powerful opera in almost every theatre in the peninsula." *Manon Lescaut* was performed twenty times in Naples that season.

If Naples had changed its mind about Puccini, so too had the composer changed his mind about Naples. Instead of hurrying away this time, he remained for three performances and reluctantly left only because of the approaching première of his opera at La Scala. His presence in Milan meant having to miss successful productions of his work in Lisbon and Leipzig, but the production at La Scala was clearly of paramount importance. Though acceptance by that theatre's unusually critical public was not easily won, *Manon Lescaut* captured the hearts of the Milanesi—in spite of what the composer felt was a far from perfect performance. Puccini was repeatedly called before the curtain, and a few nights later, on February 21, he was honored at a banquet attended by more than one hundred guests, among them the cast of the Scala production, Giovanni Verga, Boito, and the justifiably proud Ricordi. At the end of the evening, instead of the usual speeches which so pained the composer, Puccini was carried to the piano where he accompanied the singers in a number of arias from his opera.

In the middle of March, the composer was in Pisa for a performance of his opera, which was of special importance because it was conducted by the young Arturo Toscanini, who had also conducted *Le Villi* in Brescia in 1890. The composer and the conductor were to have personal and political disagreements, but when it came to the interpretation of Puccini's scores, they were of one mind. The composer had an aversion to dragging tempos—"If you fall asleep, we all fall asleep," he reportedly told a conductor. "The music must never doze off."—and in this Toscanini was in complete agreement. In this performance of *Manon Lescaut*, the music did not doze off, and both Puccini and the audience were delighted with the twenty-three-year-old conductor's interpretation of the youthful score.

The following month, Puccini again left Italy, this time for Budapest and the Hungarian première of *Manon*. It was still another triumph, and after the première he returned home by way of Vienna where he signed a contract for the production of his latest work in the Austrian capital. Throughout 1894 and 1895, there were other equally successful productions of his opera. Italian theatres in Bari, Livorno, Terni, Ravenna, Parma, San Remo, Venice, Trieste, and Fiume produced *Manon Lescaut*, and the work also achieved success in such distant places as Moscow, Odessa, Warsaw, Prague, Montevideo, Alexandria, Malta, and Mexico City. No foreign production, however, was more significant than that given at London's Covent Garden in May 1894, in the presence of the composer, who was making his first trip to the British capital.

The occasion of the première was a memorable one, in spite of the fact that the directors of the London opera house were, it seems, coerced into staging the work by Ricordi, who would not permit a performance of *Falstaff* unless the new work by the younger composer, too, was performed. No matter how it was arranged, Puccini's opera opened the season in the newly renovated, sparkling clean opera house. The audience was an elegant one, and the importance of the occasion was marked, before the new curtain rose, by the singing of the national anthem by members of the chorus, who gathered around a bust of the queen. In spite of a mediocre cast, hastily put together by Ricordi and imported from Italy, the audience greeted Puccini and his work with enthusiasm. The shy composer was called before the curtain after each act, and for the most part the British press echoed the public's satisfaction with the opera. "Signor Puccini possesses the gift of melody, is a master of orchestration and has rare comprehension of dramatic effect," wrote the critic for the *Standard*, while the reviewer for the *Morning Post* praised the composer's "Strong dramatic power," as well as his "innate feeling for stage effect and considerable melodic expression." The critic for the influential *Times*, while expressing serious reservations, felt that Puccini showed himself on the whole to be superior to the other members of the "young Italian school," but the most important and most perceptive review was that written for *The World* by a man who professed little admiration for Italian opera, far preferring the works of Wagner and Mozart—George Bernard Shaw. Shaw's review, dated May 23, 1894, read in part: ". . . The first act, which is as gay and effective and romantic as the opening of any version of Manon need be, is also unmistakeably symphonic in its treatment. There is genuine symphonic modification, development, and occasionally combination of the thematic material, all in a dramatic way, but also in a musically homogeneous way, so that the act is really a single movement with episodes instead of being a succession of separate numbers, linked together to conform to the modern fashion, by substituting interrupted cadences for full closes and parading a leitmotiv occasionally. . . .

"Puccini shows no signs of atrophy of the melodic faculty: he breaks out into catching melodies quite in the vein of Verdi. . . . On that and other accounts, Puccini looks to me more like the heir of Verdi than any of his rivals. . . ."

Puccini could not have understood the importance of Shaw, who was still little known in most of the world, but he was delighted with his trip to

London, and the reception accorded him by the British. "For me, London will always be a treasured memory," he wrote a pianist friend, Giuseppe Buonamici. "What a town!"

All of these travels, repeated confirmations of his newfound success, were a source of great pleasure to Puccini. He was a shy man, and in many ways a genuinely modest one, but he could not help enjoying the acclamation which greeted him wherever he went; he had worked long and hard for it. Even more important than fame, the opera's success meant that he was at last free from the financial worries that had plagued him most of his life. Because of the considerable royalties he was earning, he was finally in a position to stabilize his family situation by settling—with Elvira, Fosca, and Antonio—into a permanent home of his own.

First, however, just a few months after the première of his opera, Puccini hastened to fulfill his long-standing pledge to redeem the family home in Lucca, which had been sold after his mother's death. He had never forgotten that pledge—continually reminding his family of it—and the home was repurchased as quickly as possible, in spite of the indifference of his sisters. "I care about the four cracked walls, the disjointed beams, and even the ruins of my home," he wrote Ramelde. "I will redeem my home, of this you can be certain."

The house, however, became Puccini's in name only; he saw to it that it was repaired and, subsequently, that it was rented, but he never lived in it—or in the city of Lucca itself. In spite of the special pride—or was it revenge?—that he felt when his operas were performed in the city of his birth, he never forgave Lucca or its citizens for their treatment of him after his elopement with Elvira. Besides, what he craved was a home in the country, a quiet oasis in which he might work, far from the cities in which he would earn his fame and to which he would have to travel for the remainder of his life.

He found that oasis in a small, unpretentious lakeside village—Torre del Lago. In English, the name means Tower of the Lake, but the name was more romantic than the village—the tower no longer existed, and the lake, Lago di Massaciuccoli, was small, shallow, and not inaccurately described by Illica as a swamp. Nonetheless, for Puccini it was, until his last years, the home he had sought and the home he always treasured. Little more than a detour on the road that leads from Viareggio to Pisa, for Puccini this humble village was, in his own words, "supreme bliss, paradise, Eden, Emphrean, ivory tower, spiritual vessel, and royal palace. . . ." Wherever he traveled, his thoughts turned to Torre del Lago, his spiritual base and refuge. When in Milan, he wrote to friends that he lived only through memories of that small Tuscan town; in Paris, he noted that the only thing wrong with the Eiffel Tower was that it was not Torre del Lago; and while in Vienna he noted his longing for "the green Torre which, from afar, seems even more beautiful, with its green, smelly marshes, filled with singing frogs, more melodious than the music by the great one from Leipzig. . . ."

Today the village has been renamed Torre del Lago Puccini, in honor of its most famous—its only famous—resident. It consists of a number of seedy second-class boarding houses, a few decent restaurants (among them the "Butterfly"), and some undistinguished cafés, including the "Bar Liù." An outdoor theatre has been built on the insect-infested lake; each summer it is the site of a Puccini festival, during which some of the maestro's works are performed, often competing with the sounds of transister radios from a nearby camping site. These productions, though sometimes boasting some of the world's finest singers, are usually more notable for the uninhibited enthusiasm of the local audiences than for the artistic level attained.

When Puccini first visited the village, however, in 1884, it was a sleepy little town with, according to his count, one hundred and twenty inhabitants and twelve houses. The edge of the marshy lake, a body of water often invisible because of the heavy mist that periodically invaded it, was dotted with small fisherman's huts, constructed of bog grass, and tall reeds grew in abundance along its shores.

The village and its lake had a kind of mysterious and unspoiled charm, but among the many scenic splendors of Tuscany, Torre del Lago undoubtedly ranked low. The view from it—toward the mountains across the lake—was more attractive than the view of it. Yet for Puccini the very insignificance of the place meant that it would never attract the casual visitor, and that he would seldom be disturbed by curious outsiders. In addition, the reeds and marshes gave shelter to a large variety of wildfowl, which the composer avidly liked to hunt. During the season at Torre del Lago, there were few early mornings when the composer was not seen, cigarette dangling from his mouth, hat tilted over his forehead, and wearing high boots, as he patrolled the shores of Lake Massaciuccoli in search of coots and other game birds which he later delighted in eating, roasted, with a plate of beans or polenta. Though an enthusiastic gourmet, the haute cuisine of the world's capitals could never compare to the rough, hearty cooking of his own town.

When Puccini first stayed at Torre del Lago, he rented the modest old home of Venanzio Barsuglia, a custodian of the estate of the Marchese Carlo Ginori-Lisci, owner of the lake. Later, as his fortunes and his needs grew, the composer rented a more elaborate villa belonging to a Count Grottanelli of Siena. Finally, in 1900 construction was completed on an even more luxurious villa of his own, a villa which still stands today, a small Puccini museum which also houses the tombs of the composer, Elvira, and Tonio.

Throughout his lifetime, Puccini suffered from what he called "mal della pietra"—which can be translated as "builder's disease." He was to own houses at Abetone, high in the mountains; he fought for and finally bought the ancient Torre della Tagliata, in the rugged Maremma area of Tuscany south of Pisa; and he had a splendid and ornate villa built near the isolated village of Chiatri. The total isolation of this last-mentioned residence, where the composer was able to work undisturbed, so upset his family that Elvira solicited friends to wear sheets and wander up and down the stairs to convince Puccini that the house was haunted. Finally, Puccini maintained an apartment of via Verdi 4 in Milan, around the corner from La Scala, which was often convenient for his work and as a base for his dealings with his publisher.

Torre del Lago, however, was home, as no other place could be. In his early years, following his first real success, he especially enjoyed the company of the competent but rather undistinguished artists, writers, and musicians who lived in the town. They were a simple and carefree group, among whom the often harried composer could relax in his old clothes, far from the formalities required elsewhere by his increasing fame. Their meeting place was a broken-down hut, which served as a café and was owned by an amiable shoemaker Giovanni Gragnani, nicknamed "Gambe di Merlo." There they passed their evenings drinking, playing cards and exchanging jokes. These jokes were ones the composer could never repeat in public; examples of early Lucchese humor which would contradict the image of the gentleman which Puccini cultivated in public. Following the evening's entertainment, the composer and his friends would move on to the Puccini home, and the festivities would continue in the living room, while the composer set to work, with his hat always on his head, in the adjoining studio. The lively chatter of his companions was a pleasant accompaniment rather than a distraction for the composer during his periods of creativity.

When the shoemaker was forced to leave his home and emigrate to Brazil, instead of abandoning his shack, he sold it to his friends for use as their clubhouse. Some remodeling was done; the room was furnished with wooden tables and benches, members of the group decorated the walls with their own sketches and caricatures; sausages were hung from the ceiling, and second-hand Algerian drapes hung around the windows. The club was officially constituted, and among its rules were the following:

Article 1: The members, faithful interpreters of the spirit in which the club was founded, swear to drink well and eat better.

Article 2: Grouches, pedants, weak stomachs, the poor in spirit, the squeamish, and other unfortunates of this kind are not permitted or are thrown out at the rage of the members.

Article 3: The president acts as conciliator but is responsible for hindering the treasurer in the collection of dues.

Article 4: The treasurer is authorized to abscond with the funds.

Article 5: Illumination is to be provided by an oil lamp. If there is no oil, the *moccoli* of the members can be used. [*Moccoli* means both wax tapers and swear words in Italian.]
Article 6: All lawful games are strictly prohibited.
Article 7: Silence is forbidden.
Article 8: Wisdom is not allowed, even in exceptional cases.

This club, too, was given a formal name; it was called the Club La Bohème, named for the spirit in which it was founded and in expectation of the new opera its most illustrious member was at that time composing.

This new opera was to be based on Henri Murger's *Scènes de la vie de Bohème*, a somewhat romanticized but often honest account of the life of the struggling artists and writers in the Paris of the 1840s. A series of loosely connected vignettes, Murger's work had first been published serially in the magazine *Le Corsaire* between 1845 and 1848 and, a few years later, reprinted in book form. It had brought its twenty-seven-year-old author—himself desperately poor—neither fame nor fortune until 1849 when, under the title *La vie de Bohème*, it was dramatized by the playwright Théodore Barrière (who had, incidentally, also adapted *Manon Lescaut* for the theatre). The play was an enormous success, and because of it Murger became both rich and well known, not only in France but throughout all of Europe.

Puccini and Illica had apparently made their decision to base an opera on Murger's stories even before the première of *Manon Lescaut*, but no formal announcement of their plans had been made, nor, they felt, was there any need for one at the time. In March 1893, however, fresh from his triumph in Turin, Puccini had a chance meeting with his friend Leoncavallo in Milan, as a result of which an announcement became more than urgently necessary. In the course of a casual conversation with his Neapolitan colleague, Puccini mentioned that he was working on an opera based on *La vie de Bohème*. Stunned, Leoncavallo replied that he too was preparing an opera based on Murger's work; in addition, he claimed that Puccini already knew this because he himself had first suggested the idea to Puccini, who had rejected it. Angry words and accusations followed, and as a result a bitter war was declared between these two men, who had been occasional collaborators in the past.

Both felt that concrete steps had to be taken at once. On March 19, *Il Secolo*, a Milanese newspaper owned by Sonzogno, Leoncavallo's publisher, officially announced that Ruggero Leoncavallo was hard at work on an opera to be based on *La vie de Bohème*; at the same time the *Corriere della Sera* announced that Giacomo Puccini was preparing an opera based on the same work.

The following day, Sonzogno's newspaper published a detailed explanation, which read: "Maestro Leoncavallo wants to make it known that he contracted for the new opera last December and has since that time been working on the music for that subject. He had not announced the opera previously only because he wanted to retain an element of surprise. As proof of this, the distinguished artist Maurel can testify that at the time of his arrival in Milan for the rehearsals of *Falstaff*, Maestro Leoncavallo told him he was writing for him the part of Schaunard, just as Signora Frandin is able to testify that four months ago the maestro spoke to her of the role of Musette, which was destined for her. Maestro Puccini, to whom Maestro Leoncavallo declared two days ago that he was writing *Bohème*, confessed that only upon his return from Turin a few days ago did he have the idea of putting *La Bohème* to music and that he spoke of it to Illica and Giacosa who, according to him, have not yet finished the libretto. Maestro Leoncavallo's priority as regards this opera is thus indisputable."

Puccini's reply, printed in the *Corriere della Sera* on March 21, was addressed to the director of the newspaper. "The declaration made by Maestro Leoncavallo in yesterday's *Il Secolo* must have made the public understand my complete good faith; because it is clear that if Maestro Leoncavallo, to whom I have been attached for some time by strong feelings of friendship, had told me before what he suddenly let me know the other evening, I would then not have considered Murger's *Bohème*.

"Now—for reasons easy to understand—it is too late for me to allow myself to be courteous as I would like to be toward a friend and a musician.

"Furthermore, why does this matter to Maestro Leoncavallo? Let him write his music and I will write mine. The public will judge. Priority in art does not imply that the same subject has to be interpreted with the same artistic ideas. I only want it known that for about two months, that is from the time of the first performances of *Manon Lescaut* in Turin, I have worked seriously on my idea and have not kept this secret from anyone."

The truth concerning who had the idea first is difficult to establish, but it is a fact that Puccini never shied away from an idea first conceived by another composer—indeed, this seemed to stimulate him. Nonetheless, he was worried about Leoncavallo's competition, or "challenge" as he called it, and an undated letter to Illica shows that he attempted to obtain exclusive rights to the Murger stories—impossible because they were in the public domain. On the basis of the popularity of *I Pagliacci*, Leoncavallo certainly seemed to be a serious threat to Puccini, though the former's version of the Murger book would never approach the popularity of Puccini's opera. Puccini, in the end, clearly won what Ricordi termed the "derby," and his friendship with Leoncavallo was never again resumed. In fact, Puccini's deep contempt for his rival lasted until the end of his days and was reflected in the colorful and malicious word games he played with the name—Leoncavallo (*leone* means lion, and *cavallo* means horse in Italian) became for Puccini *Leonbestia* (Lion-beast) or *Leonasino* (Lion-ass).

Because of the nature of Murger's original—it is little more than a series of anecdotes—it is strange that not only Puccini and Leoncavallo but also Théodore Barrière, the dramatist, saw in it a subject that could be adapted for the theatre. Murger's work overflows with more characters than any theatrical work could possibly accommodate. As for any kind of dramatic unity, it was a complex and difficult task to weave a plot from the large number of often disconnected incidents fashioned by the French author. In undertaking the adaptation of Murger's work to the operatic stage, the librettists of Puccini's opera faced a formidable challenge: it was their job to convey the spirit and atmosphere of the original work and remain true to the essence of Murger's Bohemians, just as it was essential to make of the many fragments of the original a convincing dramatic entity.

For help in this difficult task, Puccini and Illica sought and obtained the full collaboration of Giuseppe Giacosa, and it proved to be invaluable. Giacosa was a major literary figure, a distinguished poet, essayist, and dramatist, whose plays were performed by both Duse and Bernhardt. A close friend of Boito, Verga, and Carducci as well as Emile Zola, to whom he introduced Puccini in December 1894 when the Frenchman paid a visit to Milan, Giacosa lectured at the Conservatory and was editor of *La Lettura*, an influential literary periodical.

His role in the collaboration was to set to verse and give literary form and polish to Illica's libretto; he did so superbly, contributing his full share to the success not only of *La Bohème*, but also of Puccini's next two operas. More than ten years older than either Puccini or Illica, the short, heavyset man with a bald head, full beard, and thick paunch (Puccini playfully referred to him as Buddha) was a slow and careful worker—this sometimes irritated the often impatient Puccini. But he was also a generous man, quick to forgive, and he was often able to calm the nerves of his more impulsive colleagues— when his own weren't on edge.

Upon the death of Giacosa in 1906, Puccini affectionately recalled what he termed their always peaceful and cloudless collaboration—more than a slight exaggeration, understandable, perhaps, because of Puccini's sadness at the death of his friend—but even Ricordi remembered the many tense moments which were overcome by Giacosa's gentle, often conciliatory manner, and his personal warmth. The long discussions held in the publisher's office were best remembered by Illica in an obituary written for *La Lettura* in October 1906. "Those meetings of ours," Illica wrote. "Real battles, during which suddenly entire acts were torn to pieces; scene after scene might be sacrificed; ideas which had seemed beautiful and dazzling moments before could be thrown out, and thus the long hard work of months destroyed in one minute.

Giacosa, Puccini, Giulio Ricordi and I—four of us, because Giulio Ricordi, who was supposed to preside at those meetings, would always abandon the president's chair and come down to the semicircle (two very narrow meters in circumference, made even more narrow, crowded, and uncomfortable by Giacosa's sturdy presence) to become one of the most obstinate and energetic belligerents. . . . Giacosa was the balancing factor; in the dark moments he was the sun; on stormy days the rainbow. In the uproar of different opinions, of different ways of seeing, of feeling, of expressing, Giacosa's was the delightful and convincing song of the nightingale."

As for the composer, Illica added: "After each meeting, Puccini had to run to the manicurist to have his nails done. He would have bitten them off to the bone."

La Bohème

The team of Puccini, Illica, and Giacosa—with considerable help from Ricordi—was to be one of the most successful in the history of opera, and the development of their first collaboration, *La Bohème*, can be closely followed through the large amount of correspondence which has been preserved. This correspondence, while providing valuable insights into the characters of all four men, clearly shows that this collaboration was far from "cloudless," and that Giacosa's voice was often not that of the "delightful nightingale." Nonetheless, the often painful and difficult struggles which took place were more than compensated for by the results obtained.

Illica, it seems, had started work on his scenario in the late fall of 1892, months before the première of *Manon Lescaut*. In March of 1893, he sent that scenario to Giacosa for the latter's comments. Giacosa was pleased, and on March 22 he wrote that he especially admired Illica's ability to dramatize what he believed was a fine book but one that was far from easy to adapt to the lyric theatre. He thought that the early acts had been "stupendously" done, but he had serious reservations concerning the last act, which he believed was rather too similar to the last acts of many other operas. Nonetheless, he was on the whole enthusiastic about the prospects of the collaboration.

At the same time, Puccini, because of the challenge of Leoncavallo's version of the same story, was feeling pressed for time. He was eager to move ahead, indicating that he too had new ideas concerning that last act and begging Illica to reread Murger's book so as to be completely familiar with

80

the subject in order to avoid further delays. Illica and Giacosa, however, were calm; they worked together harmoniously and peacefully, perhaps because they had as yet had little contact with Puccini — Giacosa did not even know the composer's address.

By May, however, the composer's nervous impatience began to worry Giacosa, who felt that Illica might well deserve a more effective partner. He admitted that he had been too much involved with other commitments, and he asked Boito to see Ricordi and explain his problems to the publisher. Boito, most probably, was not the right man for the job, since he had earlier tried to dissuade Puccini from setting to music the story of "those five or six rag-dressed men who debate in an attic." (After the opera's success, Boito pledged never again to offer his advice concerning a libretto.)

In spite of his doubts, Giacosa went on with his work, and by the end of May he had completed his versification of the first act, which he read to Ricordi. Early the following month, Puccini wrote to Illica of his reaction to this first act:

> Still impressed with your splendid *verbal plot*, I remind you of the episodes which are my constant preoccupation. . . . Anxiously await developments and confident in your vast and boiling, not to mention phosphorescent, talent, I send regards to you and your subjects.
>
> P.S. Remember the beginning. It is useless, I know, because you will undoubtedly do it this way, but it is one of the things I want to make sure of. When the curtain goes up, the three men — Colline, Schaunard, Rodolfo — are facing the window and meditate on the *smoking chimneys.* All of a sudden their ardent desire for warmth is broken by the unexpected movement of one of them who grabs a chair and throws it into the fire — but is there any paper? Rodolfo sacrifices his drama — commenting on each act — then after the brief fire, dejection; seated around the table, in distress, they complain about misery. It is Christmas eve; everybody is rejoicing, and they haven't a cent! Marcello comes in, they don't even turn their heads — just one more desperate person, they think. But instead, Marcello, who has made money, throws a coin at the feet of one of them. [In the final libretto, it is Schaunard who arrives with the money.] They freeze — another coin — still no one moves (maybe they think they are counterfeit). Then Marcello, impatient, noisily throws a handful of coins on the table. Everyone gets up and shows surprise. Interrogations, etc. Good-bye, I'm going to bed.

If the composer was somewhat overanxious reminding his librettist of something already agreed upon, it was nonetheless done with good humor. That he was encouraged by the work done on the first act is attested to by a letter from Ricordi to Puccini, dated June 5:

I am content with what you write me concerning the first scene of
Bohème. If there are a few words to be changed here and there, it
doesn't matter; it is the whole which is important. . . . It is absolutely necessary that you keep *secret* the progress of the libretto from
everybody, friends, admirers. If to trust is good, not to trust is better.
An inadvertent word which slips out may serve as a guide to your
rival in *Bohème* and give him ideas for his libretto. That would be a
real misfortune. Prudence, therefore, and a great deal of it! . . .

By July 28, 1893, Ricordi no longer seemed worried by any competition.
"It's fine," he wrote to Illica, upon receiving more material. "I await the
'Quartier Latin' and the 'Cortile' after the revisions you're planning. If
everything works out . . . it seems to me we will not only have a very new
kind of opera, but a real masterpiece."

In writing the "Quartier Latin" and the "Cortile" scenes, Ricordi was
referring to the original scheme of *La Bohème* and not the one that was finally
used. The first act had originally been divided into two scenes—"La Soffitta"
(The Garret) and "Quartier Latin" (The Latin Quarter). The second act was to
be called the "Barrière d'Enfer," (The Gate of Hell); the third "Il Cortile della
casa di via Labruyère" (The Courtyard of the House on the rue Labruyère),
and the final act "La Soffitta" or "La Morte di Mimi" (The Death of Mimi).
As we know the opera today, the two scenes of the original first act each
became an act. The third act, which took place in the courtyard, was
eliminated and replaced by the second act, and the final act, though extensively revised, remained basically the same. The rejected third act would
have been dramatically effective in showing concrete reasons for Rodolfo's
jealousy—Mimi being courted by a young nobleman—but it would have
been musically repetitive, its mood too similar to that of the scene at the café
in Act Two, since it too was highlighted by festive street dancing and
singing.

At the same time that Ricordi was expressing his optimism, Giacosa's
doubts returned. He worried about his own slowness, and admitted to Ricordi
that he lacked Illica's facility and was incapable of going ahead unless he was
completely satisfied with what he had already done. Though prepared to
deliver the second act, he felt he needed to take another look at the third act
before submitting anything to the publisher. He was temperamentally
unable to work at the same pace as were his collaborators, and he hoped this
would not become a serious problem.

The months of August and September were calm and untroubled ones,
with both librettists at work on the opera. By October, however, the conscientious Giacosa was once again troubled by his slowness and the conflict he felt
between his own plays and the work he had to do for Puccini's opera. On
October 2, he wrote to Ricordi:

You say that you can sympathize with the slowness required for a work of art. But the problem is that what I am doing with this libretto is not a work of art, but minute, indispensable, and exhausting pedantry. It is work that must be done, and work that requires an artist, but it is work without stimulation and inner warmth. A work of art has its painful and laborious hours, but in compensation it has its periods of inspiration. . . . Here, there is nothing to raise the spirit. . . .

I came back to Milan last night. I should now go to Paris for my play. I will give that up for many reasons, not the least of which is the thought of you and the libretto. . . . I'll get back to work on *Bohème* tomorrow and if nothing happens, I plan to finish the second act the day after tomorrow. Just a few verses are left for the third. Believe me, I don't lack goodwill.

A few days later, Giacosa, near exhaustion, reached a difficult decision — fortunately, for the sake of the opera, it was not a firm one. Completely discouraged, feeling he was being hopelessly rushed, he wrote to Ricordi on October 6 that he was giving up the job.

. . . Unfortunately for me, I am not and have never been a facile worker. I need time to think and to redo a hundred times whatever I write. I will have lost two months of hard work, but I won't make you wait impatiently any longer. I have thought a great deal before taking this step. It saddens me deeply, but at this time my imagina-Tion seems dried up, or at least dried up as regards this act of lyric comedy. There is one thing I ask you and that is, considering the serious damage I have caused to myself, that you will not add to this by remaining angry at me. I depend, as a very precious thing, upon having you as a strong and excellent friend.

Giacosa ended this moving and dignified letter by telling Ricordi that he would leave that evening for Colleretto Parella, his hometown, hoping there to rest and recover his strength. Fortunately, the rest was beneficial, and his resignation was withdrawn.

Before Giacosa had changed his mind, word of his resignation reached Puccini in Hamburg, where he was supervising rehearsals of *Manon Lescaut*. He was stunned and profoundly upset, so much so that he even considered abandoning the entire project, and from Germany he sent a postcard to Illica in which he said that if they didn't continue with *La Bohème*, they would find some other opera to do together. This card, a reflection of Puccini's casual attitude, came as a blow to Illica, who enclosed it in a letter he sent to Ricordi, then in Paris:

Is Puccini already tired of *Bohème*? A few days ago Elvira came to have lunch with me, and I learned from her — I was not surprised — that Puccini had worked very, very little. But there is a great difference between working very, very little and contemplating work on something else, especially if one realizes how essential speed, both in conception and in actual work, is, for a thousand and one reasons. . . . I know very well that Puccini is a watch that winds and unwinds easily. But in any kind of watch time passes very quickly and does not turn back, and each loss of enthusiasm is a disappointment and a further discouragement. In *Bohème*, furthermore, there is (pay no heed to my slightly dramatic presentation) a little of our honor, of all of us. I can't hide from you the fact that abandoning a battle which we entered into willingly and started with so much publicity would burn me up. . . . I therefore beg you not to give in to Puccini. Puccini must do *Bohème*; not only that, he has to do it quickly and well, and it must achieve the success of which you and I are already certain.

Ricordi, too, was upset at Puccini's apparent indifference, and he wrote to Illica from Paris on November 2:

> . . . I am very sorry about what you tell me of Puccini, but I am not surprised, because I foresaw it. . . . You know very well how filled with fervor Puccini was, how he absolutely wanted *that* subject, and the subsequent angry exchange of letters with Leoncavallo. And now — excuse the expression — is he shaking in his pants at the first difficulties? And should Illica and Giacosa first, and I last, appear to be real fools? Add to this the fact that I have very serious interests to take care of: first subject, second subject, accept, discard, put aside, make commitments . . . and someone pays! Not only the hundreds but the thousands of lire that are wasted because of regrets and hesitations.
>
> To sum up: we are faced with a matter concerning art and interests, and a very serious one. I, however, hope this is merely one of those doubts common to all composers, and very common in Puccini, and that it will pass quickly; of course, it is essential that Puccini work energetically and quickly, all in one breath, otherwise the opera will not succeed.

By December 8, the revised version of the entire first act was completed and delivered to Ricordi, who forwarded it on to the composer, hoping that his enthusiasm might return. It was accompanied by a poem which begged Puccini not to swerve while "running the Grand Derby." By the end of the year, Giacosa was more relaxed and again at work, finishing up his version of the "Quartier Latin" scene. Illica, however, continued to have doubts about Puccini, which were expressed in his letter of January 5, 1894, to Ricordi:

Do you really believe that once we put together the "Quartier Latin" Puccini will be happy with it? Allow me to doubt it. There is no one blinder than the one who does not want to see, just as there is no one more difficult to please than the one who finds pleasure in making others work in order to avoid his own work. I think it is time to cut this short and reach some decision. So I thought of writing down a new plot—a sketch—based on the existing one, taking into account what Puccini wanted (the little episodes) and what you and I decided, with very minor modifications made along the way. I am enclosing a sketch of the scene. Look at it and judge. . . . Puccini should examine the new plot on the basis of what has already been done . . . and make a decision. . . .

Illica's suspicion that Puccini was creating new work for his librettists in order to avoid working himself might have been well founded. The composer was certainly deriving great pleasure from following productions of *Manon Lescaut* from city to city. The cheers and the laurel crowns were new to him; a special pride in his accomplishment was understandable, and at that time, while his collaborators were struggling with their libretto in Milan, the composer was especially enjoying a triumphant visit to Naples. Upon his return to Milan, he was warmly welcomed by his librettists, certain that work could resume in an orderly fashion, but soon new and serious problems emerged, as can be learned from an angry letter concerning the last act, written to Ricordi by Illica:

. . . Well, Puccini doesn't like the solution found Sunday night at all. He wants to begin—and he is very stubborn about it—with Mimi in bed, Rodolfo writing at a table, and a stump of candle to light the scene. This means no separation between Rodolfo and Mimi! This way, then, there is really no more *Bohème*—not only that, but there is no more Mimi as portrayed by Murger! We have a meeting in a garret between a poet-journalist and a dressmaker. They fall in love, they have a fight, and then the dressmaker dies. . . . It's a sad story, but it's not *Bohème*. The love story is a tearjerker (and romantic) . . . but Murger's Mimi is more complicated. One must have a little compassion for the librettists, too!

Now, since I maintain that it is an error not to have the separation between Mimi and Rodolfo take place before the eyes of the public, you can imagine what I think about no separation at all. Because the essential element of Murger's book is precisely that great freedom in love (supreme characteristic of *Bohème*) which pervades the behavior of all the characters. Think how much greater and more moving would be a Mimi who—though able to live with a lover who gives her silks and velvets—when feeling herself close to death goes to die in a desolate and cold garret, just so she can die in the arms of

Rodolfo. It seems to me impossible that Puccini doesn't see the grandeur of this.

And yet this is Murger's Mimi!

And please note (and this would seem to me a real find) how novel it would be to start the last act in the way that the first began. Only it's not winter, but autumn. The snow-whitened rooftops of all Paris are not seen from the large window; instead Rodolfo would pick up a leaf carried there by the wind, and his thoughts would again turn to Mimi.

We would start with Rodolfo alone — at the same time letting the public know of the separation — this blessed separation which is so necessary. (Up to now there is not one solo for the tenor.)

In the whole play, our Bohemians do nothing but eat well and drink better. Here would be the opportunity to show the four of them sharing one herring. . . .

Finally, if wanted, here there is the chance to round out the libretto and heal the great wound that was caused by cutting "Il Cortile."

But here I feel you should take our side rather than Puccini's. Believe me when I say the press will be extremely severe. They will say it was useless to give two people the task of writing a libretto — or rather, extracting an incomplete libretto from a book.

Instead, this way, and giving Giacosa all possible freedom, every-thing falls into place and not only that, but this last act would be extremely moving and poetic. This way — as was decided on Sun-day — we too would have a chance to breathe. Because if we had to cut "Il Cortile," replacing it with "Il Niente" (The Nothing), it would really be too little.

I am sorry for all this fuss, but that Puccini can scare people off. Unfortunately (and it must be admitted) you almost always let him do what he wants.

It is necessary to tell the truth, however, and the black sheep are always Giacosa and your most devoted. . . .

The composer, at least for the record, was uncharacteristically quiet throughout this period of hurt feelings and recriminations. It seems likely that Ricordi was right that he was not sufficiently involved in his new opera and that, excited by the success of Manon Lescaut, he needed more time before he could settle down. The librettists, too, needed time off to recover strength — Illica, ironically, set to work on a libretto for Tosca, which the Baron Alberto Franchetti was setting to music, and Giacosa busied himself with his own plays. Before too long, however, Puccini again expressed a desire to get back to work, peacefully this time at Torre del Lago, and in April, Giacosa and Illica were again at work on Bohème, amicably exchanging ideas for changes with the composer.

Just when all seemed to be going smoothly again, Puccini had another change of heart, this time a most serious one. Unable to come to grips satisfactorily with Murger's book, his thoughts turned to an entirely new idea, that of turning Giovanni Verga's short story, *La Lupa*, into an opera. The similarity of *La Lupa* to the immensely popular *Cavalleria Rusticana*, also based on a tale of passion and violence in Sicily and also written by Verga, obviously influenced him in this as did the fact that the story was soon to be adapted for the theatre. Puccini hastily notified Ricordi of his decision, and asked that Verga prepare for him a scenario that might be used as the basis of the opera. His enthusiasm was such that he decided to leave for Sicily at once, to soak up the local color needed for the new opera and to consult with the author.

The trip, which he made in the company of two of his closest childhood friends from Lucca, Alfredo Caselli and Cleto Bevilacqua, turned out to be a cheerful vacation and little more. The three men acted like wide-eyed tourists, and they enjoyed themselves immensely. On June 29, the composer wrote to Guido Vandini in Lucca, "We are in Catania and feel like lions — we are enjoying the splendid and luxuriant vegetation while getting drunk on gusts of African wind." Puccini met with Verga while in Catania — the noted author had already sketched out a scenario for the opera — but little came of the meeting, and on July 1, Puccini and his friends were in Malta, on a sightseeing trip, where they encountered a bit of adventure, which resulted in the composer's arrest on charges of having photographed military installations. Within a few hours, however, Puccini was able to convince the British authorities that his knowledge of military matters was so slight that he could not possibly qualify as a spy.

By the time Puccini was ready to leave Sicily, he had lost most of his enthusiasm for setting Verga's story to music. A chance meeting, during the trip to the mainland, with the Countess Blandine Gravina, daughter of Cosima Wagner, just about settled the matter, the Countess feeling strongly that the subject matter was unsuited both to the composer and to the operatic stage.

Further correspondence with Verga followed, but on July 13 Puccini, properly embarrassed, wrote Ricordi that he had reached a new decision:

> . . . For *La Lupa* it is better to wait for public reaction to the play. I didn't pick up anything musical in Sicily, but I photographed people, farms, etc. which I will show you later. Meanwhile, I need a letter from you which will put my mind at rest by not condemning my change of mind, which I would call a *belated* insight. But better late than never. . . .

In this same letter, Puccini promised that he would throw himself into *La Bohème* with all his heart, now that the Verga story had been discarded. He asked the publisher to talk to Illica about the "Quartier Latin" scene, on

which they were in agreement, and he expressed serious doubts about the
scene at the *Barrière*, then the second act. He was worried that it contained far
too many irrelevant episodes, and suggested that Illica again read Murger's
book in order to find new ideas. All this was proof that he wanted to go ahead
with *Bohème*; all that mattered, he claimed, was that the libretto be completed quickly and satisfactorily.

Ricordi, justifiably irritated, replied to Puccini on July 18:

> . . . No, I don't wonder that you made the decision that you did,
> though it saddens me. Again, so many months lost, unfruitful! At
> least, I see your strong and resolute decision in favor of *Bohème*. You
> discard the second act. Very well. What remains to be done? I will
> see Illica, I will speak to him at once. Let us hope that we will come
> to an understanding. Permit me, however, my dear Doge, to observe
> with my usual frankness that you have waited long to come to the
> realization that the dialogue in *La Lupa* is excessive — after you have
> begun to set it to music, after the newspapers have already
> announced the imminent appearance of the opera, after your voyage
> to Catania! Well, these are useless observations. . . . I wish you a
> ticket for the most direct train to take you to station *Bohème*.

If Ricordi had accepted Puccini's explanation, Illica had not; in a meeting
with Ricordi he expressed his anger at the composer in no uncertain terms,
and on July 19, Ricordi reported the outcome of that meeting to Puccini:

> Following my last letter, I had a long talk with Illica. I am writing
> much perturbed, having found that Illica is very irritated with you.
> He has almost decided to have nothing further to do with *Bohème*.
> He complains because he has expended much work and time fruit-
> lessly, and sees himself used, cast aside, taken up again, and once
> more shoved away like a dog. I need not belabor the point. The
> conclusion was this: I succeeded in making Illica go back to work on
> the "Quartier Latin" But he wants me to tell you this: he is resuming
> his work solely out of regard for me! . . . I am writing immediately
> to Giacosa to send me the second act. In all this hubbub and during
> all this storm, I see but one consoling ray of sunshine: that is the
> assurance that you are working at full speed and well. Avanti, then! I
> remember the very beautiful beginning of the "Quartier Latin." Ah!
> Doge, Doge!! How much, how much time is lost!

On July 21, Puccini replied to Ricordi; instead of showing regret for the
delays he had caused, he expressed his own anger at the librettist's attitude
and little sympathy for his suggestions concerning the libretto:

> Must I blindly accept the gospel according to Illica? I have my

vision of *La Bohème* but it includes the "Quartier Latin" act, as I said the last time I discussed the matter with Illica, with Musetta's scene, *which was my idea*. I want the death to be as I have envisaged it, and I am sure then of creating an original and vital piece of work. As for the act at the Barrière, I am still of the same opinion that I do not like it. There is very little that is musical in it. Only the drama has movement, and that isn't enough. I should have liked to introduce a more musical element. We must remember that there is plenty of drama in the other acts. In this one I wanted a canvas that would allow me to spread my colors a little more lyrically. . . .

I hope that Illica will cool down, and we shall get to work. But I too want to have my say when the necessity arises, and I shall accept nobody's dictation. . . .

Ricordi began to lose patience. The temperamental outbursts on the part of Illica and Puccini consumed too much time and energy, and it was essential that an agreement of some kind be reached between the two men. He joked that he sought, since it was a matter of music, a perfect *acchord*, but he was serious in his awareness of the difficulties of working with Puccini.

In spite of Ricordi's worries and perhaps because of his growing impatience, the relationship between Puccini and Illica improved to such an extent that by early August the composer was able to write his librettist a cheerful letter, expressing renewed confidence that their collaboration would result in a true masterpiece, an opera that would be at the same time humorous and deeply moving. Later that month, Illica sent the entire libretto on to Puccini. "I am certain of great success," he wrote Ricordi. "Now he has no more excuses — he has the entire *Bohème*. Certainly there are things here and there to be polished, but we will do those while Puccini is working on other parts."

Another meeting was held at Ricordi's office, and the publisher reported to Puccini on August 22:

> Yesterday Illica read to me the whole of *Bohème*. He himself brought it to me. It seems to me that now we have really succeeded! The last act and the death of Mimi, especially, ought to call forth torrents of tears. I myself was much, much moved. Although it is only in three acts, the libretto seems to me long, but Illica and I already have come to an understanding, and it will be easy to shorten it here and there. Moreover, you can do it according to the dictates of musical necessity, as they will appear in the course of composition. Illica told me that you finished the first part [probably in a revised version]. How anxious I am to hear the duet. . . .

Puccini, too, in spite of certain inevitable reservations, was pleased and wrote to Ricordi from Torre del Lago on September 7:

I am now awaiting Giacosa's cuts and revisions (which are absolutely necessary to give the work a unity, and because with added
thought the libretto gains, etc., etc.). Now we do have an original
work! And how! The last act is very beautiful. The "Quartier" too,
but it is very difficult. I've had the acrobat cut, but still more has to
be eliminated. It would be fine if you too could give it a reading to
get rid of certain odd parts that are not at all necessary. For example:
The horse is the king of the animals, Rivers are wine made of water,
and many others which Illica is too devoted to as if they were his
own children (if he had any). What we must shorten a great deal is
the second act, "La Barrière": all that business in the beginning is
unnecessary, and we have agreed to shorten not only that but the
rest and the final quartet. This is the weak act—in my opinion. I
might be wrong; I hope so. But what seems to me most successful is
the last act; the death and all that comes before it are *really moving.*
    . . . Awaiting the revised, shortened, and corrected version of the
"Quartier Latin," with the intervention of the Giacosian Buddha. . . .

In late September, Ricordi accompanied Verdi to Paris to work on the first
French production of *Otello,* but even the distance between him and Puccini
did not prevent the latter from keeping his publisher up to date on his own
problems with *Bohème.* In a letter written to Ricordi on September 25,
Puccini stated:

    I have received the new script—how can I set to music such long,
    drawn-out verses that should at least be condensed, or possibly even
    rewritten . . . ? Illica himself said that Giacosa would have to make
    revisions. It's unrealistic to think that this can be done later. I must
    have the exact words for each character and situation—if I do it in
    the manner suggested to me, it seems to me that it would be a double
    effort to make corrections later on the already established meter.
    Because of this, I hope you will be able to persuade Giacosa to do
    four or five verses a day and send them to me; I don't need the whole
    work right away—two or three pages of the "Quartier Latin" are
    enough. . . .

Ricordi, preoccupied with preparations for *Otello,* was in no position to
deal with Giacosa from Paris. He wrote the composer that he feared matters
might drag out endlessly if he waited for Giacosa's revisions before going
ahead, and he suggested that Puccini enlist the aid of Tito Ricordi, his son
who would one day inherit the business, in getting Giacosa to send on the
corrected verses page by page. As for the opera itself, the publisher remained
enthusiastic. "The more I think of it, the more I like *Bohème,*" he wrote

Puccini. "In my modest opinion, the Quartier Latin act is a difficult undertaking, since to give the entire scene a lively shape, to make it move quickly
without leaving holes into which a cold wind might blow and create a void, is
hard. But Puccini has good shoulders and strong lungs! And then, are you or
are you not the Doge?"

In spite of Tito Ricordi's pleas, Giacosa stubbornly refused to go ahead with
any corrections unless Puccini withdrew certain changes he had made in the
first act. Once again, there loomed the possibility of Giacosa's withdrawal
from the project, but, temporarily at least, Puccini smoothed things over, and
a crisis was avoided. Because of this, Ricordi remained optimistic after his
return from Paris, and on October 28, he wrote to Puccini:

> So much the better if you have succeeded in calming the suscep-
> tibility of Giacosa: we shall see him do good work — and that finally
> you are planning to sit down to work and not turn away from it. It
> seems to me with your *Bohème* that I am at a ball game, in which the
> libretto is substituted for the ball! . . . I hold that before the Holy
> Trinity will be reunited in Milan, nothing really useful will be
> accomplished.
>
> I have to admit that the "Quartier Latin," in its new form, has
> gained much. Giacosa ought to be convinced of that also. It is more
> rapid, more logical, more easy.
>
> You are still finding the Barrière act indigestible: I hope the
> obstacle is not insurmountable. What do you want? To me it seems
> good, but it is not I who have to digest it and set it to music! It is
> difficult, but what is not difficult in the singular *Bohème?* Difficult,
> difficult, I have said it 10, 100, 1000 times! . . .

Ricordi's elation was such that a few weeks later he was able to send
Puccini a lighthearted if somewhat chiding note, written in Latin. Translated, it reads:

> Knock, knock!
> What are you looking for?
> Jacopus Puccinius.
> Why?
> To see if he is working.
> He is working.
> He is working? On *Bohème?*
> On *Bohème.*
> That's good.

The year 1895 began well. On January 12, Illica wrote Ricordi that the
libretto was not only finished but that Puccini was satisfied with it at last.
Illica felt that *Bohème* was now behind him, and most of his letter was

devoted to problems he was having with the *Tosca* libretto he had been writing for Franchetti. He mentioned that a sure way of getting Franchetti to work was to talk to him about *Bohème*; and he added that he wished that a sure way of getting Puccini to work was to talk to him about *Tosca*.

Puccini did work, now that he proclaimed his satisfaction with the libretto, and by the end of January he was busy on the final orchestration of the first act. However, he still found problems in the final act, and throughout the months of March and April he urged Giacosa to study these problems carefully and make the necessary cuts.

By June, Giacosa was tired of the composer's never-ending demands for revisions, but Ricordi, fearing another crisis, did his best to hide the librettist's irritation from Puccini. Instead, he wrote the composer that Giacosa was delighted with the music he had heard and could well understand the reasons for Puccini's demands for perfection. At the same time, he suggested that Puccini might write Giacosa a few lines of encouragement and, as an added incentive, send him a small present to show his appreciation for what the librettist had done.

The publisher's efforts at diplomacy did not quite succeed — Puccini was spared, but Giacosa was not placated. There is no record of Puccini sending his weary librettist a gift, or even a few words of encouragement, and on June 25 the latter was both bitter and discouraged. He wrote to Ricordi:

> . . . I confess to you that I am exhausted from this continual redoing, retouching, adding, correcting, cutting, piecing together, blowing up on the one hand in order to thin out on the other. If it hadn't been for my great friendship for you and the fact that I wish Puccini well, I would by now be liberated from this — with ill will. I've done this whole blessed libretto, from beginning to end, *three times*, and parts of it four and five. How can I go ahead at this pace? . . .
> I swear to you that I will never again be caught writing a libretto. . . . In a few days, I will have finished. But will it really be finished then? Or will I have to begin from the beginning again?

In late June, Puccini, unaware of Giacosa's anger, installed himself in a luxurious forty-room villa — the Villa del Castellaccio, which belonged to the Count Orsi-Bertolini — in the Val di Nievole, near Pescia. In this spacious villa, amidst a forest and a garden and a stream, the composer hoped to find the peace and isolation that would permit him to finish *La Bohème*. There was a great deal to do — only the first act of the opera had been completed, but Puccini showed signs of tiring of the opera and was eager to complete it. He hated his summer home, which he called an "internment camp," but he admitted to Ricordi that it was the best thing for his work, which was going both well and quickly.

The orchestration of the second act was completed on July 19, and the third act was finished on the eighteenth of September. Puccini was so certain that the end was in sight that he wrote to Carlo Clausetti, Ricordi's representative in Naples, to say that his new work would be performed in Rome, Turin, Naples, Trieste, and Warsaw, among other cities; and he even made suggestions as to which singers he felt would be suited for the various roles.

The composer had every reason to feel optimistic, but when he began work on the last act, he came to realize that more changes would have to be made before he could be completely satisfied. These changes concerned a toast the four Bohemians (singing simultaneously, in four different meters) were to make at the beginning of the act, an aria — apparently a tirade against women — that was to be sung by Schaunard, and various aspects of Mimi's role in that final act. In late October, Puccini complained to Ricordi that he did not like Schaunard's aria — "It isn't worth changing the old one to have him say foolish and boring things," and that the toast would be his "*death.*" He added: "Look over the part where Mimi is given the muff; doesn't this seem to you rather weak at the moment of death? A few words more, an affectionate word to Rodolfo would be sufficient. This might be quibbling on my part, but at the moment this girl, for whom I have worked so hard, dies, I would like her to leave the world thinking less of herself and a bit more of the man who loved her. . . ."

He explained his objections to Illica in greater detail:

> I told you, I think, to do the toast, in rapid form, with witty retorts, with ideas started by one and completed by another character. I also wrote you about Schaunard's aria. . . . I told you I didn't think it would be a good idea for Schaunard to say all those negative things about women — I told you that I believed it would be better if those criticisms of the fair sex came from those who had been betrayed — Rodolfo and Marcello. . . . For the toast, I repeat that it is almost impossible to set it to music as it stands — I say "almost" because if you want to you can even set the tailor's bill to music. You can retain Giacosa's ideas, but shape them so that they are more suited to a quartet, and cut all that chatter in the last act, where we have to cut it short and quickly reach Mimi's arrival. The episode of the Bohemians all together is only there for contrast, since if we wanted we could have Mimi appear as soon as the curtain rises, and to hell with the herring, and screw Demosthenes. . . . Goodbye! . . .

These were not the composer's final words. A few days later, while awaiting Illica's changes in response to his letter, he wrote to Ricordi of still another problem. Why, toward the end of the opera, when the muff was given to Mimi, does Musetta try to take it back? It was a valid question. In the final version of the opera, Mimi asks Rodolfo if he had bought the muff for her, and Musetta quickly answers yes—while the truth is that it was she who traded her own earrings for that muff.

Happily, for all concerned, Puccini made a major decision only a few days later: he informed Ricordi that he had finally come to the conclusion that the long-disputed toast had to be eliminated. After all the many worries that this toast had caused all those concerned, the composer realized that it did nothing but hold up the action, to the detriment of the drama. The whole point of the last act was the death of Mimi. After a short scene of merriment—effective as a contrast to what would follow—Musetta would enter as would the dying Mimi and the story could rapidly reach its tragic conclusion.

Further suggestions, minor ones coming from both Ricordi and Illica, followed but the composer rejected them all. At this point, he felt that further changes—Ricordi believed the last act might be too short, and Illica wanted to give Schaunard and Colline more to do—were unnecessary. He was, finally, satisfied.

By early November, Ricordi was certain that the long struggle had been worth it. "If this time you have not succeeded in hitting the nail squarely on the head," he wrote Puccini, "I will change my profession and will sell salami." The publisher was still worried that word of Puccini's version might reach Leoncavallo, but he was above all anxious for it all to end. "Has our Mimi finally died?" he asked Puccini in a letter of November 13, as the composer was reaching the end of the orchestration of the final act. "I get stomach cramps from curiosity. I want to hear and to admire. . . . I am here with my mouth open, ready to howl, 'Viva Puccini, glory to the Doge!' "

As late as November 25, the composer suggested changes to Illica that would add to the poignancy of Mimi's death, and one of these, Mimi's repetition of parts of Rodolfo's first-act aria, proved to be one of the most moving moments of the opera. Finally, at midnight on December 10, 1895, Puccini put the finishing touches on La Bohème. It was reported that he broke down and sobbed at the death of his beloved Mimi, but he recovered quickly and was soon able to participate in a wild, joyful masked ball, given in celebration by his friends at the Club La Bohème.

Christmas 1895 was celebrated with even more joy than usual in the homes of the weary men who had created La Bohème. Their task had been completed, and each was convinced that the endless conferences, the struggles over each revision, the outbursts of temper, and the impulsive threats of resignation had resulted in a masterpiece. To commemorate the holiday, Ricordi sent a huge panettone—the traditional Italian Christmas cake—to the home of Giuseppe Giacosa. The librettist appropriately thanked his publisher in verse, which read in part: "No wreath has ever been as sweet as the one with which you crown my table today. If this is the monument which is awarded to the unpublished Bohemia, with what will it be awarded when it will shine on the stage?"

Puccini had been worried about his opera's "shining on the stage" as early as October, when the opera had not yet been completed. If *Bohème* were to fail, the consequences to his career would be serious. From his point of view, one way to ensure success would be to obtain the services of the finest and best-known singers available. In addition, he believed that the première should be held in Rome or Naples, and not in Turin (in spite of the success of *Manon Lescaut* there) where he was unhappy about the opera house and its acoustics as well as its proximity to what he felt were the hostile Milanese critics. Ricordi, expert in these matters, disagreed in both cases and wrote his views to Puccini:

> Regarding the cast and the observations you made, let me tell you with my usual frankness, and don't take it badly, that they are uncalled for and unfair. Oh yes, there was a time when everything depended on the true virtuosity of the throat. Specialists were needed for *Norma* and *Sonnambula* and similar works. Today an opera needs a homogeneous cast, the more intelligent the better. It is not the artist who makes the opera successful, but really the opera itself. . . . Look at Mascagni, who had De Lucia in *Silvano*. Was the opera a success? Did it survive? Not at all. . . . Who talks to me about *Falstaff*? There was only one real artist in it, Maurel; all the others were almost mediocrities—including the diva Pasqua, who was never right in the ensembles, and including Pini-Corsi, who had a good voice, but no better than a dozen others, and was a trivial, second-rate actor. These and even that same star Maurel were *very bad* in the first performance.
>
> It was the monklike patience of Verdi which gave them blood day by day, hour by hour, teaching them to pronounce the words; it was that extraordinary patience which finally succeeded in obtaining a vivacious, spirited, and persuasive performance. . . .
>
> Let us put together a cast which is homogeneous, willing, animated by enthusiasm, and we will get what we need. Let us not force theatres into impossible expenditures. . . . Do not think that I am moved by tenderness toward the impresarios. Not at all! But I am speaking as a businessman, of long experience. . . .

As for the theatre in which the première would take place, Ricordi made it clear in this letter that it would be Turin's Teatro Regio, to be followed shortly by Rome, no matter what the composer said or wanted.

Puccini went to Turin in early January to help with preparations for the première of his opera. The cast did not include the well-known tenor, Fernando De Lucia, whom he had wanted (Evan Gorga was instead chosen to sing the role of Rodolfo) nor was Puccini's choice, Leopoldo Mugnone, able to conduct at the première. That task fell to the lesser known Arturo Toscanini. But Mimi would be sung by Cesira Ferrani, who had successfully sung the role of Manon at its première, and the composer was more than pleased with that choice; it was in fact rumored that he was in love with her (not the last of the sopranos with whom he would fall in love, nor probably the first), though the Torinese soprano was said to love not Puccini but the young Toscanini!

In light of this, it is interesting that Elvira did not join him during these preparations, and that Puccini did nothing to encourage her to do so. "You always talk to me of coming here," Puccini wrote her. "Are you crazy? With the life I'm leading! You would have to eat alone, and you would hardly see me, I am so busy. You'll come in time. . . ." He did, however, keep her informed of his everyday problems, such as his need for a new suit and some white shirts, and he also kept her up to date on the progress of the rehearsals. From the very beginning, he was pleased with Toscanini, whom he described as "highly intelligent," "a very sweet and nice man," and "extraordinary," and in spite of his earlier doubts, the cast pleased him, with one exception — the baritone, Tieste Wilmant, who was to sing Marcello. He is "vile," he wrote to Illica in one letter, and in another letter to his librettist he said "This Marcello is no good. He understands nothing and will not get better — even if we were to have as many rehearsals as they have in Bayreuth." Wilmant's "voice is coarse, and Marcello is such a gentle man," he wrote to Elvira, hinting to her that he would ask Ricordi to have him replaced by a more suitable baritone. By the time Illica arrived in Turin for the rehearsals, however, Puccini seemed resigned. "Wilmant is still a dog," he wrote Elvira, "but Illica hopes to succeed in teaching him at least to act less awkwardly."

In this same letter to Elvira, the composer complained of his hectic work schedule. "We are working like dogs," he wrote her. "We rehearsed today from eleven to four-thirty. Tonight we rehearse from eight-thirty to midnight." In spite of his fatigue and his dissatisfaction with the baritone, Puccini was confident as the première of the opera approached. "I foresee a great and sensational success — if the artists do their part," he wrote Elvira, though he worried that "enemies" from Milan — friends of Leoncavallo? — might be out to get him.

His worries were, to some extent, justified. A great deal depended on the fate of La Bohème — more than the success or failure of one single opera was involved, since the musical world was eager, once and for all, to crown a successor to Verdi. The huge and continuing success of Manon Lescaut had made Puccini the leading contender for this title, but a further confirmation of his talent was still needed. Puccini's rivals, too, were a factor, though Puccini was sufficiently sure of himself to feel neither jealousy nor anger towards his competitors — with the obvious exception of Leoncavallo, whose fortunes had declined steadily after the success of *I Pagliacci*, but who could not yet be counted out.

Catalani, long a serious contender, had died in August of 1893, and until the very end, the moody and gifted composer had resented his fellow Lucchese. While close to death, he repeated to his intensely loyal friend Toscanini that *Manon Lescaut* was not a "sincere" opera and that its composer was not an honest man. In spite of this, Puccini continued to speak well of Catalani, even admitting that he had been influenced by *La Wally*, his one successful opera. Puccini, too, was among those who had accompanied the composer's body to the cemetery and in later years, when he made his frequent visits to the Lucca cemetery to place flowers on the grave of his mother, he would quietly place flowers, too, on the nearby grave of Catalani.

Mascagni, still living, was a more threatening rival, but his relationship with Puccini was a generally warm one, in spite of occasional attempts by outsiders to disrupt it. One example of an attempt to create a feud between the two composers is found in a letter written to Mascagni by Eugenio Checchi, following the success of Mascagni's *Guglielmo Ratcliff* in 1895, a letter which commented on the "terrible flame of jealousy" in Puccini's eyes at a banquet following the opera's première. Mascagni, however, was quick to admonish Checchi not to pit the two men against each other, saying that no attempt on the part of anyone could succeed in loosening the bonds of their friendship. Although these bonds were strained on several occasions, always followed by well-publicized reconciliations, Puccini was openly enthusiastic about *Ratcliff* (as was Verdi), calling it a fine work and a giant step forward for the Livornese composer.

But if Puccini had nothing to fear from a deceased Catalani or a friendly Mascagni, there still remained Leoncavallo, whose own version of *La Vie de Bohème* had not yet been completed and whose supporters, Puccini felt, might try to disrupt the first performance of his own work.

The première of the new, eagerly awaited opera took place on the night of February 1, 1896 — exactly three years after the first performance of *Manon Lescaut* at the same theatre. It was a gala occasion — the newest work by the "hope" of Italian opera — and it had been widely heralded as such by the press and advertised to the public by means of colored posters — the first use of such posters to announce the première of an opera in Italy. Tickets were especially priced — the best seats in the house cost sixty lire each, an enormously high figure at the time.

The audience which filled Turin's opera house was suited to the occasion. There were members of the royal family — Isabella, Duchess of Genoa, the Count of Turin, the Duke and Duchess of Aosta, and Princess Letizia (Puccini, nervously, spent the third act in her box) — as well as Italy's most distinguished musicians, among them Mascagni, Boito, and Franchetti. Expectations, thus, were high as the curtain rose on the Bohemians' garret and the orchestra played the lively melody (taken directly from the composer's *Capriccio Sinfonico*, a reminder of his own *vie de Bohème*) which is the theme of the inhabitants of the garret, the symbol of their carefree way of life.

Nonetheless, it was clear from the very beginning that something was wrong. The audience, throughout the whole performance, was polite and appreciative, but there was none of the warmth and spontaneous enthusiasm which had marked the première of *Manon Lescaut*. Word spread during the intermissions that the opera had been a failure, that it could not possibly have a long life, and by the end of the evening Puccini was heartbroken. Many years later, he spoke of that evening to his friend and biographer Fraccaroli:

> "It was a very strange evening," he said. "It had undoubtedly been a success, yet at the end of the opera I felt a kind of melancholy which I couldn't explain. However, thinking about it, there was an explanation. The public had been generous with its applause, and its enjoyment during the performance had been obvious. There had been gusts of youthful joy and moments of profound emotion. It was exactly what I wanted, the result I had hoped for. But I didn't feel that warmth, that excitement I had desired. And then, I don't know, the malicious voices that had been heard during rehearsals, the campaign of diffidence and advance hostility which certain people had expressed . . . had succeeded in dampening the public's wish to proclaim another success. There were many people who came eager to enjoy themselves and applaud, but who did not show their pleasure for fear of seeming ingenuous or easily satisfied. And other people hoped to be present at, if not a catastrophe, a half-failure. . . . Envy is an ugly thing, especially impotent, arrogant envy. . . ."

Puccini was on the verge of tears when he returned to his hotel room. Toscanini's assurances that the opera would eventually achieve the success it deserved had not consoled him; this labor of love, to which he felt he had given his soul, had been received with near-indifference, and by the same public which had once greeted him as a hero.

There was no consolation to be found, either, in the reviews by Turin's three most important newspapers the following day. They were angry—even spiteful. In view of the huge success *La Bohème* was to have with the public and eventually the press, these severe judgments of Puccini's work are difficult to explain, though certain hypotheses are worth considering.

First of all, there was a certain amount of resentment at the unusual publicity—including the colored posters—that preceded the première of

Bohème. The poor reviews might well have been a reaction against all this ballyhoo.

Next, there was the all too common problem of any artist in following up an immensely successful earlier work. On the one hand, there were the abnormally high expectations; on the other, a residue of resentment at that earlier success.

Finally, the première of La Bohème followed by only six weeks the first Italian performance of Götterdämmerung—also conducted at the Teatro Regio by Toscanini. Wagner's massive, heroic drama had been greeted with wild enthusiasm—it had virtually numbed the public and forced it to reconsider its whole concept of what opera should be. Compared to it, Puccini's work undoubtedly seemed small and "not serious"—by comparison, it could be considered a kind of operetta.

Whatever the reasons for the lukewarm reception accorded La Bohème at its première, it is worthwhile to quote at length from the hostile press that greeted Puccini following the first performance of an opera that is today generally considered a masterpiece, if a small one, of musical theatre.

To begin with, there was E. A. Berta, reporting fully, in a most unusual way, on the events of the night before in the Gazzetta del Popolo. This eminent critic, it must be noted, had once been considered as a possible librettist for Bohème but had been finally rejected. His review began with an attack on the extraordinary publicity that had surrounded the première and above all on the use of the posters which, he felt, must have embarrassed even Puccini. He then began his account of the performance itself, which he noted began at precisely 8:35 to three rounds of applause. At the end of that first act, at 9:15, there were three rounds of applause for the singers and for the composer, who also took a solo bow. The critic continued in this vein. "The second act began at 9:35 and ended at 9:50. No interruptions other than at the moment when all join together to sing Musetta's song. At the end of the act, two curtain calls for the singers and Puccini. A lot of chatter in the lobby. There is no lack of zealots, but many people note that the finale, with drums and soldiers, reminiscent of operetta, is not very convincing. There is recognition, however, that the work abounds in a kind of pleasant geniality when the inspiration is drowsy. . . ."

The critic continued his precise account of the previous evening's events, noting that in all there had been fifteen curtain calls. He concluded by admonishing the composer: "We ask ourselves what could have moved Puccini along the deplorable path of this Bohème. The question is a bitter one, and we ask with pain, we who applauded and will always applaud Manon which revealed a composer who was able to wed orchestral skills to the healthiest of Italian conceptions. Maestro, you are young and strong, you have talent, culture, and imagination as few others do. Today you have capriciously forced the public to applaud when and where you wanted. To do this once is all right; but in the future, return to the great and difficult battles of art."

The critic for *La Stampa*, Carlo Bersenzio, was even more acrid. "To say that this *Bohème* is an artistically successful opera is (and I am sorry to say so) impossible. . . . An innate facility of invention and a great rush of ideas have pushed Puccini to write his music hurriedly (it seems to me) and with little attention to selection. . . ." Clearly, this critic was unaware of the painful process of creation that had marked each stage of *La Bohème*, and he ended his scathing review with what must be one of the least sound prophesies in the history of musical criticism. "*Bohème*," he wrote, "just as it makes little impression on the emotions of the listener, will leave few traces in the history of our lyric theatre."

L. A. Villanis, the reviewer for the *Gazzetta di Torino*, was somewhat kinder; he recognized that the public had seemed to enjoy the opera, though he felt that this could be explained by the excellent level of the performance. (It is noteworthy that neither he nor any of his Torinese colleagues even mentioned Toscanini's conducting.) Personally, however, he deplored the opera, accusing the composer of currying public favor, and, in conclusion, he stated that "the music of *Bohème* is intuitive music, made for immediate enjoyment; saying this is an expression both of praise and of condemnation."

Many years later, Claude Debussy, writing of *La Bohème*, noted that "if one did not keep a grip on oneself, one would be swept away by the sheer verve of the music." Even later, H. L. Mencken (who defined Puccini's music as "silver macaroni, exquisitely entangled") commented that "anyone who fails to get pleasure out of it must be tone deaf." The critics for Turin's three most influential newspapers certainly managed to keep a grip on themselves, and perhaps they were even tone deaf. Perhaps, too, they were, even unconsciously, part of a subtle plot against the composer and his "popular" appeal. These reviews caused Puccini great pain on the day following the première of his opera, but he had every reason to be cheered by further reviews which appeared later in other parts of Italy, many of which hailed the new work as a sign of the composer's progress and predicted that it would meet with success wherever it was performed. That the public agreed with these later reviews was obvious; that month alone, *La Bohème* was performed twenty-four times (only eight performances had been originally scheduled), to packed houses, in Turin's Teatro Regio.

Tosca

Even before La Bohème had been completed, Puccini had made up his mind to base his next opera on Sardou's La Tosca, the same play he had once desperately wanted and then given up—after some problems concerning the rights—several years before. It was a surprising choice, since Puccini must have known that Illica, his own librettist, while occupied with Bohème, had also been busily working on a Tosca libretto for another of Ricordi's composers, Alberto Franchetti, for whom the publisher had bought the operatic rights after Puccini had apparently lost interest. In spite of, or because of, this, Puccini's interest in Tosca had suddenly been revived—not only by Ricordi's and Illica's enthusiasms, but even more by reports that the great Verdi had agreed that the idea was an excellent one, only regretting that he himself was too old to set the drama to music. This additional seal of approval was too much for Puccini; it no longer mattered that Tosca belonged to Franchetti. He, the crown prince, wanted it, and it was up to Ricordi to see that Franchetti abandoned the idea. According to a popular legend, the wily Ricordi accomplished this by convincing the good-natured Franchetti that the subject was, after all, not really the right one for an opera—immediately after which Puccini signed an agreement to turn the play into one. However, Franchetti's heirs assert, more convincingly, that the reasonable Franchetti was simply persuaded by his publisher that Puccini was better suited to the task than he was.

However it happened, Tosca belonged to Puccini by the time La Bohème had had its first performance. The composer was delighted with Illica's already completed libretto and believed that it was even an improvement over the original play—which he again saw in Florence toward the end of 1895. Giacosa, too, in spite of his earlier vow to never again work on a libretto, had joined the team, agreeing to versify and make minor changes in Illica's libretto. Few problems were anticipated, and the restructuring of the original play seemed minimal. A relatively tight theatrical work, it was far easier to adapt to the needs of the operatic stage than the sprawling, episodic Bohème had been. The strong-willed Sardou had the right to approve of any changes made in his play, but given his enthusiasm for the project and his sure knowledge of the theatre, this seemed to present no serious problem. It was merely a matter of getting to work.

In early 1896, however, Puccini was not yet able to put his heart and mind into a new opera; first he had to see La Bohème successfully launched. Though not pleased by the severe judgment of the Torinese critics, he was not discouraged—nor should he have been, given the public's warm response to later performances of the opera. Audience reaction was of utmost importance to the composer, and if he tirelessly attended innumerable stagings of his works, he did so not only because of the publicity value of his presence and because he could in that way make certain that the opera was performed as he intended, but also in order to assess the advisability of revisions, based on the reaction of the public to each segment of his work. For Puccini, the process of creating an opera did not end with the work's première; revision, based on how the opera played in a theatre before an audience, was an essential part of this process, and he never hesitated to make changes where he felt them necessary.

Such was the case with Bohème after its lukewarm reception in Turin. Its next production took place in Rome, on February 23, giving the composer another chance to hear and evaluate his opera, with, he believed, a stronger cast than that which performed at the opera's première. He was particularly delighted with the Musetta, sung by the twenty-one-year-old Rosina Storchio. Ricordi, too, was certain that the opera would be enthusiastically acclaimed in Rome. "It is a new and daring work of art," he wrote Illica, "and therefore argued about and little understood by the intelligentsia, who can never be impartial, while the public loves and is moved by it." In spite of this optimism, the Italian capital was not to be the scene of the opera's first triumph. The audience was cool following acts one and two and only slightly warmer after the last two acts. The press complained that it all sounded too familiar and that it was, in the words of one critic, a "medley of reminiscences, a paraphrase of already popular fragments, a transcription of entire scenes from Manon Lescaut." Puccini, proud of having been named Commendatore della Corona d'Italia for the occasion, was again disappointed. However, this further chance to see and hear the opera led him to believe that the work's weakness was to be found in the second act, the scene of the Quartier

Latin. He alerted both Ricordi and Illica that he would add an aria, to be sung by Schaunard, in the middle of that act, and that he would also redo the finale of the act, which had been greeted coldly at each performance. These changes, and perhaps others, would not be made, however, until the composer had had a chance to hear the opera performed in mid-April in Palermo, which he felt would be its crucial test.

The composer was so certain of the importance of the Palermo production that he precipitously left Naples—where *Bohème* had been performed—in order to reach the Sicilian capital as soon as possible. There was an air of triumph from the moment of his arrival. He threw himself energetically into rehearsals and was unusually pleased with the entire cast and with the conducting of his old friend Leopoldo Mugnone. He felt confident that the performance would be exemplary and that the opera would be shown at its best.

All concerned with the production shared his optimism as the crowds began to fill Palermo's Teatro Massimo on the night of the première; all, that is, except for Mugnone. High-strung and nervous under the best of circumstances, the Neapolitan maestro was also incurably superstitious, and the date set for the première—not only the thirteenth, but a Friday as well—had upset him from the start. Foreseeing disaster, he felt his fears had been justified when the late arrival of the first oboeist caused what seemed an interminable delay in the start of the performance. As the audience grew restless and impatient, the conductor repeatedly threatened to step off the podium, in spite of every effort by Puccini to calm him.

Finally, the missing musician arrived, and the performance began. Within a short time, it was clear that the premonition of triumph—on the part of all but Mugnone—was to be resoundingly confirmed. The principals were wildly cheered, encores were insistently demanded, and the composer was repeatedly called before the curtain. At the end of the opera, pandemonium broke loose, and much of the audience simply refused to leave the theatre until the entire finale had been repeated—in spite of the fact that the tenor and soprano, already in their street clothes, had to be recalled from their dressing rooms, and half the orchestra had left for home.

La Bohème had finally been accorded the unqualified acclaim that its composer had sought, and Puccini was able to give some thought to his future. When the May 17 issue of the *Gazzetta Musicale* announced his return to Milan after several months of travel, it also noted that the composer's words to those friends who came to greet him at the station were, "And now to *Tosca* . . ."

He was a bit premature in his pronouncement, not yet ready to throw himself into the work on his next opera as he would have to. At first he put the blame on Giacosa, who was not sending the libretto as he had promised, but even when, during the summer, that material did begin to arrive,

Puccini, though setting to work, was unable to give his undivided attention to the new opera. He still kept more than a careful eye on new productions of *Bohème*, which were being given not only throughout Italy, but in every part of the world. Of special interest, as always, was the opera's first production in Lucca, an event which meant so much to Puccini that he even convinced Mugnone to conduct the opera in that small provincial capital. For Lucca, this was a major event, and money was raised by public subscription so that the performance might be worthy of the growing fame of the city's distinguished son, who was personally supervising rehearsals. Large crowds attended each of thirteen performances, and so many out-of-towners showed up that local train schedules had to be rearranged to coincide with the beginning and end of each performance.

The fame of Puccini and his new opera spread far beyond the walls of Lucca. In December 1896, *La Bohème* was performed in Buenos Aires; this was the first of the many foreign productions of the opera to be staged in every corner of the world, each new triumph proving the Torinese critics had been wrong in foreseeing a short life for the opera. The list of cities in which the work was given in 1897, the year after its première, is a long one and included Alexandria, Moscow, Lisbon, Manchester, Berlin, Rio de Janeiro, Mexico City, London, Vienna, Los Angeles, and The Hague. In today's jet age, it is entirely possible that the indefatigable composer might have attended each of these performances, carefully supervising production details wherever he went. In 1897, this was obviously impossible, but Puccini, delighted at his success, traveled wherever he could. "How my stars keep shining," he wrote jubilantly to his brother-in-law Raffaello Franceschini in February, as he prepared for *Bohème*'s première at La Scala, adding with that trace of melancholy that was to pervade his thinking even when at the height of success, "Let us hope that it will continue this way . . . but there is the problem of growing old, and that is a ball breaker." These are strange words from a man in the throes of international fame, a man who had not yet reached his fortieth birthday, yet they accurately reflect the doubts and fears that afflicted Puccini throughout his career.

In April 1897, Puccini, still unable to put all of his energies into *Tosca* because of his preoccupation with the many productions of his earlier opera, set off on his first lengthy trip outside of Italy. He briefly visited Paris, London, and Belgium. In Belgium he tried, unsuccessfully, to conclude arrangements for a production of *Bohème* in Brussels, and he took a side trip to Ghent in an effort to obtain operatic rights to *Pelléas et Mélisande* from Maurice Maeterlinck, who had already granted them to Debussy. The main purpose of this extended trip, however, was to attend the British première of *La Bohème* in Manchester. Under the title of *The Bohemians*, the opera was to be performed in English by the traveling Carl Rosa company, an earnest but hardly distinguished group. The composer was horrified when he arrived in the cold and rainy fogbound industrial city. Though he was traveling with Tito Ricordi, Giulio's son, he felt alone and lost in an ugly climate, surrounded by people who spoke a language which was totally foreign to him. As for the artists who were to sing in his opera, he wrote to his sister Ramelde, "You should hear them . . . what dogs!" A few years later, he spoke to Wakeling Dry, his earliest biographer, of this first British experience. "I always feel about past performances in the same way as I do about dead people. Let us say nothing about them but good. But I shall never forget the shock it was to me on arriving at the theatre to find the disposition of the orchestra in a fashion which I have never seen except at a circus. Out of two boxes at each end the brass on the one side and the drum on the other gave forth detached blares and pops that really frightened the life out of me. . . ."

Hermann Klein, the noted critic for the *Times* of London, traveled to Manchester for the first performance of the opera; a few hours before the curtain rose, he met Ricordi and Puccini and reported that he had never before seen two men in such a despondent mood, so certain of a total fiasco. To their surprise, however, the performance was so animated and spirited that it won enthusiastic cheers from the audience, who even seemed unconcerned that Robert Cunningham, the tenor, was suffering from such a bad cold that he was unable to do more than whisper his way through the role of Rodolfo. In Klein's words, "It was well worth the journey to Manchester and back. . . . The Carl Rosa directors had spared no pains in the endeavour to do the production justice. . . . Then the composer (accompanied by the indefatigable Sig. Tito Ricordi, who can sing every part in the opera and act it, too, if necessary) came upon the scene in the nick of time to put the finishing touches to his work. . . . Final result: admirable rendering of a delightful opera; a crowded house, unmistakable enthusiasm, innumerable recalls, and unqualified success all round."

The following morning Klein returned to London in the same railway car as did Puccini; he found the composer a changed man after the Manchester success. He was, according the Klein, a "merry, smiling fellow, with a plentiful supply of Italian jokes, and radiant with the recollection of genuine Lancashire cheering." The Carl Rosa production of *La Bohème* toured successfully throughout Britain, going on to Glasgow and Edinburgh, and finally reaching London's Covent Garden in October, where it opened the company's four-week season. Both press and public in the capital were somewhat reserved, and it was not until *Bohème* was performed a few years later in Italian that it achieved complete success in the British capital.

By early May, Puccini returned to Italy — fat from eating too much in Paris and drinking too much whiskey in Manchester, the city of soil-colored fog, he confessed in a letter to Ramelde. In spite of his approaching old age, he told his sister, he was still vigorous, though he had found a half dozen white hairs in his head, his teeth were a little thinned out, and he carried a few more pounds in his paunch. To correct this latter condition, he had bought a bicycle with which to exercise.

His success on an international scale had been confirmed, and he was further cheered to learn that Leoncavallo's *La Bohème* had failed in its Venice première, which meant that there was, after all, only one *Bohème* — his own. Now it was time to get down to work on *Tosca* and to enjoy the peace and quiet of his home in Torre del Lago. He was able to do this, however, only after a short trip to Berlin in the middle of June, where he supervised the rehearsals and attended the première of the first German-language production of *Bohème*.

The summer was a relaxed one; though he made little progress on the new opera, Puccini had a chance to visit with old friends, and he was able, for a short while at least, to return to his hunting. There was one noteworthy and altogether pleasant interruption — an unexpected visit by a twenty-five-year-old Neapolitan tenor who was eager to earn the composer's permission to sing the role of Rodolfo in Livorno that summer. Charming his way into the maestro's home, the young man proceeded to sing Rodolfo's first-act aria so movingly that the composer was only able to say, "Who sent you to me? God?" The tenor, who would become an outstanding interpreter of his music, was Enrico Caruso, and the two men were to become good friends. Before taking on the role of Rodolfo, however, Caruso expressed misgivings about the poet's high C in that first-act narrative, to which Puccini replied that the note was optional and that he disapproved of those singers who saved themselves for that one high note, far preferring that the entire aria be well sung, with or without its high C.

Puccini's period of isolation came to an end on September 18, when he again left Italy — this time for Vienna to attend the rehearsals of *Bohème*, which was to be performed at the Theater an der Wien and not, significantly, at the more important Hofoper. The latter was controlled by Gustav Mahler who, though he had conducted *Le Villi* in Hamburg in 1892, was no admirer of Puccini's work and had professed a preference for Leoncavallo's version of the Murger book. The distinguished Austrian composer-conductor, however, was present at the première of Puccini's opera at the Theater an der Wien on the night of October 5, managing to offend the composer by laughing derisively throughout the performance. In spite of Mahler's contempt and in spite of Puccini's own dissatisfaction with the production, the Viennese public enjoyed both the opera and the composer — "a distinctly attractive, elegant young man," according to Vienna's leading newspaper, "who was enthusiastically acclaimed by the audience after each act."

By early 1898, Puccini was tired of traveling; for almost two years he had journeyed from city to city on behalf of his opera, which was by then most successfully launched in most of the major capitals of Europe. Nonetheless, one further trip—this time to Paris—was necessary, and it turned out to be a very long and tiring one.

When the composer, together with Elvira and Fosca, left for Paris in early April 1898, it was to be his third trip to the French capital. He had stopped there briefly on his way to Manchester and had spent a few days there again in February to arrange for the première of *La Bohème* at the Opéra-Comique—the reason for this latest visit. Originally scheduled to take place around the tenth of May, the première was repeatedly postponed, forcing Puccini to spend more than two and a half months away from home and from his work.

This extended visit, however, proved to be an important one. As a result of it, the composer came to realize that no matter how great his fame or his wealth, he could only be truly at home in Torre del Lago, among simple, unpretentious people who spoke, in every way, his own language. It was also conclusive evidence, if such was needed, that he could never feel comfortable in his role of "celebrity" with all the parties, receptions, and interviews that that role entailed. As an artist he was sure of himself—though he was plagued by those doubts which are common to all creative people—and he wanted the recognition he felt was his due; however, the formalities and publicity that went along with that recognition merely embarrassed him. He was an attractive public figure—dignified and soft-spoken, a well-mannered gentleman who did all he could to avoid falling into the stereotype of the loud, gesticulating Italian artist in the manner of Leoncavallo and Mascagni. Though eager for applause and honors—he constantly sought and cherished formal recognition whether it be a Legion of Honor in France or a royal citation in England—he was genuinely ill at ease on official occasions.

His long visit to Paris, marked by frustration at the slow pace of the rehearsals of *Bohème* and the constant postponement of the première, bored him. Ill at ease with the French language, he showed little interest in the city or in the hectic social life he was forced to lead. "I came into this world to be born in and live in Torre," he wrote Ferrucio Pagni. "I cry out—as the snow does for the sun, as coffee does for sugar—for the peace of the mountains, the valleys, the greenery, and red sunset." Poetically, he summed up his feelings in a letter written to Alfredo Caselli one month after his arrival in the French capital:

I am fed up with Paris. I yearn for the scented woods, with their fragrance, for the undulation of my paunch within loose trousers, wtihout a vest. I yearn for the free and fragrant wind that reaches me from the sea. I savor its salty air with dilated nostrils and wide-open lungs.
I hate pavements.
I hate large buildings.

I hate capitals.
I hate columns.
I love the beautiful columns of the poplar and the fir; the arches of
shaded avenues . . . there to create my temple, my home, my
studio. I love the green expanse of the cool shelter of the woods—old
and young. I love the blackbird, the blackcap, the woodpecker. I hate
the horse, the cat, the tamed sparrow, the house dog. I hate the
steamer, the top hat, the tails. . . .

The composer was not unhappy with the rehearsals, which were more
careful than usual because of the various cast changes which had made the
postponements necessary. What upset him was the enormous publicity
campaign which entailed his attendance at endless receptions where he was
introduced to the *tout Paris*, and after which he was wined and dined,
interviewed and applauded . . . but bored and made increasingly nervous.
"I am worried," he wrote unhappily to Ricordi. "I would like to be gone from
here for the sake of my work. I am too nervously excited and lack the peace
which I need. An invitation to dinner makes me sick for a week. I am like
that and cannot be changed at almost forty years of age. It is futile to keep
trying; I wasn't born for the life of drawing rooms and receptions. What good
does it do to expose myself to the risk of behaving like a cretin and imbecile? I
see that is how I act, and it upsets me very much. But, I repeat, I am made this
way. . . ."
Complaining that Ricordi's son Tito, who was in Paris during much of this
rehearsal period, did not understand him and only made matters worse by
forcing him to make these social engagements, Puccini went on to tell his
publisher that Verdi had always done what he wanted, without pandering to
publicity, and that so far his own success had been based on his music and not
on his social and public relations activities. "I am here," he concluded in this
letter, "only to see that my music is played as it is written."
If Puccini's complaint was one common to all creative artists, so was
Ricordi's reply one common to all those whose business it is to sell the works
of creative artists. "I read your litanies about invitations, dinners, receptions,
presentations, etc. You cite Verdi but your citation is not exact. From his
youth Verdi was assiduous in frequenting the high society of Milan, and
when he went to Paris, Petersburg, London, Madrid, and Vienna for his
operas, he submitted to the necessary consequences! Certainly without pleasure! . . . But even he had to bow his head to the uses and abuses of
society." The publisher concluded by adding that times had changed, too;
that in light of greater competition, public relations was playing an increasingly large part in artistic success.
On June 4, Luigi Illica arrived in Paris to look in on the rehearsals and,
more important, to give whatever moral support he could to his colleague,

whom he had learned was suffering profoundly from the lengthy stay in the French capital. The librettist was pleasantly surprised with what he found. Most favorably impressed with the production, he was delighted that the translation of his work into French did not diminish the opera's effectiveness. He found the composer, too, in good spirits, his morale greatly improved, no doubt because, the première finally having been set for June 13, the end of the interminable Paris visit was in sight. The composer, who in his suffering had repeatedly asked to see a doctor, no longer felt the need for one; the cure for his illness, his return to Tuscany, was imminent.

Both men believed that the opera would succeed in Paris as it had throughout Europe—in spite of the hostility of the French press to the idea that an Italian composer had dared set a French work of literature to music. They were right; the audience at the première was enthusiastic, and the noisy dissenters who tried to protest the Italianization of Murger after the first act were drowned out.

The following day, Arthur Pougin, writing in *Le Ménestrel* reflected the feelings of most of his colleagues when he stated that the opera was a sincere and honest work, which owed its success to the fact that it was an opera with real people in it. It was, for him, not a masterpiece, but it was acceptable. Of course, he concluded, perhaps a French composer would have done a better job.

With the exception of Gabriel Fauré, who found it to be a "frightful Italian opera," Puccini's French colleagues were generous in their praise. Ravel and Messager spoke well of it, as did Massenet, who later told Nellie Melba that it was a perfect opera—melodious, full of feeling, and exquisitely scored. *L'Assiette au beurre*, a popular magazine, however, did not agree, calling *La vie de Bohème* (as it was known in France) *La vide Bohème—The Empty Bohème*—but it was their joke that was empty. Puccini's opera soon established itself as a much-performed favorite of the French public, a part of the standard repertory from the time of its première.

It had been useful for Puccini to enhance his reputation by means of a successful debut at the Opéra-Comique, but the visit to Paris had been even more fruitful because of the opportunity it gave the composer to meet and confer with Victorien Sardou, the author of *La Tosca*. Sardou was a formidable figure. The most popular playwright of his time, he took great pleasure in responding to his critics—who accused him of not being "serious" and writing mere melodramas—by producing statistics on the astounding number of times his plays had been performed, inevitably with great success. The charge of being a "popular" writer never disturbed him, and he was pleased that an increasingly popular young Italian composer would be extending the life of one of his own plays.

The two men got along extremely well, and Puccini was not cowed by the venerable, cantankerous Frenchman. He respected Sardou's theatrical gifts and was keenly aware of the importance of involving him in the creation of the new opera, never forgetting that the Frenchman had a contractual right to veto any changes that were made in his play. At their very first meeting, Sardou, after having exacted a most favorable contract (a fifteen percent royalty for the rights) asked to hear samples of what Puccini had already written for his new opera. The composer, having actually written nothing at all, proceeded to go to the piano and play excerpts from his earlier operas for the playwright. Sardou was enchanted. In the discussions that followed, Puccini proved to be a superb listener — partially perhaps, because his knowledge of French was more than limited. He was greatly impressed by the older man's energy — Sardou was in his late sixties — and by his elegance and wit; and in Puccini the Frenchman believed he had found an understanding and responsive collaborator. There were relatively few concrete problems to be settled. Sardou's original drama was spread over five acts. Illica and Puccini wanted it condensed into three — eliminating one and condensing two others into one. Sardou, wise in the ways of the theatre, understood at once. His was not a great play. It was, and he knew it, a vehicle for Sarah Bernhardt, and without her it would have little life — except as an opera by Puccini. Nonetheless, the playwright was, with good reason, sufficiently confident of his own knowledge of the theatre to participate fully in the lyrical adaptation of his play. Illica was present at some of the first meetings with the Frenchman, able to present his own ideas and also to act as interpreter for Puccini. At one point, the librettist told Sardou of his intentions of having Tosca sing a long aria over the dead body of her lover before killing herself. Sardou objected strenuously, feeling that at that point the opera should quickly come to an end. He turned to Puccini for his opinion, at which point the composer opened his copy of the libretto and pointed to his own words, written in the margin of the aria as envisaged by the librettist. The words were: "This is the overcoat aria." Asked to explain the meaning of this comment, the composer stated that an overcoat aria was one which would never be heard by the audience, who would be too busy putting on their overcoats. Sardou was impressed, now completely convinced that Puccini was himself a man with a sure sense of theatre.

Puccini even felt sufficiently comfortable with Sardou to confide in him his doubts concerning his ability to do justice to *La Tosca*. The following conversation was reported to Lucio D'Ambra by Puccini and published in the critic's *Lives of Italian Musicians*:

PUCCINI: Perhaps it would be better if a Frenchman were to set your play to music.

SARDOU: No, better an Italian. *Tosca* is a Roman work. It needs your Italian song.

PUCCINI: Verdi, our great Verdi, once thought of Tosca and gave it up, a sign that the subject intimidated him. Do you wonder, M. Sardou, that I am afraid?

SARDOU: Verdi wasn't intimidated, but Verdi is old, Verdi is tired. You ought to be encouraged by the fact that a great composer for the theatre such as he had confidence in *Tosca* and recognized in it the opera, the good opera, which it is.

PUCCINI: Alberto Franchetti, also, considered *Tosca* and gave it up in his turn.

SARDOU: That, my dear Maestro, certainly means nothing. Two men considered it: well, that is the best guarantee of *Tosca*'s vitality.

PUCCINI: But my music is tenuous, it is delicate, it is written in a different register.

SARDOU (*shouting*): There are no registers, M. Puccini, there's only talent!

PUCCINI: My previous heroines, Manon and Mimi, are different from Tosca.

SARDOU: Manon, Mimi, Tosca, it is all the same thing! . . . Women in love all belong to the same family. I have created Marcella and Fernanda, I have created Fedora, Theodora, and Cleopatra. They are all the same woman.

These meetings with Sardou went extraordinarily well, but things didn't go quite so smoothly at a subsequent conference in January of 1899 when Puccini reported to Ricordi:

I spent an hour at Sardou's this morning, and he told me what he felt was wrong with the finale. He wants [Tosca] dead at all costs. But I certainly do not agree to that. He accepts her madness but wants her to swoon and die like a fluttering bird. Then, in the revival that Sarah will be in, Sardou has introduced a huge flag over the Castello, fluttering and flashing, which (he says) will make a marvelous effect: go for the flag (he is more interested in that than in the play right now). But I am still in favor of Tito's cry, and for the end, a delicate one and not too *éclatante*. In sketching the scenery, he wanted to show the Tiber flow between the Castello and San Pietro! I told him that the river flowed on the other side, but he, calm as a fish, retorted, "Oh, that's nothing." A strange man, all full of vitality and fire, and full of historico-topo-panoramic inexactitudes!

Puccini had his way. At times, the playwright voiced stern objections to portions of the libretto, but they were overruled, and there was never any real conflict among the composer, librettists, and playwright.

Stimulated by his contacts with Sardou, Puccini returned to Italy as soon as *Bohème* had been successfully launched at the Opéra-Comique. The country was in the midst of serious political and social turmoil, but the composer felt relaxed and happy to be home once again, finally freed of his top hat and tails and his exhausting social obligations. He was eager, too, to apply all of his energies to the composition of his new opera.

He was certainly far behind; with a minimum amount of participation on his part, Illica and Giacosa had completed the libretto of *Tosca*, to their satisfaction, during 1896. The composer had feigned impatience, especially with Giacosa, but, preoccupied as he had been with performances of *Bohème*, it is most unlikely that he would have worked seriously even if he had had the material on hand. Nonetheless, even without Puccini, there had already been problems, most of which stemmed from Giacosa's lack of enthusiasm for the entire project. He had never felt the play was suited to the lyric stage, nor was he enthusiastic about the prospects of working again with Puccini; he had, he said, agreed to collaborate only out of respect for Ricordi. In addition, he felt he was being rushed again, and this time for no reason. His letter to Ricordi of July 6, 1896, showed his irritation:

> Tonight or, at the latest, tomorrow morning I will bring you a great deal of work, but believe me this is a terrible job. . . . I am working desperately, but on the one hand clarity must be respected and on the other the act cannot contain more than three hundred verses.
>
> That's already too many, and nothing at all, not a single incident can be omitted. I will succeed but is a real torture. The more I go ahead, the more difficult it becomes. Please don't get angry and be of ill humor. I am doing all I can.
>
> Just think that this morning I got up at 4, worked till 6:30, then I took my family, who left for the country, to the station, and at 7:30 I was back at my desk. All that to put together eight verses. But there had been twenty and I had to cut them to eight. I again solemnly promise to give to you tonight or tomorrow morning a large amount of finished work. Finished except for the changes that Puccini will propose! Because of which I'll begin again at the beginning.

Giacosa's unhappiness was understandable; he could foresee the same struggles he had suffered throughout the creation of *Bohème*, and this time for a work he had little faith in. Ricordi, apparently, however, had little sympathy for the librettist, who grew increasingly bitter as evidenced in another letter written to Ricordi on August 23:

> . . . I have been working on nothing but *Tosca* for the past two months, and I assure you that your harsh words fill me with bitterness and surprise. . . . I am profoundly convinced that *Tosca* is not a good subject for an opera. On first reading it seems to be so because of the rapidity and clarity of the dramatic action. And it

seems even more so after reading the clever synthesis prepared by Illica. But the more one enters into the action and penetrates into each scene, trying to extract lyrical and poetic movements from them, the more one realizes its absolute inadaptability for the musical theatre. I am glad to have written this, because I am sure I will have opportunities in the future to remind you of this letter of mine. . . . It is a drama of emotional events without poetry. It is completely different from *Bohème*, where the events were not at all important but where there was an overabundance of poetic and lyrical moments. In *Tosca*, on the other hand, there is a need to point up the chain of events, which takes more space than it should, leaving little room for the development of emotions. Although convinced of this basic shortcoming, I began to work—in deference to you and with the greatest zeal. . . . I don't feel like just tossing something off. If you, Illica, and Puccini came to me, it is because you wanted me to give the libretto the proper form and poetry. If it weren't for that, my contribution would be of no use. The effort to include in a very few words all of those small, complex parts is a very difficult and exacting task. Each scene is very difficult, and many times I have to do one over again because I will not part with anything until I am satisfied with it. You expressed your dissatisfaction very crudely, and, if I read correctly between the lines, you seem willing to do without my contribution. Well then, dear Ricordi, let us be frank and open as two good friends should. I, for my part, do not give up, but I do not want any obligation you feel toward me to prevent you from acting freely. If you have better options, if the artistic scruples which cause my delays bother you, I am willing not only to stop working, but I am also willing to return part of the advance given me. I have not failed in my obligation to you. But a work of art is not a product of manual labor that can be completed in a day. . . . By the beginning of September you will have all of the second act. I've already done a good part of the third; I have started to do the lyric, flowing parts and am saving for the end the task of putting it all together. But I repeat, if you prefer to do without my contribution, you are always the boss and we are always friends. . . .

Giacosa's by-now familiar offer to resign was not accepted by Ricordi, and the librettist continued work on the opera, but he was never to do so in a completely happy frame of mind; nor was he ever able to accept *Tosca* as proper subject for an opera. By December, he was still upset and chided Ricordi for accusing him of being slow, of wasting time. He reminded him that Puccini wasted more than his share of time in hunting, and that even when he had completed his job he knew he had Puccini's last-minute corrections to look forward to. In a letter of December 14, he complained about the characterization of Scarpia, ending that letter with a phrase that summed up his attitude throughout the writing of the entire opera: "I shall do it, but I decline all responsibility."

As promised, Giacosa completed his job by the end of 1896, but he was fully aware that once (and if) Puccini started work revisions would be called for. He also had the not mistaken idea that the composer's enthusiasm for the work was less than it should have been. Nonetheless, Puccini claimed that he was going ahead; he had written Ricordi in early November that his work was really getting under way, but later that winter he had been forced to admit that he had accomplsihed nothing—promising only to make up for the loss of time as soon as possible.

From all available evidence, it seems unlikely that the composer managed to make up for lost time during the following year; he was still too busy with *Bohème* to give much serious thought to *Tosca*. By the spring of 1898, however, he was more than ready to devote full time to the new opera, particularly after the long period of creative inactivity in Paris.

To do so, he felt that he needed to find a temporary home away from both Milan and Torre del Lago. Milan was out of the question—he could never work successfully in any large city; and Torre del Lago, in addition to its oppressive summer heat, was too filled with friends and the temptations of hunting. The small village had been the ideal setting for his work on *Bohème*, since the hearty camaraderie there had been well suited to the theme of his earlier opera. To re-create the dark, brooding atmosphere of *Tosca*, on the other hand, he felt the need for almost total isolation.

"I will," he wrote Illica, "seclude myself in a Lucchese villa, where I will at last rest my forearm on the *toscano* table."

The villa in which Puccini worked that summer belonged to his friend the Marchese Raffaello Mansi. It was located in the small village of Monsagrati, one of the many tiny villages that dot the hills surrounding Lucca, villages which though not far from the provincial capital remain even today, because of difficult access, remarkably untouched by modern comforts. A stone placed on the side of the Villa Mansi proclaims that it was there that the composer wrote the first act of *Tosca*; it does not state that it was, in effect, a kind of prison for the composer, Elvira, and Fosca.

All three hated it, but at least Puccini had his work to keep him occupied, while his family had nothing to fill the long gloomy days. Portions of the completed libretto kept arriving, and they were for the most part satisfactory. Occasionally, there were problems. In July, for example, Puccini was shocked to find that the last line of the second act, "*E avanti a lui tremava tutta Roma,*" had been eliminated. Happily, he insisted that this line, among the best known and most chillingly effective in all opera, be restored. In addition to small changes sought by Ricordi and his two librettists, Sardou came forth with suggestions, none of major importance, and Puccini was perfectly willing to agree to them in order to please the playwright—both because he respected him as a dramatist and because he was eager to have Sardou's full endorsement of the finished opera.

The villa was large and comfortable, but the surroundings were ugly and oppressive. The days were blisteringly hot, so hot that the composer was forced to work at night—usually from ten o'clock till four in the morning. Shut in among the woods, between the mountains, there was nothing to do but work; few human beings came near the place. Nonetheless, it was just what he wanted, and he planned to stay there until October—if he could last and if Elvira and Fosca could sustain their martyrdom and remain there for that length of time.

The work proceeded smoothly, and by August 18 Puccini was ready to set to music the finale to the first act, a relatively short scene which was to be one of the dramatic high points of the opera. The setting is Rome's magnificent Church of Sant'Andrea della Valle. Word has come of the Royalist victory over Napoleon, and a mob of priests, monks, and choristers are entering the church, preparing to sing the *Te Deum*, the thanksgiving hymn in celebration of the victory. Scarpia, the villainous police chief, arrives, and the plot moves quickly and dramatically forward with the appearance of Tosca who, provoked to jealousy, apparently yields to the police chief's attempts at seduction. At the end of the act, the cardinal and his escort appear; the *Te Deum* is sung, and over it the voice of Scarpia can be heard, rejoicing at his conquest of Tosca. Suddenly, he stops himself, realizing that he is preoccupied with thoughts of lust while in the midst of a church service. "Tosca, you make me forget God," he cries out as he joins the religious chanting.

It is a tremendous and overwhelming spectacle, and it called for all of Puccini's gifts as a musician and dramatist. To do it properly, too, the composer felt the need for advice from those more knowledgeable in ecclesiastical matters than he was. Accuracy was of the utmost importance, and what the composer required was the text of a prayer which could be recited during the cardinal's procession to the altar in preparation for the celebration of the *Te Deum*. He felt that his friend, the musician Guido Vandini, could supply him with the necessary prayer, and he wrote him from Monsagrati. "I need a written version of the *Ecce sacerdos magnus*," he pleaded. "Go to any priest or monk and copy it and ask, too, what priests recite when a cortège, with a bishop, goes from the sacristy to the high altar to sing the solemn *Te Deum* in honor of a military victory. I thought of having the Chapter or even the people mutter the *Ecce sacerdos magnus*, but I don't know if it's right." When Vandini did not answer at once, Puccini wrote again, a frantic but also very amusing letter, telling his friend to go to the bishop with the request, adding that, if he didn't supply it, he would write to the pope and have him fired like any imbecilic employee. If those verses weren't found or invented, he would also, he threatened, write a funeral march for religion; and if the verses didn't reach him soon, he would become a Protestant and swear for the rest of his life!

Vandini did not satisfy Puccini's request, nor, as it turned out, did the composer really want the *Ecce sacerdos*. It was, he felt, too powerful a prayer to be muttered, and, for dramatic purposes, the text used had to be muttered.

Never hesitating to call upon his friends and acquaintances for help, the composer next turned to a Dominican priest, Father Pietro Panichelli, an opera lover he had first met in 1897 and who was an excellent adviser on ecclesiastical matters. He had already supplied Puccini with the exact pitch of the largest bell of St. Peter's and had furnished him with the version of the plainsong to which the *Te Deum* was sung in Roman churches; he was later to offer advice on the correct order of the cardinal's procession as well as the costumes for the Swiss Guards. Late in August, Puccini wrote to Panichelli, outlining his specific needs: "I know it is not common for anything to be said or sung before beginning the solemn *Te Deum* which is done as soon as they reach the High Altar, but I repeat (right or wrong) I would like to find *something to be muttered*, when they go from the sacristy to the altar, either by the Chapter or the people. The latter would be better because there are more of them and it is thus more effective musically."

As it turned out, it was Puccini himself who finally found, in an old prayer book, the verses containing the sounds that he required; they proved to be highly effective. His insistence upon accuracy was extraordinary, and it also explained his turning to a poet other than his librettists for the shepherd's short song at the beginning of *Tosca*'s third act. In this case, the text needed had to be in keeping with the pastorals sung in the Roman countryside at the beginning of the nineteenth century; and the composer commissioned Luigi Zanazzo, a poet and scholar employed at the Ministry of Education, to supply him with the appropriate words in the Roman dialect.

In spite of personal discomfort, the summer had been a productive one, and Puccini almost maintained his promise to remain in the mountain retreat until October, not leaving there until September 22. When he left — for Torre del Lago, where he could ease the burden of work with the pleasures of hunting — he was well satisfied with the progress he had made.

The composer was able to stay in Torre until the end of the year; as always it provided him with the breathing space he badly needed. He complained that he was not moving ahead as quickly as he had wanted, and Giacosa complained about almost every aspect of the opera, but there were no serious problems. After completing the first act, the composer made another trip — this time a short one — to Paris in early January of 1899. While there he looked in on performances of *Bohème* at the Opéra-Comique, and he took part in further discussions with Sardou, during which the Frenchman suggested that Tosca perform a miracle by falling into the far too distant Tiber from the Castel Sant'Angelo.

On his return to Torre del Lago in February, he began work on the second act; this was, according to notes on the score, completed on July 16. During this period, there were the usual battles with Giacosa, whose ill-temper was only made worse by Puccini's harassment and never-ending requests for revisions, but these were by now an accepted part of the collaboration. Illica, too, caused problems, insisting on retaining a lengthy philosophical farewell to life and art, the contents of which had deeply moved both Verdi and Sardou when they had heard it in Paris, to be sung by Mario at the beginning of the last act. (It was, fortunately, not retained and was substituted by *E lucevan le stelle*, one of the most popular of all of Puccini's arias.) Nonetheless, work on the opera went forward, with Ricordi, once again, placating all concerned and tactfully offering suggestions when called for. On September 29, the third and final act of *Tosca* was completed. Relieved that his work had come to an end and confident of its success, Puccini sent the score off to Ricordi. There was no way he could have anticipated the violent response from his publisher and friend, which was contained in an extraordinarily emotional letter written from Milan on October 10. It is worth quoting at length because of the insight it provides into the relationship between these two men. Ricordi wrote:

> The true and intense affection that I feel toward you, which makes you as dear to me as a son; the greatest esteem and faith which I have always felt toward you as an artist; these encourage me, persuade me to write you things I would not write to anyone but to Puccini. Just because it is Puccini, I would be failing in my duty as a truly cordial friend if I did not write such things to you. And I write you fully convinced that only Puccini, and no one else in the world, will accept this letter of mine as a sincere expression of an intimacy which, perhaps, never before has anyone been able to inspire in me.
>
> And I, with a beating heart, but with clear conscience, have the courage to say to you: the third act of *Tosca*, as it stands, seems to me a serious error of conception and execution . . . such a serious error that, to my way of thinking, it would cancel out the good impression of the first act. It would cancel out the very powerful impact that the second act, a true masterpiece of power and tragic expression, will surely have. . . .
>
> Cavaradossi's scene and Tosca's entrance are fine and effective, just as the shooting at the end is certainly effective, a real find. But my God, what is the actual luminous center of this act? . . . the Tosca-Cavaradossi duet. What did I find? A fragmentary duet, of short lines which diminishes the characters; I found one of the most beautiful fragments of lyric poetry, that of the hands, accompanied

only by a fragmentary and modest melody, which, to make matters worse, comes right from *Edgar!* Sung by a Tyrolese peasant, it would be stupendous, but it is completely out of place coming from a Tosca and a Cavaradossi. In short, what should have been a kind of hymn, Latin or not, but a hymn of love, is reduced to a few bars. In this way, the heart of the piece is made up of three fragments, one after another, yet interrupted, and lacking in effectiveness. Really, where is the Puccini of the noble, warm, and vigorous inspiration? What's going on? His imagination, in one of the most striking moments of the drama, forced full back on another opera? What will be said about this way of getting out of a difficult situation?

Maybe you'll tell me I'm crazy, that I can't see straight . . . and that no one is a better judge in these matters than you are. I wish to God it were like that. I would be happy and deserving of harsh punishment. However, in the light of cold reason, I ask myself: How can my feelings about the first act be explained? And the intense emotion I felt at the second act? And at the same time how can the terribly painful doubts I have about the third act be explained? Please note that I didn't want to be bound by my first impression. I let a day pass before reading it a second time, a third time, calmly, hoping that I would find I had been wrong. But, unfortunately, no. . . .

And if, unfortunately, my opinion were not wrong, what would the consequences be? Disastrous for my publishing house; bad for you, as far as the material side is concerned, and incommensurable as a reflection of the artistic nature, the good name, and the glory of Giacomo Puccini. These are so important to me that I stayed awake all night, wondering if I should or shouldn't open my soul to you. I decided to do so, and I feel I've done the right thing and have acted honestly. Now either you, having calmly re-examined this third act, will again find your artistic conscience satisfied—and then will be able to convince me of my error, and I will gladly join you in this great event which will forever solidify your fame and bring added radiance to your name; or else the doubts I have expressed will in some way influence you, and we are still in time. No half measures, no mere polishing, but putting aside all those pages in the middle of the duet from the words "O dolci mani" until the words "Gli occhi ti chiuderò," etc. (Concerning these I know Giacosa's point of view, a reasonable one, which it is useless to pass on to you now.)

Oh, is it possible that for these stupendously lyrical moments, Giacomo Puccini is unable to find one of his heartrending, exultant inspirations, which move us to tears of pity or tenderness? My God, Puccini must succeed, and suddenly, like a jet of water from an unexpected source . . . as long as he wants to!

To write so much to the man who has created *Manon Lescaut* and *La Bohème* certainly requires a great deal of courage. . . and I've always had it . . . and so I don't have friends . . . . But I don't fear saying this to you . . . my friendship toward you is so great that you must understand and listen, so that we can apply the verse of the great poet, "Amor, che a nullo Amato amar perdona."

Saints make miracles, and there are no more saints! That's an error. You are among the saints of music and you can make a miracle! . . .

Puccini was stunned by this severe if affectionate rebuke from his publisher, but his reply, sent the following day from Torre del Lago, is remarkable for its display of calm self-confidence.

Your letter came as an extraordinary surprise; I am still deeply affected by it. All the same, I remain calm and convinced that if you examine this third act again you will change your opinion of it. This is not a question of pride on my part. No, it is the conviction of having brought to life as best as I could the drama which was before me. You know how scrupulous I am in interpreting each situation and each word, and you know how carefully I select before putting anything down. The matter of having taken something from *Edgar* can be criticized by you and those few who can recognize it to whom it might seem a work-saving device. As it is, ridding oneself of the idea that it belongs to another work (the eliminated fourth act of *Edgar*), it seems to me full of that poetry which grows out of the words. I am sure of this, and you will be convinced when you hear it where it belongs, on the stage. As to its fragmentary nature, this is intentional; it can't be a steady and calm flow as in other conversations of love. Tosca's preoccupation keeps returning, the well-acted-out fall of Mario, and his behavior before the firing squad. As to the final duet, the so-called Latin hymn (which I have not yet seen written by the poets), I too have my doubts, but I hope it will work on the stage, perhaps even very well. The third-act duet has always been the great obstacle. The poets have not been able to give me (I speak of the end) anything good and, above all, honest. Always academic, academic, with the usual amorous embroideries. I have had to do what I could to reach the end without boring the listeners too much, avoiding all the academic elements.

Mugnone, who has heard this third act sung by me many times, is so enthusiastic that he prefers it to the fourth act of *Bohème*. Friends and people at home have been very favorably impressed by it. I, based on the experience I have had, am not unhappy with it. I really don't know how to explain your negative feelings. Before I take steps to redo it (and would there be time?) I will run up to Milan and we two will talk about it alone, with the piano and the music in front of us, and if your impression persists, we will try, as good friends, to save ourselves, as Scarpia says. I repeat that this is not a matter of my pride, but only a defense of a work about which I have thought and which has cost me much concern. I always find in my dear papà

Giulio a great feeling of delicacy and an affection which (you can be sure) is most fully reciprocated. And I am grateful for the interest you show in me and have always demonstrated since I was fortunate enough to meet you. I disagree with you about the third act; this must be the first time we are not in agreement. But I hope and will say that I am sure you will change your opinion; we'll see!

This exchange of letters between the composer and his publisher marked a turning point in the relationship between these two men. Puccini, while maintaining not only respect but also deep affection for the man he calls papà Giulio, asserted his independence, his coming of age; and Ricordi, in not insisting that the changes he wanted be made, thereby recognized the mastery of his protégé. It is a tribute to the intelligence and maturity of both men that this serious difference of opinion in no way loosened the strong bond between them.

By November, the disagreement between Puccini and Ricordi had been forgotten; the composer had had his way. Both Illica and Giacosa, too, were uncharacteristically silent, quite simply because they had been excluded from taking part in any further decisions concerning *Tosca*, and thus had no way of knowing that the opera soon to be presented was, in several ways, different from what they had expected. There were none of the long, exhausting, but profitable discussions that had marked the creation of *La Bohème*. It was enough that the opera had been completed to Puccini's satisfaction, after which arrangements were made to have the work performed in January.

The time before the première passed slowly for Puccini. He was bored, with little to do but hunt, and he was so confident of *Tosca*'s success that he was already eager to consider new projects to occupy his time. Both Illica and Carlo Clausetti, Ricordi's representative in Naples, presented him with ideas, the latter especially enthusiastic about a one-act play by Roberto Bracco entitled *Don Pietro Caruso*. Puccini was intrigued by the idea of writing a one-act opera, an idea which later came to pass, but he found Bracco's play lacking in originality. Illica's suggestions, works by Dostoevsky, Zola, Pierre Louÿs, and Balzac among them, were more interesting but were finally discarded as was a dramatic poem by a Frenchman named Jean Richepin, *La Glu*.

By the end of the year, it was time for him to give all of his attention to the forthcoming première of *Tosca*, and he traveled to Rome to supervise the new production. Rehearsals were, as always, long and tiring, but they went smoothly, and the composer was pleased with the cast, which included the Rumanian soprano Hariclea Darclée, the tenor Emilio De Marchi, and the baritone Eugenio Giraldoni. He was more than pleased, too, that Leopoldo Mugnone would be conducting the first performance of the opera at Rome's Teatro Costanzi.

Rome had been Illica's choice for the début of the new opera, and Ricordi had readily agreed to it. It seemed logical that a new opera, set in the capital, by the man who was then universally considered Italy's foremost operatic composer, be first presented there. The choice might have been logical, but it was not wise. The mood in the Italian capital had been a turbulent one throughout the period preceding the première. Revolution was in the air, strikes and riots had plagued the country, and the Italian government had repeatedly been threatened with collapse. The monarchy, too, was in danger, and there had been assassination attempts on the life of King Umberto (several months after the première, one of these succeeded). The first performance of Puccini's opera, the major cultural event of the year in the Italian capital, took on an almost official character — the queen was expected to attend as were other members of the royal family and important members of the government — and as such it was dangerously susceptible to noisy or even violent disruptions.

On the morning of the première, January 14, Puccini gave little thought to social or political problems. He was somewhat worried by rumors that a group of critics and rival musicians were conspiring against him and his opera, but he felt that these rumors were exaggerated and that the merits of his opera would overcome any attempts at hostility. Mugnone, on the other hand, was seriously disturbed. This time his fears were not based on superstition — the première was not taking place on Friday the thirteenth — but on his awareness of the explosive climate which pervaded the capital and on personal experience; only a few years before, politically motivated bombs had caused several deaths while he was conducting a performance in Barcelona's opera house.

The conductor's fears were heightened when, a quarter of an hour before the curtain was to rise, he was visited by a delegation from the Roman police. They reported that there were persistent rumors of demonstrations and even bombs that could very possibly interrupt the performance and advised him, at the first sign of anything suspicious, to lead the orchestra in the playing of the Royal March in order to calm the audience. Though assured by the police that the rumors were most probably without foundation, Mugnone was anything but calmed by this visit.

The large, distinguished crowd that filed into the theatre that evening was either unaware of or unconcerned by these rumors. Tickets had been bought up weeks in advance, and by eleven in the morning of the première throngs had literally stormed the box office in hopes of last-minute cancellations. Contrary to its usual habits, the gala audience began to arrive well before eight o'clock, when the performance was scheduled to begin. (Among those not to arrive early was Queen Margherita, who missed the first act because of a dinner at the Quirinale.) Among them were well-known members of the worlds of art, literature, diplomacy, the government, and the clergy, as well as musicians — Mascagni, Franchetti, and Cilea, and many others. The only attempt at a demonstration — as Mascagni was about to take his place in a box, a small group of his supporters, seated in the upper gallery, began to shout "Viva Mascagni" — created hardly a ripple, as the members of the audience settled into their seats, intent upon judging the new opera.

They would not judge it under the best of conditions. Word of possible problems had reached the performers, who were understandably shaken. Mugnone, as he stepped to the podium, was trembling — he was worried not about artistic success but for his life and for the lives of all the participants. Once the curtain was up, he saw no reason not to be concerned. The audience refused to settle down — whispered conversation filled the house during the first few minutes of the opera. By the time the basso, who sang the role of Angelotti, started to sing, the whispers had become a series of scattered angry cries. Something was brewing, and before the situation got out of hand, the conductor ordered the curtain to be lowered. Inquiries were made, and within a few minutes the cause of the disorder was ascertained. It had not been a bomb threat or the start of an angry political demonstration. It was merely a battle, a vociferous one, between those who had arrived early and had promptly taken their seats, and those who had arrived late and caused a disturbance in scrambling for their places.

Before long, the audience had taken their places, and a somewhat shaken conductor signaled for the opera to begin again. There were no further incidents, but neither was there the unbridled enthusiasm that all the participants had anticipated. The major arias were warmly applauded and encored, and the composer was called to the stage and before the curtain several times, but the evening could best be termed a mild success rather than a triumph. Puccini was disappointed but not dismayed, as he had been at the opening night of Bohème.

The following day, the major critics reflected the feelings of the first-night audience. They were satisfied, but they expressed many reservations. The main problem, they agreed, was to be found in the subject and the libretto. The plot overwhelmed the music; there was too much violence, too much torture, and too little lyricism — in brief, too much rage and too little poetry. The music had been subordinated to the drama, and for many reviewers, the result was a melodrama with musical accompaniment.

Nonetheless, the première of Puccini's latest opera was treated as a major event. The Corriere d'Italia, though expressing disappointment which it blamed on the libretto, devoted its entire front page to the evening. In another minutely detailed review of the opera, Alessandro Parisotti of the Popolo Romano, though not wholly enthusiastic, found much to praise. "The gentle lyrical passages," he noted, "coming between the dark and sadly heavy colors of the drama, almost always win out, creating music of beauty and durability." The critic for L'Avanti echoed the general consensus that the subject matter was not suited to the composer's temperament, while Eugenio

Checchi, writing in *Nuovo Fanfulla,* though acknowledging that the subject matter tended to overwhelm the music, felt that the piece could be better judged in later performances, when the anxieties of the first night had passed.

Perhaps the most perceptive judgment was written by the Milanese critic, Alfredo Colombani, who noted in the *Corriere della Sera* that the libretto limited the possibilities of the music that was needed to accompany the rapid, broken, and agitated dialogue. "Events follow one another, almost tumultuously, and the music cannot afford to linger," he commented. "In *Bohème,* Puccini overcame such difficulties, but in that earlier opera the requirements of the drama were not so overwhelming. There were in that libretto elements which described the ambiance, the situations, and the characters; while here there are only bare facts and a rapid succession of events. The capability of the Lucchese maestro has not been daunted by these, and the musical commentary with which he has embellished Sardou's drama could not, in fact, be more appropriate and effective."

By far the worst review came not from a newspaper critic, but from Illica. Embittered by the reviews, which almost unanimously blamed the opera's shortcomings on the libretto, he wrote a furious letter to Ricordi on the day following the première. He complained that the opera was unrecognizable, that some of the most effective parts of the libretto (Mario's farewell to life and art and the Latin hymn) had been discarded without his consent, and that the few melodies in the score had been taken from work already done on the abandoned *La Lupa.* Puccini, in ignoring his librettists, had treated them like mere stagehands. He accused Ricordi, too, of mistreating him, of hiding the final libretto from him until the day before the première, "a libretto so mutilated and antimusical that it must be considered just the shadow, the outline of the libretto which had so enraptured Giulio Ricordi."

In conclusion, the outraged librettist wrote: "For these reasons, and for others of which you are certainly aware, I am sure that you will not be surprised if, since it seems questionable whether my humble work would or would not be acceptable, I take my leave of you, dear Signor Giulio—taking with me, however, together with my present sorrow, precious memories of the affectionate kindnesses of the unforgettable days not long past."

Illica did not take leave of his publisher, nor of Puccini; neither did the equally disappointed Giacosa. *Tosca,* in spite of the reservations of the press, was sung at the Teatro Costanzi twenty more times that season to packed houses. The combination of Puccini-Giacosa-Illica-Ricordi was too successful for any of the partners to seriously consider breaking it up. Whatever their differences, no matter how painful their clashes of temperament, it was clearly in their interest to work together.

Madama Butterfly

As was always the case, Puccini spent the period following the première of his latest opera seeing that it was successfully launched in Italy and throughout Europe, as well as worrying about what would be his next project.

After Rome, there was the important opening at La Scala to be supervised. The production was much the same as that in Rome, but with a new tenor and with Toscanini conducting instead of Mugnone. The composer felt on the whole that the performance was better than the first ones in Rome, and the audience, initially cool, was most enthusiastic by the end of the evening. Once again, however, the press was somewhat hostile, one critic noting that "in *Tosca* there is only one piece of real music, and that is the *Te Deum* at the end of the first act. And, after all, that piece does not belong to Puccini but really to Saint Ambrose, who wrote it several centuries ago." Once again, too, however, the opera was a huge popular success—there were twelve sold-out performances that season alone at La Scala.

After Milan, there was a production in Verona, followed by one in Genoa. For this latter, the composer once again demonstrated his insistence on perfection. There was no organ at the opera house, so one had to be specially purchased at a local piano shop for use in the first act finale. During the first orchestra rehearsal, however, the new instrument was drowned out by the orchestra. A frantic search began, and for a while it seemed they would have to send to Milan for an organ. Before doing so, the conductor, Edoardo Vitale, had another idea: borrow the large organ from Genoa's Church of Santa Zita. After much wrangling with church authorities, permission was given and

124

the organ taken from the church into the opera house. But the sound of the church's organ, too, was overwhelmed by the orchestra, and, in the end, two organs were used simultaneously for the finale to the first act of *Tosca*.

On June 10, Puccini left for London; *Tosca* was to be performed at Covent Garden only six months after its Roman première, and the composer wanted to be there to supervise the new production, which was to star the brilliant soprano Milka Ternina. This trip was to be an important one; not only was London to be the scene of *Tosca's* first great triumph, but it was there that the composer would find the subject for his next opera.

After a few days in Paris, where he stopped to visit the spectacular Exposition, he arrived in the British capital, where he was to remain for over a month. Though hampered by his inability to speak English—he said he could only manage the numbers from one to ten—he was wined and dined and treated like a celebrity. There was an official dinner given in his honor by the Italian ambassador, a visit to Rothschild's country home, and a dinner party at which he met the fabled Adelina Patti. During this visit, too, he renewed a friendship with Francesco Paolo Tosti, the Italian composer who was teacher of singing to the royal family, and who took him in hand during his visits to England, introducing him to the right people in the right places. Puccini charmed them all; he was good-looking, elegant, well-mannered and self-effacing—in every way a gentleman.

At the age of forty-two he was firmly established as a celebrity; he had traveled extensively throughout Europe and had triumphed wherever he went. His mixed feelings about these trips, and about his status as a celebrity are strikingly illustrated in a letter he wrote to his old friend Alfredo Caselli in Lucca during this visit to London.

"London," he wrote, "is a city of six million inhabitants. Immense, hellish, indescribable movement. Paris is nothing in comparison. Impossible language, beautiful women, splendid shows . . . and an abundance of entertainments. Not a beautiful city, but a fascinating one. In Paris, a more beautiful city, there is less movement, but one can live in it splendidly." As if astonished, he adds: "I am a friend of Zola, Sardou, and Daudet; who would ever have thought this would happen to the poor organist of Mutigliano?"

The Covent Garden *Tosca* was an important one, for it established, once and for all, Puccini's immense popularity in England. The performance, conducted by the composer's good friend Luigi Mancinelli, was a superb one, with Ternina proving herself to be one of the greatest of all Toscas. In reviewing it the following day, the critic for *The Times* wrote: "In his *Manon Lescaut*, and again in his *Bohème*, the composer has proved himself a master in the art of poignant expression, and it is most gratifying to find that he can handle the larger passion of the cantatrice with as certain a touch as he displayed in treating the less strenuous grief of his two former heroines. Such scenes as the love-making of the first act, the horrible scene of torture in the second, or the tragic dénouement of the whole are treated with wonderful skill and sustained power so that each rises to its natural climax and therefore makes a tremendous effect. . . ."

The composer, too, made a tremendous personal effect, shyly responding to the tumultuous cheering that followed each act, dragged repeatedly before the curtain, apparently unwillingly, by the principals and the conductor. The audiences and press were especially taken by this quality of reticence and apparent lack of what they felt should be Latin temperament, and Nellie Melba, who sat beside Puccini in a box during one performance of the opera noted, "Puccini was an extremely simple man. I do not think that it is anything to his discredit to say that he was really a peasant of genius. He very rarely talked, except in short staccato sentences, while he sat shyly on the edge of his chair." It is hard to say whether or not this was the real Puccini. Toscanini noted that the composer insisted on sharing bows with him at the Scala première of Tosca, and Puccini at times implied that this modesty was intentional; but if it was an act, it was an effective one and again proved his sense of theatre.

Even more important to Puccini than the Covent Garden triumph was a visit he paid to the Duke of York's Theatre to attend a performance of two plays by the American producer-director-dramatist-showman David Belasco—a farce called Naughty Anthony, which was followed by the tragedy, Madame Butterfly. The latter work had been recommended to him by Frank Nielson, stage manager of Covent Garden, as a possible basis for a new opera. (In his book, Fifty Years of Music, William Boosey claims credit for first suggesting the Belasco play to the composer.) The pathetic story of a young Japanese girl who marries and is then abandoned by an American naval officer had first appeared as a short story in the Century Magazine in January 1898; its author was a lawyer from Philadelphia named John Luther Long. Its theatrical possibilities were recognized by the flamboyant and brilliant Belasco, who adapted it for stage. First produced at the Herald Square Theatre in New York on March 5, 1900, it was an immediate success. After a month's run in New York, the play opened in London on April 28, starring the eminent British actress Evelyn Millard as the tragic Cho-Cho-San.

Though he understood no English, Puccini was enchanted with the play; indeed, he might not have been if he had understood what was being said on stage. (Even Belasco admitted that Puccini was not seeing the play but only hearing the music he would write for it.) To substantiate this, one need not print the text of the entire play; excerpts will do. When Butterfly's faithful servant Suzuki wonders whether or not the American officer, Pinkerton, will ever return—he had left on a tour of duty shortly after their marriage—Butterfly replies: "Course he come back! He's gone so long accoun' he's got business in those his large country. If he's not come back to his house, why he sign lease for nine hundred and ninety nine year for me to live? Why he put 'Merican lock to bolt it door, to shut it window? Answer me those question. . . . I know w'en he comes back—he told me. W'en he goin' 'way, he say in tha's doors: 'Madam Butterfly, I have had ver' nice times with my Japanese sweets heart, so now I goin' back to my own country and here's moaney—an' don' worry 'bout me—I come back w'en "Robins nes' again!" ' "

Anticipating an early return, Butterfly tells Suzuki: "But soon they nes' now. Suzuki, w'en we see that ship comin' in—sa-ey—then we goin' put flowers every where, an' if it's night, we goin' hang up mos' one thousan' laterns—en-ha?"

Within a short time, Sharpless, the American consul, appears and Butterfly wonders about his knowledge of American birds—specifically robins. " 'Bout when do they nes' again? Me, I think it mus' be mor' early in Japan as in America, accoun' they nestin' here now."

The tragic tale unfolds; there is a baby, a blue-eyed American one named Trouble, whose name will, on the day the officer returns, change to Joy. And Butterfly sings to the child the lullaby "all 'merican sing for bebby," the one her husband sang for her: "Rog' a bye bebby, Off in Japan, You jus' a picture, Off of a fan."

Finally, at the very end, when the officer has returned with his new American wife, the loyal Butterfly turns her child over to the Americans and dies in her husband's arms, saying faintly, "Too bad those robins didn' nes' again."

The tragedy of the story was a poignant one, and Puccini was able to perceive that without being embarrassed by the dialogue. And he was clearly taken by Belasco's masterful theatrical effects. The drama began with picture drops of ricefields, flower gardens, fishing boats and a snow-capped volcano in the moonlight. In the midst of the one-act play, when the officer's return is awaited, there was a night vigil, lasting fourteen minutes on stage—without one word of dialogue. Butterfly, Suzuki, and the child were poised at the window, awaiting the return. Night fell slowly, stars appeared, and the lanterns celebrating her husband's return gradually went out one by one until the stage was enveloped in darkness. Slowly, the grey light of dawn appeared, revealing Butterfly awake at the window, Suzuki and the child at her feet asleep, the birds beginning to sing from the cherry trees in the garden. . . .

The audience was spellbound at this heart-rending spectacle—so was Puccini. The brilliant theatrical effects, the theme of the love-stricken, beautiful, defenseless young woman, the exotic setting of Japan—all appealed to his imagination, and it might well be that he really was putting the incomprehensible play to music while it was being performed. Belasco told his biographer, William Winter, that Puccini saw the play in London and "after the curtain fell he came behind the scene to embrace me enthusiastically and to beg me to let him use 'Madame Butterfly' as an opera libretto. I agreed at once and told him he could do anything he liked with the play and make any sort of contract he liked, because it is not possible to discuss business arrangements with an impulsive Italian who has tears in his eyes and both arms around your neck."

Belasco's account is colorful but not believable; the reticent Puccini would not have begged him to use the play for an opera, nor would he have embraced him. His approach was more cautious and realistic. Though obviously attracted to the theme, he was not ready to make up his mind nor, he knew, could contractual arrangements be made that easily—especially with a man whose success and business acumen were well known in the English-speaking theatre.

By the time Puccini returned to Italy—via Paris and Brussels—he was still thinking of *Madame Butterfly*, but he had not given up other possibilities. He was uncharacteristically optimistic after *Tosca*'s London triumph—"Let us hope to live another forty or fifty years," he wrote to his sister Ramelde—but he was still uncertain about his next opera.

By the middle of August, however, back at Torre del Lago without a subject, he was again gloomy—and bored because he was without work. "I have had no word from Illica or from Giacosa," he wrote Ricordi. "Not even one proposal. I am truly a forgotten man. . . . I don't know where to turn. The best years (the last of my youth) are passing. It's a pity."

Briefly, he turned to an old idea of writing an opera about Marie Antoinette—he had considered it since 1897 and would not finally discard the idea for several more years—but he felt that the subject of the Revolution was already overworked. More seriously, there was the possibility of adapting Alphonse Daudet's stories about the colorful Tartarin de Tarascon, a kind of Provençal Don Quixote, whose humorous, exuberant adventures were immensely popular thoughout Europe during the last quarter of the nineteenth century. These tales, filled with bizarre and unusual characters, would have resulted in Puccini's first comic opera, a welcome change of pace from his succession of tragic stories of thwarted love. Even before going to London, he had written Illica of his enthusiasm for the project—while at the same time recognizing that in *Tartarin* there might be the danger of a comparison with Verdi's *Falstaff*. By May, Illica had gone so far as to write a rough draft for the proposed opera. Knowing his composer, however, he at the same time was giving thought to other subjects—among them two plays by Carlo Goldoni. But Puccini was for a while completely in favor of *Tartarin*; even the press spread the word that it would indeed be the next subject of a Puccini-Illica-Giacosa opera, something that Giacosa, completely against the project, officially denied. In spite of this, the composer persevered. A day before leaving for London, he wrote Illica a detailed description of the last scene of the opera. "A large square, filled with trees, many-colored oleanders, white ground like that in Malta and Palermo, a dark cobalt sky, sun, sun, sun, a large passable bridge over the Rhone in the background" — this was to be the setting. And the ending would be "gay, warm, radiant, colorful, and clamorous, to an opera we will make original, entertaining, and youthful," he wrote the librettist.

In spite of Puccini's enthusiasm, Illica grew cool toward the project, and Ricordi was far from enthusiastic. The reason it was abandoned, however, was a simple one of legalities, for it was learned that the operatic rights to Daudet's books had already been acquired by a minor French composer named Emile Pessard.

Once he had returned from London, Puccini didn't seem to care too much. He had continued to think of *Butterfly* and urged Ricordi to keep after the firm's New York representative concerning the rights, which Belasco clearly had not given him in a burst of generosity that night at the theatre.

In the months that followed, there were other possibilities, among them Gerhart Hauptmann's *The Weavers*, Hugo's *Les Miserables*, Rostand's *Cyrano de Bergerac*, and Benjamin Constant's *Adolphe*. But as time passed the composer was increasingly determined to use *Madame Butterfly*, if only Ricordi could obtain rights for him. "If at least some reply would come from New York," he wrote Ricordi in November. "The more I think of *Butterfly*, the more I am irresistibly attracted. If only I had it here so that I could set to work on it." He already had specific ideas, planning to turn the one-act play into a two-act opera—the first act set in America and the second in Japan.

While waiting for word from America, Puccini, though nervous and "inoperatic"—his play on words combining the Italian "out of work" and without an opera—kept busy supervising productions of his newest opera. As always, and it was by now a ritual, special attention was paid to the Lucca première of *Tosca*, which took place on September 3; he had shown his usual concern for the proper casting of this production even when he was in London several months before. As always, too, it was a triumph. In the presence of D'Annunzio and Eleonora Duse, the composer was summoned to the stage twenty-seven times. After one of the eighteen performances given of the work, he was presented with a sculpture—of himself—done by Giuseppe Bianchi and donated to the composer by public subscription.

Shortly after Lucca, Puccini traveled to Brussels, this time for the first performance at the Théâtre de la Monnaie of *La Bohème*. It was a great success, and again the composer was praised as a man of remarkable modesty and simplicity, an artist without pretensions.

On the evening of December 9, Puccini was in Bologna for the last of twelve performances of *Tosca* given at the Teatro Comunale; it was an evening in his honor, and he was called to the stage repeatedly. The performance was a superb one—Mugnone conducting, with Ada Giachetti and Caruso at their best. The twenty-seven-year-old Caruso was already making a reputation as an uncommonly gifted singer, but not until December 26, 1900, did he make his début at La Scala. It was the opening night; the Scala season was to have opened with a performance of *Tristan und Isolde*, but due to the illness of the heldentenor, *Bohème* was hurriedly substituted for the Wagnerian opera. With Toscanini conducting, the well-thought-of soprano Emma Carelli singing Mimi, and the much-heralded Caruso in the role of Rodolfo, success seemed assured. Instead, the evening was a disaster. Caruso was ill, but he neglected to mention the fact to anyone. Each aria and each act was greeted with total silence. Puccini, who had been at rehearsals, left the opera house at the beginning of the last act — he was too upset to stay until the end. The following day, a critic, Giovanni Borrelli, writing in *L'Alba*, noted that the "little tenor," trying to take a step that was too long for his leg, managed to break the leg.

Within a short time, Caruso's health had improved, and further performances were successful.

In January of 1901, two Italian musicians died — both of whom were of importance to Giacomo Puccini. The first, who died on January 13, was Carlo Angeloni, a pupil of Puccini's father as well as Puccini's own teacher. It was an occasion for bitterness. Lucca planned to commemorate Angeloni's death with all honors. There were to be plaques, and a bust of the Lucchese maestro was to be installed in the Palazzo Pretorio. Unwillingly, Puccini was appointed to the committee; he went along with it, but angrily commented to his sister Ramelde, "To think that Boccherini has no more than a tablet on the walls of a brothel." Ramelde was even more upset. Michele Puccini was, she believed, far superior as a musician to Angeloni and went entirely unrecognized. "Angeloni's masses," she wrote in her diary, "put people to sleep, while those of my father are a part of the classical repertory." Even her uncle, Fortunato Magi, was far more talented than was Angeloni, she believed.

Two weeks later, on January 27, Giuseppe Verdi, whose talent could not be contested, died. The entire country entered into a period of mourning. The Senate was convoked, a state funeral decreed, and the execution of a bust of the composer, to be placed in the Senate, was commissioned — a tribute worthy of a national hero.

Puccini was — there was no longer any doubt — the successor to the great man of Italian opera, but there is some question as to whether the two men ever met — if so, it was probably a brief meeting at the première of *Falstaff*, which the younger composer attended with Giulio Ricordi. In any case, their meeting was of no importance to either man. Verdi preferred Mascagni and felt that the composer of *Cavalleria Rusticana* was the musician most likely to follow in his footsteps. As for Puccini, he admired *Falstaff*, but little else of Verdi's including *Aida*, the opera that presumably convinced him to write for the stage. His preference, often expressed, was Wagner—the Wagner of *Parsifal* and *Die Meistersinger.*

Ricordi, a great friend of both, was upset about this lack of rapport between the two composers, and it seems likely that he had to exert pressure to convince the younger man to represent the city of Viareggio at Verdi's funeral—just as he had to almost force Puccini to compose a short piece in memory of Verdi for the fourth anniversary of the latter's death. Nonetheless, upon Verdi's death, Puccini formally noted that "with him the purest and most luminous glory of Italy was extinguished." He added: "For the true greatness of our country, let us hope that the virtues of the man and the artist will be imitated and carried on."

Puccini was certainly eager to carry on where Verdi had left off, but in early 1901, he was still without a subject for a new opera. *Tartarin* had been abandoned, and the composer once again (it would not be the last time) decided against *Marie Antoinette;* in doing the latter he somewhat irritated Illica, who had already put in a great deal of work on it. He continued to busy himself with *Tosca*—trying his best to arrange for a production in Vienna and going to Palermo to supervise rehearsals there. But his main concern was *Madame Butterfly,* and an agreement from New York that would allow him to begin work on a theme that was close to his heart.

Even without an agreement, by the beginning of March he started doing his best to interest Illica in the project. On March 7, commenting that he himself was completely taken with it, he sent the librettist a translation of the John Luther Long story on which it was based. He emphasized that in the play Belasco had made some major changes, with which he completely agreed—among these was the ending. In the play, Butterfly succeeds in committing suicide, while in the story the child prevents the suicide.

Illica was favorably impressed, so much so that he immediately began making suggestions for revisions—he felt that the American wife should be eliminated (she very briefly appears in the opera) and that a scene with the American consul should be deleted.

Though he disagreed with most of these suggestions, Puccini was heartened by Illica's response and urged him to write of his enthusiasm to Ricordi, who apparently had serious doubts about the project. The librettist complied and shortly after wrote to Ricordi that he was sure that *Butterfly* would be a strong and beautiful opera, that he was already working out the first act, the finale of which would be "almost more poetic than the scene between Mimi and Rodolfo in the first act of *Bohème.*"

On April 7, Puccini was finally able to write Illica that "*Butterfly* is ours. Agreements have been received from America." The third Puccini-Illica-Giacosa-Ricordi collaboration was to begin officially, and with it the normal share of disagreements. At first it was Illica who argued that Belasco's role was somewhat less important than that generally accorded him. He felt that Puccini was overimpressed with the American's theatrical effects, that the story itself had more than enough drama without gimmicky staging. And he felt that Puccini himself would have realized this if he had been able to understand the words of the play. He and Giacosa, he wrote Ricordi, could surpass Belasco's contribution if only they were supported by Puccini and their publishers. "I repeat," he wrote, "*Butterfly* is the strongest plot Puccini has ever had, strong and new but not easy. We must find a way to have mutually beneficial conferences as we had for *Bohème*. I said strong and new, and I would also add the most suited to Puccini's elegance . . . even without Belasco. And our self-esteem would lead us to work wonders!"

In June, when Ricordi had had a chance to read a translation of the play itself, he too was convinced of its merits; so was Giacosa, to whom the publisher wrote that he was joyfully anticipating another *Bohème*, another *Tosca*. "With the trinity of authors we will also have a trinity of operas," he said. They all looked forward to a joint meeting to discuss the work.

Before long, the usual period of waiting, of impatience on the part of Puccini, began. On August 14, he wrote three letters, one to Ricordi, one to Illica, and one to Giacosa, complaining of the lack of material from the latter. The summer period, one of calm, was coming to an end, and the composer was desperate for the first act so that he might start work. Giacosa, for his part, seemed in no great hurry—he was taking the cure at Salsomaggiore and working on another libretto. But by November, the composer had received almost all of the first act from Giacosa—almost all, but not all; the final duet was still to come. In the meantime, Illica had gone ahead and was well into the second act.

This pattern continued, with Illica and Puccini going ahead and Giacosa dragging behind. Puccini, however, was in good spirits, responding to his friend Alfredo Vandini's request for publicity information in a jocular fashion: "*Willy, Edgar, Manon Lescaut, Bohème, Tosca*—these are my five crimes. For my date of birth, omit the year . . . say I am twenty-two years old."

He was disturbed by Giacosa's delays, but because he was pleased with the way the opera was going, he remained calm. Giacosa, for his part, was apologetic. He had had personal problems—his son-in-law had been involved in a scandalous duel—but he would meet with Puccini and they would make up for lost time.

Puccini might have been temporarily placated, but Ricordi continued to put pressure on Giacosa. On May 20, Giacosa answered his publisher's criticism in a letter that sounds all too familiar to those who have followed the progress of the two earlier collaborations:

. . . It wasn't the second act that Giacosa was supposed to to finish by July 1901, but the 1st, the First, the First. So much so that the very first sketch of the second, or rather of the first part of the second, was read by Illica in the study of Commendatore Ricordi either at the end of October or the beginning of November. And that reading did not obtain the complete approval of Puccini, so that Illica had to take it back to the country and do it over again. In the meantime, Giacosa was making changes in the first act, according to certain suggestions agreed upon by Puccini and Mr. Giulio.

Now as far as the first part of the second act is concerned (which later, according to my suggestion, became the entire second act), the slandered Giacosa read it in its entirety only in February of 1902 — and only then was it approved, except the further addition of the brief episode of the threats to Goro. Then, before I even had in hand the two scenes of the third act, Puccini requested further changes in the first act (nothing less than the entire final scene — the love duet — which was redone from scratch) and the complete overhauling of the second half of the second act. This is the true, genuine, documented story. . . .

Before long, it was Puccini who was offended. Not only was there no word from Giacosa, but even Ricordi had stopped writing to him. Nonetheless, he kept working on the first scene and was particularly pleased with Butterfly's entrance. His only reservation was that the music was too Italian, something he must have known was inevitable. He did consult various experts on matters Japanese, however, to make the opera somewhat more authentic. Among these was a Madame Ohyama, the wife of the Japanese ambassador, whom he saw several times. She filled him in on local color and sang a few songs for him — promising to have more songs sent to him. (Puccini did obtain a number of recordings of Japanese songs, but they were apparently of little use to him.) The ambassador's wife liked what he told her of the libretto but claimed that some of the names of the characters were not really appropriate. She did not approve of Yamadori because it was feminine, but for some reason Puccini retained it as the name of Butterfly's rich Japanese suitor; she felt the names of Yaxonpide, Sarundapiki, Izaghi, and Sganami were also wrong.

In the early fall of 1902, the composer was happy — he was working hard on the beginning of the second act, and he was delighted with the libretto. There seemed to be none of the problems that had tormented him during his work in the past. But after a short trip to Dresden for the very successful première of *Tosca*, he returned home and realized there was a problem — a serious one. On November 14, he wrote to Giacosa to warn him of radical changes and to ask him for a meeting. Two days later, he explained to Ricordi and to Illica the reasons for his concern. As originally conceived by Illica, the opera would have been in three acts, the last act set in the American Consulate in Nagasaki. As he worked on it, Puccini came to feel that the last act had to be eliminated, that it served no purpose and merely weakened the impact of the drama. Illica had wanted the scene in the Consulate to contrast with the Oriental atmosphere of the rest of the opera, but the composer had come to feel that two acts were stronger; one, a kind of prologue which depicted the marriage, and the second showing the period of anxious waiting and the terrible climax. He realized the problem of a two-act opera with two very long acts, but he felt it would work.

Illica agreed, but he believed that the long second act should be divided into two acts — in that way *Butterfly* would remain a three-act opera, and the problem of an over-long second act would be solved. Only Ricordi remained unconvinced, fearing that the opera would be too short if the Consulate scene were eliminated, but he was heartened by the harmony that resulted from a series of meetings in Torre del Lago between composer and librettist.

By the end of 1902, Illica and Puccini were almost euphoric; they felt certain that they were on a road that would lead to their greatest success. *Butterfly*, Illica wrote to Ricordi, was surrounded by the fragrance of success.

There was only one obstacle, and that was Giacosa who, in the course of a meeting with the composer in mid-January, threatened to withdraw if the long second act were not divided in two. After the meeting, Puccini was deeply depressed and hurt — his heart was in *Butterfly* as it had been in no other opera, and he wanted nothing to disturb the process of its creation. "Don't abandon me in the most beautiful of my operas," he pleaded with Giacosa in a letter of January 16, 1903, at the same time writing to Illica that he felt Giacosa was dissenting largely because he had not been informed of the change until after Illica and Puccini had already agreed upon it.

Giacosa might well have been offended — in the past, too, he had often felt left out — but in a letter of January 17, he provided Puccini with serious and well-thought-out reasons for his refusal to accept the opera's new structure. He was convinced that there had to be a break between the night vigil and the return of Pinkerton; that combining the two acts into one would result in an act that would be far too long and tedious and would not give the action sufficient time for development. He also felt that the changes would eliminate "many exquisite poetic details . . . poetry of an intimate, essential character." However good the music might be, he foresaw a disaster with the public. Suggesting once again that he give up his role in the collaboration, he concluded with a threat. "To maintain my artistic integrity and also not to claim a merit which is not mine, I must let the public know what my part in the collaboration consisted of, so I reserve the right to publish my scenes, all those which had already met with your enthusiastic approval as well as that of Illica and Signor Giulio. . . ."

As in the past, however, Giacosa finally gave in; there was no resignation and Puccini's changes were accepted, though Giacosa's suggestions were, later, to be heeded. So it was that Puccini was a happy man when, toward the end of February, he left Milan for Torre del Lago and a few days of hunting and relaxation. His opera, in which he was deeply involved, was coming along well. There had been problems—they were inevitable—but for the most part all concerned were satisfied that the work was coming to an end and that the result would be a huge success.

What was meant to be an idyllic holiday in his beloved Torre del Lago turned into a near tragedy. On the morning of February 25, the composer, Elvira, and Tonio were driven by their young chauffeur, Guido Barsuglia, a local mechanic befriended by Puccini, to Lucca, where the maestro was to be examined by a throat specialist. For years he had suffered from frequent attacks of laryngitis, a condition undoubtedly aggravated by his incessant smoking, a habit he had acquired in early adolescence in Lucca. His latest bout with the illness had worried him, and he hoped for help from the local doctor.

The trip to Lucca also gave Puccini a chance to visit with his childhood friends, and after the visit to the doctor, the Puccinis dined with Alfredo Caselli and a few others in one of the city's oldest restaurants, Rebecchino. The meal did not come to an end until past ten o'clock. The road to Torre del Lago was a treacherous one, especially on a pitch-black, foggy night, and Caselli urged Puccini and his family to stay with him and return home the following morning. Puccini would have none of it. His passion for automobiles equaled his passion for hunting, and his faith in them was complete. This passion was shared by other composers, by Umberto Giordano, with whom he paid daily visits to the international automobile show in 1901 in Milan, and by Alberto Franchetti, who in 1900 had been named president of the Club Italiano degli Automobilisti and was the first of the composers to have his own auto. Puccini's beloved auto—he first owned a four-and-a-half horsepower, one-cylinder De Didion-Bouton and then a two-cylinder Clement—would surely get them home safely.

He was wrong. Only a few miles out of Lucca, near the village of San Macario, the young driver, having just crossed a small bridge, missed a sharp, sudden curve. The car plunged into a field, more than fifteen feet below, turning over. Fortunately, the accident was witnessed by a nearby resident, a Dr. Sbragia, who had come to his window at the sound of an approaching car—not many cars traveled that road in those days. He quickly summoned some neighboring farmers and together they ran to the scene of the accident. Elvira and Tonio were, miraculously, well; they suffered only minor bruises and, most of all, shock. The driver was howling with pain, due to serious injuries to his thigh and shin. (The accident, he later said from his home in Grimes, California, left him with a permanent limp.) But Puccini, at first, was missing. Fearing he had been hurled far from the car, the rescuers took their lanterns and went in search of him.

Finally, he was found, under the overturned car, but fortunately not crushed by it since his body was lying in a depressed ditch, the car above it resting on a fallen tree trunk which protected the composer from what would have been a fatal blow. Nonetheless, he was gravely wounded; unconscious, unable to cry for help, almost asphyxiated by the fumes from the broken gas tank.

In agony, he was transported to the doctor's home, where he spent the night. Early the next day, a noted surgeon from Lucca was summoned. The immediate diagnosis showed a fracture of the right shin as well as a number of contusions. At noon, he was carried by stretcher to the Villa Piaggetta of his friend the Marchese Ginori-Lisci on the shores of Lake Massaciuccoli; from there he was transported, comforted by Elvira and the Marchese, by means of a flat-bottom boat to his own home on the other side of the lake. Two days later, a well-known Florentine surgeon joined the doctor from Lucca in making a further diagnosis: not only was there a continuing inflammation in the right leg, but there was also considerable damage to the left leg.

As word of the terrible accident spread, more than three hundred cables of concern arrived at Torre del Lago—from the king, from members of the government, from Sardou and from Albert Carré, the director of the Opéra-Comique, and even from Mascagni, who was in San Francisco at the time.

Treatment was long and difficult; the broken leg had been poorly set immediately following the accident; this necessitated breaking the bone again and resetting it. Even worse, when a wound refused to heal, tests were taken and it was determined that Puccini was suffering from diabetes.

The period of convalescence was a torture to Puccini. His creative powers, the driving force of his existence, were curbed. Much of the time he was in physical pain, but even more than that he suffered from boredom and from anxiety over the fact that work on *Butterfly*, which had been going so well, had come to a halt. A restless, active, energetic man, he was suddenly immobile, totally dependent on Elvira, her sister Ida, and his sister Nitteti. They behaved as loyal and efficient but insensitive prison guards.

After a few weeks, the temporary bandages were removed, and the composer's emaciated and weakened legs were put in a cast; a few weeks after the accident he wrote to a friend, "I am all plaster cast." His mind however, was active, and he found some consolation in a few pieces of good news from Paris. A cable from Carré informed him of the Opéra-Comique's wish to produce *Tosca* in the fall and Mugnone visited him, reporting that he had just attended the Opéra-Comique's 102nd performance of *La Bohème*, given before a packed and enthusiastic house. In addition, the conductor said he had met Massenet, who had remarked that no Frenchman had done for opera what Puccini had.

In spite of his discomfort, the days passed quickly at first. There was an enormous amount of mail from all over the world, affectionate tributes of concern addressed to the composer, and an endless stream of visitors came to Torre del Lago to cheer him up as best they could. But the nights were different: unable to sleep, his thoughts turned to his work, and his frustration at not being able to go forward with it threw him into moods of black despair. Without his opera, he was nothing.

In May, there was further bad news. The doctor came to examine his leg and found that there had been little progress; he predicted that it would be at least three months before he could put his foot on the floor — essential for his work at the piano, where he did all of his composing. "Farewell to everything, farewell to *Butterfly*, farewell to my life," he wrote to Illica. "How can I endure the terrible summer months? What will I do? My God, this is enough to age a newborn child."

As time slowly passed, the number of visitors decreased, and his illness seemed to drag on endlessly. Begging him to come and stay with him for a few days, Puccini wrote a desperate letter to his old friend Caselli. "I am alone with my eternal boredom and sadness. Nothing interests me. Even the tepid springtime irritates me. I feel I am in prison, constantly guarded and watched. Damn my life. . . . No one understands me. I would speak, if I should speak, to people who don't understand me and don't want to. My very existence is ruined."

By June there was improvement, some cause for optimism. Tito Ricordi and Giacosa arrived in Torre del Lago with the finished libretto at the time the composer had found a way of sitting at the piano and working for a few hours a day. Even this limited resumption of work helped him regain his self-confidence, and he was able to begin to think beyond *Butterfly*, of future operas — this time he showed interest in Victor Hugo's *Notre-Dame de Paris*.

Later that month, too, the doctors noted further improvement, and a steel brace was devised so that he might rest one foot comfortably on the floor. By August, Puccini and Elvira were able to escape the summer heat and go to his home at Boscolungo, near Abetone, where the composer first discarded his crutches and learned to walk with the aid of canes. Blood tests showed an improvement in his diabetes, he had gained weight, and his energy was renewed. He could realistically look forward to the completion of *Butterfly* and think of its first production early in 1904. He was even able to plan, tentatively, to go to Paris for the première of *Tosca* in the French capital; while there, his Italian doctor suggested that he might consult a French physician about his leg.

On September 10, Tito Ricordi, Giulio Gatti-Casazza (then managing director of La Scala), and the conductor Cleofonte Campanini visited him to go over the score of *Madama Butterfly*. Plans were being made for its première in Milan. Puccini was stimulated and excited by this prospect, yet he was exhausted by the long day's session. He had not yet, he realized, regained his former strength; the healing process, hindered by his diabetic condition, had been slow and therefore debilitating. He lacked energy, and, even now, seven months after the accident, he could only walk with the aid of canes. This long period of enforced inactivity had taken its toll; it had also given him much time to think of his health, a preoccupation since he was a young man, and to wonder if his premonitions of an early physical decline were not based on fact. Even worse, those months of immobility made him realize that he was basically alone. His friendships were largely superficial ones, his family life far from satisfactory — Fosca, Elvira's daughter whom he adored, had married and gone to Milan; Tonio, with whom he had found it less easy to have a comfortable rapport, was away at school in Switzerland; and Elvira, who excluded herself from his professional life, was increasingly unable to provide the sympathetic companionship he required.

The trip to Paris proved to be as effective a medicine as any prescribed by the doctors. He was lionized in the French capital, *Bohème* having achieved such astounding popularity that he was known even beyond operatic circles. Recognized as a celebrity, he was treated as such; even Elvira, once her identity was revealed, was greeted warmly by the usually less than friendly French shopkeepers and, most surprisingly, in order to please her she was offered merchandise at reduced prices!

The composer's physical condition seemed to improve as well; he was given daily massages, and a lighter and less cumbersome brace was designed for his leg, which enabled him to get around more easily. He was, according to Louis Schneider, who interviewed him for *La Revue Musicale*, a courageous and stubborn man who had rested his leg but not his brain during the long convalescence.

Rehearsals went well, and Puccini was friendly but meticulous and demanding with the French cast. Very much present at these rehearsals was the seventy-two-year-old Sardou, whose energy and vitality delighted Puccini. At the very beginning of these rehearsals, the Frenchman made it clear that he, as author of the play, was in charge of the action on the stage, and that Puccini need only concern himself with the music. The composer readily agreed and the two men got along famously. Puccini worked harmoniously, too, with André Messager, artistic director of the Opéra-Comique who was to conduct the première of *Tosca*. The two men studied the score together at Puccini's hotel on the rue Danou, where the conductor also had a chance to hear excerpts from *Butterfly*.

The opening performance of *Tosca*, on the night of October 13, was, in Puccini's own words, "a veritable triumph . . . Italian-style with shouts and calls for encores." The king and queen of Italy had arrived in the French capital the day before, and the composer was greeted as royally as they had been by a cheering public. The critics, not unexpectedly, were not so friendly, though all had to admit that the audience had greeted the work enthusiastically. It was clear from the reviews that Puccini's problem was simply that he was Italian—though *Le Guide Musical*'s critic grudgingly admitted that he was an Italian who knew what was going on outside of Italy. Writing in *Le Ménestrel*, Arthur Pougin felt the subject was not really suited to the composer's talents, and in this two distinguished composers agreed. Paul Dukas felt the opera lacked cohesion and style, while Gabriel Fauré, writing in *Le Figaro*, was disturbed by certain "disconcerting vulgarities." During this visit to Paris, Puccini had an opportunity to meet France's most distinguished composer, Claude Debussy, and to hear *Pelléas et Mélisande*, which had first been produced the year before. Messager, to whom *Pelléas* had been dedicated and who conducted the performance, introduced the two men. Puccini was moved and impressed; though he complained that the opera contained not one aria, he was full of admiration for the texture of the Frenchman's orchestration, which he would soon imitate to some extent. Debussy, for his part, was not impressed. Writing about *Bohème* in *Gil Blas* on February 16, 1903, he had said: "Even if Monsieur Puccini is attempting to recapture the atmosphere of the streets and people of Paris, it is still an Italian noise he makes. Now I wouldn't hold the fact of his being Italian against him, but why the devil choose *Bohème*?" And after hearing *Tosca*, he could find nothing in Puccini but "an almost complete imitation of our own masters," though he admitted finding an element of charm.

In spite of the critics, *Tosca* was a huge success. Puccini stayed in Paris another two weeks and proudly noted that one week's schedule at the Opéra-Comique showed that *Tosca* would be performed on Tuesday, Thursday, and Saturday and that on Friday night there would be a performance of *La Bohème*. The critics didn't really matter; each of these performances was sold out.

However, *Butterfly* had to be completed, and he wanted to go home. As always, success exhilarated and then tired him. He yearned for Torre where he could complete his new opera—it was quieter there than in Milan, where he also had to worry about the problem of climbing the stairs to his apartment on his still-weakened leg. Tired of Paris and of his demanding fame, he looked forward to returning to the simple life in the country. Yet, he was sufficiently aware of his worldly obligations to write a diplomatic letter to Albert Carré of the Opéra-Comique: "With great regrets, I leave Paris, to which I am tied by recollections of memorable days, which have made my heart—that of an artist and an Italian—quiver. . . . Before leaving, I address myself to you and ask you to convey all my admiration and gratitude to André Messager, the valiant interpreters of *Tosca*, the orchestra, the chorus—in short, all those who, with talent and good will, worked together to make the performance of my opera a perfect and pulsating one. And what shall I say to you, the entire soul of all of this? Thank you again, from the bottom of my heart, which is deeply moved. . . ."

On December 27, 1903, at 11:10 P.M. *Madama Butterfly* was completed at
Torre del Lago. "It's not bad," Puccini wrote to Carlo Clausetti in Naples.
"We'll see."

Everything was set — or almost so; there had to be one final protest from
Giacosa. At the last moment, just when the libretto was about to be printed,
Ricordi asked the librettist for permission to omit several of his verses, which
were to have been sung by Pinkerton in the last act, but had not been set to
music by the composer. Giacosa was furious and his anger must be understood in light of his reputation as an important poet and man of letters — not
merely a librettist.

> I insist with all my strength that the entire libretto be printed.
> This mutilation might serve the musician, but it profoundly offends
> the poet. I cannot approve of a scene without rhyme, without syntax,
> without common sense. . . . Where Pinkerton says, O *l'amara fra-*
> *granza,*" the poetic movement proceeds in tercines. Now the third
> verse of each tercine has been removed. What is wrong with printing
> it, even if the composer omits it? . . .
> . . . the libretto is my responsibility. Put those verses in paren-
> theses if you like, but print the text as it stands. I am very sorry to
> throw a wrench into things at the very beginning of the year, but if
> you think about it I am sure you will agree with me.

Ricordi's reply, on January 3, was an annoyed one:

> Yes, it is a wrench which saddens me very much. It presents a risk
> of confusing the public and ruining the scenic and musical effect,
> because it will surely be noticed that either the composer made a
> mistake by not setting verses to music or that the poet wrote unnec-
> essary verses. . . . If the verses are not found in the libretto, no one
> will make any comment, no matter how beautiful or ugly they may
> be. I am speaking from practical musical experience, and I tell you
> that what Puccini has done is good, very good, and we would ruin for
> him the effect of a scene which is necessarily hurried. . . . But
> how, how could you, a man of the theatre, think that at that
> moment the tenor would stop at the prompter's box to ponder on the
> qualities of poor Butterfly! You are Giacosa, and therefore a splendid
> poet; but not even Apollo who, as the Sun, is more splendid than you
> could produce verses fit for that occasion! . . .

Giacosa answered Ricordi's letter at once. Tired, not feeling well physically, he had no choice but to give in. He had accepted the fact that the two
last acts would become one — an error, he felt — and now he would accept this.
But he refused to agree that it would be wrong for Pinkerton to sing at the
end — after all, Cavaradossi was allowed to sing at some length near the end of

Tosca, and neither Puccini nor Ricordi found that to be a dramatic error. But none of this mattered, and composer and publisher could have their way; he, Giacosa, nonetheless, would reserve the right, in answer to the inevitable criticisms of the libretto, to let the public know exactly what had happened and what his role in the writing had been. "Now," he concluded, "go ahead and butcher my work."

Ricordi, however, had the last word. Writing to Giacosa on January 5, he expressed his belief that far too much was being made of a relatively simple change, and that no valid comparison with the last act of *Tosca* could be made. He agreed to print some of the poet's unused verses in the libretto, but without calling attention to them, by the use of parentheses or any other device. Giacosa gave in, as always, but he had at least asserted, if without effect, his beliefs as poet-librettist. By January 18, when Giacosa was ill, Ricordi wrote to him in jest: "It's time to end this! Either you get well or there will be a war to the death between us."

During the month of January, a few finishing touches were put on the opera. There was a meeting at La Scala described by Puccini, in a letter to Illica: "Conducted by Cardinal Buddha [Giacosa], assisted by the Indian Rajah [Giulio Ricordi] and by the little Parisian [Tito Ricordi]. You and I will be altar boys. . . ."

The parts were not printed until toward the end of the month, and a veil of secrecy surrounded the libretto. Puccini, sending a copy to his sister Ramelde, asked her to see that no journalists or strangers be allowed to see it. It was for the family only. Rehearsals went well, and there was an air of optimism. Puccini was especially pleased with the soprano, Rosina Storchio, whom he believed perfectly personified Butterfly. He himself had been ill in Milan, with an intestinal flu, but he kept up with what happened at the theatre, and several meetings took place at his sickbed.

The first stage rehearsal of the opera took place in early February; the tenor, Giovanni Zenatello, was ill, and his place in the rehearsal was taken by Tito Ricordi, the stage director. Puccini and Giacosa attended, satisfied with the results of their labors. Also present, of course, was Giulio Ricordi, a bit concerned that his son was paying too much attention to unimportant details. But producer, director, composer, the entire cast, and even the somewhat battered librettists were certain that the opera would triumph.

On the day of the première, February 17, Puccini, Illica, and Giacosa wrote a note to Rosina Storchio: "Dear Butterfly, We are forced to kill you on stage, but you, with your profound and exquisite art, will make our opera live." And a few hours before the performance, the composer sent a personal note to the soprano, which read: "My wishes are superfluous! Your great art is so real, delicate, and impressive that the public will certainly be conquered; and I hope, through you, to speed toward victory."

Puccini did not speed toward victory on the night of February 17. Indeed, the first performance of *Butterfly* must be considered a complete defeat for all concerned. In the midst of the almost euphoric confidence on the part of the creators of the opera and the artists who were to perform it, there were a few warnings of what was to come, but little attention was paid to them. Gatti-Casazza, for one, felt it was a serious mistake to divide the opera into only two acts, with the second being too long. In fact, after the rehearsal that preceded the dress rehearsal, the managing director met with Puccini, Giacosa, Illica, Ricordi, and Campanini to discuss the possibility of dividing the second act into two parts. But he was overruled; only Giacosa agreed with him. In addition, when Gatti-Casazza first heard Puccini go through the score at Torre del Lago, he had been worried by its similarities with earlier Puccini operas.

Another important figure who had doubts about the new opera was Toscanini. The conductor, in the presence of the composer, had gone over the score several weeks before the première, at the apartment of Rosina Storchio. (The slim and beautiful young soprano and Toscanini were lovers.) He was disturbed by the length of the work as well as the fact that it was to be presented in two long acts. Not wanting to offend Puccini, however, he refrained from any negative comments, merely pointing out what he liked about the opera and wishing the composer well. He did not attend the opening performance.

But neither Gatti-Casazza nor Toscanini could have foreseen what happened the night of the première. The house was packed; journalists from all over the world waited expectantly for the latest triumph from the pen of the man who was then indisputedly the world's best-loved operatic composer. From the moment the curtain rose, at 8:45, it was clear that something was wrong, however. Apathetic at first, the public soon became hostile—there were frequent shouts of derision and outbursts of laughter. At the end of the first act, there was a scattering of mild applause. Puccini was called before the curtain only twice; his face was sad, he was trembling, and he bowed to the lukewarm reception with difficulty, leaning on his cane.

During intermission, the crowded lobby was the scene of what seemed to be angry quarreling. Backstage, Gatti-Casazza was speechless, Puccini distraught, Campanini close to shock, and Storchio in tears.

Displaying a great deal of courage, the performers took their places for the second act. Things were even worse. There was mild applause for *"Un bel dì"* and for the flower duet, but for the most part the performance was interrupted by catcalls, groans, shouts, and giggles. In fact, laughter broke out often, and for apparently no reason; the public roared with special joy when an on-stage breeze made Storchio's kimono swell, causing someone to shout out, "She's pregnant . . . Toscanini's baby!"

When the final curtain fell, there were no more shouts and no more protests; a glacial silence filled the house.

There have been many reasons given, but no conclusive explanation for this catastrophic failure. The opera, as Toscanini and Gatti-Casazza and Giacosa felt, had its defects, but the worst of them, the fact that the second act was too long, could hardly explain the public's hostility from the very beginning of Act One. That phrases here and there reminded the audience of other Puccini operas is hardly a plausible explanation for the violent protests. Gatti-Casazza felt that an unfriendly atmosphere had been created because of the unusual secrecy that had surrounded the work before its first performance. The singers were not allowed to take the score home and had to study their roles within the confines of the opera house. No one except the composer and librettists was permitted to hear a preliminary rehearsal — even the manager of the opera had to listen, almost hidden, from the back of a box. And the press was excluded from the dress rehearsal, something unprecedented. This, too, however, is not sufficient explanation for the extraordinarily angry reception that was given to Puccini's newest opera.

It is clear, whatever the cause, that this hostility had been carefully, and very well, organized. A claque had been hired, a claque well trained in stirring up an audience, one that even called occasionally for encores when it was certain that such calls would be met by counter-demonstrations of anger. Puccini had enemies — he was too successful not to have them — but there is no evidence pointing to the identity of these enemies on that terrible first night of *Madama Butterfly*. "The show in the auditorium," wrote the correspondent for *Musica e Musicisti*, "seems to have been as well orchestrated as the one on stage." And the public seems to have left the theatre most satisfied that the destruction of Puccini's latest work had been efficiently accomplished.

Of all the many accounts of that disastrous evening, the most moving was written by Puccini's sister Ramelde to her husband Raffaello. For the first time, Puccini had been so sure of success that he had urged members of his family and his friends in Lucca to attend the première of one of his operas. Ramelde came, accompanied by her eldest daughter, Albina, and a nephew, Antonio. (In an interview, many years later, Albina noted that even before the performance began she and her cousin had felt the hostility of the audience in the air.) Unable to sleep after the première, Puccini's favorite sister, "more dead than alive," wrote to her husband at four in the morning:

> . . . We were all so sure. Giacomo didn't even talk about the opera. We went there with only the slightest trepidation, and fortunately we were in a box, otherwise I would have made a spectacle of myself because we were so distressed. The public was hostile from the beginning. We realized that immediately. We never even saw poor Giacomo because it was impossible to go backstage. I don't

know how we made it to the end. I didn't even hear the second act, and before the opera ended we fled from the theatre.

What a disgusting, vile, ignorant public! Not even a show of respect. Giacomo, two hours ago, that is after the theatre, was gaining strength. I thought it would be worse (we saw him two hours after the end of the opera). Giacomo is certain that he has worked well and hopes the opera will be salvaged. I don't know what to tell you because I was so upset from the time of the first difficulties that I didn't understand a thing. Mascagni and Giordano were there — you can imagine their pleasure! Well, that's how it went! We were really unlucky, we, too. I would like to be home, but how can I abandon Giacomo at this time? Damn the moment they thought of opening at La Scala! Damn the moment I decided to come! But, of course I would have suffered at home, too.

Our trip is ruined, but that's not important. Don't let anyone read and don't discuss this confidential letter. If anyone asks, answer that Giacomo calmly feels that the public has been very severe, but he knows he has done a good job, that this is really his best opera. This is what he cabled to many people. I didn't send a telegram because I lacked the courage, and because I had lost my head. . . . Damn the professions that depend on the public. You should bless your job as a tax collector.

According to Puccini's early biographers, the composer returned to his apartment immediately following the performance, accompanied by Illica. He walked into his studio and took down from the wall a painting of the head of Butterfly which had been reproduced on the cover of the score. On the back of it he wrote: *"Rinnegata e felice,"* (rejected and happy) — a quotation from his opera.

The following morning, on awakening after a restless night, Puccini was greeted by the sound of newsboys, shouting out their headlines under the windows of his apartment on the via Verdi. "Read the details of Puccini's great fiasco . . . Puccini's diabetic opera . . . The result of an accident . . ." The première of a new Puccini opera was big news; the demolition of this opera by the first-night audience was even bigger news.

The critics, with few exceptions, were as harsh as the audience had been. E. A. of *Il Tempo* questioned the author's sincerity, accusing him of applying his "somewhat mawkish sentimentality" to a subject far from his heart. This was about a work which was, of all his works, closest to his heart! The anonymous critic for *Il Secolo* complained that the opera bored the public. He wrote that the first act, in spite of a beautiful but overlong love duet, seemed more like operetta, but lacked the gaiety of operetta. And the second act, in spite of some good moments, among them *"Un bel dì,"* was far too reminiscent of the composer's earlier works. *"Butterfly,"* he concluded, "is an interval between the past and what Puccini can give us in the future. . . ."

Nappi, in *La Perseveranza*, was somewhat kinder, though he did immediately proclaim the work a fiasco. "But," he asked his readers, "even if dressed with Giacosa's verses, how is it possible to put to music irrelevant episodes and inconclusive scenes which have no lyrical purpose?" He complained that, in spite of the composer's gifts, all of his characters were more or less the same, that *Butterfly* was little more than a somewhat wilted copy of *Bohème*. Ending on a more positive note, the reviewer stated: "I am convinced, though, that the public will later appreciate the many beautiful passages which yesterday were either overlooked or, perhaps, intentionally ignored."

The most perceptive, as well as the most positive, review was that of Giovanni Pozza, writing in the *Corriere della Sera*, who in the beginning of his article reminded the readers of the lukewarm reception accorded *Bohème* at its première, and further reminded them of the enormous success of that opera, in every part of the world, in the years following that première. Suggesting that many of those present at the first night of *Butterfly* would do well to listen to the work again and would be surprised by what they heard—some of the best music ever written by Puccini—he admitted that the opera did have its shortcomings. The first act, he found, was somewhat slow; there were too many details, more suited to a play than to an opera. The second act, too, in spite of an elegance of form and an abundance of melodic inspiration, went on too long. The intermezzo did not please the public, which wanted the opera to reach its climax as quickly as possible. For all these reasons, Pozza felt, the composer had failed to meet completely the challenge presented to him. "I still believe" he concluded, "that the opera, once shortened and lightened, will recover—there are too many beautiful pages in it, its structure is too elegant and exquisite. . . . It would be best to wait before pronouncing the final word, better to wait for a calmer and more carefully considered judgment."

A look at the history of opera might have consoled Puccini. In 1816, in Rome, Rossini's *Barbiere di Siviglia* had been almost booed off the stage, a victim of a rival's claque, and the composer rushed home, certain his work had failed. A revised version of Wagner's *Tannhäuser*, produced in 1861, had fared so poorly that it had to be withdrawn after three performances. An even closer parallel could be drawn with the première of Bellini's *Norma*, which took place at the same La Scala on the night of December 26, 1831. With everyone involved convinced of its success—Bellini was a favorite in Milan—the opera was received with the same kind of cold indifference that later greeted Puccini's work. Heartbroken, Bellini went home and that same night wrote a letter to his close friend, Francesco Florimo, a letter that is startlingly similar to those written by Puccini after the première of *Butterfly*. "I am writing to you under the shock of sorrow," Bellini wrote, "of a sorrow that I cannot put into words for you, but that only you can understand. . . . Fiasco! . . . fiasco! . . . solemn fiasco! To tell the truth, the audience was harsh, and seemed to have come to pass sentence upon me. . . . I hope to appeal against the sentence pronounced against me, and if I succeed in changing its mind, I shall have won my case, and then I'll proclaim *Norma* the best of my operas."

There was, of course, no consolation, for Puccini, to be found in history. The composer was heartbroken. "I was in the depths of despair," he told Fraccaroli. "It was not for three years of hope that I wept, but for the shattering of all my hopes, of the dream of poetry which I had so tenderly nursed. For a moment, I thought I would never again touch a note."

That same morning, Ricordi, Giacosa, Illica, and Puccini made a decision. The opera was to be withdrawn at once and the advance which had been paid would be returned — there would be no further performances at La Scala. In the evening, the composer was visited by Gatti-Casazza. "He was in his studio," the impresario wrote in his memoirs, "the room being almost entirely dark. His hands were running over the keyboard of a piano. Seeing me enter, he greeted me with a wave of the hand. I saw that he was very upset, that his eyes were full of tears. He sat there without saying a word for some minutes, then pulling himself together he said to me: 'See here, Gatti, does it really seem to you that this poor *Butterfly* was such an ugly thing and so ill conceived?' "

Gatti assured him that once some changes were made — specifically the division of the opera into three acts rather than two — the opera would have the success it deserved; the composer seemed somewhat comforted.

Certainly, neither Puccini nor his collaborators had any intention of abandoning *Butterfly* — they would make revisions and present the work again, in a smaller theatre. Puccini was angry and hurt, but he was also certain that his beloved opera would survive. "I can assure you that I was hurt by this unjust blow," he wrote to Alfredo Caselli after the première. "But I did not lose hope and will never lose hope. I have faith in what I have done — now more than ever because I have heard the opera performed and have a precise conception of it. You will see that there will be a glorious resurrection." To another old friend, Alfredo Vandini, he wrote, in the same vein: "The press, the public can say what they want, they can throw stones at me . . . but they cannot kill my *Butterfly*, who will rise again, healthier and more alive than before." Upset by the anger that his work had engendered — anger at him as well as at the opera — he was nonetheless determined to obtain his revenge through a successful production of the opera.

Less than a week after the disastrous première, the composer and his librettists were at work on the revisions, readying their "revenge." A projected Rome production of the opera was postponed—all concerned believed it was best to present *Butterfly* next in a smaller theatre.

In the aftermath of the Scala production, there was fortunately some good news. The king and queen of Italy had attended a performance of *Tosca* in Rome; the composer had dedicated *Butterfly* to Queen Elena and was heartened by this royal gesture of support. There were further encouraging signs—later reviews of the opera were more favorable than those immediately following the opening night, and many individuals rallied to its support, among them the poet Giovanni Pascoli, who addressed a little poem to the composer in praise of his opera. It began: "Our dear, great maestro, the little butterfly will take wing. . . ."

By early March, plans had been made. The revised *Madama Butterfly* would be performed for the first time in Brescia, on May 28. Its location—not too far from Milan and easily reached by critics—and the size of its Teatro Grande (about 1000 seats as contrasted with the more than 3000 at La Scala) were the determining factors. On March 2, Puccini wrote to Alfredo Caselli that the revisions would be minor ones: a few cuts in the first act, a few more verses for the tenor near the end, and the division of the second act into two parts, making it a three-act opera. "I don't say I am calm, because my temperament precludes that," he added, "but I am completely confident as far as my work is concerned."

The months before the Brescia première passed slowly. Puccini was restless and unhappy in his Milan apartment, but his leg was bothering him and it was best for him to remain there. Because of this, it wasn't till late March that he returned to Torre del Lago and the tranquil joys of hunting and boating on the lake. This was a welcome change from his existence in Milan, with its constant reminders of that terrible night at La Scala. Not that all was well, even in the country. He was unable to find a decent cook to prepare the meals, and the weather was cold and damp. He was worried about his next opera and whether the public wanted more of what he labeled his "sugary" music. His health troubled him—his leg, his throat, an attack of the flu—and he worried that he was growing old. Though only forty-six at the time, he wrote to Ramelde: "I have white hairs in my mustache. I yank them out, but they keep coming back, even more than before."

On May 5, Puccini left for Brescia, for the rehearsals and the long-awaited second première of *Butterfly*. He did so with surprisingly little enthusiasm. Certain that his opera would be vindicated and that its initial failure was due to a well-organized plot rather than the defects of the opera, there seemed to be something anticlimatic about this attempt—which seemed almost certain to succeed—to resurrect his opera.

Once rehearsals began, the composer was excited. The conductor was again his friend Campanini, and the tenor was again Zenatello, whom he found to be in better voice than he had been in Milan. Storchio was not, however, available to sing *Butterfly* in Brescia. Shortly after the Milan première, she had embarked with Toscanini on a tour of South America. Butterfly without her, the composer felt, would be a creature without soul, and he was deeply disappointed in spite of the fact that the soprano would be singing the first Butterfly outside of Europe, in Buenos Aires, as part of the tour. Instead of Storchio, there would be, however, another powerful singer, Salomea Krusceniski, a tall and beautiful young Ukrainian-born singer who had sung in Vienna and had achieved great success as an interpreter of Wagner. The soprano's voice was superb, and her magnetic classical beauty had won the praises of all those who had seen her. It was even reported that Toscanini had said she was the only woman he had ever been madly in love with who had refused him. The conductor was never as enthusiastic about *Madama Butterfly* as he was about the first two Butterflies.

The Teatro Grande was packed on the night of May 28. Among the audience were, once again, critics from all over the world, prepared to re-evaluate *Butterfly*. Among the many notables were Boito, Gatti-Casazza, and the soprano Luisa Tetrazzini. The public was well aware that it was asked to sit in judgment of an appeal to the harsh sentence pronounced by the Milanese public a few months before. And the verdict, from the very beginning of the performance, was overwhelmingly in favor of the composer and his opera. The triumph was complete; there were thirty-two curtain calls and seven encores. Even some reviewers who had damned the work in Milan now changed their minds. For this, they credited the changes made by the composer (which were minor ones) and the fact that the opera could be best appreciated in a more intimate setting (*Butterfly* is a small opera, whose many details are indeed lost in a large theatre).

Puccini was overjoyed; not only for the success of his opera, but for the embarrassment of those who had hastily condemned his work. On the night of the second performance, King Vittorio Emanuele III occupied the royal box; he enthusiastically complimented the composer and told him how fond the queen was of his latest work, and that she would often play through the score on her piano.

On the night of June 16, *Butterfly* was performed for the tenth time in Brescia; it was a special evening in honor of the composer, who was showered with gifts, among them a precious gold medal. His beloved little Butterfly was no longer rejected.

"We Are the Victims of Our Temperaments"

In early January 1904, less than a week after the completion of *Madama Butterfly*, members of Puccini's family and a few friends received a curious and somewhat vulgar caricature, made for the occasion by the painter Plinio Nomellini. It showed the composer, naked but for a sheet of music draped around his waist, a string over his shoulder on which hung a toy automobile, and his arms around his formally dressed bride, Elvira. In one hand was the ever-present, lighted cigarette. In the background, naked musicians serenaded the couple from a cloud, and a bubble announced their words: "Long live the bride and groom."

This was the wedding announcement of Elvira Bonturi, widow of Narciso Gemignani, and Giacomo Puccini. On January 3, the couple, accompanied by two witnesses — the bride's brother and a local doctor — had gone to the villa of Cesare Riccioni, mayor of Viareggio, who had performed the civil ceremony uniting the two, after which they traveled the short distance to Torre del Lago where the religious rites were performed by the parish priest, Giuseppe Michelucci.

The previous February 26, ironically the day following the composer's accident, Narciso Gemignani had died, after a long illness, in Lucca. Lucca had, according to the local newspaper, lost one of its most honest and active residents. There was a mob at the funeral; flowers arrived from Gemignani's daughter and son-in-law, and among the mourners was a representative of the Banda G. Puccini, a fact that might not have delighted the deceased.

The death of this well-loved businessman meant that his wife, Elvira, who

149

had left him many years before, was finally free to marry the man for whom she had abandoned him. According to Italian law, a widow could not remarry until ten months after her husband's death, and that was the only reason for the delay in the marriage of Elvira and Giacomo Puccini. "I took the leap," the composer wrote to his friend Bastiani, on December 31, 1903, but it might have been more accurate to say that he had been pushed.

Puccini's relationship with Elvira had begun to deteriorate only a few years after they had left Lucca together. At the beginning, theirs was a passionate romance, intensified by the scandal and by the fact that financial problems forced them to spend a great deal of time apart. With the composer's success, and with the establishment of a home—actually two, since their time was divided between Milan and Torre del Lago—differences began to emerge and the couple grew apart. During their first few years together, Puccini wrote a series of ardent, teasing letters to Elvira, letters filled with loneliness and a longing to be with her whenever they were forced by his work to be apart. Soon, however, the letters became far more formal; they contained few of the endearments that had filled the earlier correspondence. Finally, Elvira almost disappeared and was rarely referred to in public or private pronouncements by or about the composer and his activities.

Most important, Elvira seems to have played no role in his life as an artist. There is no evidence that she took any interest in his work nor that he ever confided to her about his professional problems. He was a moody man, one given to bouts of despair; he could not get from her the comfort and reassurance he so often needed, and she was unable to lighten the burden of his anxieties.

If he was unable to share his creative life with her, he was also unable to enjoy with her the simpler pleasures of the rural life at Torre del Lago. His paradise was, to her, a bore; she enjoyed far more the time spent in their Milan apartment, and to relieve her boredom in the country, she filled their home with her relatives, whom she invited to stay with them as often as possible. A letter written to Elvira by the composer in early 1900 is evidence of the strain that had already developed between them.

You write me a letter full of discomfort and sadness. And I? We are two strange beings. But a little of the guilt is yours, dear Elvira. You are no longer the same, your nerves dominate you, no longer a smile, no longer an open mien. In my own house I feel myself more of a stranger than you do. Oh, the beautiful intimacy of our first years! Now we pass months (at least I do) in a house which belongs to others. I do not say this in order to complain about Ida, Beppe, etc. No. They are all good people, very sweet people. But their continuous presence in our midst has expelled our intimacy. You are always bored in the country and I love it so. You have need of your relatives in order to make the heavy burden of green nature seem lighter. This is what has given a shock, I hope not an irreparable one, to our dear past intimacy. . . .

. . . I think always of the beautiful times which are past. In those days we were materially not well off, but for all that we were not less content. You are unhappy? I am doubly so . . . I see no way out. . . . Your letter gave me so much pain. . . .

In recalling their early days, when they were not materially well off, the composer indicated another serious problem in their relationship. Not only had a disparity in interests come between them; they had also matured at a different pace and in different ways. When they first met, Elvira was an attractive young woman, with a good figure and an elegant bearing, passionate and headstrong enough to give up her secure home life, with her husband and children, to set out on what must have seemed a risky adventure with a young, struggling composer. For his part, Puccini was a tall, thin, somewhat nervous young man—good-looking, obviously talented, but inexperienced and unworldly. With success, and with the years, everything changed. Elvira became dowdy and matronly—she lost her zest for life, and she became increasingly tense and unable to relax and enjoy herself. At the same time, Puccini, his confidence buoyed by success, grew another dimension. All traces of provincialism disappeared as he traveled from city to city and country to country for the productions of his operas. In spite of the immense pleasures he continued to find in the life of a village—Torre del Lago—he was to become a man of the world, at home through his work wherever he went. His meetings, too, with the important musical and literary figures of Paris and London and Vienna—as well as those of Italy—produced profound changes in him.

He was no longer shy (though he was always reserved in public) and he was no longer awkward; as he matured, he acquired a bit of a paunch, but he also acquired an elegance and a bearing which, added to his status as a celebrity, made him a more than attractive figure. He was pursued by women wherever he went, and he was often willing to be caught. Because of this, Elvira grew jealous—and sometimes with good reason. Her jealousy, however, turned to near-paranoia; she became, in Puccini's words, "a nervous policeman," and she spied on him relentlessly, following his every move and even opening his letters. If she was often right in her suspicions, she was also often wrong. But right or wrong, she made his life a tense and difficult one when they were together.

In spite of this, and without the formal ties of marriage, they did remain together. Basically, Puccini was conventional—he saw nothing wrong in having his women on the side as long as he fulfilled his duties at home. Then, too, there were the children. Tonio, their own son, spent most of his time away at school, and thus was not much of a factor in the home; however, Puccini was eager to remove from the boy the stigma of having unmarried parents. Fosca, Elvira's daughter by Gemignani, was the source of enormous pleasure to the composer, and her presence, to a great extent, held the family together. When in 1902 she married Salvatore Leonardi and moved to Milan, Puccini was crushed. "You left us with a great emptiness," he wrote the young woman, "and the life that Elvira and I live is a terrible one. We are the victims of our temperaments, and you were the mitigating factor."

Even before Fosca's marriage and departure, however, Puccini had met and fallen in love with a woman who came close to breaking up his union with Elvira. Referred to in correspondence as "the Piemontese," little is known about her except that her real name was Corinna, she was a law student from Turin, and she first met the composer on a train. Women had come and gone in the past, and been of little importance to Puccini, but his almost three-year involvement with Corinna was serious and might have led to a final separation from Elvira, had it not been for the intervention of those closest to him — Ricordi, Illica, and his sisters, as well as Elvira, who was determined to do anything to fight for their continued coexistence, troubled as it was.

Each of these had a different motive, but they were all united in wanting the relationship between Puccini and Corinna to come to an end. Ricordi, who had taken the composer's many short-lived affairs with women in his stride in the past, became seriously alarmed in late 1901, when Puccini was starting work on *Butterfly*; he saw the Piemontese as a threat to his composer's creative powers, and in a letter of October 18 he confided his fears to Illica. "I am afraid the Puccini tragedy is becoming more serious," he wrote, "and it is impossible that a man who is preparing his own physical and moral downfall with his own hands can compose. I write this with the greatest pain and sorrow. However, in Puccini's present state I don't believe he can possess that vitality of thought which is needed to give birth to a creation."

The affair continued into the next year. Elvira suffered from it deeply, and Puccini, in a letter written in early 1902, begged her not to be so "exclusive and exigent." He assured her of his love and went on to say that "the Turin affair has become very — but very — weak on my part, believe me. I hope soon to acquire my tranquillity and serenity." Nonetheless, it was clear even by spring that the affair had not come to an end; Elvira's spying confirmed the fact that the composer had seen Corinna in Viareggio in May.

Ricordi, the only one close to Puccini who felt affection for Elvira, became increasingly angry. He felt that the composer had deteriorated both physically and morally through the affair, and he was hurt that a man he had treated as his own son had refused to follow his advice. On December 2, 1902, he gave vent to his feelings in a furious letter to Illica, in which he wrote that he did not want to speak to Puccini again. "I don't want to say or do more than what I've already said and done," he went on. "They are words thrown to the wind, and as a consequence I have been forced to judge as vulgar and dishonest a man I highly esteem and for whom I care. I don't want this to happen again. . . . Puccini is a man lost to his art and to his friends. It is noticeable in his looks, the flabbiness of the muscles in his jaw, the movements of his body, his restlessness, his sudden boredom. How I wish I were a mistaken prophet!"

A few months later, the publisher was even more disturbed, his prophecy confirmed, he believed, by the composer's slow recovery from the automobile accident. He put the blame for this slow recovery on Puccini's relationship with Corinna, and the physical decay, and possible venereal disease, that had resulted from it.

Puccini's sisters were no less upset. Iginia, who as a nun was known as Sister Giulia Enrichetta, wrote to another sister, Tomaide, shortly after the accident from her convent in Vicopelago near Lucca:

> I can open my heart to you. God didn't send this blow in vain. It could be read as a sign of his justice, but I think it is a sign of his mercy, of his love for him so that he might not be lost. We have to help him. I can only do what I can from here, but you sisters who are out in the world can talk to him. You have to do all you can to show him his way as a good Christian. . . . Mother blesses us from heaven. She loved Giacomo so much. Is it possible that his soul should be lost? No, certainly not; this grace will be granted, it is for his soul and Jesus cannot deny it. Now it is time for grace and I beg you, Tomaide, with tears in my eyes, to help that poor child who is fundamentally good. . . .

Ramelde, the most worldly of the sisters, was also eager for the affair to come to an end. However, she did not feel that bringing her brother's soul "back to the fold of Jesus" was the answer. Instead, she believed that a quick marriage to Elvira was the best solution, and she wrote to Illica to ask if he could possibly help in obtaining a royal dispensation to circumvent that 1865 law (still, in 1980, in effect) that forbade a widow to marry until ten months after her husband's death. Time, she was sure, was important.

The librettist replied to Ramelde that an early marriage was impossible, that neither the king nor any of his ministers would grant a dispensation since it would clearly be an abuse of power. Nonetheless, Illica informed Ramelde that he had been in touch with her brother, who, now almost tied to his bed and guarded by Elvira, her family, and his own family, had assured him that the affair was coming to an end. Illica wrote Ramelde, too, that he had told Puccini "a return to the Piemontese could be very dangerous for him, because it seemed certain that she, if the affair began once again, would realize how easily the fish was able to get away and would start thinking things over, figuring out a way to prepare a net that would entrap the fish, no matter what his wishes."

In other words, Illica was apparently telling Puccini to seize the occasion of his enforced imprisonment to rid himself, once and for all, of Corinna. At the same time, he repeated to Ramelde what he had told Puccini: that the composer, now sufficiently recovered from the accident, no longer needed moralizing, preaching friends. He was able to take care of his own affairs. "I can't hide from you," he wrote Ramelde, "the fact that Elvira gets on my nerves. I think that if Puccini acts this way, it means that Elvira has been unable to inspire him to greater respect. People have the governments they deserve; and so does Elvira."

Nonetheless, from Ramelde's letters to Illica, it is clear that the weary and distraught composer had already taken legal steps to get out of his entanglement with the young woman. He had hired a lawyer, and ugly negotiations had begun—the injured woman had letters sent by the composer which she would not hesitate to use against him, if necessary, as a basis for an official settlement. The settlement consisted of Puccini making a formal announcement of his forthcoming marriage to Elvira, while at the same time making certain not to damage the feelings of the Piemontese. Corinna also requested a meeting with Elvira, but that was denied. As matters seemed to come to a standstill, Ramelde regretted only that Ricordi had not been heard from—he was the one person who might move her brother on to positive action. Before long, however, the publisher broke his carefully calculated silence in an altogether remarkable letter written to Puccini on May 31, 1903, and worth quoting at length:

Dear beloved Puccini,

Certainly you must be very surprised by my long silence: I wonder what you must have thought of me. Well, my silence will now be explained to you by what happened last Sunday, and that is by the unbandaging and rebandaging and by the predictions of the doctors, predictions which grieved you as well as your friends, especially me who followed each step of your *via crucis*. In fact, from my continued questioning of doctors, and from the daily bulletins I received, I always feared that there had not yet been that reaction of vitality which alone leads to a relatively rapid healing. Of course, the unforeseen and cursed catastrophe is the primary cause of your present condition, but this was already predisposed by the previous events, just as later circumstances helped to prolong it.

Dear Puccini, you have to look well into your conscience, the hidden parts of it, the most intimate, and then you will have to say: *mea culpa!* And you will also remember what I told you many times, and the sacrosanct promises you made, and how many times you offended me by not keeping your word, your promises.

You know very well that I am not a rhetorician, a pedant, a preacher; I am a man of the world, and I've had enough experience to observe and keep quiet, to evaluate and condone. But, in the life of a man, among our duties to ourselves, there are limits which should not be passed because that would mean the abasement of all morals, physical prostration, the decay of thoughts, insanity, or idiocy! . . .

You, my dear Giacomo, have certainly had your battles to fight and you have endured hardship—this is true of all artists—but you have had the good fortune to reach very early that goal which many others, who later achieved greatness, had to struggle much longer to achieve. Your innate goodness, your genial disposition, and your good looks brought you even more good luck: that of having loving and loyal friends, which is indeed a rare thing. However, all this good fortune, whether or not truly earned by you, created, little by little, a spoiled and willful boy. Unfortunately, it was too late for a spanking. Puccini, who could have been the modern Rossini, that is the real Emperor of Music, was about to become the unhappy Donizetti!

But remember, in the name of God, how many times I told it to you, when you were there, in my office, facing me, in an armchair, depressed, exhausted physically and morally. You were not the same Puccini, full of life, in love with his art. . . .

Oh, I know well . . . You will think, you will say that I was a dreamer, a madman then, just as I am a nuisance now! This is the way stubborn children think, and they shout: Bad daddy! But fortunate are those whom bad daddy succeeds in leading on the right path.

But was I really insane? What would have been the reason to see in you another Donizetti? No, no, no: it was the sacred truth. Your strong organism was capable of reacting from time to time; but it was also true that you were rushing toward a terrible abyss.

The terrible catastrophe happened! . . . And with it the truth of my fears were proven by cruel evidence! . . . Here is a man, so beautiful and vigorous in appearance, in the prime of life, provided with all possible medical treatment, who shows no vital strength, no recovery: his constitution is used, worn out—and we spend hours and days consumed by a terrible fear of the announcement of the disease which signals a dangerous, very often irreversible, decay. And the tears which are shed are real . . . while other painful, unhealthy wounds appear, pounding at me so that I am surprised to find myself still willing to fight for art . . . and friendship.

Yes, dear Giacomo, friendship, because it is you I am fighting, and I ask myself, afraid, if I am perhaps dealing too hard a blow at such a great friendship. Nonetheless, my conscience, the real affection I feel for you, the limitless esteem I feel for the artist, the personal fondness, everything urges me to speak, to tell you what for months has been oppressing my heart and saddening my soul. And it is true that you are betraying yourself, that you show no gratitude to your friends, your country, your art! You, with your own hands, are tearing up your flag, and you are so blind that you are mistaking friends for enemies and creating infinite pain and discomfort.

And shouldn't those who love you complain about this? And shouldn't they feel the pain? And shouldn't I have the courage to face every danger and speak up? ¡

During the long hours and endless days that you unfortunately had to spend motionless, I don't think that you made an honest assessment of your own physical condition. I can understand that; up to now, with the aid of good health, you were always able to abuse life a little, without suffering the consequences. Because of this, your hope of now overcoming, even slowly, the serious and dangerous crisis can be justified. But your physical constitution turned out to be in worse condition than your morals; and the latter, in turn, intolerant of any opposition, excited by childish and stimulating subterfuges, did not help the former. And now you see the very sad consequences of this. Will these now, at least, have sufficient power to make you look at the future with a true picture of how things are, with resolution in your soul, and honesty in your heart?

How is it possible that a man like Puccini, an artist who has made millions of people palpitate and cry with the strength and charm of his creations, can have become a faint-hearted and ridiculous toy in the meretricious hands of a vulgar and unworthy woman? Is it possible that this man has no more discernment? No ability to judge wisely? Is it possible that sadistic lust has more of a grip on him than does his pride as an artist and as a man, than the insistent, pressing, and frightened pleas of his friends? And doesn't this man understand the immense difference between love and the filthy obscenity which destroys the moral perception and the physical vigor of a man? To think that a low creature, with whorelike instincts, can become the master of the heart, mind, and body of such a chosen artist, and by means of obscene sensual pleasures, which would have driven him to moral and then physical death, can make him her toy, appearing in his eyes to be a beneficent, lovable and inspiring fairy! The lowest and most vile creature, I say, and I shout it out loud: vile, low, a creature who, to reach obscene lust and possess the person, does not refrain from killing the brilliantly Italian artist, who honored Italy as he was honored by Italy. And that's not all! Vulgar letters, hackneyed phrases from which no truth emerges and no loftiness of soul transpires, appear in the eyes of a Puccini as the exaltation of an insurpassable love!

Oh, what painful blindness! What pain for all of us who love in you the dear friend, the kind friend, the amiable Giacomone, the chosen artist, a real example of the Italian spirit which gave life to the Risorgimento . . . and a corrupt woman drives out this marvelous individuality, by means of influence, and like a filthy vampire sucks from it all thought, all blood, all life?

Oh! . . . By God! . . . this is too much. Come on, Puccini. Come on, my dear Giacomo, or rather our dear Giacomo — as painful as it might seem at this moment, break this chain of lewd excitement, and rise up to nobler and higher ideals. . . .

That is the way — and no other — that Giacomo Puccini must act. And don't be the skeptic and say that you take art and squeeze it dry and then discard it for an idle life. No, it is art that will not leave you — as it is Puccini who cannot leave art! And let there be disappointments and battles; the resulting victory will make the road traveled even grander. But just see for a moment if now your thoughts — when not inspired by obscene memories but by the feelings of art — don't turn eagerly and with real desire to the job so sadly interrupted . . . and see also if your thoughts don't look towards the future?

Here, and here alone, lies your salvation and your health! . . .

Think of me what you want, that my words are inspired either by true affection or dictated by commercial interests — it doesn't matter to me. Just because of this they are an expression of truth. I don't care whether you welcome them or not. I have given vent to what has been in my heart for a long time, making me cry time and again and forcing me to spend countless sleepless nights. And there must be tears for a beloved artist who wastes away, little by little, for that maestro whom the country, the world, and art still want so much, because there is still so much he must and can give. Isn't this a terrible thing? Doesn't this move you and open your mind to the true vision of what it is your sacred duty to do?

I won't go any further. If what I have dared write to you today does not move your soul, there's nothing left but for me to shout: God help us!

The excellent, kind Dr. Guarneri has always kept me informed, knowing how anxiously I awaited news. If the results of his last examination have been so unsettling for us, I can imagine what they must have meant for you, poor man. But it is not the time to lose heart; you must react with strength and courage, both physically and morally; it is a victory which can be attained, which must be attained. Never more than now, is it the time to say, "Where there's a will, there's a way."

I think the doctors have explained to you the reasons that have delayed the healing; yours is an exhausted body, that lacks the elements that connect and fortify bones. (You have reached this point!) But the organism in general is there ready to improve, and to begin the vital organs working again. Of course, this condition is painful, very painful. But you will overcome it, with will, with iron will. . . . Let beneficial, moral distractions come to your aid. Aren't we all here to help you? The poor leg still needs to be bandaged? And you must still remain motionless? All right, let's find a way to enable you to work on a piano, distract your mind, discover sounds, invent melodies, and slowly start working again. All this without strain, without worries, without irritating nervousness — and this would be a large factor in your recovery.

And wouldn't it be possible later, in the summer, to go to the mountains, to breathe some pure, regenerative air? It might be a kind of sacrifice, but the recovery of your health is worth any sacrifice.

Tito just came back yesterday; in two or three days we meet with Giacosa, and then he and Tito will come to see you. And I hope too that our dear Butterfly will soon come to you and will draw you in her arms in a healthy and glorious embrace.

I wonder how many times, while reading this interminable letter of mine, you drew back with impatience, with rebellion. My poor son! But I do not regret it. My conscience is at peace, my heart is lighter and I say this to what I have written: Go and penetrate his heart and persuade him, in the name of God, that you have been dictated by my real, great, and loyal affection, and it is with such affection that I embrace him tenderly.

Puccini, both stunned and moved by this extraordinary letter, never answered Ricordi directly. Instead, he wrote a letter to Illica, which he felt certain — and he was right — would be forwarded to his publisher, friend, and mentor. The letter, a firm denial of the lightly veiled charges that a venereal disease, caused by his relationship with Corinna, had resulted in his decline, as well as a gentlemanly defense of a woman he had loved, was also a plea to be taken back into the fold by a man he had long considered a father. It read, in part:

At last, Signor Giulio has written a long letter, a real indictment. But it was not at all convincing nor did it conform to the truth. It was, also, somewhat ungenerous toward a certain person. . . . One shouldn't make these accusations without evidence, but I imagine that undue influences and unfair rumors have made him judge too harshly. He is wrong, too, about my illness — I would like to answer him, but at the moment I have a toothache which does not permit me to think clearly. If only I could talk to him!

Nonetheless, his affection for me shines forth from his letter like the sun, and this has greatly consoled me. You must know how I have suffered from his silence toward me! It was a real cross. I wish I could talk to him! I can't refute his charges, especially by means of a letter. He is a man of the world, and certain judgments he made could be changed if I could only talk to him. These judgments are very painful when not substantiated by truth or by solid evidence and leave one's soul either puzzled or rebellious. I wish I could write the way my soul dictates on a subject that even you don't want to hear about. All right! What really saddens me is to be here with my thoughts and without one person to whom I can open my heart. . . .

It was, of course, not a toothache that prevented Puccini from responding to Ricordi; instead, the composer was obviously exhausted by the controversy, the fights, even tired of the affair itself. He had had enough, and would make every effort to resolve the problem, but he could no longer spend the energy to justify the complicated, unpleasant situation. He was, however, determined to end it, though it obviously meant a difficult battle—Corinna was not a common whore as Ricordi believed, but an intelligent law student. It is impossible to ascertain exactly what the humiliated young woman's demands were—though it seems clear that she would not let her little fish out of the net without some monetary compensation, as Illica had suggested. The problem was bothering Puccini even as late as the following October, during his visit to Paris, when he wrote troubled letters to his friends in Italy, wondering how the matter would be resolved.

In November, the composer was still distraught; on the twenty-fourth, he wrote the following letter, that of a weary and tormented man, to Illica, from Torre del Lago:

Write me often. I am here alone and sad. If you knew how I suffer! I so badly need a friend, and I have none, and if there is one who loves me, that person doesn't understand me. My temperament is so different from that of many others. Only I understand myself, and I suffer; but mine is a constant suffering, which never leaves me. Even my work gives me no relief, and I work because I must. My life is a sea of sadness, in which I am immersed. I feel I am loved by no one; understood by no one, and so many people tell me I am to be envied. Something went wrong at birth. Even you don't understand me as I would like, and perhaps you don't even sympathize with me. I would like to talk to you and unburden myself. But you are so far away and to listen to lamentations is certainly not amusing.

If you could only come down here. We're alone, come with your wife, stay a few days. Your company would do me so much good, and our friendship would be further cemented. You tell me to read? I can't. I jot down a few notes because I have to, and I spend my time in an atmosphere of complete darkness.

On the same day, Elvira wrote to Illica, a letter which proves that she was still examining her husband's mail before sending it out. She noted that she had guessed the tone of Puccini's letter and had looked at it to make certain that she was right; and she begged Illica not to betray her, since that would result in a fight between the couple which would serve no purpose.

Giacomo is going through a very sad period because of the Piemontese, who will give him a great deal of trouble, since she has (as we
had foreseen) already started to blackmail him. In spite of all the
evidence concerning the behavior of that perfidious woman, he still
hopes in his heart that what he has been told is merely the result of
an exaggerated zeal on the part of those people whose task it has been
to unmask her. But this morning the blinders were removed when
he received a letter from a lawyer [from Turin] requesting a meeting
and informing him that he had in his possession all his correspondence, including his insulting letter dismissing the young lady. He
was deeply affected by it, partially because he is afraid of trouble, but
largely because he has seen his idol fall completely from the pedestal
on which he had placed her. Now I join with Giacomo in begging
you to accept the invitation and come here to try to help him
understand that it is a waste for him to grieve for such a person. If I
tried to console him, it would only irritate him—it is different
coming from a friend. Don't you agree? If we want him to finish the
opera, we must try to give him back the serenity he needs. If you
think it best, talk to Sig. Giulio about this—he knows everything.
Answer me by registered letter in care of the post office, and I will
instruct the postman to give it only to me. . . .

There is no further correspondence concerning Corinna—she had been
successfully eliminated from the composer's life. Certainly, as Elvira pointed
out, Ricordi knew everything; he had been the leader in the carefully
planned campaign to remove this powerful threat to Puccini's stability, and
he had waged the campaign brilliantly. At every point, he had been in touch
with Illica and with Puccini's sisters—all of the letters pertaining to the affair
have been found in the Ricordi files.

The day after his wedding, Puccini sent Ramelde an announcement,
writing, "Are you happy now?" and adding that Iginia, too, must be happy.
He might have added that the happiest and most relieved of all the participants in the drama must have been Giulio Ricordi.

A student at the Istituto Pacini, 1874.
(Metropolitan Opera Archives)

Below, the Villa Puccini at Torre del
Lago, 1905. *(Foto Magrini)*

With Elvira and Tonio at Torre del Lago, 1908. *(Foto Magrini)*

The Club La Bohème. *(Foto Magrini)*

With Luigi Illica. *(Foto Magrini)*

With Tonio in Viareggio.

Below, in one of his first cars. *(Foto Magrini)*

With Belasco and Toscanini, 1910. *(Metropolitan Opera Archives)*

The hanging scene from *La Fanciulla del West*, with Caruso, Destinn, and Amato. *(Metropolitan Opera Archives)*

Elvira Puccini. *(Museo Teatrale alla Scala; courtesy* Opera News)

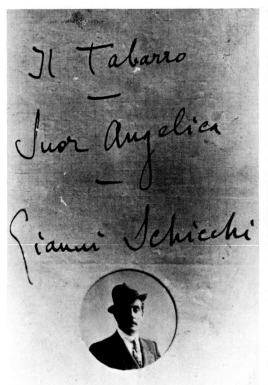

Above, illustrated postcard from the period. *(Anna Landi, Lucca)*

Right, Giulio Ricordi. *(G. Ricordi, courtesy* Opera News)

One of the most popular, and most photographed, figures of his time. *(Top left, Foto Ripari; bottom left, Anna Landi, Lucca)*

In his last year. *(Foto Ripari)*

Below, the funeral procession.
(Metropolitan Opera Archives)

Interlude: The Search
for New Subjects

Three of the most trying episodes in Puccini's life had come to an end by the summer of 1904, but certain scars, inevitably, remained. He was again able to get about easily, but the accident had taken its toll and he would never recover from it completely. Corinna was no longer in the picture, but his relationship with Elvira continued to be an uncomfortable one. Finally, with the success of his opera at Brescia, *Butterfly* had taken wing, as Pascoli had poetically predicted. The opera's hostile reception at La Scala would, however, remain a bitter memory and cause the composer serious doubts concerning the direction of his future work.

He was unquestionably both wealthy and successful, but he was far from the contented, self-confident man pictured by the press. His preoccupation with death and his feeling of inner loneliness, long part of his nature, increased with the years. He was often troubled, torn between pride in his achievements — a normal attitude considering his immense fame and popularity — and the deepest despair over what he considered his inadequacies as a man and as an artist. His suffering, rather than strengthening his creative powers as it had for other composers (Schubert noted that the world seemed to like best what he had written out of distress and misery), was an almost paralyzing factor against which he had to struggle frequently.

The summer following the Brescia *Butterfly* afforded him a much-needed rest. It was a period of recovery and a time for the private Puccini to replace the public image of Puccini. Shortly after that second première, he spent a few weeks at Acqui Termi, a popular spa where he took the mud baths in an

161

effort to regain his physical strength. After that, he divided his time between his mountain home at Boscolungo and, when the heat subsided, at Torre del Lago. At Boscolungo, with little to keep him busy, he found his greatest pleasure in racing his new car—a De Dion-Bouton—dangerously up and down the curved, narrow mountain roads, as if he had never had a near-fatal crash. At Torre del Lago, there was the inevitable hunting, and, even more important, he was able to pass the evenings with his old friends in the village, men who had no place in the life of Puccini, the international celebrity, and with whom he had been able to spend less and less time in recent years. With them, he tried to recapture a simpler past, indulging in adolescent pranks, exchanging dirty stories, happily able to forget the image of the suave, dignified celebrity that he so carefully—and uncomfortably—cultivated in public.

Once the relatively carefree summer had ended, Puccini resumed the life he had led following each of his successes—the search for a new subject on which to base his next opera, and the travels in aid of his already established works. This time, however, the search was more complicated, more desperate, and more frantic—from Mirbeau to Poe to Wilde; and the trips—in addition to what had become routine visits to Paris and London—were longer, bringing him to such faraway places as Buenos Aires, Cairo, and New York.

In the past, in his relentless quest for a new subject, Puccini seemed to have a reasonably clear idea of what he wanted. This time, however, he was floundering. Ever ready to explore new ideas, he only seemed to know what he didn't want—and he wasn't always certain of that. In answer to the many critics—including Ricordi—who felt that Butterfly was too small and fragile, he seriously considered looking for a larger work, in spite of his often-expressed belief that he was not really made for grand opera, for "heroic gestures." Also, after having killed off the tragic figures of Manon, Mimi, Tosca, and Cio-cio-san, he felt he might have had enough of what he called "teary-eyed" heroines; as a contrast he returned to the idea of a comic opera, to entertain his public. In addition, the idea of doing a few short operas, which had presented itself a few years before, once again seemed to be a possibility.

There was one more problem. Giacosa was seriously ill—he was to die in the summer of 1906—and there seemed little likelihood that the successful partnership that had created his three greatest masterpieces could continue. Illica remained, of course, and very many other librettists offered their services—to be associated with Puccini was almost certain to mean success—but changes in his method of working were inevitable.

At first, Puccini leaned towards a large dramatic theme—"something grand, new, emotional, something never before seen"—he wrote to the journalist and playwright Valentino Soldani, who for a while seemed a strong possibility as the successor to Illica and Giacosa, if there had to be such a successor. The composer considered Soldani's *Ciompi*, *Calendimaggio*, and even more seriously, his medieval drama, *Margherita da Cortona*, and carried on a long correspondence with the writer concerning future projects—but nothing materialized. Ricordi suggested *Romeo and Juliet*, a story which did not move Puccini as he felt it should, and the publisher also suggested a large-scale work based on the legend of William Tell, but that too failed to arouse the composer's enthusiasm. More interesting was an adaptation of *Notre-Dame de Paris*, which had been thought of even before *Butterfly* had been completed. Puccini had even asked Illica to sketch out a libretto based on the Victor Hugo novel as early as May, and for several months he had offered the librettist specific suggestions for what he felt certain would be his next opera. He felt less certain by July and more certain in September—when he called for serious discussions with Illica and Ricordi—but later in the fall he had lost interest, completely convinced this time that it was not for him.

In early 1905, he returned to the idea of a comic opera, a complete change of pace which he would enjoy. On March 2, he wrote to Illica: "Tonight, I feel like writing a comic opera, a real *opera buffa*, an Italian one, with no historical background and no moral lessons for anyone. Something comic, merry, gay, carefree; not biting but funny, a work to make the world double up with laughter." He was so delighted with the idea that he wrote to Giacosa about it, urging him to come up with a good idea. He thought again about *Tartarin*, which he learned was again free for possible adaptation, but neither this nor any other idea for a comic work bore fruit. Neither did his scheme for an operetta, consisting of twenty short pieces, and only many years later would he write both a comic opera and an opera that had started out as an operetta.

An almost infinite number of projects were presented to Puccini in the years following *Butterfly*, and of them a few are worthy of special attention, if only because they illustrate the composer's conflicts during this period. One idea that preoccupied him for almost three years was that of setting to music a few short stories by Maxim Gorki. Russian literature was enjoying a popular vogue in Italy during this period, and the composer buried himself in the stories of Tolstoy, Turgenev, and Gorki, finally reaching the conclusion that the ideas of Gorki were most closely attuned to his own. He felt it would be effective to bring together three short operas in one evening and decided upon the Russian master's "The Khan and His Son," "On a Raft," and "Twenty-six and One" as suitable for his purposes. The first resembles an Oriental fable, and the second and third are works of social realism. The whole work would be known as *Tales of the Steppes*. Puccini was fascinated by the exotic setting; he would have an opportunity to depict the sea, the Volga, the hovering sea gulls, a raft, and all the sufferings of mankind. It didn't matter that he hadn't been to Russia; after all he had never been to Japan, and yet *Butterfly* had not suffered. By 1907, however, he had lost interest in the Oriental tale, and he sought a way to reach Gorki, then on Capri, to see if he had any suggestions for the third opera. Before the Russian could come up with any ideas, however, Puccini had lost interest in the whole project—the Gorki stories were not, after all, what he wanted.

Another persistent idea was that of a collaboration with Gabriele D'Annunzio. This possibility particularly intrigued Tito Ricordi, who greatly admired the poet's work. Of course, too, the result of a partnership between Italy's most popular writer and her most popular composer was almost certain to be commercially successful. It had been considered in 1894 and again in 1900, when it had come to naught; it was, in 1906, once again under serious consideration.

In February, the two men met, and Puccini was encouraged. "He will," he wrote to Giulio Ricordi, "give me a theme created specially for music—a human drama in an exalted lyrical vein—three acts, interesting and moving—so he says." At this meeting, in Florence, D'Annunzio promised to prepare an outline, after which they would enter into a contractual agreement. The poet, too, was encouraged, writing his admirer Tito Ricordi that he and Puccini were in perfect agreement about the conception of the work.

In March, there was another conference, this time in Milan. The occasion was the première of an opera based on D'Annunzio's *La Figlia di Jorio*, which had been set to music by Alberto Franchetti. The opera was, in Puccini's words, a semi-fiasco, but he put the blame solely on the music and continued to hope for a collaboration with Gabriele D'Annunzio. At the same time, he did not want to risk falling out of favor with Illica, with whom he was already involved in several new projects. Afraid that his faithful librettist would learn of the negotiations with D'Annunzio, the composer wrote him a letter noting that no firm agreement had been reached with the poet as yet, and adding that if indeed the opera materialized it should not at all interfere with his additional collaborations with Illica.

In the summer, however, certain irreconcilable differences between the poet and composer began to emerge. Puccini had already rejected D'Annunzio's *Parisina* (later put to music by Mascagni) as too grandiose; and by August, the poet was working on another subject, tentatively called *The Rose of Cyprus*. After the two met in Pietrasanta, not far from Lucca, the composer was again encouraged, feeling that D'Annunzio's ideas were now approaching his own. The poet, too, was ecstatic about his new work—he could already hear the music, he said.

But there was to be no music. In a matter of days, Puccini decided against *The Rose of Cyprus*. D'Annunzio's reaction was entirely in keeping with his renowned ego. When they first met in Florence, he wrote Puccini, "You expressed your aspiration toward a higher form of human poetry, toward a profound renewal of your whole style, and I felt that the spring of your melody deserved to water a poem wherein life and dream intertwine mysteriously, as in the soul of man. . . ."

Obviously, for D'Annunzio, Puccini was not up the formidable task, though he rather condescendingly offered the composer the warmth of his continuing friendship. Puccini still held out hopes for a future collaboration, but by the end of August, D'Annunzio wrote a letter to Camillo Bondi which all but ruled out such a collaboration:

> My contacts with the Maestro from Lucca have been sterile. He is overwhelmed by the power of Poetry. Two excellent outlines — *Parisina* and the *Rose of Cyprus* — seemed too grandiose for him. He went so far as to confess to me that he needs a "small, light thing, to be put to music in a few months, between one trip and another." And for this he came to the poet of *Francesca da Rimini!*
>
> The delusion has been very sad. Not art, but commerce. Ah me!
>
> I, with great cordiality, without regretting the time that had been lost (it was not entirely lost, because I learned many new things), gave him back that liberty which I love so dearly and respect in art and in life. Now he writes me a letter begging me not to abandon him and to give him a third outline, a more humble one, and more suited to his strength. I shall try one of these days.

The two men did keep in touch, but it should have been clear that nothing could come of it. Their temperaments — personal as well as artistic — differed too greatly. Puccini demanded that his librettists submit to him entirely — and this would have been impossible for D'Annunzio. In addition, there could never be room in a Puccini opera for the poet's heroic superman.

Another project which held Puccini's interest for a number of years was that of making an opera from Pierre Louÿs' *La Femme et le Pantin*; it had first come to his attention in 1903. A short novel, published in 1898, it is the story of a teasing femme fatale, Conchita (*Conchita* was to be the name of Puccini's opera) who sadistically taunts a distinguished rich, old man, teasing him but finally refusing to yield to his desires. This leads to his insanity and to eventual violence. The novel, in some ways reminiscent of *Carmen* — a factor which must have encouraged Puccini — had been successfully dramatized for the stage by Maurice Vaucaire. Its validity as a theatrical work is confirmed by the fact that it has subsequently served as the subject for no less than five movies: in the films, Conchita has been portrayed by Geraldine Farrar (1920), Conchita Montenegro (1929), Marlene Dietrich (1935), Brigitte Bardot (1958), and the play was the basis for Luis Buñuel's *That Obscure Object of Desire* in 1977.

Puccini was so taken with the idea that he actually signed an agreement in June of 1906, to write the opera. Vaucaire was to prepare the libretto in French and turn it over to Illica for the Italian adaptation. With that in mind, Vaucaire had come to Boscolungo in August to work with the composer. "It is turning out to be very beautiful," the composer wrote to Ricordi, who was all in favor of the project. "Difficult, but, I think, convincing and original."

A month later, Puccini was discouraged about Conchita—he didn't really like his heroine, so different from his others, nor did he find any of the characters lovable. On October 1, Conchita was still weak, but the composer hoped she might recover her strength; a few days later, she had recovered her strength and was coming to life. He still had his own doubts, but he was too embarrassed to confide them to Ricordi, preferring to blame all problems on Illica, who was doing all he could to complete his adaptation. While the composer was in Paris in late 1906, he had several meetings with both Vaucaire and Louÿs. They worked together harmoniously—and they agreed that the problem was Illica's adaptation. There were good things in what he had done, Puccini felt, but essentially it was too far from Louÿs' original intentions. "We are," Puccini wrote to Ricordi, "in a glorious mess." Illica's ideas were simply not in keeping with the subject and the composer believed he would have to be replaced.

In the end, however, the blame for the failure was placed on Puccini's vacillations. It was he who had confused the issue—and Vaucaire and Louÿs as well as Ricordi and Illica felt themselves hurt and injured by what had happened.

Puccini had originally made a firm decision: Conchita was to be his next opera. He had put Louÿs, Vaucaire, and Illica to a great deal of trouble—and then had decided the subject might not be right. Ricordi was not unduly disturbed about the hurt feelings of the Frenchmen; but he felt that this change of heart might mean a complete break with Illica, who had spent so much time on the projected opera, and was still potentially of great help to the composer. In a harsh but realistic letter of November 19, 1906, Ricordi reminded Puccini that things were not as simple as he might have assumed:

> Take care; if you renounce Illica you will not be able to use any of his ideas, and that means da capo. . . .
> Perhaps you will be astonished to read this. But between friends, as people who esteem each other and who love each other, one may be frank and call things by their right names. Regarding the millions that my firm is earning—just like that!—do you want to know, my dear Puccini, the truth? Up to now, Butterfly is a liability. . . . What with the administrative expense, the personal representation, the voyages, more voyages, regal suites, banquets, and all other incidental nuisances.

I am saying this because if all our affairs were to go like this, I would be constrained to roam "homeless and poor," and perhaps the good Giacomo would come occasionally and take me out in his 275 H.P. automobile for a ride around the bastions. . . .

Nonetheless, long live *Madama Butterfly* and Giacomo, Doge, and Imperator. You know very well that you are like a son to me, and my affection for you will always be the same, as well as my trust. I only wish to see clearly in this murky fog of the future. I cannot discern when the sun of *Conchita* will break through.

You can never say of me that I have not lent myself to all your desires. Even recently I resumed friendly relations with Illica just so that we might succeed in getting some results. Now we are at *sicut erat in principio*. That is the reason why today my liver is manufacturing enough bile to supply a whole stock company. . . .As to all composers, French, English, German, Turkish, and Abyssinian—
A BUNCH OF IDIOTS!!

In spite of Ricordi's pleas, Puccini's grave doubts about *Conchita* lingered; his heart was not in it. Nonetheless, he was not willing to abandon the project entirely until he had another more promising subject at hand.

That subject might be, he felt, *Marie Antoinette*, which had first been considered after the completion of *La Bohème*, and which had already occupied a great deal of Illica's time. So, of course, had Gorki and so had *Conchita*, and it is a tribute to the librettist's patience—or his desire at all costs to continue a collaboration with Puccini—that he even considered working again with the changeable composer.

Ricordi had always seen in *Marie Antoinette* the perfect vehicle for Puccini's talents, and as early as March of 1904 he had expressed his regrets to Illica that the composer had apparently abandoned the idea of an opera based on the French Revolution. Nonetheless, he had no choice but to resign himself to Puccini's rejection of the idea. A year later, however, other composers—chief among them Mascagni—showed interest in the subject. Both Ricordi and Illica knew their composer, and knew that interest on the part of other composers could only stimulate his own interest; therefore they resumed pressure on Puccini to resurrect the project, this time successfully convincing him that only he could bring the dramatic story of the queen to life. Unfortunately, however, this resurrection of a discarded project resulted in little but hurt feelings, bitter disagreements, and a great deal of lost time.

Even Ricordi, in spite of his enthusiasm for the idea, seemed to sense failure when he proposed a meeting with Illica and Puccini in March 1905 to discuss the matter in detail; at the last minute he canceled the meeting, declaring it would be useless since Puccini obviously did not share his enthusiasm. The composer's feelings were hurt; he felt he was misunderstood, that his reservations concerning the opera did not mean final rejection of the idea. While repeating his misgivings, he claimed he was prepared to be convinced he was wrong and couldn't understand why his publisher refused to give him a chance to change his mind. Once given the chance, he exercised the privilege—too many times, for all concerned. Hardly a month after seriously reconsidering the project, he came to the conclusion that the opera was not for him, that it was "frighteningly enormous." Two weeks after that, he urgently requested a meeting with Illica, to discuss the often-rejected work again. Throughout the summer that followed, while in South America, he continued to think about it. When in doubt, and he was most often in doubt during this period that followed *Butterfly*, his thoughts kept turning to Marie Antoinette.

By November, Illica was exasperated, and with good reason. He had worked for eight years on this libretto, and because of that he was reluctant to give up. However, he was unable to understand Puccini's endless vacillations. The subject was, he wrote Ricordi, perfectly suited to Puccini. "So majestic, so extra-grand opera on the surface, yet so humanly gentle and feminine. . . .And Marie Antoinette, the character, is a perfect link, a golden one, to the literary creatures that form Puccini's glory: Manon, Mimi, Musetta, and I would even add Tosca. . . .But she would be even stronger because of the historic truth, because of the more powerful drama that surrounds her. . . ."

The librettist's enthusiasm was apparently for a short time contagious, and Puccini began to offer a series of constructive ideas, as well as a detailed scene-by-scene outline of how he saw the opera. Basically, however, he was still torn—the enormity and the length of the proposed opera frightened him, but he remained fascinated by many of its individual episodes. Something else was wrong, and he suggested it might have been the fact that it was a one-woman opera, so he was still unprepared to commit himself completely to this new undertaking. In early 1906, he wrote to Illica that the opera, at least temporarily, had to be put aside.

The composer's instincts were right in postponing and, finally, giving up both *Conchita* and *Marie Antoinette*. The former was a psychological drama, calling for the portrayal of intense inner emotions, too modern in theme and approach for the creator of Mimi and Tosca; the latter subject called for a grand opera, more suited to Verdi's temperament, and too old-fashioned for a composer who sought something new and different. This was a problem that was to plague him for the rest of his life: he was not a nineteenth-century composer—much of his music was written during the first quarter of the twentieth century—but neither did he belong completely to the following century. Schoenberg, Debussy, Richard Strauss, among others, brought music into the twentieth century, while Puccini remained on the brink. The composer was well aware of this conflict in his temperament—he paid close attention to what was being done by other composers—and this awareness troubled him throughout his long search for a libretto. He badly wanted something new and different, but he was uncertain of his ability to achieve it. When, during the first decade of the twentieth century, that search finally came to an end, in the course of one of his many trips, his decision and the opera that resulted from that decision reflected musically his position as a composer who bridged two centuries.

No matter what his place in the history of music might have been, and no matter what inner turmoil this might have caused him, Puccini's astounding popularity could not be questioned, and in the years that followed *Butterfly* he traveled far to solidify that popularity, also hoping to find the subject for his next opera in the course of those travels. The longest trip was undertaken in the summer of 1905, when at the invitation of the Argentinian newspaper *La Prensa*, he and Elvira embarked for South America. He was to be paid the then enormous sum of 50,000 francs, in addition to the money for his passage and that of Elvira, and they were to be provided with luxurious accommodations in the newspaper's own building. He was promised hunting parties, a round of tourist excursions, and the production of five of his operas, including a newly revised version of *Edgar*, at the Teatro de la Opera in Buenos Aires. Even the fact that the visit would be "poisoned by banquets and speeches" (he asked Illica's help in preparing a few words that he might say in addition to his customary "Thank you very much") did not dim his enthusiasm as he embarked on this exotic adventure on June 1.

The trip was an unqualified triumph. After a stop at Montevideo, the couple landed at Buenos Aires on June 23, Elvira somewhat weakened by a prolonged bout of seasickness. The reception at the pier was overwhelming. There were cheering mobs, and local bands played excerpts from the composer's operas; it was a hero's welcome in every way. In a city whose cultural life was dominated by a large and affluent Italian colony, Puccini's every move was front-page news throughout his entire stay. At the opera house, too, all went well, except for *Edgar* which, once again, was not a success. But this failure was compensated for by the enthusiastically acclaimed performance of Rosina Storchio as Butterfly—a more than welcome contrast to the La Scala fiasco.

After more than a month in the Argentinian capital, the composer was—as after all his trips—more than happy to return to the quiet of his own home. He had had enough of formal banquets, speechmaking, and never-ending adulation. However, before long, he was again ready to leave Torre del Lago, this time for London and another season of his operas at Covent Garden. Most important for Puccini would be the performance of *Butterfly*, since the South American trip had forced him to miss the Covent Garden première of July 10. That première had been most successful, with audiences and critics both applauding the opera and its cast—Emmy Destinn was Butterfly and Caruso sang the role of Pinkerton. *Punch* felt that the soprano was "destinn'd for the part," and the reviewer for the *Daily Telegraph* thought it was the composer's finest opera. The *Times'* critic found the music original and distinguished; he especially praised the intervals of pseudo-Japanese music, which he felt conveyed genuine emotion. At a banquet following the première, Tito Ricordi, who had supervised the production in place of the composer, spoke: "The wound still open in Puccini's heart will draw a greatly beneficial balm from the flattering and exceptionally decisive judgment of this evening."

Puccini would have thoroughly enjoyed *Butterfly's* vindication in England, but he had a second chance to savor it on October 25, 1905, when it was again given with great success at Covent Garden. He had carefully supervised the production — this time starring Rina Giachetti and Zenatello, the original Scala Pinkerton — and following each act, he was repeatedly called before the curtain to accept the cheers of the audience. He was more than ever ecstatic about England, which he contrasted with Italy in a letter written from his room at the Hotel Savoy to Alfredo Caselli: "I'm in my real country," he wrote. "How well one lives here, in spite of the fog which, however, has its own poetry. I have been fêted, wooed, and applauded to the point of delirium. Here my soul breathes."

In addition to Puccini's pleasure at his triumphs in London, this visit gave him a chance to meet and be interviewed by his first biographer, Wakeling Dry, an Englishman. Published in 1906, Dry's slim volume is of no great importance — the author admits his knowledge of Italian was somewhat limited — but it provides an amusing picture of the composer in 1905. "A big broad man, with a frank open countenance, dark kindly eyes of a lazy, lustrous depth, and a shy retiring manner," the author begins. "Such is Giacomo Puccini, who is operatically the man of the moment." Dry notes that while *Butterfly* was the sensation of London at the time, the composer spoke not of his own work but of the achievements of the interpreters, and of the excellence of the production. "He has a quiet sense of fun, too," Dry goes on. "Let us step quietly,' he said — as we came into the range of the scene that was being enacted — 'like Butterflies.' " Sense of humor apart — and it is clear that Dry did not have access to Puccini's earthy and sometimes scatological verses which he penned on various occasions — the author enlisted from his subject a statement of some significance: "I am determined not to go beyond the place in art where I find myself at home," he told Dry.

Most important of all during this stay in the British capital, Puccini formed a lasting friendship with a woman who would play a vital part in his life. Her name was Sybil Seligman; the wife of an immensely wealthy banker, David Seligman, she was to be an unfailing source of compassion, and of intelligent understanding for all of the composer's remaining years.

The daughter of a noted pianist, Zillah Beddington, Sybil was a leading figure in London's social and cultural world, known for her beauty and her elegance as well as for her tireless devotion to the arts. A singer of some talent—she had studied with Francesco Paolo Tosti—she was an ardent Italophile. Both she and her husband spoke fluent Italian, and their home was a meeting place for every visiting Italian artist. Caruso was one of their closest friends.

The relationship between Sybil and Puccini was, however, a special one; it has been recorded in letters from the composer which were collected, translated, and selected by the Seligmans' son Vincent. Though this collection of letters is only a selection of those written by Puccini and includes none written by Vincent Seligman's mother, it is evidence of a warmth and mutual understanding that was unique in the composer's relationships with women. Rightly or wrongly, because of Sybil's extraordinary tact, Elvira seemed to feel no jealousy toward her husband's English friend. This was a tribute to Sybil, who went out of her way to become a friend of the family; Puccini never returned to Italy from one of his many short trips to London without bringing with him a gift from the cultured Englishwoman to Elvira. The Puccinis and the Seligmans spend holidays together—in Nice and in Abetone; they shared their personal problems and offered each other comfort in times of stress.

However, it was the love between Sybil and Puccini that served as the basis for this family friendship. They had first met at Tosti's home in the spring of 1905; they renewed their acquaintance in the fall, after which their friendship grew to become an important element in both of their lives. The composer's letters, especially at the beginning of this friendship, are remarkably touching and gentle. "How I remember everything—the sweetness of your character, the walks in the park, the melodiousness of your voice, and your radiant beauty," he wrote from Torre del Lago shortly after returning from London in November 1905. Obviously, he was in love, but it was a different kind of love for him—no fleeting sexual adventure this time, but a love based on admiration, respect, and deep friendship.

Whether or not there was any sexual relationship between the two—and if there was, it was of short duration—Puccini was able to confide to Sybil his innermost thoughts, certain that she would respond sympathetically. On April 6, 1906, he wrote her a letter similar to those written previously to Illica and Caselli, yet far different in tone. "I make the mistake of being too sensitive," he wrote, "and I suffer too when people don't understand me or misjudge me. Even my friends don't know what sort of man I am—it's a punishment that has been visited on me since the day of my birth. It seems to me that you are the person who has come closest to understanding my nature—and you are so far away from me. . . . I am sending you a little photograph to remember me by—a thousand affectionate thoughts for that exquisite and beautiful creature who is the best friend I have."

To Sybil he was able to write freely of his frustrations in his search for a new libretto, certain that she would respond with intelligence. "I am so utterly depressed by this feverish and disheartening period of searching; not only I, but those who are near me, my publishers and many others, are losing heart," he wrote her in January of 1906.

Sybil responded, doing her best — then and later — to find a subject suited to his temperament and talents. Among her first suggestions were *Anna Karenina*, *The Light that Failed*, *Enoch Arden*, and *The Last Days of Pompeii*. Puccini, however, quickly rejected Tolstoy, Kipling, Tennyson, and Bulwer-Lytton. Far more interesting to him was Sybil's proposal of a play by Oscar Wilde — either *The Duchess of Padua* or the unfinished *A Florentine Tragedy*. Wilde was then in vogue, with Richard Strauss' *Salome* the talk of musical circles throughout the world, and Puccini was particularly drawn to *A Florentine Tragedy*, a copy of which Sybil had obtained from Robert Ross, Wilde's literary executor, and sent on to Puccini. He eventually gave up the idea, but before doing so, he expressed a belief that it would rival *Salome* but that it would be more real and human and thus have more meaning for the average man.

In spite of Sybil's enthusiastic help, by the beginning of 1906 Puccini was no closer than ever to finding the right subject for his next opera — though he had not completely given up on either *Conchita* or *Marie Antoinette*. The public, too, was beginning to wonder what had happened, and false reports and rumors circulated with increasing frequency. Among these was the startling announcement in the February 24 issue of New York's authoritative *Musical America* that Puccini's *The Roman Empire* would be completed by August and that the composer had already entered into negotiations for an opera to be based on *Cyrano de Bergerac*.

No opera, of course, would be completed by August, and the composer filled his time by continuing to travel in aid of his earlier works. *Butterfly* had taken wing throughout Italy, and Puccini followed her from Milan (where the opera was successfully launched, not at La Scala but at the Teatro Dal Verme) to Bologna (where Toscanini conducted), Turin, and Naples. In March 1906, he crossed the border and went to Nice for the French première of *Manon Lescaut*. The performance was poor, and he was embarrassed. In spite of this, Massenet's irritated publisher withdrew from Nice permission to perform any of the French composer's operas, an action with which Massenet was in total disagreement — he admired Puccini and felt there was room for two versions of the Manon story, even in France.

In May, Puccini traveled to Budapest for what amounted to a Puccini festival, with one week devoted to performances of *Bohème*, *Tosca*, and *Butterfly*. The latter was an outstanding success; there were a total of forty curtain calls. On his way home, the composer found time to stop in Austria to hear Strauss' *Salome*, which he found very interesting, but finally very tiring. Afterward, there were short visits, several of them, to London, to hear his operas, which dominated the stage of Covent Garden, and to see Sybil. On the way back to Italy after one of these visits, he stopped in Paris to make final arrangements for the Opéra-Comique production of *Butterfly*, for which he would once again travel to the French capital in the fall.

Puccini hoped that the Paris visit would be a short one, for it was to be followed in a few months by an extended trip to the United States, and he badly needed a rest in between. Unfortunately, as had happened before, the visit, begun in October, lasted for more than two months. Everything went slowly, and the première of his opera was subject to innumerable delays. Puccini was again pleased by the meticulous care given to the production by the director Carré, but he was eager to finish his work. He was far less pleased, however, with the Butterfly, Marguerite Carré, the director's wife. He found *Madame pomme de terre*, as he called her, unconvincing, weak, and unintelligent, but he knew that there would be no production without her and valiantly made every effort to encourage and compliment her, no matter how much her actions on and off the stage irritated him.

It was not a happy time, and he felt depressed. "I see everything through dark-colored spectacles," he wrote Sybil. "I'm tired to death of everything — including Opera," and he begged his friend to join him in the French capital, or, failing that, to find him some kind of medicine to raise his spirits. "Such a medicine must exist in London," he pleaded, "and you who know everything will find it for me — for your faithful friend who cares for you so much."

Sybil promised to join him in Paris, and in the meantime she sent on an elixir — it relieved the composer's depression to some extent, undoubtedly because it came from Sybil. Nonetheless, he continued to be plagued by both ill humor and ill health. The seemingly endless waiting for the première discouraged him and unnerved him; he felt he was wasting time which would have been better spent in his quest for a new libretto. To this end, while in Paris, he did manage to have several meetings with Vaucaire and Louÿs about *Conchita*, and he even talked Illica into joining them for a few of their conferences, but it was becoming clear that their differences in approach to the subject were irreconcilable.

Again, there was the round of parties, receptions, official occasions which continued to bore and tire the composer. He yearned for the peace and informality of Torre del Lago and wondered why he continued to make engagements that he invariably regretted later. He was also confused. "I am fine when I am in Torre," he wrote Ramelde; "that is the life for me. Yet when I am there I get bored, and now I long for it because I cannot go there." Elvira, who had accompanied him, helped as much as she could during his periods of depression yet she was often unwilling to join him at formal dinners, preferring to eat alone in her room. "She is happy when she can put her ass in bed and sleep for nine or ten hours," he wrote Ramelde.

By late November, a short visit from Sybil cheered him up, but shortly after her departure he wrote her another letter filled with sadness. "I'm not at

all well—since the moment you left, I've had nothing but days of discouragement, filled with the usual unhappiness. All I ask is to be allowed to retire into my shell—if only I could get out of going to America, or put it off...."
At the very least, he hoped for a few days at home to relax before his overseas trip began.

This was not to be. The première, finally rescheduled for mid-December, had to be postponed again, this time because Madame Carré had come down with a sore throat and fever. The new date was December 28, by which time the composer was so exhausted and discouraged that he had almost lost interest in French reaction to his opera. Paris, however, had always been a special challenge for him. The French had resented both *Bohème* and *Tosca*—how, they wondered, could an Italian accurately interpret works first conceived by Frenchmen? The management of the Opéra-Comique had not even dared put on *Manon Lescaut*. These problems, at least, did not seem to exist in the case of *Butterfly*, based on an American story and play, with apparently no French associations, and the composer still hoped that this latest opera of his would meet with critical approval in France. (He was not worried about the Parisian public, which had already taken to its heart his earlier works and had made them a mainstay of their opera house.)

Unfortunately, the French critics had many reservations even about Puccini's latest work. Some even commented that its source was, after all, French once again, noting, with good reason, similarities to Pierre Loti's novel *Madame Chrysanthème*—"One can bet anything that without this first Madame the second Madame could never have seen the light of day," Arthur Pougin pointed out in *Le Ménestrel*.

The composer did not remain in Paris to answer his critics. Once free of his commitment to be present at the première, he and Elvira hurriedly returned to Italy where they purchased heavy winter clothing—they had been warned of New York winters—and prepared to embark almost at once on their first trip to the United States. In spite of all the effort and rush involved, the trip would prove to be worthwhile, for there the composer was to find at last the subject for his next opera.

"The Girl Is More Difficult than I Thought"

When Puccini boarded the *Kaiserin Auguste Victoria* for New York on January 9, he was close to nervous exhaustion. The frustrating search for a new libretto and the incessant traveling had culminated in two months of near inactivity in Paris after which, he wrote Sybil, he was "bored to tears with Opéra-Comique, Ritz, Rue de la Paix, Faubourg St. Honoré, Champs-Elysées. . . ." He had also had more than enough of the disagreeable Madame Carré and Pierre Louÿs, who had plagued him throughout his visit.

Though he desperately needed the peace and quiet of Torre del Lago, he knew that the trip to New York was important for his career. The Metropolitan Opera had offered him the considerable sum of eight thousand dollars to supervise the first performances there of *Manon Lescaut* and *Madama Butterfly* and to help in whatever way possible with the current productions of *Bohème* and *Tosca*, already well-established favorites at the New York opera house. Not only profit but prestige would result from his trip; the finest singers—above all Caruso—would be performing his music at what many considered the world's leading opera house. In addition, he realized that in America he might find the new and exotic setting he had sought for his next opera.

In any case, the ocean crossing was sure to provide time for relaxation—a luxurious cabin, with adjoining bath and sitting room, had been booked for the journey, together with a "vomitorium" for Elvira, who had not forgotten the trip to South America. As expected, the composer was immediately delighted with the luxury liner's amenities which included, he wrote

175

Ramelde, "a winter garden with real palms and flowers . . . and a room for gymnastics, with wooden horses that trot electrically—the American ladies go there every day and ride the horses to have their uteruses shaken."

Elvira had ample opportunity to use her vomitorium. The last days were marked by such rough seas and heavy fog that the ship's arrival was delayed by more than twenty-four hours, which meant that there was no chance of the composer supervising rehearsals of *Manon Lescaut* and even doubts that he would make the opening night curtain. When he finally disembarked, at six o'clock on the evening of January 18, it was a scant two hours before the performance was to begin. He was tired and nervous, having spent the day sending frantic wireless messages to officers of the Met. After a short statement to the press—"I am thinking of writing an opera with Western America as a background and want to get in touch with David Belasco"—the composer and his wife were rushed to their tenth-floor suite at the Hotel Astor and then to the Metropolitan. The first act had already started, and the Puccinis and their party—officials of the Metropolitan—slipped quietly into the director's box. At the end of the act, the composer's presence was noted, and the orchestra broke out in a tremendous fanfare, after which the *Herald* reported, "one of the most brilliant audiences of the season applauded and cheered for nearly five minutes. . . . All over the house people rose, women in the boxes waved their handkerchiefs, and there was what looked like a perilous craning of necks over the upper balcony in the general endeavor to catch a glimpse of the famous composer."

Puccini was overwhelmed by this reception, rising to bow from his chair in the box at frequent intervals. "Every time there was applause I had to get up and sit down I don't know how many times. I felt like one of those puppets you see in a circus," he was to tell a friend.

At the conclusion of the second act, the composer was dragged before the footlights between Caruso and Lina Cavalieri, the Manon. At one point, the two singers left him there alone. "He stood very much embarrassed," the *Times* reported, "and the applause was deafening." According to the *Herald*, "enthusiasm surpassed anything the opera house has echoed to in many a moon." Before Puccini was allowed to return to his box for the third act, he was encircled in a wreath and deluged with bouquets.

After Act Three, the opera's most dramatic and rousing one, the composer did not make an appearance before the curtain; he remained in the director's box and vigorously applauded the singers. This display of modesty, which further endeared him to the public, was not quite as innocent as it seemed; Puccini confided in a letter to Tito Ricordi that he purposely wanted to behave in a "serious and dignified way" as a contrast to the behavior of Mascagni and Leoncavallo, both of whom had been full of their own importance during their visits to New York.

At the end of the performance, there was tumultuous applause, and again

Puccini bowed several times from the stage. He then returned to his box, greeted his admirers and issued a formal statement, expressing his delight with every aspect of the evening.

The composer must have been delighted, too, with the New York critics' response to *Manon Lescaut* the next day. The *Sun* felt that "what will appeal most forcibly to the musical listener to this work are the crystalline transparency of the scoring, the dainty, delicate, and piquant conceptions of the comedy scenes, the perfect adaptation of means to end in the treatment of the subsidiary voice parts in the concerted bits and ensembles, the virile breadth and force of the love music, and the poignant dramatic expressiveness of the final scene." The *Tribune* preferred *Manon Lescaut* to all of Puccini's operas, finding it "fresher, more spontaneous, more unaffected." The critic for the *Times* called it "an unqualified success," commending the composer for the many "moments of passion and uplifted emotion," as well as "the numerous mellifluous and sonorous airs, finely expressive of such emotions."

Puccini's first formal press conference took place the next day. At this meeting with reporters, he again expressed interest in composing an opera with an American theme. "If I could get a good Western American libretto, I would undoubtedly write the music for it. The Indian does not appeal to me, however. Real Americans mean much more, and there are costume effects to think of. I should think that something stunning could be made of the '40 period."

Apparently, none of the reporters bothered to question Puccini about his definition of "real" Americans, but the composer did admit that he knew the West only through translations of Bret Harte. He went on to say that he would not necessarily visit the West if he chose a Western subject. "Human nature is very much the same everywhere," he stated, "and while I shall endeavor to indicate the color, it is not essential that I should visit the place to do that."

The journalists at this first formal press conference were most favorably impressed by the maestro. The representative of the *Times* was especially, and agreeably, surprised by his attitudes and appearance, commenting that "Mr. Puccini in talking used no temperamental or foreign gestures. He adopted no affectations. Even his hair is cut!"

The composer also made a strongly favorable impression on New York's musical world. He was tireless in working with the principals of his operas, driving them to perform as they had never performed before. After Emma Eames had sung an especially moving Tosca, the reviewer for the *Sun* noted that "the presence of Mr. Puccini in this city is not without its influence." Critics noted, too, that Marcella Sembrich had made noticeable alterations in the interpretation of Mimi, as a result of her rehearsals with Puccini, leading to her finest performance in the role to date. The Met's prima donnas were working hard, forced to go over each detail of their roles with painstaking care. Some complained, while others grudgingly praised the composer's efforts. One unidentified artist told W.J. Henderson of the *Sun:* "We spent an hour and a half this morning on something that takes a minute and a half to do. You know we have not been in the habit of doing such things in this house." The singer admitted, however, that "when he was through with us it went exactly right, and it is going to make its effect."

As much time as he devoted to his already established operas, he lavished even more attention on *Butterfly*. An Engligh-language version of the opera, directed by Tito Ricordi, was in the midst of an extraordinary tour that was to cover more than sixty cities in the United States and Canada—a distance of 14,000 miles and a total of more than two hundred performances. But the first Met performance, in Italian, was to take place on February 11, and Puccini worked day and night with the orchestra and the chorus, as well as with the principals—Caruso, Antonio Scotti, Louise Homer, and Geraldine Farrar, the Cio-cio-san. Chief victim of his relentless drive for perfection was Farrar. The young American soprano, already well known for her performances in Europe's leading opera houses, had made a spectacular début at the Metropolitan a few months earlier as Juliette. Never before had she been subject to such harassment as she was at the hands of Puccini. The composer seemed to find no aspect of her interpretation of the young Japanese heroine satisfactory, in spite of the fact that she had spent months studying the figures on Japanese vases and working with a noted Japanese actress. Furthermore, he was angry that she refused to sing at full voice during rehearsals and made repeated visits to her hotel room to urge her to do so. Years later, in her autobiography, the soprano wrote that she had "slaved with ardor and enthusiasm," but that she was almost out of her mind before the première. Though Cio-cio-san was to become one of her most popular roles, she wrote that at the time of rehearsals "no such encouraging and pleasing vision was vouchsafed me."

For his part, Puccini, too, was not encouraged. Only a few days before the première he wrote a letter to Sybil saying that "rehearsals are going fairly well, but not too well, partly on account of the imbecility of the conductor, and partly on account of Butterfly's lack of *souplesse*. . . . I'm half dead," he continued. "I'm so tired of this life; I've had to arrange the whole mise-en-scene—all the musical side of it—and my nerves are torn to shreds. How I long for a little calm. Believe me, our life is not to be envied—the texture of our nerves, or at any rate of mine, can no longer stand up to this drudgery, these anxieties and fatigues. . . ."

In spite of his apprehensions, a large and glittering audience greeted *Butterfly* with unqualified enthusiasm on the night of the première. The reviews, too, were excellent, the *Herald* reporting that "the charming work made what may be fairly called a sensation." Each member of the cast came in for special praise, but the critics were unanimous in giving the composer much credit for the fine performance, due to his presence at the rehearsals. The *Times* noted that "through every measure of the performance, both in the orchestra and in the action upon the stage, was to be perceived the fine Italian hand of Mr. Puccini himself, who had molded it according to his own ideas and had refined and beautified it into one of the most finished performances seen at the Metropolitan for many a long day." The *Tribune's* critic felt that "a higher intelligence than that ordinarily at work in the Italian operas at the Metropolitan Opera House was influential." Finally, the *Herald* reported: "At every point in the score the composer's personal influence on the rehearsals could be felt in every detail of the performance and in general by its spirited movement." And it quoted the composer as saying from the wings during Act One that "everything seems to be going very well indeed. And I say so with the memory of many previous performances of my favorite opera in mind."

The reporter from the *Herald* must have misunderstood, for Puccini was far from satisfied with the performance. "*Butterfly* went very well as far as the press and public are concerned," he wrote to Tito Ricordi, "*but not so as to please me.*" He complained, too, to Sybil, saying the performance had lacked poetry, and that "the woman was not what she should have been." As for Caruso, he wrote, "I make you a present of him. He won't learn anything, he's too lazy, and he's too pleased with himself." But he did admit that the tenor's voice was magnificent.

After that first performance of *Butterfly*, Geraldine Farrar remembered in her autobiography that she somehow got home and sobbed herself to sleep on her mother's shoulders, "utterly worn out by the nervous strain and cruel fatigue of the previous weeks."

Puccini, too was worn out. He had had little time for pleasure or relaxation on this trip to America. He enjoyed walking along Fifth Avenue and looking in the shop windows and admiring the gadgets, he was impressed by the city's bright lights and tall buildings, he spent a pleasant evening in Chinatown and visited Wall Street to pay a call on Sybil's relatives; but most of his time was spent either at the opera house or in search of a subject for his new opera, preferably with an American theme, as he had told the press on arrival. This meant several evenings at the theatre, which involved no little effort on his part, for he knew no English and could judge the plays he saw only with the aid of rough summaries provided by his theatre companions, plus his own theatrical instincts. Of all the plays he saw, he was most interested in two by David Belasco — largely, of course, because of his experience with *Butterfly*. The playwright-director, too, encouraged him, remarking in an interview that the Italian composer could "give the truest and loftiest expresson to our national characteristics and ideals."

The two Belasco plays were *The Music Master* and *The Girl of the Golden West*. The latter had been recommended to him by his friend the Marchese

Antinori, and of all the plays that he saw in New York it was the one that intrigued him the most. It was filled with Belasco's spectacular dramatic and scenic effects—there was a raging blizzard on top of Cloudy Mountain, and the shrieking wind as the snow began to enter the heroine's cabin through its cracks. There were the remarkably advanced cinematic effects for which Belasco was famous, and there was Western music, with "Camptown Races," "Old Dog Tray," "The Prairie Flower," and "Coal Oil Tommy" among the songs played by an onstage band consisting of concertina, banjo and "bones." Even more appealing, and a change from Conchita and Marie Antoinette, there was a potential Puccini heroine in Minnie, the Bible-reading saloon-keeper, in love with the reformed outlaw Ramerrez, or Johnson, and loved by the rough sheriff Jack Rance. The play clearly had possibilities.

Nonetheless, Puccini was not convinced that this play was the answer to his problem. He wrote Tito Ricordi that the Wild West attracted him, but he had not seen one single drama that fulfilled his needs. Ten days before leaving America, he was desperate. "I haven't found a single new subject; I'm wandering in the darkness as usual—it's a sad thing," he wrote Sybil. "I'm so tired of my old operas that it makes me positively sick to hear them torn to pieces again. I shall either have to change my profession or find a good libretto." On the same day, Puccini wrote to Tito Ricordi. "The world is expecting an opera from me, and it is about time it were ready. We've had enough of *Bohème*, *Butter*, and Company. Even I am sick of them. . . . I am really very worried, very. I am tormented not only for myself, but for you, for Signor Giulio, and for the house of Ricordi to whom I wish to give and must give an opera that is sure to be good."

The Puccinis' departure was set for February 28, and on the day before the composer held a final press conference at the Hotel Astor. He spoke at length of his quest for a new libretto. He mentioned that *As You Like It*, *The Tempest*, and *King Lear* had been suggested to him, but that he was wary of Shakespeare. "I have thought of *King Lear*," he said, "but who could act it?" A helpful reporter suggested that Caruso and Alessandro Bonci, another popular tenor, would do admirably as the ungrateful daughters.

Italian subjects, Puccini noted, did not interest him, though he mentioned he had once seriously considered an opera based on the life of Cellini, rejecting it because of unsatisfactory love interest, and "love cannot be invented." As for *La Femme et le Pantin*, he felt that after the furor created by *Salome*, which had recently caused a major scandal at the Met and had been withdrawn, there was little hope that such a risqué plot would be accepted by the American public, an audience very much on his mind. He expressed disappointment that his search for an American theme had so far failed, but he still hoped that Belasco might soon write something that he could use. As for *The Girl of the Golden West*, which he enjoyed, he was most taken by the heroine, whose naïveté he found "refreshing" and "charming" and "adorable." He further told the press that he had been most impressed by American women in general and believed that much of the success of American men was due to the interest and help provided by their women. He did not mention to the reporters what he had written to his sister Ramelde about these same women: "The women here have some shapes! What protruding behinds, and what figures and what hair. . . . Enough to make the Tower of Pisa straighten up."

When Puccini and Elvira, the latter's arms filled with roses and carnations, boarded *La Provence* the following day for the journey home, the *World* reported that he departed with "golden memories of America in his mind and her golden dollars in his pocket." He left with more than that, however, for though still unaware of it he had found the American girl who would be the subject for his new opera. He thought about it during the crossing and upon his arrival in Paris, he wrote the following letter to David Belasco: "I have been thinking so much of your play, *The Girl of the Golden West*, and I cannot help thinking that with certain modifications it might easily be adapted for the operatic stage. Would you be good enough to send me a copy of the play to Torre del Lago, Pisa, Italia? I could then have it translated, study it more carefully, and write to you my further impressions."

In less than three years, Puccini would return to New York for the world première of his own tribute to the "adorable" American woman, *La Fanciulla del West.*

When Puccini wrote to Belasco, however, he was still a long way from making up his mind. As is clear from past experiences, an expression of interest was not the equivalent of making a decision to proceed with the serious work of creating an opera. Once back in the relaxed atmosphere of Torre del Lago, the composer's first task was to kill off two of his would-be heroines — Conchita and Marie Antoinette, whom he had refused to eliminate entirely until another project was in sight.

By March he had made his decision to abandon, once and for all, *La femme et le pantin;* he was even thinking again of turning to a work by Gorki. Pierre Louÿs was furious — he felt Puccini had made a firm commitment and even threatened to sue the composer for moral and material damages. Ricordi was no less angry, and tried as best he could to persuade his composer to go on with the adaptation of Louÿs' novel. Pressed by his publisher to give an explanation for his rejection of the opera, Puccini denied that fear of Anglo-Saxon prudery or the failure of *Salome* in New York had in any way influenced his decision. In a letter of April 11, he gave his precise reasons for his decision:

My reasons are based on practical and theatrical considerations. If there had been anything (I won't call it fear) that worried me, it was the thought of comparison with the musical color and brilliance of

Carmen. This is the only point which would trouble any composer. During the many long hours of reflection, I have examined the matter critically, from the point of view of the spectator as well as that of the composer. I believe that the character of Conchita would be inexplicable for the spectator, who must be thought of as one who had not read the novel. . . .

I don't deny that Louÿs' work is more than attractive. Perhaps it was necessary to depart more from the novel or treat it differently in order to make it clearer for the public. Doing this we might have found other contrasts, other variations, and other episodes which would have relieved the monotony that the work now seems to possess. . . .

Vaucaire brought me a completely French Conchita, lacking any original character. It was I who set the poet back on the right track, and perhaps we followed the novel too closely instead of using our imagination a bit more. . . .

In spite of the well-considered reasons for not continuing his work on the opera, Puccini graciously offered to discuss the matter again with his publisher, admitting that in the past enormous difficulties had been overcome by means of calm discussions. All this in spite of the fact that he was tired of fighting over the woman he now called his "Spanish slut." The promised meeting was held, and Puccini did his best to ward off the "Spanish assault," as he wrote to Sybil. He won — if only because he absolutely refused to go any further with the opera — and he joyfully wrote to London on May 9 that "I have sidetracked *Conchita* and I have even convinced Ricordi. Today I can breathe again — after so many days of struggle and the vilest temper." He had a new idea, but it wasn't so new — his next opera was to deal with Marie Antoinette, not the grand opera originally planned but merely the queen's last, tragic days. There would be three short acts: the prison, the trial, and the execution. And the title would be changed to *The Austrian Woman.* It would be the "new" opera he had sought, original in that it would be dominated by the soprano and a chorus, with no important role for a tenor or a baritone. Puccini was immensely enthusiastic, envisioning each scene down to the smallest detail. He bought himself a large portfolio and collected in it all possible material about the queen — letters, clippings, drawings, anything relevant to his theme. Illica was overjoyed — perhaps, after all, something might come out of all the work he had already put into the project. A formal contract was drawn up, and there was an energetic and furious exchange of letters between the two men. When, for a short time, Illica failed to respond to the composer's letters (he fortunately had other projects to work on), Puccini wrote in desperation, "I behead asparagus to keep myself in the mood."

In early June, Puccini took a short trip to London where he announced to the press his plans to write *The Austrian Woman*. He had not forgotten the American woman, however, and while in England Sybil arranged to have a rough Italian translation made of the Belasco play, which she felt was more suited to the composer than was the story of Marie Antoinette's last days. Sybil's influence on the composer was great but not great enough for him to abandon *The Austrian Woman*. Instead, he would do both operas, he decided, and on his way home he sent Sybil a short poem, which read in part:

> Dearest Syb, I'm far from sorry
> To leave at once for rural Torre,
> There to bare my manly form
> To the sun, the rain, the storm;
> While my Maiden from the West
> Lies uneasy on my chest,
> And I study "con amore"
> France's Revolution's story. . . .

By the end of June, the composer was able to start reading parts of the translation of *The Girl*, which Sybil forwarded on to him. He liked it, and on July 12 he wrote to Sybil, who had obviously been urging him to adapt the American drama: "It's quite certain that *The Girl* is the opera I'm going to do! You can rest assured, and please say whatever you like for it gives me the greatest pleasure that you should enter into my most initimate affairs." In that same letter, he asked her to find some early American music for him so that he might absorb the atmosphere of the times.

In a short time, the composer threw himself into his work with enthusiasm. He felt that he would have to make many changes in the original play, particularly in the last act, but if Belasco would agree to give him that freedom he was ready to enter into an agreement. Since Illica was busy working on *The Austrian Woman*, Puccini turned to Carlo Zangarini, a poet and journalist from Bologna, to write the libretto. His precise reasons for choosing this librettist are unknown, but he was undoubtedly influenced by the fact that the Bolognese poet had a good knowledge of English and that his mother was American. (Zangarini, incidentally, was later to write the libretto for *Conchita* for the composer Riccardo Zandonai.)

Throughout the summer, the composer and his new librettist met several times and worked in complete harmony. Puccini was completely taken with his subject and spoke of it incessantly to the Seligmans during their visit to Abetone during the month of August. At the end of that month, he wrote to Ricordi, "*The Girl* promises to become a second *Bohème*, but more vigorous, more daring, and on an altogether larger scale. I have in mind a magnificent set, a clearing in the great California forest, with colossal trees, but we will need eight or ten horses on the stage."

In the meantime, he had not forgotten Marie Antoinette; his energy was such, after his long hiatus, that he felt he could do both works at the same time. He believed, however, that Illica, who had submitted the first act of *The Austrian Woman*, would need the help of a collaborator as he had in the past. He found that first act "laconic," and suggested to Illica that he himself find the collaborator as he had said he would do when they finally reached agreement to complete the project. That way, Puccini wrote, "the work could be shared as was done in the times of poor Giacosa."

Illica was furious. He replied that he had never suggested that there might be need of a collaborator, and that he had written the first act according to Puccini's own specifications. Perhaps, he continued, it was Puccini who needed to find a good musician as a collaborator. The composer was angered, reminding Illica of the precise circumstances under which they had mutually agreed to find a poet to do the verses when the time came. "I ask you," he concluded, "which are the operas that are most remunerative to you, the ones that are known all over the world? Those by the librettists Illica and Giacosa, with music by Puccini alone."

The battle continued, with copies of all correspondence, from both sides, sent to Giulio Ricordi, whose efforts to bring the two men together again were of no avail. Either the opera would be done the way Illica felt they had envisioned it, or he would abandon the project entirely. In October of 1907, the librettist sent a letter to Ricordi, enclosing a copy of a letter he had sent to Puccini. It was to mark the end of their collaboration. In it, he defined what he believed were the differences of opinion between him and Puccini and his own feelings about the role of any libretto. "The form of a libretto is given to it by the music, only the music, and nothing but the music. That alone, Puccini, is the form. A libretto is merely the outline. Méry [the French librettist of Verdi's *Don Carlo*] is right when he declares, 'Verses in opera are written only for the convenience of the deaf.' And that is why I continue to give importance in my libretto only to the delineation of the characters, the cut of the scenes, and the verisimilitude of the dialogue, the passions, and the situations. . . .

"On the top of a libretto, there used to be written, 'Words by so-and-so,' and there was in that line a profound truth. The verse in a libretto is merely a custom of our times, a fashion which has become a rule just as has that of calling 'poets' those who write libretti. What is of real value in a libretto is the word. The words should correspond to the truth of the moment (the situation) and of the passion (the character). Everything is there, the rest is nonsense. . . ."

The matter ended there; though Illica asked that they part company as friends, they were never again to work together. Nor would Puccini ever compose *The Austrian Woman*.

Nonetheless, work continued on *The Girl*. Zangarini spent a great deal of time that fall at Torre del Lago; all was going well, and the composer was only impatient to begin writing the music. While waiting for the finished libretto he took time out to go to Vienna for the first performance of *Butterfly* in the Austrian capital. In spite of what he felt was a less than perfect performance, the opera was a great success. It was a great success, too, in Berlin, Prague, and Madrid and was being performed in twelve different opera houses in Germany. There was no longer any question of its future.

Just as his Japanese girl was taking her place alongside his other heroines, Puccini was encouraged about the American girl's prospects. On November 5, he wrote to Sybil that it was well on its way and he was certain that it would be a great success. "How I adore the subject," he wrote. "The first act is finished now, but it will be necessary to return to it later, as it needs to be made clearer and to be smartened up. The second act is nearly finished, and, as for the third act, I'm going to create that magnificent scene in the great California forest. . . ." On the eighth, he wrote her that he was completely taken up by Minnie. "The poet hasn't quite finished, but I shall soon have the libretto complete. I think the third act is going to be simply marvelous — if only the poet will understand me; but I'm going to make every conceivable effort so as to be certain of getting what I want."

Later that month, he expressed his first reservations concerning Zangarini, in another letter to Sybil, noting that he had taken too many liberties with the original and therefore the characterization and language of the cowboys and Minnie were not quite what they should be. However, he was pleased that the librettist's mother, who taught English, was helping him, and by the end of the year he was able to report that it would be a "chic" libretto. With the libretto for his new opera nearly completed, he was optimistic and light-hearted again, and his holiday poem to Ramelde ended with the lines, "Oh, people of Lucca, if you love farts, I send you one: Merry Christmas!"

By early January 1908, with the holiday euphoria at an end, Puccini began to express irritation at Zangarini's delays in sending on the completed libretto. He wrote Sybil that his new librettist was a pig, and that if the finished work were not in by the fifteenth, he would find someone else to do it. When it arrived, however, and he had had a chance to go over it with Zangarini, he was delighted. "The result is a really beautiful libretto," he wrote Sybil. "It is not fully built, but the foundations have been laid." He wrote to Giulio Ricordi, too, on February 2, declaring that he had reached the conclusion that the librettist had done a good job. "Of couse," he continued, "there have to be some literary and scenic corrections, and I will make comments in the margins. I am already savoring the moment I can finally get to work. Never have I had such a fever for it as now. . . ."

Before settling down to work, however, Puccini took one more trip abroad, this time, accompanied by Elvira, to Egypt. Outside of his attendance at a performance of *Butterfly* in Alexandria, it was to be a pleasure trip, a chance to visit another exotic setting and to relax before commencing the composition of his new opera. His impressions of the two-week visit, during which he had a chance to cover all the high spots of the tourist's Egypt, were brilliantly conveyed in a letter to Ramelde, a letter that deserves a place among the masterpieces of travel literature for its conciseness, marvelous confusion, and final exhaustion:

> The pyramids, camels, palms, turbans, sunsets, sarcophagi, mummies, beetles, colossi, columns, tombs of the kings, boats on the Nile, which are nothing but our Freddane enlarged, the fez, large gowns men wear, the blacks, the mulattos, the veiled women, the sun, yellow sand, ostriches, the English, the museums, Aida-style arches, Ramses I, II, III, etc., the fertile mud of the Nile, the cataracts, the mosques, the flies, the hotels, the Nile Valley, the ibis, the buffalo, the nagging street vendors, the stench of fat, minarets, Copt churches, the tree of the Virgin Mary, Cook's ferries, donkeys, sugar cane, cotton, acacias, sycamores, Turkish coffee, bands of pipes and drums, religious processions, bazaars, belly dancing, crows, blackhawks, ballerinas, Dervishes, Levantines, Bedouins, the Kedive, Ahebes, cigarettes, narghile, hashish, bashish, sphinxes, the immense Fta, Isis, Osiris—they've all broken my balls, and on the 20th I leave to take a rest. Ciao, your Egyptologist.

Once back home, it was time to resume work. Just before leaving for Egypt, the composer had had a chance to hear *Salome* again, this time in Naples, and his comments are of interest in light of his concern with creating something "new" in his next opera. He wrote to Ricordi following the performance: "Last night I went to the première of *Salome* conducted by Strauss, and sung (?) by Bellincioni whose dance was marvelous. It was a success . . . but how many really were convinced of that? The playing of the orchestra was a kind of badly seasoned Russian salad; the composer was there, and, everyone says, it was perfect. . . . Strauss, at the rehearsals, trying to rouse the orchestra to a rough and violent performance, said: 'Gentlemen, this is not a matter of music, this has to be a zoo: make noise and blow into your instruments!'"

A month later, in an interview printed in the *Giornale d'Italia*, he offered further opinions of Strauss, and of Debussy; these, too, are of special interest because they were given at the time Puccini was composing *The Girl*, an opera in some ways influenced by the French master. "Richard Strauss is a derivation pure and simple of Wagnerian theories. He differs from the Bayreuth master only in that he is less profound and less inspired. Through the abuse of contrasts, he becomes monotonous, but one cannot fail to recognize his genius in the first part of *Salome*.

"Debussy is more original. He has opened up to us hitherto unexplored realms. His orchestration is so ingenious that he makes dissonances agreeable and softens austerities. He has enriched the musical palette with nuances that would have remained unknown but for him, but in admiring both Debussy and Strauss I cannot forget that I am an Italian, and I remain a convinced partisan of melody. . . ."

Puccini kept this in mind while working on his new opera. After the trip to Egypt, all seemed to go well — miraculously so after the composer's long battles with Giacosa and Illica. However, by April, he was again at odds with his librettist. Zangarini, he felt, could not do it alone, and he suggested they look for a collaborator. When Zangarini disagreed, Puccini, without wasting time, decided to take the matter to a lawyer. "I *will* have a collaborator," the composer wrote to Sybil on April 8. Three days later, all parties reached an accord. A second librettist would be called in to help out, and Zangarini was rarely heard from again. In fact, the despondent poet reported many years later that the libretto was really written by Puccini himself. Nonetheless, there was a second librettist — suggested by Tito Ricordi, as was Zangarini — and his name was Guelfo Civinini, a thirty-five-year-old poet and novelist from Livorno. He was, for Puccini, satisfactory, if not much more. In May, he wrote to Sybil that the "new Poet" had redone the first two acts and that he was able to work again. A month later he admitted that "the *Girl* is more difficult than I thought — it's on account of the distinctive and characteristic features with which I want to endow the opera that for the time being I've lost my way and don't go straight ahead as I would like." Shortly afterward, he remarked that he was somewhat less unhappy but he complained of the difficulties of writing an opera at that time.

By July, he seemed to tire of his work; it was far more difficult than he had expected, and he only wanted to go ahead with it and come to the end. He was annoyed, too, at the librettists. He complained to Sybil that they were a plague and that they paid no attention to what he wanted. In spite of all this, he still liked the *Girl* and by early summer he was sufficiently satisfied with it to invite Caselli to listen to his rendition, on the piano, of the nearly completed first act. Caselli was moved as were the other friends who had listened to it; there seemed no doubt that another Puccini masterpiece was in the making.

The year 1908 had certainly been a hugely successful one for the composer's earlier operas. The French periodical *Le Guide Musical* reported that *Tosca* had been performed in fifty-three opera houses in France, twelve in Spain, eight in Austria, eight in Germany, and three in Switzerland. *La Bohème* had been heard in thirty-eight theatres in France and thirty-eight in Spain, twenty in Germany and twenty in Austria, ten in Belgium, and two in Switzerland. In addition, twenty-four European cities had already heard *Madama Butterfly*. These figures do not include the large number of houses in which the composer's operas had been performed in Italy or in Eastern Europe, or outside the continent.

Understandably, music lovers throughout the world eagerly awaited Puccini's new opera, and rumors had begun to circulate as to the time and place of the work's première. The word was that *The Girl* would first be performed at Covent Garden . . . at New York's Metropolitan . . . or in Budapest. There was speculation, too, as to which soprano would have the honor of first interpreting Puccini's latest heroine. According to some, it would be Geraldine Farrar; others reported that Emmy Destinn had been set for the role; and still others authoritatively announced that Elsa Szamosy, the first Hungarian Butterfly, would be the world's first Minnie.

Wherever it was first performed or whoever first sang it, it was known that Puccini's opera was well on its way to completion. There had been minor problems with the librettists over the summer ("One has disappeared, and the other doesn't even answer my letters," the composer complained to Ricordi at one point), but by late autumn of 1908, the composer had every reason to feel confident that Minnie would soon take her place among the galaxy of Puccini heroines.

Doria: A Scandal

In that fall of 1908, as he approached his fiftieth birthday, Puccini seemed to be—as the press insisted—the happiest of men. His work was once again going well, and even he and Elvira, though basically ill-suited to one another, seemed to have reached an understanding after the drama of Corinna had been resolved. He certainly continued to have what the Italians call "flirts"—he remained an attractive and elegant man and was much sought after by women wherever he traveled—but none of these was serious enough to threaten his marriage with Elvira. He foresaw no immediate problem other than that of completing his newest opera, and as he reached the end of that task he could not envision that his wife's jealousy was such that it would come close to destroying not only *The Girl* but their marriage and the composer's entire existence.

Elvira was never good with servants. She was demanding and imperious, totally lacking in compassion for or understanding of those who worked in her home. Her own role outside of that home—in the opera capitals of the world—was a minor one; though she accompanied her husband on many of his trips, she was most often too tired or too uninterested to participate in any of the official or formal functions that were an essential part of his career. Nor did these functions seem to interest her any more than did any aspect of Puccini's creative life.

Their home was something else—it was there that she was in command and there that she could assert her authority and play the dominant role. Servants, and they could afford to have as many as they wanted, came and

189

went, most of them having been ill treated and harassed by Elvira, whom many townspeople even felt was possessed of the evil eye. Still, the Puccini villa was the center of the small, sleepy community, and to work there was an honor, even if it meant being subjected to Elvira's tantrums and unfair demands.

Of all the many servants who had worked in the villa, none was more loyal and hardworking than a young girl who took on the job of caring for the composer after his automobile accident in 1903. Her name was Doria Manfredi, and when she accepted employment at the Villa Puccini, she was sixteen years old. A year before that, her father had died, leaving her mother almost penniless and with several small children to support. The entire village took pity on the unfortunate family, and if no one wanted Doria to become a servant girl, there was little choice. At least she would be working in the home of an illustrious man.

Doria was, by all accounts, a loving and gentle young girl, so much so that in time she became almost a member of the family and was treated, even by Elvira, as a daughter of the house. During the composer's illness and convalescence, Elvira and her family as well as Puccini's sisters were efficient and conscientious, but it was Doria who provided affection and compassion and who managed to cheer up the distraught composer. Throughout the years, Doria's responsibilities in the home increased, and her devotion to the composer never failed.

If Doria had been somewhat emaciated and sickly when she first went to work at the Puccinis, by 1908, when she was twenty-one, she had developed into a strikingly attractive young woman. Suddenly, Elvira saw her in a new light; she was no longer a pathetic servant girl, she must inevitably be her husband's latest mistress. Elvira's jealousy was often justified, but in this case what can only be described as her insane rage was turned upon a blameless, naïve young woman.

With apparently no provocation, Elvira began to torment the young servant, angrily and incessantly hurling accusations at her. In spite of Puccini's pleas, she seemed unable to control herself. She insisted that Doria leave the house; the composer insisted that she stay. Life became miserable for all three of them, and without giving details of the ugly situation Puccini wrote to Sybil on October 4 that "there are days when I should like to leave my home — but the opportunity never occurs because I lack the moral strength to do it. And yet I *want* to do it — and I'm certain that you would understand if you knew the circumstances. . . ." His work, too, suffered, and he added in this letter to Sybil that The Girl had completely dried up.

By the end of the month, the composer could stand it no longer; he fled to Paris, and from there he wrote to Sybil: "I'm all by myself and I've taken refuge here. Elvira has given Doria notice, saying that she is a . . . without *a shadow* of proof. Life at Torre has become absolutely unbearable for me; I'm only telling you the truth when I say that I have often lovingly fingered my revolver."

He knew, however, that he would have to return to what he called "that Hell," and he did so after a short visit to Milan — from there he wrote Sybil, "I only manage to sleep with the help of veronal, and my face is mottled like a Winchester gun."

Once home, things were no better, and Doria's dismissal from the house had in no way diminished Elvira's wrath. Consumed by her fury, she spread vile rumors about the girl throughout the village, rumors which were, given Puccini's reputation, inevitably believed by some who heard them. Even Doria's family began to doubt the girl, and Puccini, horrified by his wife's behavior, felt it necessary to put the true facts on the record. In the late fall he wrote two letters, one to Doria and one to her mother. The former began, "I am writing to you at home. I don't care if your mother knows about it. I know that I have a clean conscience in regards to you, and I am desolate to see you thus sacrificed and slandered. I declare openly that I am fond of you because you were always a good girl in my house. Nobody can say anything bad about you. Whoever does, lies and commits the greatest injustice. . . ." In the letter to the girl's mother, Puccini wrote that "There is not the shadow of truth in all that has been whispered. It is the result of vicious people who have turned my wife's head. I have always considered your daughter as a member of my family."

This mention of "vicious people" is the first hint that the composer believed — or wanted to believe — that Elvira was not solely responsible for her behavior. In fact, he was so alarmed by his wife's lack of reason that he felt it necessary to put some of the blame on outsiders, in this case the many members of Elvira's family who spent long periods of time in the villa at Torre del Lago.

Whoever was to blame, Elvira's rage only increased. She publicly taunted the girl, following her down the street, cursing at her as she went. In the presence of townspeople, she accused her of being a slut and a whore, and she warned her that sooner or later she would drown her in the lake. All efforts on the part of Puccini, his friends, and his relatives to calm her failed, and on December 20 the distraught composer reported to Sybil:

My work goes on, but so slowly as to make me wonder if it will ever be finished — perhaps I shall be finished first! As for the "Affaire Doria," Elvira's persecution continues unabated; she has also been to see the Priest to get him to talk to her mother, and is doing everything she can to drive her out of the village. I've seen the poor girl secretly once or twice — and the sight is enough to make one cry; in addition to everything else she's in a very poor state of health. My spirit rebels against all this brutality — and I have to stay on in the midst of it!! If it hadn't been for my work which keeps me here, I should have gone away, and perhaps for ever. . . . But I lack the courage to take action, as you know. Besides, I'm not well either; all these upsets are bound to leave their mark in the end, and it's my work especially that suffers. How can one keep one's brain clear for work and hope to find inspiration? It's impossible — impossible! I can only go on, hoping for the best and that things will settle down again. . . .

Things did not settle down; over the next two weeks they only worsened, and on January 4, the composer again wrote to Sybil:

I'm still in a state of the greatest unhappiness — if you only knew the things my wife has been doing and the way she has been spying on me! It's an appalling torment, and I am passing through the saddest time of my life! I should like to tell you everything, but I don't want to torture myself further; it's enough if I tell you that I don't want to live any longer — certainly not with her. To go far away and create a new life; to breathe the air freely and rid myself of this prison atmosphere which is killing me — Elvira keeps on talking of leaving, but she doesn't go. I wouldn't mind staying here by myself; I could work and shoot — but if I go, where should I go to? And how should I spend my time — I who have now grown accustomed to the comforts of my own house? In short, my life is a martyrdom! I'm working, yes, but not as I could have wished.

That Elvira had indeed been spying on her husband is attested to in recently discovered letters to Caselli, the old family friend who remained on close terms with both Puccinis during this period. In a letter written the night of January 22, Elvira wrote to Caselli that "last night's expedition was a failure. The pigeons didn't come home to nest. I waited uselessly for one hour. And today he left for Rome. There is no hope of catching them another time since I too will leave, for Milan, on Saturday, and who knows when I will be back here."

A few days later, it was Puccini, then in Rome, who wrote to Caselli, bringing him up to date.

. . . We had a kind of reconciliation, and I said I would let bygones be bygones. This was agreed upon, and after such a long time I finally had a reasonably good day. Next night I went out as usual after dinner — I swear I had no secret meeting. I went to Emilio's and then I talked for a while with a hunter, and after a half an hour I came back but did not find Elvira. I looked for her everywhere, but she was nowhere to be found. So I positioned myself near the door, in the dark, to wait for her. Soon I heard footsteps, and

I saw in front of me Elvira, dressed in my clothes! She had been out to spy on me. I was nauseated and sadly upset by this. . . . I didn't say a thing and left the next day for Rome, depressed.

As soon as I arrived here, I received a letter from one of Doria's brothers containing serious threats—among other things, he says he knows that Elvira has affirmed that I have meetings with his sister at eight at night outside in the dark. Can you imagine that? Now what do I do? I wrote to Elvira and I wait here. My God, this is too much! After promising not to spy anymore, she has insisted on doing things her way until the very end, and this way something tragic or certainly very unpleasant is bound to happen.

Within a few days, something tragic did happen. Under Elvira's relentless assault, Doria's health had begun to fail. She grew pale and thin. Increasingly nervous, she was reported as fainting on several occasions. Finally no longer able to withstand the terrible strain, she took poison on the morning of January 23. On the twenty-eighth, she was dead. In view of the outraged reaction of the townspeople, it is well that the Puccinis were not in Torre del Lago at the time of the tragedy.

When, in Rome, the composer learned of Doria's suicide, he was grief-stricken and in a state of despair. He wrote to Sybil that he was "irretrievably ruined," that it was the end of his family life, of Torre del Lago, "the end of everything." He added that he never wanted to have anything more to do with Elvira.

Immediately following the girl's tragic death, an autopsy was ordered, and it was determined that Doria had indeed been innocent of the charges brought against her, that she had died a virgin and, in the words of the local newspaper, that "she had been an honest girl in the full meaning of the word." Thus, Doria was vindicated as was the composer. It was clear that Elvira's senseless persecution of the young woman had led to the latter's death as well as to what seemed the inevitable dissolution of her own marriage. However, Puccini, though deeply scarred, emerged innocent in the eyes of the curious public.

There were now practical considerations to be faced. Puccini, separated emotionally and geographically from his wife, asked Ricordi to straighten out her financial matters, and he asked his long-time friend and lawyer, Carlo Nasi, to look into the situation at Torre del Lago and to deal with the formalities of a separation from Elvira. Nasi wrote to him from Torre on January 31:

I cannot hide from you the fact that I was very worried by the story going around (of which I was informed by a letter I will show you) that there had been an abortion. . . . But now even the slightest doubt has been erased, and the absolute integrity of that poor creature has been ascertained. That is a great deal, from every point of view — hers, yours, and that of your wife. It is for your wife that we must be concerned most seriously. . . . This is the situation: the entire village openly curses her, and expresses extremely hostile feelings toward her. Stories of her rows and accusations abound. Because of this it is absolutely essential that she not come here. There would be very unpleasant scenes. This is not true as far as you are concerned; you are wanted here. The family not only wants to bring charges against your wife, but they have already consulted two lawyers in order to do so. . . .

There must be a legal separation, one signed in front of the court, though without fault. One that is signed by the court after mature deliberations. Henceforth, your wife will not be able to return here. But you, on the other hand, will have to stay here after a certain period of time. It is impossible to go on living with a daily poison, and not to arrange things for the best would be folly. I have already spoken along these lines to your wife, who cabled me asking me to go to Milan. I went, I spoke to her, I told her not to move. So I am going to write to her now and tell her again that I think a separation is indispensable, especially now. . . .

On the same day that Nasi wrote to Puccini, the composer sent a letter to Sybil in London:

I'm still here and I shall remain on until the necessary arrangements for the separation with Elvira have been completed. Tosti, of whom I see a lot, cheers me up a little for all the unhappiness I have undergone. I'm a little calmer now, and my health isn't bad.

Apart from the arrangement with Elvira, it appears that other misfortunes are to follow; poor Doria's family intend to bring an action against my wife as being directly responsible for her suicide. . . .

The action which may be brought against my wife can have very serious consequences for her and — morally — for me too. God grant that the friends who have taken the matter in hand succeed in dissuading the family from bringing the suit!

My state of mind, although I have entered on a period of relative calm, is deplorably sad and pitiable. I am a wounded man — and perhaps one who may never recover.

Doria's family was not, however, to be dissuaded from taking action against Elvira — their hurt had been too deep. On February 1, a suit charging defamation of character, leading to suicide, was filed against Elvira Puccini. The deceased's mother submitted a lengthy deposition, honestly, if in florid terms, setting forth the complaint. Puccini's letters written to her and to Doria were submitted as further evidence, as was a crudely written letter penned by Doria before her death in which she protested her innocence. A character reference from Doria's school was included in the brief as were the testimonies of other friends and relatives as well as the doctor's report that the girl on her death was in "perfect physiological state of virginal innocence." The brief submitted by Elvira's lawyers was unconvincing, claiming that the defendant did not recall ever having unfairly defamed the deceased and vaguely promising concrete evidence to be produced in the future. The trial was set for the following summer.

In the meantime, Puccini and his lawyer maintained that there must be a legal separation and that the charges against Elvira should be allowed to cool off so that the court case might be avoided.

Elvira had reservations on both counts. She stated that she would agree to a legal separation, but her financial demands were so unreasonable that it was clear that she really did not accept the idea of a formal rupture of the marriage. She had mixed feelings, too, about making an effort to avoid a court case — on one hand, she seemed to agree that it was not advisable to have everything brought out into the open, with the gossip-hungry press covering every aspect of the case; and on the other hand, she stubbornly felt that, given the chance of a hearing, she could prove her innocence.

During these weeks following the death of Doria, Puccini was miserable. He didn't know where to turn. Efforts to bribe the Manfredi family into withdrawing the charges against Elvira had not been successful; and Elvira herself, in Milan, continued to make unreasonable demands, still blaming her husband and Doria for what had happened. Curiously, at the same time, Puccini was increasingly putting the blame not on Elvira but on those who had incited her to what he labeled her "insane passion."

In the meantime, the case had created an international scandal; it was news all over the world, and especially so throughout Italy. Puccini's friends rallied to his aid. Illica came forth with practical advice, suggesting that the composer take the first ship for New York. In his opinion, it would be only logical for him to go to America to work on his American opera, at the same time absenting himself from the center of the storm. Ervin Lendvai, a young Hungarian musician living in Berlin, who was a close friend, advised him to come to the German capital where he would be warmly welcomed and could work in peace. Ironically, he reminded the composer that Elvira's jealousy had been so intense that at one time she had even torn up letters from and pictures of his innocent young sister, Blanka. The irony here lies in the fact that recently discovered letters prove that the composer's relationship with Blanka Lendvai had been far more than the casual, platonic friendship her brother believed. It was for many years a profoundly passionate one.

Escape, however, was not the answer, and by the middle of February it was clear that it was time for Puccini, though greatly comforted by his friends in Rome, to return to Torre del Lago. He had been assured that he would be welcomed in the village—all resentment toward him had passed—and it was only there that he could seriously attempt to get back to his work. Nonetheless, his fear of being alone among so many tragic memories was such that he begged his sister Ramelde to join him at the Villa Puccini for a few days.

"I go back to Torre tomorrow," he wrote Sybil on February 22, in a letter summarizing the situation. "The separation is not yet definite; I expect news of it any moment now. And the lawsuit has not been withdrawn—I hope the trial will be put off, if for no other reason so that the press may stop writing about this beastly business. I'm still dominated by thoughts of the tragedy. . . ."

Once back home, life was far from normal. Puccini's family spent a great deal of time with him; Tonio, too, though for the most part siding with his mother, at first divided his time between Torre del Lago and Milan. Worst of all, the composer was unable to get back to work. "Perhaps I shall never work again. I think my life is finished, done for," he wrote Sybil on March 3. "I only want to die." He was obsessed with the tragedy, and on March 6 wrote to Sybil again:

> I can't work anymore! I feel so sad and discouraged! My nights are horrible; I cry—and am in despair. Always I have before my eyes the vision of that poor victim; I can't get her out of my mind—it's a continual torment. The fate of that poor child was too cruel; she killed herself because she could no longer bear the unceasing flow of calumny which was spread about to her mother and her relations, Elvira saying that she had caught me in the act—the most infamous lies! I defy anyone to say that he ever saw me give Doria even the most innocent caress! She was so persecuted that she preferred to die—and her strength and her courage were great. If Elvira has the slightest heart, she must feel remorse!
>
> Forgive me if I am always harping on the same subject.

In time, though, his loneliness and desolation became so overwhelming that his stand on the question of a permanent separation weakened; he still wanted a separation but only a temporary one in order to punish Elvira—after that he would take her back. He was more convinced than ever that the real culprits were those members of her family who had driven her to her unreasonable behavior. Elvira, however, was hysterical and unyielding in her anger. On March 25—apparently unaware that efforts had been made to settle the case out of court—she wrote a devastating letter to her husband. She called him selfish, hardhearted, and cowardly. She accused him of standing by and doing nothing to prevent her from being taken to court. "Something you never should have permitted to happen is that the mother of your son should appear on the defendant's dock, between carabinieri and police, just like a common criminal," she said. She reminded him that she had come to his aid during the Corinna affair, and had defended him when the spurned Torinese had threatened a suit. She was upset and confused by her lawyers' conflicting advice, she wrote him, and concluded even more angrily:

> For much too long, you have made me your victim, you have always trampled on the good and loving feelings I have had for you, and you have always offended me as the loving wife and passionate lover I have always been. But if God exists you will pay for Laving made me suffer, and there will be a punishment for you too, and then you will be sorry for all the evil you have done to me, but it will be too late. Through your selfishness, you have destroyed a family and have caused very serious damage, and if it is true that everything in this world is called to account, you too will be called to account for this. You are no longer twenty years old and no longer in good health, and soon the day will come when your loneliness will be a burden to you and you will look for the care and love of an affectionate person, but it will be too late and you will end your days alone, abandoned by everybody. Your theory that with money one can have everything is mistaken because love and the security of having loving people around you cannot be bought. Not even your son, when he thinks of the suffering you have caused his mother, will be able to forgive you. . . .

After this lengthy tirade, it is not surprising that Puccini did not see Elvira when he traveled to Milan for a new production of *Manon Lescaut* at the end of March; while there, however, he did see a good deal of Tonio, who reported that his mother was thin and worn-out and unhappy. Relations between father and son, however, were far from ideal. In spite of the love he felt for his son, who was then already in his early twenties, Puccini was clearly disappointed in him. Wanting him to follow the family tradition by becoming a musician, he was dismayed when the boy showed neither interest in nor talent for music. (It is said that the composer gave Tonio, when still a young boy, a violin and was delighted that the boy immediately began spending hours by the lake with his new instrument. Instead of studying the techniques of a violinist, however, Tonio, his father learned, had rigged the instrument up as a sailboat and had spent his time playing with it along the shores of the lake.) He was further distressed that the boy, ostensibly studying to be an engineer, was actually drifting aimlessly in search of a career. Now, more and more, with his parents divided, Tonio sided with his mother against his father. From a letter written by Puccini to his son in Munich in early April, it is clear that the relationship between the two was not, temporarily at least, a close one. "What have I done to deserve this treatment?" the composer asked. "To others you confide that you will go to

Munich, from me you hide your plan. . . . You are hurting me and your-self. I did not deserve this new affront added to all those which I have received from my family. . . . As to what is going on in our house, you judge wrongly. Very wrongly. You have let yourself be led astray by asser-tions which are contrary to the truth. . . . I love your mother in spite of everything, and I do not wish for any other outcome than a reunion with her. But this will only happen when she agrees to tell the truth according to the facts."

Tonio was deeply disturbed by the conflict between his parents. He was so torn that he even contemplated going to Africa to escape the various pres-sures, but his father was able to dissuade him, and in the end the young man returned to the family home in Torre del Lago. Before then, however, he was joined by his mother in Munich; from there the two set out on a tour of the country. From there, too, Elvira wrote what seemed like a conciliatory letter to Caselli, informing him that if she did indeed return to Torre del Lago, it would mean that many people would in the future be kept away from their home. "It seems incredible," she wrote, "that my charming husband feels comfortable only with his enemies and mine." In a sense, she too was beginning to blame "others" for the rupture of their marriage.

In late May, Puccini decided to take a trip to London and Paris; the change would do him good, and he had the excuse of checking on recent perform-ances of his operas. Before leaving, he stopped in Milan to meet with Elvira, for the first time since January. The meeting was not successful, and on May 24, from London, he wrote to Tonio:

> After having met with your mother, I became very sad because I see that her behavior towards me remains the same, nothing concil-iatory, always the same violence, and above all an unwillingness to recognize that the cause, the principal cause, of her and our misfor-tune is she herself. . . . Believe me, dear Tonio, the future looks black for us. I have every intention of returning to her, but I do not wish to humiliate myself. . . . I repeat that my best advice is for her to say that she treated the girl badly, having been deceived by appearances, and that she deplores the tragic outcome, not having had the slightest idea that such could be possible. That is what Burresi, Attalla [lawyers], and all the others are advising. Tell that to your mother, so that once and for all she will be convinced. . . .

Elvira could not be convinced; she was relentless in pressing her point of view, which she repeated in a letter written to London. The composer answered her on June 2:

> I expected quite another letter from you. I had hoped that finally you would write me, saying that you'd be happy to return and that

you will consent to what I have asked of you without further
to-do—and without contradicting all of my ideas, ideas which are
just, conciliatory, and inspired by truth and honesty. Instead, you
propose a rendezvous with witnesses on neutral territory (in Switzerland?!), etc., etc. But my dear wife, with all these discussions and
speeches, we will begin all over again where we started. There must
be no further speeches and discussions. Let's confine this to us two;
let's not drag in others. . . .

After a few days in the British capital, where he spent much of his time
with Sybil and her family, Puccini went on to Paris. By doing so, he avoided a
meeting in Milan with the lawyers who were making plans to counter the
suit to be brought against Elvira. But, still conciliatory, if only for the sake of
Tonio, he planned shortly afterwards to meet with Elvira, not at their Milan
apartment but in a hotel—thus partially fulfilling Elvira's request to meet on
neutral territory. This meeting, too, was a failure. The composer wanted the
reconciliation to take place after the trial, while Elvira insisted on reconciling
before the trial; she believed that he would abandon her again after the trial
unless a firm agreement had been worked out beforehand.

The depth of misunderstanding between the two was profound, as was
their mutual lack of trust. Following this latest discussion, Elvira wrote
another letter in which she restated her innocence and demanded that her
husband accept the blame. Puccini had no other choice than to leave Milan
for Torre del Lago, but before he did so, he wrote a firm letter to his wife on
June 12:

> I have no wish to quarrel. You write me a letter which does not
> even deserve an answer, so unjust and false is it. . . . *I* repair the
> harm that I have done? That's really too much! You who, with your
> sick jealousy and with your entourage, have poisoned my existence,
> now demand that I prostrate myself and beg your pardon? You are
> mad! Very well, do as you like. I am leaving. . . . If you wish to
> return to me, I shall always be ready to take you back. If you want to
> conduct your defense [at the trial] in the way you say you do, go
> ahead. I have nothing to fear—nothing. . . . I will not write to you
> again. . . .

Once back in Torre del Lago, he found he was still unable to work. The
months of emotional turmoil had taken their toll, and though a reconciliation with Elvira now seemed certain—he had gone so far as to make arrangements to go with her and Tonio to Bagni di Lucca after the trial—he was still
in a state of depression. In a letter to Sybil on June 16, he wrote:

> Forgive me for having ceased to write to you. I came on here from
> Milan and I'm all alone, my sister having left today. It's raining, and

I'm unhappy, with *The Girl* in front of me — silent. It's eleven o'clock at night — what great, what immense sadness!

Elvira's lawyers are doing their best to ruin her and me by giving conflicting advice, but I can understand that they want to pile up the costs so as to make a better meal, and in order that the case should be more sensational, thus giving them additional advertisement. The lawsuit, which looks rather black for Elvira, will be heard on July 6; I've done everything I possibly can here by speaking to Doria's brother, but he is implacable. He's determined to bring the action, failing which he has sworn to kill Elvira — and I believe he is quite capable of carrying out his threat. I am not personally involved; in fact he told me that he wishes me well, but that, before she died, Doria bade him avenge her on her mistress, though no harm must befall her master. . . .

If Puccini was miserable, so was Elvira. Traces of her anger remained, but as the date for the hearing neared, her attitude toward her husband mellowed and her tone at last became conciliatory. She was exhausted and lonely, and she was frightened at what might happen to her. On the advice of her lawyers, she did not travel to Pisa for the trial; she stayed in Milan, pleading illness, and thus offered no defense.

As Puccini had feared, she was found guilty of defamation of character, libel, and threat to life and limb. The sentence was a heavy one — five months and five days of imprisonment, a fine of seven hundred lire, and payment of all legal expenses. She had planned to rejoin her husband in Bagni di Lucca, but Tonio was not well, and she was forced to remain with him in Milan. On July 8, she wrote Puccini a letter that is remarkable because in it she continues to imply his guilt in the matter: "And now what do we do?" she wrote. "Appeal? What will be my defense? Tell the truth? But you know that this, now more than ever, is impossible without hurting chiefly you. What will the world say? That you let your wife be condemned? And will I have to go to prison? That you do not desire, I hope. . . ." In this same letter, she attacked her lawyer for incompetence and insisted the Manfredi family not be given a cent, that instead they be exposed for having tried to blackmail the composer.

Two days later, she declared that she no longer wanted to discuss the matter with her husband, that she no longer wanted a confession from him and that she no longer doubted him. She was distraught, and soon wrote to Puccini that she only wished she had the courage to throw herself out of the window.

In the meantime, two concrete measures were taken. An appeal, which was filed on July 21, was prepared; and talks resumed with the Manfredi family in an effort to get them to accept a large sum of money in exchange for withdrawing the charges. That latter was done, initially at least, without

Elvira's knowledge. On July 26, the entire family was at Bagni di Lucca, and Puccini was able to write to Sybil: "Now all three of us are reunited again here, and it seems as if life is going to be less unpleasant. Elvira seems to me to have changed a great deal as a result of the hardships of the separation which she has endured — and so I hope to have a little peace and to be able to get on with my work." In a few weeks, the Manfredi family accepted Puccini's offer of an out-of-court settlement, and the action against Elvira was officially declared extinct. Doria's family had had their revenge; the girl had been officially exonorated of any wrongdoing by the court, which had at the same time declared Elvira guilty as charged by the family. Now, the considerable amount of money would be useful.

The matter was closed, but for the Puccinis it could not soon be forgotten. Over a period of many months, there had been too much anger and too many recriminations for the couple to resume their former life together — precarious as even that had been. Not until the composer's last years could it be truthfully said that a degree of real affection and mutual understanding between them returned.

"I Have Minnie—the Rest Is Emptiness"

It was time to return to work, the composer's only real salvation. The public had begun to wonder about the delay in the completion of Puccini's latest work, unaware of the shattering effect of the crisis in the composer's personal life. Nor did Puccini want to divulge the real reason for his inactivity, and, in the midst of the Doria scandal, he explained to the *Giornale d'Italia:* "I have been accused of being lazy because for a few years I have remained silent. Of the many propositions I have received from librettists—some of them very well known—not only from Italy but from the rest of Europe and from America, none has corresponded to my idea of passion which my musical spirit requires, and therefore I have rejected them all. However, I fell in love with this *Girl* at once, and I will find no peace until I complete it." He concluded by declaring that he could write only when his imagination was stimulated and when melodic ideas came to him, without his having to look for them. This took time, but he was confident of his new opera because its key element was "love, always love, which reigns throughout the world."

The first act had already been completed when Puccini resumed work in August 1909; the opera was, he wrote Sybil, "beginning to take on life and strength." By the end of September, when peace if not love reigned at home, he had nearly completed all of Act Two. Only the last act remained, but he foresaw difficulties because of that act's complexities, and he also feared that the orchestration, vastly different from that of his earlier operas, would take him a considerable amount of time.

In late October, pleased with the progress made on *Fanciulla*, the composer took time out to travel to Brussels for the Belgian première of *Butterfly*. As always, he worked arduously to see that the production was a satisfactory one, but as so often happened, the première was delayed so that by the time it took place he was interested only in going home. He was, he wrote Sybil from Brussels, getting on reasonably well with Elvira—"life is fairly boring, but at least we don't have squabbles and rows—of which I have had more than my fair share." In any case, he was eager to be back at Torre del Lago, so that he might return to Minnie, if not Elvira. In that same letter, he regretted that Elvira "has taken our friendship amiss." This is the only suggestion that, for a short time, Puccini's wife did feel jealousy toward the woman who was actually her only serious competition.

At the end of the year, his New Year's wishes to Sybil ended with the words: "Am I alive? I don't know myself. For the time being, I have Minnie—the rest is emptiness."

Work on Minnie was exhausting; it occupied him to such an extent that he worried what he would do once the opera was completed and he would be alone, without his girl, and with nothing to replace her. By April the second act had been completed as had two hundred pages of orchestration. Fatigue and a bit of boredom began to set in. "I'm living like a hermit *without emotions and without anything else,*" he wrote Sybil on April 9. "I've still got the whole of the third act to do, and I'm beginning to be a little fed up with Minnie and her friends. Let's hope that the third act will satisfy me as much as the other two—if only it were finished soon."

To break the monotony, the composer, Elvira, and Tonio traveled to Paris in late spring to be present at a season of Italian opera to be given at the Théâtre du Châtelet by the Metropolitan Opera Company. Gatti-Casazza, then managing director of the New York company, had been accused of discriminating against French singers, and the audience demonstrated its hostility by booing Toscanini at the opening performance of *Aida*. The Met's brilliant singers—Caruso, Destinn, Homer, Farrar, Amato, and Scotti among them—managed to overcome this initial hostility, and the *saison italienne* was a huge success. Most surprising was the triumph of *Manon Lescaut*, which no one had dared before to present in the French capital, for fear of comparisons with Massenet's opera. The public was delighted with the score, Toscanini's conducting, Caruso's Des Grieux, and, especially the enchanting Manon of the twenty-two-year-old Lucrezia Bori—Puccini himself found the performance uniquely beautiful and the young soprano "exquisite." In fact, his only reservation, following the dress rehearsal, concerned Bori's costume, which had been made in Paris. Noting that this last-act custume, worn when Manon was starving and penniless on the plains of Louisiana, was far too clean, the composer proceeded to throw a cup of coffee on it, thus achieving the realistic effect he required.

The Parisian critics, predictably, found little to praise in the opera. Denying chauvinism — "It will be said that I am blinded by chauvinism," wrote E. R. in *La Revue Musicale*; "Don't accuse me of chauvinism," echoed Arthur Pougin in *Le Ménestrel* — their reviews reflected nothing but contempt for this Italian rendition of a French work. "Where we need a pastel, he gives us an etching," E. R. noted, adding that the French had a right to be exigent for they had Massenet's opera, a work which was so young and delicate. Pougin criticized the libretto and found the music totally lacking in charm and emotional appeal. Victor Debay, in *Le Courrier Musical*, was not disappointed — he knew in advance that this was not at all the subject for Puccini, since it called for a light touch that the composer of *Tosca* could never supply. The Italians, he felt, had made an image of Epinal from a Latour pastel. "If Massenet ever feared being dethroned, he should sleep soundly now," the critic concluded.

In spite of the press, the opera was a resounding success; each sold-out performance was wildly acclaimed, much to the composer's delight. Even more important, during this visit to Paris, arrangements were made for the world première of *La Fanciulla del West*. An agreement was made with Gatti-Casazza and the first performance was scheduled to take place at New York's Metropolitan, in the presence of the composer.

Refreshed by his latest success in Paris and spurred on by prospects of the performance of his newest opera, which would be conducted by Toscanini and sung by Caruso and Destinn, Puccini returned home to complete work on *Fanciulla*. On July 28, the composer was able to write to Ricordi, "The opera is finished — God be praised." And two weeks later he wrote Sybil that he felt it was his best opera.

To celebrate the completion of his new opera, and to celebrate too his somewhat uneasy reconciliation with Elvira, Puccini, accompanied by his wife and son, set off on a leisurely tour of Switzerland, by car. In the meantime, advance publicity was set in motion for the première of *Fanciulla*, which was to be given in December. As early as June, the New York *Times* heralded the event, pleased that the American public would be the first to hear the new opera by the leading Italian composer. In an editorial, it was noted that the opera "will comprise a realistic lynching scene in a forest. The chorus will be made up of vigilantes, cowboys, border ruffians, all singing Italian. Probably these personages are as romantic as the gypsies and *banditi*, the Druids, peasants, Egyptians and Nubians of the older operas." Shortly afterward, it was announced that the scenery and costumes for the opera would be designed and made in America, and that special attention would have to be paid to the last act, so that the horses used in it might be shown off to good advantage.

Those who had had the chance to read the score of the new opera were enthusiastic. Henry W. Savage, whose company had toured so successfully with *Butterfly*, immediately bought the rights to an English version of

Fanciulla, stating to the press that it was the composer's greatest opera. Riccardo Martin, the American tenor known for his interpretations of Puccini's earlier operas, too, felt it was superior to the composer's previous efforts—more mature and more dramatic. More important, Toscanini, who had gone to Torre del Lago to study the score with the composer and establish the tempos, was convinced that the opera would be an enormous success. Though they were to have major differences in the future, at this point the relationship between the composer and the conductor was characterized by mutual respect and admiration. Toscanini had publicly proclaimed the superiority of Puccini's *Manon* to that of Massenet, and the composer had nothing but praise for what he considered to be the conductor's unique genius. Gustavo Giovannetti, a young acquaintance of Puccini's who witnessed a working session at Torre del Lago, was especially impressed by the mutual understanding that existed between them, surprised that two such strongwilled men could calmly discuss and agree upon each aspect of the score.

In October 1910, finished score in hand, Toscanini left for New York to begin preliminary rehearsals. A few days after these rehearsals had begun, he cabled the anxious composer that all was going very well; Puccini was relieved.

In early November, the composer himself sailed for New York, accompanied this time by Tonio and by Tito Ricordi, who was increasingly assuming many of his father's duties. It had been reported that Elvira had not joined her husband because she had had enough of New York on their previous trip there. However, from the contents of two letters that she wrote a few weeks after his departure, it is clear that it was Puccini who did not want her to come with him. The wounds of the Doria scandal had not yet healed, and Elvira wrote to him bitterly on November 29 and then again on November 30:

> You ask me what I am doing. What should I do? I am bored and always alone. Then I go out simply to escape solitude and sadness. I get tired very quickly when I walk. So I take a carriage and do my shopping and thus pass my days. . . .
> The only thing that consoles me is the thought that at least you are happy without me—I wish that everything goes well, just as you desire, that you enjoy a great triumph, and that no shadow, even the faintest, comes to disturb your peace. Now you are a great man, and compared to you I am nothing but a pygmy. Therefore be happy and forgive me if I have annoyed you with my lamentations.

Though he wrote to her several times, Puccini did not seem to miss Elvira—either during the crossing or in the course of his visit to New York. The sea voyage was an enjoyable one, the composer again delighted with the luxury and modern conveniences, this time on board the newest luxury liner, the *George Washington*, which he jubilantly described as colossal and pyramidlike. A month before his departure, *Musical America* had published a report stating that he was so nervous about the trip that his friends had been urging him to stay home, but Puccini seemed to be completely relaxed once at sea. A fellow passenger, a writer and cartoonist named Bert Levy, wrote of the composer's romping with children on deck, graciously giving out autographs to other passengers, and thoroughly enjoying ragtime renditions of excerpts from *La Bohème* when they were played by the ship's pianist. In addition, with Tito Ricordi at the piano, he hummed parts of his new opera in the presence of fascinated passersby and allowed himself to be photographed playing shuffleboard.

On his arrival in New York, Puccini was greeted even more warmly than he had been on his previous visit. Within hours of his arrival, he was guest of honor at a tea given by the affluent directors of the Met. In the midst of this elegant party, however, Tito Ricordi grabbed the composer by the arm and led him to the door, informing the stunned hosts that they had not come to New York for time-consuming social occasions but to work and rehearse. Later, the younger Ricordi confessed that he had acted rudely so that, if only once, he could "slap a million dollars in the face." The proper, gentlemanly Puccini did not then, or later, appreciate the aggressive, businesslike Tito's bad manners, nor did he approve of his relentless efforts to obtain publicity at all costs. The behavior of these two men was diametrically opposed, and the composer felt none of the affection for Tito that had marked his relationship with Giulio Ricordi, a fact that would subsequently lead to a temporary break between Puccini and the House of Ricordi.

At his first New York press conference, Puccini was most eager to speak of his quest for a new libretto. "No more heartthrobs," he told reporters. "I want a good lusty comedy. I am going to every comedy I hear about in every city I visit in an attempt to discover a good libretto for a comic opera." This was the reason he had completely abandoned both *La Femme et le Pantin* and *Marie Antoinette*. He expressed his belief, too, that modern opera would become simpler and simpler; instead of reverting to Wagner, it would revert to Gluck, a composer he greatly admired. "How about Richard Strauss?" he was asked, and his response was a simple, "No personalities, please." In a later interview, he reiterated his desire to write a light opera, adding, "I am an Italian and I love melody. Melody must always be queen in music."

He was again delighted with the comforts New York had to offer. A few days after his arrival, he wrote to Ramelde: "New York is a marvelous city. Tonio and I go around all the time trying to see all there is to see. In this hotel, which is more than fifteen stories high, we have magnificent accommodations. We have four rooms and two baths. Plenty of lights, and delicious food, all paid for. Rehearsals are going very well. . . ."

These rehearsals were of primary importance. Though Puccini spent what little free time he had showing the sights of the city to his son, most of his time was spent at the opera house, where, with the aid of playwright Belasco, he supervised the preparations for his new opera. Initially, Belasco had come to the rehearsals out of curiosity; but before long, he was very much in charge of the stage action. Dressed in black, with a high clerical collar, he was always calm and courteous in his efforts to get the singers to act and to sing to each other and not to the audience. It was a formidable task to make himself understood, since the cast was made up of ten Italians, a Bohemian, a Pole, a Spaniard, a Frenchman, two Germans, and only one American, in addition to an unwieldy chorus. "Men and women by the score and fifties would troop out on the stage, range themselves in rows, and become merely a background for the principals," he later recounted in *My Life's Story*. "Then for no purpose they would all begin to shrug their shoulders, grimace, and gesticulate with their hands. I resolved to undo all this at once. I located the ones who shrugged too much and either backed them up against the trees and rocks or invented bits of "business" by which they were held by the others. When a chorus singer became incorrigible in the use of his arms I made him go through entire scenes with his hands in his pockets. Little by little I tamed this wriggling crowd until they themselves began to understand the value of repose."

Belasco worked tirelessly on each detail of the production; he was alarmed that in preparation for the lynching, the hero's hands were tied by an Indian, explaining that this would be impossible given the caste structure of the old West. He worked hard with the principals, too, showing Pasquale Amato, who played the villainous sheriff, just how to slap the hero—Caruso—and teaching Caruso how to kiss a young lady in a bungalow during a blizzard. He failed only in getting anyone to throw a lasso so that it would knot on a tree limb.

Throughout these stage rehearsals, Puccini watched quietly from the back of the theatre, smoking incessantly, quietly observing and jotting his observations on scraps of paper which he later showed to Toscanini. He and Belasco shared no common language, but they shared a profound mutual respect for each other's professional skills. Belasco was pleased with the results of his efforts at lending authenticity to the production and certain it would be a successful one. "Mr. Caruso is going to do the finest acting of his career, Mr. Amato is going to be a superb sheriff, and I am absolutely pleased with Miss Destinn's conception of the girl," he told reporters. For his part, too, Puccini was satisfied, and on December 7 he wrote to Elvira:

> The rehearsals are going very well. I believe it will be a success and let's hope it will be a big one. Tomorrow is dress rehearsal. After the première there will be a supper and reception at the Vanderbilts' and perhaps others to follow—what pleasure! . . . Tonio is well but

I believe he is enamored of a ballerina. It is certain that whenever he can he runs off and I find myself alone. However, he is a good boy and one ought to let him live a little. Fosca has written me a charming letter. . . . And you? How are you? I hope you are better. . . . The opera emerges splendidly, the first act a little long, but the second act magnificent and the third grandiose. Belasco has attended all the rehearsals with great love and interest. Caruso is magnificent in his part, Destinn not bad but she needs more energy. Toscanini, the zenith! — kind, good, adorable — in short, I am content with my work and I hope for the best. But how tremendously difficult it is, this music and the staging! . . . I can't wait for the hour to see my little nuisance of a wife again (I am one too, don't get offended). . . .

The dress rehearsal was a huge success. Among the more than one thousand people who attended were the leading singers of the Metropolitan and a large number of the actors and actresses who were performing on Broadway at the time — included among the latter was Blanche Bates, who first played Minnie on Broadway and who was reportedly in tears at the end of the performance.

Expectations ran high as the night of the première, December 10, approached. The press had given enormous coverage to the rehearsals, and to every remark made by the composer. No one doubted that it was an event of major importance, the first time a European composer of world renown had allowed an opera of his to be premiered in America. Furthermore, it was an American opera, but on this point the journalists seemed unduly curious in wondering just how American it was. To one interviewer, Puccini stressed that he had striven for an essentially American atmosphere and that he had inculcated in the score a few bars of Indian music and also some ragtime, but that he had made no effort to use essentially American themes. To another journalist he said, "For this drama I have composed music that, I feel sure, reflects the spirit of the American people and particularly the strong, vigorous nature of the West. I have never been West, but I have read so much about it that I know it thoroughly and have lived the feelings of my characters so intensely that I believe I have hit upon the correct musical portrayal of them. With very few exceptions, I have borrowed no themes. Practically all are of my own invention. It is American music, though it is Puccini at the same time. . . ."

When questioned on the same subject, Toscanini replied unequivocally that the music of the opera was Italian, although the play was American.

On December 10, an editorial in the *World* proclaimed: "One of the great musical events in the history of the country will occur this evening when *The Girl of the Golden West* by Puccini, the most popular of living operatic composers, will be sung at the Metropolitan Opera House for the first time."

The event lived up to its expectations in every way, and to this day the New York opera house has never again generated the excitement that it did that evening. Tickets were sold out weeks in advance, and special precautions were taken to prevent speculation, whereby tickets were paid for and signed for upon purchase but not delivered until little more than an hour before curtain time upon a matching countersignature, after which the seat holders were required to enter the theatre. This complicated system was only partially successful, since precious tickets did fall into the hands of speculators who sold them for as much as $150 apiece, but it did succeed in creating huge jams at the entrances to the theatre while signatures were being verified. The mob, either trying to get into the theatre or get a look at those getting into the theatre, was so great that it had to be pushed back repeatedly by police.

The chaos outside the Metropolitan was more than matched by the glamour inside the jam-packed auditorium, where the famed diamond horseshoe was bedecked with Italian and American flags for the occasion. The audience was a dazzling one; it included J. P. Morgan, Colonel John Jacob Astor, Mrs. August Belmont, a generous collection of Guggenheims, Vanderbilts, and Goulds, President Nicholas Murray Butler of Columbia, Walter Damrosch, pianist and composer Josef Hofmann, Engelbert Humperdinck (whose *Königskinder* was soon to make its début at the Met), and the most important stars of the contemporary opera world. In addition, the military establishment was represented by a good number of generals, and leading members of the diplomatic corps, including members of the Chinese embassy, were in attendance.

The performance was a tremendous success. There were innumerable curtain calls for all the principals, for Belasco and, above all, for Puccini. Between the second and third acts, Gatti-Casazza, on behalf of the board of directors, presented the composer with a large silver wreath. The clamor after the final curtain lasted more than fifteen minutes. Backstage, when the applause had finally subsided, the composer was jubilant. "My heart is beating like the double basses in the card scene," he commented.

The following morning, headlines in the New York press reflected the excitement of the occasion. GREAT WELCOME FOR NEW OPERA . . . BRILLIANT AUDIENCE WILDLY APPLAUDS PUCCINI'S GIRL OF THE GOLDEN WEST . . . COMPOSER, ORIGINATOR AND CONDUCTOR HAVE A TRIUMPH AFTER EACH ACT . . . THE OPERA HOUSE THRONGED, proclaimed the New York *Times*; UNDER TWO FLAGS A $22,000 HOUSE RIOTS OVER PUCCINI, THE OPERA DIRECTORS SEND A SILVER WREATH TO THE STAGE . . . CARUSO LOOKS AND ACTS HIS BEST . . . EMMY DESTINN SINGS HEROICALLY THE MOST POWERFUL WOMAN'S ROLE IN RECENT MELODRAMA, the *Sun* announced; while the *World* simply exclaimed, GOLDEN WEST IN OPERA DRAWS GOLD OF EAST.

In spite of these sensational headlines, the response of New York's music critics to the new opera was decidedly mixed. Reginald de Koven, writing in the *Sun*, stated that any success the opera had was due to the author's staging of the work and not to the composer's music. He felt that the subject had never really taken hold of Puccini and predicted that the opera would enjoy no more than a vogue of short duration. The reviewer for *The Musical Courier*, expressing a desire for American operas written by Americans, was entirely negative in his judgment of the new work. "The play caters to a depraved taste, and the music is without any appeal beyond that of emphasizing the meretricious elements in the libretto. Puccini's harmonic scheme is extremely limited and consists of intervals studiously made unconventional and tonal succession arbitrarily distorted to titillate the senses," he wrote, adding that he felt the opera should be withdrawn at the end of the season and completely revised.

Richard Aldrich, writing in the *Times*, gave a more balanced opinion. Commenting that the success of the opera was due more to Belasco's work than to that of the composer, he admitted that Puccini's task had been a most difficult one. "The place of music in such a drama as this — a drama of rapid movement, of sharply focused realistic situations, of a few tensely theatrical climaxes, in which the emotional and psychological elements rise only rarely to influential or commanding places — is not easy to find," he wrote. "In setting this drama to music, Mr. Puccini undertook a task that not so many years ago would have been deemed impossible, almost a contradiction in terms of all conceptions of what the lyric drama could or should be. . . ."

Aldrich recognized that Puccini's music for this new opera was evidence of a new step in the composer's development. "In 'Madama Butterfly,' it was observed that he had ventured far into a region of new and adventurous harmonies. He has now gone still further into this field of augmented intervals and chords of higher dissonances. He has made much use of the so-called 'whole tone' scale and the harmonies that associate themselves with it. In a word, there is a marked predeliction for the idiom that is coupled particularly with the name of Debussy. . . ."

Aldrich's long, detailed review — only a small portion has been excerpted here — was appreciative but by no means completely enthusiastic; in the end, he felt that the composer had not succeeded in his new work. However, it is noteworthy as a sign that at least one critic had recognized that Puccini was making a serious effort to break out of the pattern of his previous, and highly successful, operas.

At the time, the reviews seemed of little interest to Puccini; he was used to the mixture of critical disapproval and public acclaim, and he was thoroughly enjoying his personal triumph in America. His only comment to those who criticized the opera for not being sufficiently American was a calm, "I wrote it as I felt it, as always, without worrying about it being 'American' or not." He was undisturbed, too, by an angry letter that his librettist Civinini had written to the *Giornale d'Italia* in Italy, claiming that his work had been distorted and was no longer recognizable, a charge minimized by co-librettist Zangarini who, resigned, countered that a libretto, after all, was only a libretto, and that in an opera it was the music that counted.

On December 28, 1910, Puccini embarked for Europe a happy man. In addition to memories of the spectacular première, he was carrying with him the proof of his triumph—his silver wreath, carefully packed in a velvet-lined box. To follow would be a shiny new motorboat which he had seen on Fifth Avenue and which he had bought with three thousand dollars given to him for an autograph score of "Musetta's Waltz."

On New Year's Eve, while on board the *Lusitania*, he wrote a letter to Carla Toscanini, the conductor's wife, in which he expressed his gratitude to the musician he felt had composed his opera a second time by means of his superb interpretation of the score; and he also voiced once again his feeling of profound loneliness, even in the midst of what he believed to be a success.

> I keep thinking of the last days, the rehearsals, the première, the lights of New York. All that has passed now, but I am left with a profound fondness for both of you, and that will never pass. You have been so good and kind to me, so gentle and attentive—Toscanini so patient and affectionately friendly. My thoughts are full of you, and I envy you, for I would like to be like you, with your closely knit family, with your children who love you so, and with your friends who believe in you. I, alas, feel alone in this world, and that is why I am always sad—and yet I have always tried to love but I have never been understood, or rather, I have always been wrongly interpreted. Now it is too late: I am too far gone, too far. . . . Keep your friendship for me, so that I might at least have good and intelligent people who might tolerate and might understand me. . . .

This loneliness and melancholy had afflicted Puccini for much of his life; they would become the dominant characteristics of his remaining years. Upon his return to Italy, however, where he was given a hero's welcome as the man who had conquered America, he did his best to avoid the problems at hand—largely the important decisions concerning the direction his music would take—and busied himself by traveling throughout Europe to supervise new productions of *La Fanciulla del West*—much as he had done for his earlier operas.

The first European production of the opera was to take place in London, and the composer went there in early May to supervise the rehearsals. London was a second home to him, and, with the possible exception of Vienna, the capital in which he felt most at ease. His popularity there was immense. "His work claims more performances than that of any other composer living or dead," *The Sketch* noted, adding that "the rise of Puccini has been comparatively rapid, a matter of less than twenty years, and today it may be doubted that any living composer, with the exception of Dr. Richard Strauss, can command as great a material reward. It costs far more to satisfy the German composer, but the Italian probably has twenty performances to his great contemporary's one."

The London première of *Fanciulla* rivaled in excitement the memorable first night in New York. Special attention was attached to the fact that the opera had been dedicated to Queen Alexandra. Tickets had been sold out one hour after the performance had been announced, and an elegant, bejeweled crowd filled Covent Garden on the night of May 29. Puccini and the cast were called before the curtain countless times—it was one more gigantic popular success. The following morning, however, the press expressed serious reservations, the *Telegraph* noting that while it had all the outside semblance of a triumph, "emphatically it is not an opera that is destined for more than a limited age; certainly it is not for all time." The reviewer for the *Times*, while admiring the composer's ability to handle a melodramatic subject, complained of the lack of lyrical elements. "In numerous places," he wrote, "where Puccini in old days would have written a swinging melody, we are now given declamation over a shifting, delicately colored background." He, too, predicted that the opera would have no more than a momentary popularity.

Following London, Puccini hurried to Rome for the first Italian production of *Fanciulla*. The première was another gala occasion, and the royal box was occupied by King Victor Emmanuel and Queen Helena, who invited the composer to their box to offer their congratulations and convey to America their special appreciation for the magnificent scenery which had been sent for the Roman production from New York. The public responded enthusiastically once again, but the critics the following morning voiced surprise at what they felt was a new Puccini. On the whole, however, they were appreciative of this new development in the composer's art, and especially of his handling of the orchestra. For Lionello Spada of *Vita*, the new opera was musically the strongest of all of Puccini's operas, while Giovanni Pozza, writing in the *Corriere della Sera*, maintained that "never before as in this opera has Puccini shown a firmer control of his talent and his art." The enthusiastic reviewer for *Giornale d'Italia* found "a novelty of harmonization and a richness of instrumentation that place this score among the most exquisite and vigorous, among the most organic and pleasing, of the modern Italian theatre. . . ."

Further successes followed as the opera made its way through Italy—to Brescia, Turin, Naples, as well as to Lucca, where once again the occasion was a festive one in honor of the provincial capital's native son. Of all the important opera houses of Italy, only La Scala delayed—until late 1912—its first production of *Fanciulla*. The composer again traveled abroad, notably to

Paris, where the audience cheered while the critics condescended, and to Budapest, where, because of rehearsal problems, he almost withdrew the opera. Nonetheless, he was royally treated in the Hungarian capital, honored officially at a luncheon given by the mayor, at which the menu included *Pot-au-feu à la Madama Butterfly, Sterlet de Danube à la Bohème, Soufflé à la Fanciulla del West,* and *Choux à la Tosca.* He was, in the end, pleased too, with the execution of his opera and above all with the performance of Elsa Szamosy, to whom he presented a photo pronouncing her the best Minnie as well as the best Cio-cio-san that he had ever heard. When he was reminded that he had said this of at least five other sopranos, he was ready with a romantic explanation. "Have you ever been in love? Have you not fancied yourself at various times to be in love with several girls, or perhaps actually been in love with them? And didn't you have the feeling every time afresh that the latest adored one was, after all, the only one you had ever really loved? I can't recall the five to whom you refer, but if I have used that sentiment as an autograph for five different singers, you may rest assured that at the moment of writing it I really believed it in each case."

Neither fame nor adulation was new to Puccini, yet never before had he been so honored and acclaimed as he was during 1911 and 1912, not so much, it is true, for his latest opera—which, as many reviewers had predicted, did not achieve the popularity of his earlier works—but for the ensemble of his work. Nonetheless, it was not a happy time, but one marked by an absence of joy and enthusiasm. At the Roman première of his new opera, Mascagni's young daughter, who met him there after many years, noticed that even when he smiled his eyes were sad. At Brescia, he was depressed, preoccupied with the failing health of his sister Ramelde, and from Paris in May 1912, he wrote to Albina, Ramelde's daughter, a letter full of brooding in which he stated: "My mood is as black as a hat. I feel my years . . . that's what it is. There is nothing that makes me rejoice, not even the success of my opera makes me happy. . . ."

It was not the weight of his years that depressed Puccini; rather, it was his uncertainty over what to do with those years that remained to him. He had reached a crucial turning point in his life—as a man and as an artist—and he was entering what was to be the most trying period of his whole life, one marked not by drama but by a profound emotional, creative unrest.

Second Interlude: "Always Searching, and Finding Nothing"

After *La Fanciulla del West* had been launched, Puccini realized that he had reached another turning point in his life, that it was time to re-examine his role as an artist. He was desperate to begin work again, to find another libretto to occupy his time—"I need work just as I need food," he wrote to Sybil in early 1911, but he knew that this time he would have to come up with something that would mark a departure from his earlier successes. "At the point at which I have now arrived in art," he wrote Sybil on February 8, 1911, "I need to find something loftier, more musical, and more original."

In order to do so, however, he needed an inner tranquillity that was to be denied him. In 1912, two of the people closest to him died, and he was unable to fill the void that they left behind. The first of these was his sister Ramelde, who died on April 8. The composer had maintained good relationships with all of his sisters, but Ramelde was the only one in whom he had been able to confide. She not only understood him more than did any other member of his family, but she had also provided the link between him and his more conventional sisters. Though he remained on warm and friendly terms with Ramelde's husband and her daughter Albina, he was never able to unburden himself to them as he had been to his favorite sister.

Puccini suffered an even greater loss with the passing of Giulio Ricordi, who died, at the age of seventy-two, on June 12 of that year. Papà Giulio, as the name Puccini often called him implied, had been more than a publisher or a friend. He had discovered the composer, had helped his talent grow, and had taken a paternal pride in his success. Their relationship had been based on profound mutual affection, respect, and trust. They had quarreled—angrily about the third act of *Tosca* and about Puccini's affair with Corinna—but these had been in the nature of ill-tempered family quarrels, after which no bitterness had remained. Puccini had few real friends, and Giulio Ricordi had been one of them.

Not only did Ricordi's death constitute a deep personal sorrow for Puccini, it also meant a radical change in his dealings with the House of Ricordi. Tito, whom Puccini often referred to as Savoia, had started to manage the affairs of the firm during the last years of his father's life, and for a long time it had been clear his relationship with Puccini would be a difficult one and that he would be unable to offer the moody composer the patient understanding and unfailing support to which he had become accustomed. Giulio Ricordi had been a cultured gentleman of the nineteenth century; his son, though he had a sound knowledge of musical theatre, was a not-so-gentlemanly twentieth-century businessman. Puccini could never approve of the lattter's high-handed, aggressive manner of working, while Tito, perhaps jealous of the affection his own father had felt for the composer, only seven years his senior, considered Puccini passé and unworthy of special attention.

Immediately following Giulio Ricordi's death, Puccini wrote a letter to Sybil, telling her how deeply grieved he was and also warning of future problems. "From now on everything is in the hands of Savoia—we're in a nice fix," he wrote. "But on the very first occasion that he tries any of his tricks, I shall leave the firm—you can be quite sure of that, I promise you!"

The first problem arose only six months after Tito had taken charge. In line with his new policy of business efficiency, the new director of the firm wanted to sign a contract with Puccini for the rights to his next opera. The composer was stunned; he explained to Tito that he had never signed a formal agreement before a libretto was ready. "To commit myself is oppressive," he wrote indignantly. "I love open air and freedom. Why do I have to tie myself down, at this tender age, when it's never happened before? The House of Ricordi has proof of my fidelity, why doubt it now? Dear Tito, I beg you not to insist upon this point. I, more than anyone, want to have work. Let the libretto come, and then we will sign our agreements."

Though there were to be formal contracts, there was to be little basic agreement between the two men. Tito lost no time in making it clear that, just as his father had looked for a successor to Verdi, he was looking for a successor to Puccini. Not only that, he believed he had found one in the twenty-nine-year old Riccardo Zandonai, who, ironically, once Puccini had finally rejected it, set *La femme et le pantin* to music and who later would write an opera with a libretto by Tito Ricordi.

Puccini was hurt by all the attention being paid to Zandonai, whom he felt showed no special gifts. On January 27, 1913, he wrote to Sybil: "Savoia is more impossible than ever—I have found out he is actually my enemy—or at least the enemy of my music. I am assembling the evidence together, and then he can go and—look elsewhere for a composer!" He complained again to Sybil in May, saying that Tito treated him as if he were "nothing but a bit of scrap iron," and a few weeks later, on May 14, he wrote her:

> I am engaged in underground, but not open, warfare with Savoia, who is pleasant enough when he writes and when he sees me; but there's a storm brewing which I fear, or rather hope, will soon burst. You can believe me when I say that this fellow is a real pig, and that his behavior to me is most Jesuitical; I know that he has said of me that I shall never write any more—is that the way to behave after twenty years during which I have brought honor to his firm as well as many millions of profit? And I am treated without the least respect or consideration. It's a disgrace! I wish I were ten years younger—but although I am already getting old, I can still give him a nasty pill or two to swallow.

Tito, apparently, did little to assuage Puccini's feelings, and the composer did, for a short time, make a formal break with the House of Ricordi. The most commercially successful composer of his time, Puccini obviously could have found another publisher. Nonetheless, except for this one short period, Puccini remained with the House of Ricordi, out of a sentimental attachment to the firm, and because, as he wrote to Sybil, "at heart I'm a decent fellow, and my feelings of vindictiveness don't last long."

During this time, when his professional life was suffering from changes and from his own uncertainties, the composer's marriage, too, was far from satisfactory, and he embarked on what, from all evidence, was the last serious love affair of his life. The woman, with whom he was involved for several years, was a German baroness, Josephine von Stängel. A native of Munich, she was thirty-five years old when they met (seventeen years younger than the composer), had been separated from her husband and was the mother of two small daughters. She and the composer met on the beach at Viareggio in the summer of 1911—a fact which explains Puccini's unwillingness to spend that summer in the mountains, instead remaining at his nearby Torre del Lago home, in spite of the extreme heat which had so oppressed him in the past.

Josephine made the composer happy; she worshiped him as a man and she deeply admired him as a musician. In appreciating his qualities as an artist, she was able to provide the kind of sympathetic understanding Elvira had been unable to give him. "You sneer when the word 'art' is pronounced," the composer once wrote Elvira. "This has always offended me. . . ."

Their affair was necessarily a difficult one, of subterfuges and hastily arranged clandestine meetings. For a man of Puccini's fame, there was more than the ordinary fear of being discovered. However, by 1915, Josephine began consulting a lawyer in order to obtain a divorce, and the couple started to make plans to share a home together in Viareggio—the composer took steps to purchase the land for a house. Three letters written by Josephine during this period have been discovered, and they are evidence of a passionate bond that existed between the two. On March 16, 1915, Josephine informed her lover that she had been to a lawyer who had advised her to leave her daughters with her father-in-law in Munich so that she might be near the composer in Viareggio. (The German lawyer, an admirer of Puccini's operas, also requested a signed photo of the composer.) Josephine was ecstatic at the prospect of a union with the man she playfully called "Giacomucci" or "Mucci," and she planned to join him as soon as possible. "I would like to have your dear mouth and your tender eyes now," she wrote, "but deep in your eyes I have you forever."

Shortly afterward, she wrote that she had been deeply moved by his poetic letter, in which he called her "one thousand tender names." (The composer's favorite names for the baroness were "Josi" and "Busci.") She understood his suffering and his conflicts, but she reminded him that it was their duty to live life to the full, to enjoy their pleasures while they might. "I adore your art, your music, your great knowledge, and above all I love . . . your modesty and your simplicity in everything you do. . . . And your love for me is the most sacred of poems, and your goodness is so sweet that it makes me your slave," she added.

Josephine was interested in knowing every detail of Puccini's life when they were apart; at one point she wanted to know if by chance he was after any other women. She must have known the composer well, since he had not changed his ways and might well have answered her in the affirmative, for he was, for a while at least, carrying on a secret correspondence with Blanka Lendvai, the sister of the Hungarian friend who had come to his aid at the time of his troubles over Doria. In the course of this correspondence, he admonished Blanka to stop sending letters to his clandestine post box in Viareggio and to send them instead in care of his old friend Carignani. "I kiss your beautiful mouth," he wrote Blanka in October of 1911, a few months after he had met and fallen in love with Josephine.

In spite of temporary distractions—such as Blanka Lendvai—Puccini carried on his affair with Josephine for several years. His love for this younger woman who adored him and shared his interest in music—she was thrilled by *Die Meistersinger* and hated Strauss' *Ariadne auf Naxos*, which must have delighted Puccini—was deeply felt. However, contact between the two became increasingly complicated with the advent of the first world war—she was the citizen of an enemy country—and they were never able to live together, as they had once hoped.

Even if there had been no war, however, it seems unlikely that Puccini would have had the courage to make a final break with his wife. Though only in his mid-fifties, he felt he was getting old, and even when younger and infatuated with Corinna, he had been unable to leave Elvira. In addition, his ties to his wife were undoubtedly stronger than even he suspected. She had been his companion for many years; in spite of his unhappiness and his loneliness he was used to Elvira, and the two had managed to find a way of coexisting. There was little understanding between them, and he enjoyed the chance to be separated from Elvira during his travels, yet it is clear from two letters written her from Berlin in 1913 that the bond, even if strained, between them, was a strong one. The first one was an excuse and a plea for understanding:

> My dear Elvira: You poor thing! You always vent your feelings in a letter. You never speak to me as you write to me. . . . You complain because I did not bring you here. But good God! You do not want to understand that if a man has work to do, a woman is a hindrance. I am never in the hotel. And you would remain alone almost all the time. . . . After the rehearsals there is one reception or another (as yesterday), then an invitation to dinner (as yesterday), and you would have remained alone because you go neither to the receptions nor to the dinners and I have to go. I assure you that I would willingly do without them. Here it is not like Paris, where even if you remain alone you can enjoy yourself. Here you would have been furious. I assure you, and you know it as well as I, that you would have been on tenterhooks here and then the journey would have become feverish and painful. In short, it is time that you understand certain matters. We are always together, either at Torre or at Milan, and once in a while a man wants a mite of liberty — that is not a crime. You fabricate God knows what phantoms, and you suffer. But be tranquil. I always think of you and with you, and when you are good and less grim I remain with you very willingly. But you have a tragic soul. That is it. Your enormous pessimism, that is your enemy. It does not permit you to enjoy life. You also communicate it to me. That is why from time to time you make me wish to be alone, to rid myself of that continuous black which surrounds you and which makes you suffer morally and in consequence physically. . . . Well, if you want to come and if it makes you sad not to be here, do as you please. I cannot say more.

Four days later, he wrote her again, admitting there was no one else to whom he could write:

> . . . I have such a desire for peace and for equilibrium. Death is a great friend. I have no further interest in myself. Wherever I turn I see ugliness, evil actions. The philosophy of the world is that it

belongs to others. And the others think that it belongs to others still. Perhaps the young people (those who are intelligent) enjoy life. Now I am old, and no matter how I try not to seem old, and no matter how much I wish not to be old, that's what I am. I have suffered so in my life that now I am fed up. . . . I have no libretto, I have no work, my publisher is my enemy, the friends I have are out of favor, like Carignani, or worth little. Relatives—oh, my God! Tonio is everything but mine. . . . Children are here and there, everywhere but with their parents. What to do? Patience. Suffer and send precautions to the devil, the more so as there is no remedy either for my character or for my disease. . . .

Obviously, it was too late for Puccini to surrender himself completely to the love of another woman, even one as adoring and compassionate as Josephine. More than ever, he was obsessed with and almost paralyzed by the thought that he was declining physically and emotionally, fearing that his best years were behind him.

The composer was also keenly aware that, in the eyes of many, his operas were considered old-fashioned. Few, if any, composers had attained either his universal popularity or his material wealth during their lifetimes, yet just because of his popular acclaim, he was the target of vicious criticism during these years. From the time of *Manon Lescaut*, when the influential *Rivista Musicale Italiana* had called his music vulgar and mediocre, to 1910 when Ildebrando Pizzetti accused him of being a bourgeois composer only able to express middle-class attitudes in his music, he had been sniped at and accused of pandering to cheap public tastes. His immense success had helped him to ignore such attacks, but in 1912, when he was at his lowest, when he was without work, and when his protector Giulio Ricordi had died, he was stung by a small book, written by a young, highly respected musicologist that contained the most blistering attack of all, one that attracted worldwide attention.

The book was titled *Giacomo Puccini e l'opera internazionale*, and its author was Fausto Torrefranca, a twenty-nine-year-old Calabrese who had already gained a loyal following in Italian musical circles. Torrefranca's attack was a direct one, and in his preface he wrote: "Requested to choose a figure in Italy's musical art as the subject of a study, I have elected to take Puccini rather than any other because he seems to me to be the only one that embodies in the most complete fashion all the decadence of modern Italian music and represents all its bare-faced commercialism, all its miserable impotence and its triumphant international vogue. . . ."

In the pages that followed, the author attacked Puccini for abandoning the glorious tradition of Italian nonoperatic music; he accused him of being a "puny, anemic artist," one who was really no musician at all but merely an opportunist who eagerly sought nothing but commercial success. In conclusion, Torrefranca derided the composer's fame in other countries, especially England and Germany and added: "Puccini is the manipulator *par excellence* of international lyric drama. The ideal condition for international lyric drama is to command a music that adapts itself to all kinds of translations, into whatever languages; a music that is neither Italian nor Russian nor German nor French, but which has all the commercial advantages of an international language such as Esperanto—simplicity of grammar, brevity of words, easy syntax for those who wish to adapt it. And to these conditions Puccini's music, which requires of the spectators only the minimum of attention necessary to pass the time agreeably, conforms admirably. . . ." According to the critic, Puccini's efforts at a facile universalism had betrayed Italy's rich musical heritage.

Many years later, when he had achieved eminence in his field, Torrefranca spoke of his little book as a "necessary youthful sin." He also claimed that his attack on the composer had forced the latter to re-examine his work, resulting in the composition of his later and more original (according to Torrefranca) operas. At the time, however, Puccini was hurt by the critic's harsh words. He never responded publicly, and he only expressed his anger privately to his friends. Nonetheless, he was shaken by the realization that Torrefranca was not alone in believing that his early works were dated and no longer relevant as works of art. He was no longer competing with the memory of Verdi or with Mascagni, Leoncavallo, or even Zandonai; he was now composing for a public that was responding increasingly to the music of Schoenberg, Stravinsky, and other members of the modern school, whose compositions he respected but could never truly understand or feel. It was time, he knew, for an artistic evolution on his part.

This climate of re-examination and uncertainty made his search for a new libretto a difficult and frustrating one. It had never been easy, but this time he seemed to be floundering as he reached out in every possible direction, groping for new themes and ideas. Shortly after returning from New York, in early 1911, he wrote anxiously to Toscanini, "Everybody offers me things, but nobody hits the mark. How difficult it is, and I am in a hurry!" In March, he wrote Sybil that he was "always searching, and finding nothing. I'm in despair—I think it's the most difficult thing in the world." A year later, still searching, he asked Sybil, "Aren't you yourself ever going to get fed up with my *Tosche* and company?"

A vast number of diverse subjects were considered and rejected. Among them were *Trilby*, *The Three Musketeers*, *Lorna Doone*, Hermann Sudermann's *Johannisfeuer*, and Gerhart Hauptmann's dream play, *Hanneles Himmelfahrt*. He gave thought to *Sumurun*, a wordless play based on a tale from the Arabian nights which had been spectacularly produced by Max Reinhardt in London, and he looked into the possibilities of Hall Caine's *The*

Prodigal Son and Ferenc Molnár's *Liliom*—in the latter case the author reportedly refused, saying that he preferred *Liliom* to be remembered as a play by Molnár rather than as an opera by Puccini.

Rumors again began to appear in the press, and in July 1911 it was announced that Puccini had commissioned Herman Heijermans, a Dutch socialist playwright, to write a libretto based on the life of Frans Hals; a month later *Musical America* reported that this project had been abandoned. On December 3, 1912, the New York *Times* noted that Puccini had invited undergraduates of Cornell University to write a libretto for his next American opera; according to the newspaper, the composer believed that fresh ideas and a novel execution could be produced by amateurs with the advantages of a higher education.

During this frantic quest for work, Puccini did not hesitate to return to earlier collaborators and previously rejected ideas. In London, he went to see *The Darling of the Gods* by his old friends Belasco and Long, but this play proved to be unsatisfactory from his point of view. Far more serious thought was once again given to Oscar Wilde's *A Florentine Tragedy*, which he had discarded in 1907, and as in the past, the composer turned to Luigi Illica for this project. Illica, in spite of Tito Ricordi's discouraging words, had started work on the Wilde story in July of 1912. In August, as Puccini was about to travel to Bayreuth for a performance of *Parsifal* ("Complete enchantment," he commented on this), he wrote his librettist that he was convinced the result of their collaboration would be an interesting opera, and that same month he wrote Sybil:

> Do you know I'm thinking again about doing Wilde's *Florentine Tragedy*? So you would do me a great favor by writing to your friend, Wilde's literary executor, and asking him whether this play is still free. Illica is trying to compose a big first act, and, if he succeeds, I'll do it—as it stands, it's too small a thing, but with a preparatory act, which must also be beautiful (it must be more beautiful and more varied than the second, so Illica has a heavy task), I'll write this opera.

Sybil obediently contacted Robert Ross, Wilde's executor, at once and learned that the play was still free, though nonexclusive rights had been granted to an obscure French composer, Antoine Mariotte. Ross suggested, however, that Puccini might base his opera on a nearly completed theatrical version which was being prepared by Sturge Moore, an Irish poet, and, failing that, that the composer might like to base an opera on *The Duchess of Padua*—another previously rejected subject. The executor, it seems, showed a certain impatience, and later in August Puccini wrote a forthright letter to Sybil clarifying his own position:

Just had your telegram—I can't fix up anything definitely as yet. It depends on the poet who is trying to invent a first act to add to it, and he'll have to find something very interesting, because the second act of Wilde isn't sufficiently so—do you understand? So it all depends on this first act whether or not I do the opera.

And it's only right—I can't and won't write an opera unless it's really *taking* and *compelling*, and all this *au complet!* Puccini must compose something *extra*, and it is essential that he himself should first be convinced. So you can tell Mr. Ross all this—that is to say, to wait until I make up my mind, which will be shortly. And the only reason we asked whether Wilde's play was free was so that we could get to work on it and not start off without obtaining permission.

Before long, however, Puccini and Illica gave up, and the composer wrote to Sybil on October 7: "Alas! The *Tragedy* of Wilde has gone the way of the others—because I tried to construct a first act to it, and neither I nor Illica have succeeded—I'm here, boring myself indecently . . . and so I'm awaiting the arrival of old age. . . . It's sad, but it's true—I feel as if I were the prisoner of . . . Zenda!" That was the end of Puccini's interest in *A Florentine Tragedy*, though the validity of his interest was confirmed in 1917, when an interesting opera based on the subject was written by Alexander Zemlinsky, the Viennese conductor who had first conducted Maria Jeritza in *Tosca* at Vienna's Volksoper.

At the same time the Wilde was being reconsidered, the composer was giving further thought to another abandoned idea, that of basing an opera on a Russian subject, the libretto to be written by Illica and Giovanni Pozza of the *Corriere della Sera*. In finally rejecting this idea once again on October 3, Puccini wrote to Illica, "This subject is not the extraordinary thing I want to do, and to give to the world another opera which does not possess what is needed to make a strong effect is something I cannot do, I who, for better or for worse, call myself Giacomo Puccini. . . ." This need to do something new and powerful and important, this recognition of his position in the world of opera, was again expressed to Illica in two more letters written a few days later. On October 5, he wrote that the production and stage effects were becoming increasingly important elements in the lyric theatre, that even an unoriginal subject could be made to seem original by means of striking theatrical effects. Frustrated, he wondered if his entire output would consist of only his five operas—he himself had already discounted his first two works. On October 8, he explained further:

I'm in a terrible mood because I don't think the *quid* which is needed for *my* theatre can be found. I wrote to you about productions, not as a gospel, but as a different approach and a secondary element. . . . Our task . . . is to find a story which, with its poetry and its love and sorrow, takes hold of us and inspires us so that we might make of it an opera. I repeat to you (not that I ever doubt you) that I am a little shaken and I am beginning to lose faith. Do you think that in all this time (from the last note of *Fanciulla*) I have sat with my hands crossed? I have sounded out everything and everyone, and only the dust of the dead remains on my fingers. . . . I am bored and desperate.

Illica, apparently, had no new ideas, and Puccini was so desperate that he turned again to D'Annunzio. He had made contact with D'Annunzio in August, expressing his certainty that this time he could "make the miracle" which was needed, and in November a meeting between the two men was held at the playwright's home in Arcachon, near Bordeaux. There they agreed to adapt for the operatic stage *La Crociata degli Innocenti*, a D'Annunzio play which dealt with the Children's Crusade of 1212. This time, the playwright wrote Tito Ricordi, Puccini seemed genuinely enthusiastic and eager that their collaboration be a successful one; and work on the scenario began at once. For a few months, Puccini was encouraged and encouraging; by January 1913, however, after having seen what D'Annunzio had written, he was disappointed and forced to admit that still another effort had failed. "D'Annunzio has given birth to a small, shapeless monstrosity, unable to walk or live," he wrote Sybil. "I am as usual in midocean, without any hope of ever reaching harbor." At the same time, he wrote to the playwright, "I am desolate, because my only hope was in you, your heart, your imagination. But it was my duty to speak to you frankly, and I have done so without hesitation, certain that my bitterness is also yours."

Surprisingly, there was to be one further attempt at a joint effort between these two giants of Italian cultural life, but, not surprisingly, this too came to nothing. Later, commenting on D'Annunzio's collaboration with Mascagni on the opera *Parisina*, Puccini noted that it failed because the composer was too obsequious to the librettist, that "the musician must always be the master." D'Annunzio could clearly accept no master.

There were other false starts, some of them occupying much of the composer's time. On November 19, 1911, he wrote to Sybil: "Do you know of any grotesque novel or story or play full of humor and buffoonery? I have a desire to laugh and make other people laugh." This represented another return to an old idea, the often-expressed wish to write a comic opera, and by the end of the year he believed he had found the right subject in *Anima Allegra*, a Spanish play written by the brothers Serafin and Joaquin Alvarez Quintero. He had seen the comedy performed in Milan in the fall of 1909 and remembered it with pleasure. The story of a young woman who lives a gloomy life in the castle of her aunt, a marquise, and who runs away and finds love — her own cousin, who has come to take her back to the castle — in a rustic peasant village, the subject was an appropriately light one that lent itself ideally to the kind of opera that interested the composer at the time. On January 26, 1912, he had written Giulio Ricordi, who liked the idea, suggesting that Giuseppe Adami, a thirty-three-year-old playwright and publicist who worked for the House of Ricordi and who was at the time preparing a libretto for Ricordi himself, might be able to write the libretto, together with Puccini's own nephew, Carlo Marsili. A few weeks later, Marsili was ruled out, but Puccini was still optimistic about the project and suggested that his old librettist Zangarini might be a useful partner. Adami, the composer knew, would prove to be the subservient librettist he now wanted, and he had remembered Zangarini's own recognition of the secondary role of any librettist. "I will be the director of everything," he wrote Ricordi, "and I will make the two librettists the vassals of the Doge."

Adami worked hard on the libretto, but while he did the composer cooled to the subject. This was not surprising, since at the very beginning Puccini seemed to have a change of heart and he confided to Sybil that though he rather liked the Spanish play, "now that I can have something cheerful, I'm looking for contrast — sorrow, sorrow, sorrow, which is the very essence of life. I want to express moral sufferings without blood or strong drama."

The light comedy was hardly a vehicle through which to express "moral sufferings," and the composer became increasingly aware that the material was thin, and that the project would most likely come to nothing. He went ahead with it, but he did so only because he had nothing else to do.

In May 1912, however, he seemed to have another change of heart. While in Paris, he announced to the press that he was on his way to Spain to gather material for the new opera, which "will be much lighter in character than my previous works." There is no record of his having gone to Spain, however, and in August he wrote emphatically to Sybil that "anybody who likes can do *Anima Allegra*, not I — it was a great mistake and I've thought better of it. . . ." In spite of this, he was not willing to abandon it completely — Adami suggested it might be salvaged by moving the locale to Holland — for a few more months.

A fair amount of time was spent on *Anima Allegra* during this period of creative inactivity, but far more energy and determination were expended in Puccini's pursuit of the rights to a short novel, *Two Little Wooden Shoes*, written in 1874 by an English writer known as Ouida. Born Marie-Louise de la Ramée, Ouida herself would have been an interesting subject for a dramatic treatment: an immensely popular romantic novelist (her greatest success was *Under Two Flags*), she enjoyed a great vogue in Victorian England, which she left to spend her remaining years in Italy. After living in Florence for several years, she died in 1908, alone and penniless, in the small town of Massarosa, just across the lake from Torre del Lago.

Two Little Wooden Shoes certainly seemed an odd choice for the composer at the time he was desperately searching for something new and original, something that would place him among the school of modern composers. Its theme, the unrequited love of an innocent little flower girl from Brabant for a sophisticated Parisian painter, was anything but novel, nor would it lend itself to modern treatment; and its pathetic heroine, Bébée who finally drowns herself after walking, heartbroken, from Brabant to Paris and back in her worn-out wooden shoes, bears a striking similarity to the tragic Cio-cio-san. Nonetheless, over a period of several years, Puccini not only believed that this old-fashioned novel could serve as the basis for his new opera, but he fought stubbornly to obtain the rights for the adaptation. Under the circumstances, it is entirely possible that the complex battle to obtain these rights was more interesting to the composer than was the novel itself, and that he would not have spent so much energy on the struggle if he had had anything more stimulating to occupy his time.

Puccini had first heard about Ouida's novel in 1898, but he was then far too busy to pay attention to it. It was suggested to him again in 1911, and rejected, but in January 1913, he sent a copy of it to Illica, with a note saying that he had mulled it over for a long time without coming up with any good ideas, but that he felt the book was full of charm and had a certain potential. He added that if one day the librettist, who by then had spent almost as much time on Puccini's uncompleted works as he had on those that were finished, woke up in a good mood, he might perhaps think of a way to adapt the novel. "Even two red cheeks can give you an idea," he wrote.

Apparently, Illica was not inspired; he had no comments to make. However, a year later, in March 1914, the composer was still interested, and he turned to Sybil, announcing to her that he had definitely decided to do the opera—"which will be full of grace and extraordinarily poetical"—and that he wanted her help in obtaining the exclusive rights to it, including cinematographic rights, at once. He insisted that these rights be his and only his for two reasons: Mascagni had let it be known that he wanted to base an opera on Ouida's novel, and Tito Ricordi, too, had shown interest in purchasing the rights to the novel for his publishing house, after which, Puccini told Sybil, he would "then throw a noose around my neck." Once again, competition had acted as the stimulus in the composer's determination to initiate a new project. This competition became all the more keen after both Puccini and Mascagni officially announced their intentions to the press.

It was soon learned that not only Chatto & Windus, Ouida's British publishers, but also the German firm of Tauchnitz, who published English-language fiction on the continent, claimed ownership of these rights. These claims were not substantiated; it was a highly complicated legal matter— there was even the possibility that no copyright at all existed—and it was finally determined that the rights to Ouida's entire output—she had left no will and had been in debt at the time of her death—could only be obtained from a lawyer in Viareggio, who had been empowered to pay off all outstanding debts with whatever might be earned from the author's literary rights.

In the midst of all this, as soon as Puccini's intentions to base an opera on *Two Little Wooden Shoes* became known, a Viennese publishing firm, Herzmansky-Doblinger, made the composer a most attractive offer for his new opera. Puccini was delighted, for this meant not only a large sum of money but also a chance to free himself from Tito Ricordi. He would, of course, inform Ricordi of the offer and give him a chance to match it, but he was certain that the publisher would be unwilling to do so. "These are fantastic terms to which Savoia certainly won't agree, and then I shall be free and feel no scruples," he wrote Sybil. "Indeed, the debt of gratitude I owe to the House of Ricordi has been more than fully paid through the large and continuous revenue they derive from my old operas. . . ."

Of course, Ouida's novel still did not belong to him, but Puccini visited the Viareggio lawyer and deposited with him one thousand lire, which he felt would be sufficient to secure the necessary rights. He also set the ever-faithful Adami to work on the libretto. In spite of these moves, he was realistic enough to sign no formal agreement with either Adami or the Viennese until he was absolutely certain that *Two Little Wooden Shoes* was his—and certain, too, that Tito Ricordi would not match the Viennese offer.

He was right to be cautious. By June 1914, it became clear that it would not be possible to buy the exclusive rights to Ouida's novel, and that he was therefore in no position to conclude an agreement with the Viennese publishers. He was pleased with the progress Adami had made on the libretto, and he would still write the opera—even for Ricordi, at half the price offered by the Austrians, he wrote Sybil, "because of a certain peculiar sentimentality of mine." And he didn't care if Mascagni wrote his opera based on the same subject. "Let him if he wants to," Puccini wrote to Sybil. "I've nothing to be afraid of—by now I have become accustomed to doubles; the two *Manons*—the two *Bohèmes*—the . . . *four little wooden shoes*."

It was not quite that simple. Someone had to be dealt with, and the entire matter was eventually put in the hands of the Viareggio court, which decided that the rights should be auctioned, with the proceeds going to the late writer's creditors.

As March 18, 1915, the date of the auction, approached, confusion reigned. There was talk of fierce competition and of plots and counterplots among those interested in Ouida's hundred-page novel. Among those present on the decisive day were Puccini, Mascagni's lawyer, Ricordi's legal representative, a number of Ouida's creditors, and Giovacchino Forzano, a writer who had been appointed literary expert by the court. In the end, Ricordi's representative placed the winning bid of four thousand lire—after which he generously presented the rights to the novel to Puccini.

It was an empty gesture. By the end of 1915, after much work on Adami's part, Puccini reached the conclusion that *Two Little Wooden Shoes* was not for him. Nonetheless, Ouida's novel did later serve as the basis for an opera, *Lodoletta*, which was first performed in 1917 — the music was by Mascagni and the libretto by Giovacchino Forzano.

At the same time that Puccini was going after *Two Little Wooden Shoes*, he was also returning to another earlier idea, that of writing three one-act operas. He thought the musical presentation of three distinctly different moods in the course of one evening might be effective, and though Giulio Ricordi had earlier disagreed with him, he had never completely given up that project. Now that Ricordi was gone, he again began the search for three separate, contrasting librettos. In 1912, he found what he felt could be one of them, a chilling short play, *La Houppelande*, by Didier Gold, a French playwright. A few months later, he decided to combine it with a black comedy by Tristan Bernard, which dealt with a group of European explorers who had been captured by an African tribe, and a sweet, spiritual work to be provided by D'Annunzio. Bernard's play proved to be unworkable, and this final futile attempt to collaborate with D'Annunzio failed — as did another try at a collaboration with Valentino Soldani — but the composer was eager to begin work at once on the Didier Gold drama.

La Houppelande had first been performed at the Théâtre Marigny in Paris in September of 1910. A tale of passion and violence, ending in murder, and set on one of the barges that lined the Seine, it had achieved great success and had become part of the repertory of the Grand Guignol. According to Puccini, he first heard about it when a woman who had invited him to tea in Paris thrust a copy of the play at him, insisting that he look it over. There are other reports that he had seen a performance of the play in Paris in 1912. Whatever the origins of the idea, Puccini was taken with it and wrote the playwright of his interest in July 1912. Gold was delighted, more than willing to have his play set to music by the distinguished composer, and the two men met when Puccini came to Paris the following April to absorb local color. The playwright acted as guide; he showed the composer the darker side of Parisian life, walking with him along the banks of the Seine and pointing out the barges under the shadows of Notre-Dame, which would be the setting for his opera.

The two became friends, and final arrangements were made for Puccini to acquire the play as the basis for his one-act opera by the spring of 1913. In August, the composer contacted Ferdinando Martini, a distinguished politician, statesman, and man of letters, to write the libretto. Though the elderly Martini — he was then in his seventies — expressed serious doubts about his ability to carry out the task, Puccini persuaded him to try it. Throughout the rest of the summer, he flattered and cajoled Martini, assuring him that the samples of the libretto that he had submitted were more than satisfactory. By

November, however, he wasn't so sure; what Martini had done, he insisted, was excellent, but not quite in keeping with the demands of Gold's passionate drama. Martini seemed relieved, and within a short time he proffered his resignation—he was not and could never be a librettist, he declared—and Puccini accepted it with regrets.

Even without Martini, however, the composer determined to set La Houp-pelande to music, and he once again turned to Guiseppe Adami to undertake the writing of a libretto. Adami was competent but uninspired; he possessed a certain facility, and he worked hard; above all, he was prepared to give in to the composer's every wish.

In the fall of 1913, Puccini temporarily halted work on Il Tabarro (that was to be the Italian title) in order to supervise rehearsals for a new production of La Fanciulla del West in Vienna. The opera was a great success in the Austrian capital, where the composer was once again given a hero's welcome. Much of the opera's success was attributed to the young and glamourous soprano, Maria Jeritza, who sang the role of Minnie. Though the composer was both tired and discouraged by his frustrating quest for a new opera, he had lost almost none of his ability to work with and bring out the best in the sopranos who were to portray his heroines. He and Jeritza worked together tirelessly so that the soprano might master every aspect of the demanding role. "He went over the music step by step, phrase by phrase," Jeritza noted. "He molded me. I was his creation. Sometimes he would make me so angry I wanted to cry; then, he would get angry. 'Jeritza,' he would say, 'if I ever wake you at three in the morning and ask you to sing a high C, you will sing a high C.' " The soprano learned her lessons well; a year later her singing of Tosca caused a sensation, and in the course of it she sang her second-act aria, "Vissi d'arte," from a lying position. (She had accidentally tripped to the floor during a rehearsal and remained there while she sang her aria; the composer found this so effective that he asked her to retain it for the performance.)

In his free time, Puccini took every possible occasion to visit the city's famed operetta theatres, where he heard for the first time Franz Lehár's Der Graf von Luxemburg and Eva. After one of these performances, he was approached by Otto Eibenschütz and Heinrich Berté, the managers of the Karlstheater, who suggested that he write an operetta for Vienna. The terms they offered were most generous, and all the composer would have to do was provide eight or ten musical numbers to fit into a book that would be chosen by mutual consent. The two gentlemen did what they could to convince him that the operetta was a valid form of musical theatre, for which his talents were especially suited, but Puccini declined their offer on the spot. The writing of an operetta would hardly enhance his reputation.

Once back home, however, the composer had second thoughts. On November 6, he wrote to his close friend in Vienna, the Baron Angelo Eisner, asking him to find out if the Viennese were really serious, and, if so, if they wanted rights only for their theatre, for the whole of Austria and Germany, or for the entire world. If the latter were the case, he felt there was no point in having further discussions; if it were for Vienna alone, perhaps. . . .

Eisner learned that the managers of the Karlstheater were indeed serious, and from that time on he acted as Puccini's intermediary in the matter. After some discussion it was agreed that the composer would retain the rights for Italy, France, Belgium, England, and North America; it was also established that Puccini would have to approve of the libretto before even preliminary agreements were signed.

The Viennese lost no time, and within a few weeks a libretto was submitted—and quickly rejected. Puccini found it too banal and frivolous, totally lacking in character development and originality, and he asked them to come up with another idea, failing which he himself would make an effort to come up with something more to his liking.

In a short time, the impresarios came up with another subject, to be written by A. M. Willner and Heinz Reichert, both experienced in the ways of Vienna's lyrical theatre. The operetta would be called *La Rondine (The Swallow)*, and its plot bore a superficial resemblance to *La Traviata*. It was the story of Magda, the mistress of a wealthy Parisian banker whom she leaves to live in the country with a penniless young romantic poet, Ruggero. The two are ecstatically happy, so much so that Ruggero, wanting to legalize their union, writes to his family for permission to marry the woman he loves. In the third and last act, a letter from the poet's mother arrives; she gives her consent provided that her son's future bride is "good, meek, and pure." Ruggero is overjoyed, but Magda promptly tells her lover of her impure past and, unable to meet his mother's conditions, she leaves him. The swallow, having known true love, resumes her flight (back to the banker's home) and her suffering.

It was hardly a subject for a "new" opera, but initially at least, Puccini found it acceptable, and he enlisted the aid of the obedient Adami to put the libretto into Italian. He explained his reasons to Sybil: "It's a work that will entertain me, and which I will get through quickly," he wrote her.

Long and complicated negotiations followed, dealing not with money but with the question of precisely what rights the composer would retain; gone were the days when Giulio Ricordi would automatically take care of these matters. In fact, almost forgotten in all this was Tito Ricordi—he could, Puccini felt, eventually acquire the Italian rights from him, but he felt no obligation to the firm. Tito had, for too long, shown little respect for Puccini while showering most of his attention on Riccardo Zandonai.

In late April 1914, an agreement was signed with the Viennese. "And good-bye to Savoia—but he has really brought it on his own head," the composer wrote Sybil. Adami had started work at once, and in May he had completed the libretto for the first act of *La Rondine*. In the beginning,

Puccini was pleased and optimistic, but as early as May 26 he was disenchanted, and he wrote to Eisner. "I don't much like the libretto for the *Rondine*." He found it stale and tiresome, a story unworthy of his time and effort; yet he would continue to work on it, even if he did so without his customary passion and dedication. This was, indeed, a new Puccini; never in the past would have have continued work on an opera which involved him so superficially.

During the summer of 1914, Adami spent a good deal of time with the composer at Torre del Lago and at Viareggio. As they worked together, it became obvious that Puccini was incapable of writing an operetta, and before long Adami was reshaping rather than adapting the German libretto—he and the composer were turning an operetta into an opera, something that could not displease the Viennese, for the result would be more rather than less than they had bargained for.

That summer, war broke out in Europe, and though Italy was not yet directly involved, Puccini was inevitably shaken. On September 14, he wrote to Sybil: "During the first period of this terrible war, I felt absolutely stupefied and I was unable to work anymore; now I've started again, and I'm pleased about it." In the same letter he said that the opera would be finished in the spring and that it was "agreeable, limpid, easy to sing, with a little waltz music and lively and fetching tunes."

It is surprising that Puccini in 1914 would be willing to settle for "lively and fetching tunes," as he wrote Sybil, but his letters to Adami were not nearly so optimistic. After the librettist turned in his second act, the composer expressed his disappointment. "I am not happy, I am not laughing, I am not interested," he confessed to Adami. He was bored with the whole thing, and he was working mechanically and without real interest—something he had been unwilling and unable to do before. He resigned himself to what he felt was a mediocre second act, but in November, after having gone over the third act, he was ready to abandon the opera. On the nineteenth he wrote his librettist:

> I am completely discouraged. The third act is making me suffer so greatly that perhaps *Rondine* will remain with only two acts, and published posthumously. It doesn't work, the end doesn't convince me. Where did he find Magda, in a convent? And that great love of his collapses in an instant, when he finds out who she is? Whoever sees and hears this drama cannot believe in it and is bound to find the ending almost illogical, and certainly not convincing. And when the public is not won over, there's not a chance for the opera to succeed. . . . The third act as it stands is useless, dead. The usual duet, and a clumsy, unconvincing ending. What can be done? How can we get out of this?

I can send the contract back to Vienna and think about something else. Believe me, dear Adami, my eyes are open. The *Rondine* is a complete mess. Damn the moment I started with the Viennese.

Somehow, he found a way to keep working—even without his usual enthusiasm—and on April 9, 1915, he wrote to Sybil that the opera was nearly completed. Six weeks later, on May 23, Italy entered World War One, joining an alliance with Great Britain, France, and Russia and declaring war on Austria-Hungary.

The War Years: *La Rondine*

Puccini was not a political man; he had shown little interest in world affairs, nor had he expressed himself on Italy's domestic problems. When war had begun to engulf Europe during the summer of 1914, he was stunned and, very briefly, unable to work. The important thing for him, however, was that his own country had remained neutral and was not yet involved in the armed conflict. On December 22, 1914, he wrote to Sybil that "at least we're not at war; this is a selfish remark to make, I know, but I cannot do otherwise than make it. War is too horrible a thing whatever the results, for whether it be victory or defeat, human lives are sacrificed. We live in a terrible world, and I see no sign of this cruel state of things coming to an end! I am working — but God knows when I shall be able to give this opera, which has to have its première in Vienna."

The composer's political sentiments were, quite clearly, formed more by his concern for the fate of his music than for any deeply felt convictions. His operas earned him huge royalties from all parts of the world, but especially from Germany and Austria, where he was a popular hero; in addition, *La Rondine*, by contract, had to be first performed in Vienna. On the other hand, the French, though enjoying his music, had always treated it with a certain condescension and even contempt. Primarily for these reasons, during the period of Italian neutrality he tended to side with the Germans and Austrians, as did a large number of Italians. His expression of these sentiments, during the summer of 1914, were the cause of a bitter, if short-lived break with Toscanini, who was spending his holidays at Viareggio, close to the

Puccini home. One evening, when the two musicians were arguing about the war, Puccini complained of the state of total chaos in Italy and expressed the hope that the Germans would come in to put things to order. The passionately anti-German Toscanini was enraged. He leapt to his feet and closed himself in his house, refusing to leave it for fear of what he might do if he ever bumped into Puccini. He remained there for one week, and for many years did not forgive the composer.

Toscanini was not alone in his anti-German sentiments, which were shared by much of Europe's intellectual and artistic community; and on two occasions Puccini's refusal to join this distinguished company caused him a considerable amount of trouble. The first time was towards the end of 1914, when Hall Caine, an English novelist, was preparing a volume called *King Albert's Book*, a collective expression of condemnation of Germany's aggression against Belgium and a tribute to the Belgians and their king. Contributions to the volume were solicited from Europe's most illustrious literary and musical figures, among them Maeterlinck, Debussy, Saint-Saëns, Messager, Elgar, Paderewski, D'Annunzio, Mascagni, Leoncavallo, and Puccini. All but Puccini joined in this protest.

A letter arrived from Caine in November 1914, and Puccini was frantic at the prospect of having to take a stand. He wrote at once to Carlo Clausetti, his friend at the House of Ricordi:

> Hall Caine bombards me with letters and telegrams. I have to write something—but then what can happen? The boycott of my operas? Did you read that Leoncavallo has been banned from German theatres? . . .
> I have to write something—I think—I can't evade it—but it means running a risk. I would say that I should come up with a small humane statement, deploring that war leads to excesses, etc.— but this could irritate the Germans—and then what? Please answer quickly. I telegraphed Hall Caine signing Madame Puccini and saying (in French), "My husband is on a trip and will return in three or five days" in order to gain time.
> Send me back the letters with practical advice.
> P.S. Or should I speak of a great desire for peace . . . ?

He also sent a letter to Tito Ricordi, saying that Caine had cabled "Madame Puccini" that he eagerly awaited her husband's return and reply, and on the back of that letter Puccini sent a draft of his proposed answer to Caine:

> Upon returning from my trip, I found your letters awaiting me. You ask me for something which my spirit would willingly do, because I too have been moved by the sad fate of Belgium and have admired the heroic defense of that people, led by the courageous King Albert.

But I have already received requests to join in other tributes and protests from other parties. I have answered all of them that I wanted to stand aside and because of this did not want my name to appear in public. I tell this to you, asking you to forgive my self-restraint. . . .

If Puccini's behavior in this matter was anything but admirable, he was apparently blameless a short time later, when he was accused of taking sides by both the Germans and the French. In later December 1914, news of a German boycott of his operas reached him, based on a charge that he had signed a proclamation decrying the German bombardment of Rheims, which had almost leveled the city. On December 21 the composer wrote a short note to Arthur Wolff, secretary of the German Theatrical Society, denying the charge. "I have just heard from my publisher, Mr. Ricordi, that you are counting me among those who have taken a stand against Germany," he wrote. "I am delighted to be able to tell you that, on the contrary, I have always refrained in any manifestation against your country."

Predictably, this denial caused an uproar in France, where the composer had long been suspected of Germanophilia. He was puzzled and irritated, maintaining that he had never been invited to join the long list of intellectuals who had signed the protest. He wrote to Tito Ricordi that he had never refused to sign the proclamation, nor did he even know that there had been such a proclamation. Nonetheless, he reiterated that he preferred not to take any part in political activities, especially while his own country was still neutral, and that because of his own neutrality he felt that both the German boycott and the French anger at him were completely unjustified.

His explanations did nothing to calm the outcry, and on February 11, 1915, he wrote to Sybil:

It is some time since I had your dear news. You will have heard of the uproar in the French papers against me — they are unjust and have always been against my music because it is so successful in their theatres — I made no sort of demonstration in favor of Germany and have kept myself strictly neutral as was my duty. I have feelings of friendship and gratefulness for the reception given to my music everywhere — in France, in England, in Austria and in Germany — only I happened to read in a German paper that I was against Germany and they said that I actually signed this declaration — whereas I had in fact signed nothing, for the simple reason that I was never asked to. And so I wrote a couple of lines denying this, saying that I had never taken up a hostile attitude to Germany. That is all — and from this a whole host of the basest calumnies have poured down on my head. But patience — everything will pass — as I hope this terrible War which has shaken the whole world will also pass! . . .

Only two weeks later, he wrote to her again, claiming that it was not the French people but his jealous French colleagues who had taken a stand against him and that his position was dictated by the policies of his country:

> No, dear Sybil! — my little denial (which perhaps it would have been better if I hadn't made) has been travestied by my enemies in France into an assertion which is untrue. I repeat to you that it isn't the French — that is, the people of France — but those incapable colleagues, people like X, Y, Z and Co., who for a long time past have been working and writing against me — it is they who have let loose the storm. You know how grateful I always am to anyone who has shown me a kindness — that is why I am indebted to the people of France, of England, of Germany, of America, and I might go on until I had mentioned all the nations of the civilized world, because my music has found its way into every quarter of the globe — and so I must publicly show myself impartial and neutral. As an Italian, it is my duty to be bound by neutrality, and so I am — because, having a horror of war and loving my country as I do, I must pray God that it be preserved from this scourge. I have an additional reason for saying this, that I do not think my country is as yet in a position to take part in a big conflict. You will see that when it is over — and God will that that may be soon! — all these unjust little outbursts of rage will vanish.

Strangely, his anger was directed not at the Germans, who had banned his works, but at the French. He wrote Alfredo Vandini that his "dear French brothers" couldn't stand the idea that his operas were supporting their national theatres, and he wrote Father Panichelli that his "bilious colleagues spit venom because they are envious — and the same goes for their allied press." He was grateful for those who came to his defense, among them, according to Sybil, the English — "You people are more serious-minded and have better sense than the French," he wrote her, and he was pleased that a number of citizens of Lucca supported him, writing the mayor, in April, that he had refused to sign all petitions, including those asking him to support the cause of the Germans.

The following month, when Italy joined the war, the situation changed radically. Puccini could no longer hide behind his country's neutrality, but resentment toward him remained. Tito Ricordi accordingly suggested that the composer might make some positive statement to heal the breach with the French and mollify that part of the public which had criticized him for his prewar attitudes. The composer disagreed. Leoncavallo had throughout been outspoken in his anti-German sentiments, and Puccini did not want to appear to be following his lead. In addition, he felt that no apologies were needed, and that the storm would pass in time. As a concrete move against the enemy, now that Italy was at war with Austria, he was determined to take all possible steps to break his contract with the Viennese publishers. If this entailed legal complications, which were difficult to straighten out, he would simply change both the title and the libretto of *La Rondine*. This move, he felt certain, should satisfy his critics.

As a first step, a meeting was arranged in Switzerland between the composer and Berté, one of the Viennese impresarios, but no agreement was reached to alter their contract. Puccini explained that he was unwilling to wait until the end of the war for the première of his new opera, and Berté agreed merely to present this point of view to his board of directors in Vienna, after which a decision would be made. Shortly afterward, he notified the composer that the board had decided to postpone any decision until the hostilities had come to an end.

Nonetheless, Puccini did retain the Italian rights to *La Rondine*, and he was free to negotiate their sale—even if the opera, by agreement, had to be performed for the first time in Vienna. In spite of his less than cordial relations with Tito Ricordi at the time, he felt it his duty to offer the work, which had been completed by Easter of 1916, to the House of Ricordi. He knew that Tito had been opposed to the project from the start, but he was stunned when word reached him that his publisher wanted no part of the opera and that he considered it to be no more than "bad Lehár."

Just at this time, another Italian publisher, Sonzogno (who had years before rejected *Le Villi*), entered the picture, offering not only to publish Puccini's opera in Italy, but also to go to the trouble to buy up world rights from the Viennese publishers. From Puccini's point of view, this was the ideal solution, as it would enable *La Rondine* to be produced before the end of the war, but he felt obligated to offer the opera one more time to Ricordi. On July 31, 1916, he wrote him:

> I have just received some serious proposals to resolve the question of *Rondine*. Although you have already told me your opinion of this business, that the onerous conditions of the contract made it impossible for you to deal with it, I still wanted to inform you before making a firm commitment. Since the matter is urgent, and I have to give an answer within seven or eight days, and since I am anxious to resolve this nightmarish situation, I beg you to write to me immediately.
>
> The proposal I received would relieve me of any legal responsibility, would resolve the political question, and would bring me a considerable amount of money. I am upset that this arrangement would not be made with your firm, but I can no longer keep this work of mine on the shelf and allow it to grow stale.

Ricordi did not make a counter-offer, but several months later he apparently had some regrets for at that time Puccini wrote him that "with regards to *La Rondine*, I offered it to you a hundred times, and you rejected it, and I don't see why you should now be faced with problems because of it."

In December 1916, the composer signed a formal agreement with Sonzogno, but even before then, on December 3, he signed another agreement with the House of Ricordi granting that firm first refusal to the rights to any of his future operas, as long as Tito Ricordi was director of the publishing house, thus confirming that his break with his publisher was to be merely a temporary one.

In late February 1917, Puccini left Torre del Lago and, accompanied by Elvira, traveled to Monte Carlo to prepare for the première of *La Rondine*, which had been arranged by Sonzogno. He wrote his niece Albina that he felt "old in body but a lion as far as my head goes." His presence at the première of one of his operas was, this time, more of a duty than a pleasure. An English writer, Thomas Burke, spotted him wandering lonely on the terrace outside the opera house, and the composer wrote to his friends that he felt lost and missed his home.

The opening night, on March 27, 1917, was a gala one. Monte Carlo's impresario was the distinguished Raoul Gunsbourg, who had brought international fame to the opera house with his presentation of the first staged version of Berlioz's *La Damnation de Faust*, as well as the world premières of Massenet's *Le Jongleur de Notre-Dame* and *Don Quichotte*, and the first performance anywhere of Puccini's new opera was a worthy addition to the impresario's impressive list of firsts. The cast, too, was excellent, with Gilda Dalla Rizza, a young soprano who had first come to Puccini's attention when she sang Minnie, and Tito Schipa singing the roles of the lovers; the conductor was the Sicilian maestro, Gino Marinuzzi, a favorite of the composer's since, as a very young man, he had conducted *Tosca* in Catania.

As befitted the occasion, the small, jewel-like opera house was crowded for what was considered the musical event of the year, and Puccini sat in the royal box next to Albert I, Prince of Monaco. Missing, however, because of the war, was the usual throng of critics from all over the world.

The performance was a huge success; there were innumerable curtain calls, and the composer was called upon repeatedly to bow from his place in the box. The local press, though noting the fragility of the libretto, was full of praise for the opera. André Corneau, writing in the *Journal de Monaco*, said: "It was a triumphant gala. *La Rondine*, the first swallow of the season, follows the successful tradition which is confirmed with each work signed by the very great name of Puccini. . . . It is a work that is ever smiling, even through the honest tears which shine like pearls." The reviewer for *L'Eclaireur de Nice*, noting the opera's uninterrupted flow of melody, commented that "the swallow seems to have taken wing on its flight across the world," and Claude Trevor, one of the few foreign critics heard from, wrote in *The*

Musical Standard that "it will not be very long before the suave melodies of Puccini's last success will be heard everywhere where flowing, melodious music still appeals."

On April 3, in appreciation of his service to Monaco, the Ordre de Saint-Charles was bestowed upon Puccini, but at the same time the French press resumed its attacks not only on the composer, but on the man who had arranged for and presided over the first production of *La Rondine*. The attack was led this time by Léon Daudet, son of the author of the Tartarin stories, who wrote a series of scathing articles in the paper *L'Action Française*, protesting the presentation of work commissioned by the Viennese and demanding that Gunsbourg be condemned for commerce with the enemy. Daudet's complaint reached the courts, which exonerated the impresario, but before then, in April, Puccini himself sent a lengthy letter of explanation to the leading French newspapers. It read, in part:

> M. Léon Daudet, continuing in *L'Action Française* his campaign against M. Gunsbourg, the director of Monte Carlo's theatre, attacks the origins of my latest opera, *La Rondine*. . . . I find it essential, out of a love for the truth, to set the record straight.
>
> Long before the war, I signed a contract with a Viennese publisher for an operetta. Messrs. Willner and Reichert offered me, through the publishers, a suggestion for a libretto which I accepted as a basis. But when I set to work, I changed my mind completely. I no longer felt like writing an operetta and I therefore could not accept the libretto as presented to me. Then, in agreement with the publishers and the librettists, the original contract was changed so that not only would I write an opera rather than an operetta, but also that the libretto would be written by Giuseppe Adami, with whom I then began to work. The libretto of *La Rondine* was thus born of a continuous and assiduous collaboration between me and Adami, to which Willner and Reichert remained extraneous. The authors of the original project, in this reversal of the terms, would have become German-language translators of Adami's libretto, because the contract required that *La Rondine* be first performed in Vienna in the German language.
>
> I must add that in the contract with the foreign publishers, both my librettist and I retained the complete rights to the opera for Italy and for South America. Once the war broke out, even before Italy's intervention, I wanted to change the contract so as to have the rights to my opera not only for Italy and South America, which I had always retained, but for all countries. The publishers did not grant me this change, which I requested repeatedly and in every possible way, and I then decided not to consign the opera, which was almost completed, in spite of many requests and in spite of the fact that the publishers were to pay me a certain amount upon the delivery of

each act. I therefore kept the *Rondine* in a drawer, more than ever determined to find a way to get out of the contract which had become, because of political events, intolerable for me. Lorenzo Sonzogno, an Italian publisher, intervened; by eliciting a ministerial decree and assuming all eventual responsibilities toward the Viennese publishers, he could offer me the complete liberation of *La Rondine*, and then having annulled the original contract, could sign a completely new contract with me and with my librettist, for the absolute rights to the opera. I joyfully accepted the offer because it crowned my wishes and my insistent efforts with success. . . .

This then explains the origins and the history of my opera. Thus, the accusation of M. Daudet comes down to this: I withdrew from our enemies something which was their property, and I gave my opera to an Italian publisher. If this is my crime, I have reason to be proud of it.

Puccini had joined the reviewers in predicting a long and happy life for his newest opera, but the bird's flight was a short and not very successful one, due initially not only to the opera's defects but to the difficulty in obtaining the services of first-rate singers during the war years. The first Italian production, given at Bologna in June, was a success, but the next production, at Milan's Teatro Dal Verme, was a near disaster. Puccini blamed the cast—he thought they were all "dogs, dogs, dogs," and he also felt the conducting of his old friend Mugnone was heavy-handed and colorless—but the press blamed the opera itself for the evening's failure. The next production took place in Rome, and it was somewhat more successful. The tenor on that occasion was Beniamino Gigli, then twenty-seven years old. Puccini had considered Gigli for the role of Ruggero at the time of the opera's Italian première, but he then believed that the tenor's rotund figure might make him an unconvincing young lover. By the time of the Rome production, however, the composer decided that the public would pay little attention to Gigli's figure once they had heard his voice.

Scattered performances followed—in Turin, Bergamo, Naples, and in South America, and Puccini's "Viennese" opera finally reached Vienna in October 1920. In spite of many revisions made at different times by the composer, *La Rondine* has never become a permanent part of the repertory of any major opera house.

In 1916, even before finishing *La Rondine*, Puccini had resumed work on *Il Tabarro*. Adami's libretto, which had been hastily written, had satisfied the librettist but not the composer, however, and once again Puccini sought a co-librettist. This time he turned to Dario Niccodemi, an Italian playwright who had already made a name for himself in the French theatre. Not wanting to offend Adami, who felt there was no need of a collaborator, Puccini secretly asked Niccodemi to do what he could to enliven the script and give it the color he felt was lacking. It was a useless deception; Niccodemi showed little interest in the project and soon abandoned it. Rather than look elsewhere, the composer took matters into his own hands, and under his close supervision, Adami made the necessary changes in the libretto, and the composer completed his composition of the opera on November 25, 1916.

Puccini was pleased with the results; he believed that *Il Tabarro* was an effective theatrical work, but he still needed two more short works to complete his project. Happily, during that period he renewed his friendship with a young man, Giovacchino Forzano, who was to provide him with these remaining parts of his trilogy.

The two men had first met when Forzano, then a young journalist, had interviewed Puccini for a Florentine newspaper while the latter was composing *La Fanciulla del West*. They quickly established a friendly rapport, and at the end of the interview Forzano mentioned that someday he would like to write an original libretto for Puccini. The composer encouraged him and promised to read carefully anything Forzano sent him.

A few years later, Forzano moved to Viareggio where he frequently met the composer, who continued to remind him of his vow to submit an original idea for a libretto. At one of these meetings, Puccini suggested that Forzano might try his hand at the adaptation of *La Houppelande*, but the young man reminded him that he was interested in doing an original work and not an adaptation from a foreign source. (It was he who suggested Martini for the adaptation of the Didier Gold play.)

As time passed, the paths of the two men crossed often — Forzano, who had built a reputation in the theatre, had been the literary expert at the auction of Ouida's property and had also started writing the libretto based on *Two Little Wooden Shoes* for Mascagni. He was still eager to find an original subject for Puccini, and in the winter of 1916–1917, he presented the composer with his first idea. The short opera, which would be called *Suor Angelica*, would deal with the last day in the life of a nun, born a princess, who had been banished to a convent after having given birth to a son out of wedlock, and who, upon learning from a visiting aunt that the child had died, kills herself by drinking a concoction of poisonous herbs in order to join her child.

Puccini was deeply moved by the subject — his visits to the convent of his own sister, a nun, would be helpful in providing him with a feeling for the background — which would also represent a departure for the composer in that the opera contained no roles for male voices. He asked Forzano to begin work at once and soon after left for Milan to tell Tito Ricordi the story of his next opera. From Milan, he wrote to Forzano:

I angelically told Tito about the poison in the salad and the rain of gold pieces, and he was astonished. I'll write you again tomorrow. It's cold here and dark by seven so that one bumps into passersby because the lights are not golden as in Suor Angelica's little church. From now on, everything that is not angelic is unimportant to me.

By early 1917, Puccini was hard at work on "the new Nun" as he described her; he was excited to be at work on an opera for which he felt a good deal of his former enthusiasm. His relationship with Forzano was a good and an easy one. Living close to each other as they did, a long, complicated correspondence was unnecessary and they could easily discuss any problems that arose. By the end of February, Forzano had completed the entire libretto, and on March 3 he wrote to Tito Ricordi that Puccini had already composed a good part of the first scene, which was so "simple, noble, and so clearly Franciscan that no work could have a more auspicious beginning." In May, when Puccini's work on the score was well advanced, the librettist again wrote to Tito of his enormous enthusiasm for the opera, which he felt contained the composer's "loftiest and at the same time simplest music."

Puccini, too, was optimistic throughout the composition of *Suor Angelica*. He worked harmoniously with Forzano, and this time he felt no need for a second librettist; the only outside help he requested was from Father Panichelli, to whom he turned for advice on liturgical matters.

Suor Angelica was completed on September 14, 1917, somewhat later than anticipated, only because the composer had for several months interrupted his work on the story of the tragic nun to start on the third of his one-act operas, again based on an idea of Forzano's. This turn of events had been unexpected, but more than welcome.

Shortly after Forzano had set to work on *Suor Angelica*, reports began to circulate in the press of Puccini's continued search for a short comic opera. They told of his approaching such figures as George Bernard Shaw, a commercially successful team of French writers Robert de Flers and Armand de Caillavet, and Sacha Guitry. Forzano was disappointed that the composer was once again looking for a non-Italian subject, and he expressed his dismay to Puccini, who admitted that his search had so far been fruitless. At this point, Forzano came up with his own idea, a comedy based on a few verses drawn from Cantos XXV and XXX of Dante's *Inferno*, in which the poet condemns the deceitful Gianni Schicchi to Hell. Dante did not find Schicchi's antics humorous, but Forzano did. Puccini was intrigued, and at the end of February 1917, Forzano submitted to him an outline for the proposed opera. The story, set in thirteenth century Florence, was a simple one. The relatives of the recently deceased, and very wealthy, Buoso Donati have gathered around his deathbed to mourn him and to examine his will, in which it is rumored he has left his considerable fortune and property to a monastery. Their fears confirmed, they summon the wily Gianni Schicchi to come to their aid. Since Donati's death has not yet been announced, Schicchi proposes to impersonate the deceased and dictate a new will, which will leave the estate to his relatives. All agree, and a notary is called in to record this false will. To the horror of the powerless relatives, the disguised Schicchi leaves the bulk of the estate to . . . Gianni Schicchi.

After reading the outline, Puccini was enthusiastic. He would be able to reach two of his goals with one short opera—to make people laugh, and to base one of his works, no matter how loosely, on Dante. By June 1917, Forzano had finished writing the libretto, his only problem having come at the very end, a problem he solved by the device of having Schicchi come before the curtain and address himself to the audience, asking their forgiveness for what he had done.

Puccini accepted the libretto with but one small reservation—he wanted a short trio to be added just before Schicchi donned his disguise. Never before had he been so quickly and unconditionally satisfied. In fact, his elation was such that he wanted to interrupt his work on *Suor Angelica* so that he might immediately start the composition of *Gianni Schicchi*, and he sent off the following verses to Forzano:

Dopo *Il Tabarro* di tinta nera
Sento la voglia di buffegiare.
Lei non si picchi
Se faccio prima quel *Gianni Schicchi*.

(After the gloomy *Il Tabarro*
I feel a desire to clown.
So don't be upset
If I first do that *Gianni Schicchi*.)

It was a relief for the composer to turn his energies to the witty, light-hearted comedy, which finally gave him an opportunity to express the more cheerful, and typically Tuscan, side of his nature, and he did so with gusto. At one point during the summer, however, he returned to *Suor Angelica*, which he finished in the fall; its first audition, with the composer playing the piano and, in his deep hoarse voice, singing the words before the nuns at his sister's convent, was an unqualified success—the nuns were moved to tears. A few months later, on April 18, 1918, *Gianni Schicchi*, too, was completed.

The war years had been surprisingly productive ones for Puccini. The conflict which he had so dreaded had affected him personally—many of his relatives, including Tonio, had served at the front—yet he had managed to complete one opera, *La Rondine*, which had been produced, and his trilogy, which he would call *Il Trittico* (The Triptych), was ready to be presented as soon as a production could be arranged.

However, as the war went on, he felt increasingly trapped—his routine and his travels had been suspended for too long. As early as April 27, 1916, he had written frantically to Sybil from Torre del Lago, "How I long to travel! When will this cursed war be over. It seems to me like a suspension of life. . . . Here one languishes; between the green earth and the sea, the seeds of hatred against this enforced calm are beginning to develop within me. . . ." More than a year later, he was even more desperate, and on June 17, 1917, he wrote to Sybil that he could no longer stand being tied down and unable to make his customary trips to London or to Vienna.

Worse than that, when the *Trittico* was completed, he was forced to face the fact that his new work could not be given for the first time in Italy. Singers were not available, and wartime conditions made the elaborate preparations necessary for a new production too costly. Instead of Rome, where he wanted to present his short operas for the first time, he had to resign himself to another première, the following fall, outside of his own country. On June 8, 1918, he wrote to Sybil: "Everything is paralyzed, but don't let's talk about my art — I've finished the three operas, and they're going to be given for the first time in New York. . . . I should dearly have loved to have heard this new music of mine and I hoped that the war would be over in November — but it seems as though we shall never see the world set straight again. . . ."

Il Trittico

The armistice ending the first world war was signed on November 11, 1918. Though the première of the *Trittico* was not scheduled to take place until December 14, it was impossible for Puccini to attend its first performance in New York. For the first time in his life, he would neither supervise nor be present at the première of one of his works. "Could I have foreseen the sudden collapse of our enemies," he wrote Gatti-Casazza, "I certainly should have been helping to celebrate the glorious victory in New York." However, the difficulties of transatlantic travel immediately following the war made such a celebration impossible.

Even without the composer's personal presence at the rehearsals, the utmost care was given to the preparations of the new operas. The conductor, Roberto Moranzoni, had managed to travel to Viareggio to go over the score with Puccini, and the Metropolitan had assembled a distinguished cast for the occasion. Claudia Muzio created the role of Giorgetta in *Il Tabarro;* Geraldine Farrar sang the role of Suor Angelica; and Giuseppe De Luca starred in *Gianni Schicchi*. From early November on, Gatti-Casazza kept sending cables to the anxious composer to assure him that all was going well. Gatti, though surprisingly no great admirer of Puccini's music — "Despite the fact that neither you nor I admire his music, we cannot deny the fact that Puccini is the most popular of living composers," he had written Otto Kahn of the Met in September 1915 — obviously felt a personal loyalty to the composer and wanted, for many reasons, to stay on good terms with him.

Though the glamour which had surrounded the opening of *Fanciulla* was missing, a large audience filled the Metropolitan Opera House on December 14 and enthusiastically applauded the performers. Gatti-Casazza was able to cable the composer that each opera had been cheered and that there had been more than forty curtain calls in all, adding that the evening was a complete success.

The evening itself, as an occasion, was undoubtedly a success, though two of Puccini's three operas had been greeted with less than complete approval. The press the following day, too, was mixed. W. J. Henderson, in a mildly favorable review, made note of the relationship the operas bore to one another. "The succession is like that of symphonic movements. The first a passionate and stormy *allegro*, the second a pallid elegaic *andante*, and the third a flashing *finale*, inviting the mind to frolic in a whimsy of fantastic humors for relief after the songs of sin and sorrow." The reviewer for the *Herald*, Reginald de Koven, wrote: "I cannot think that, from his own standpoint, in these operas Mr. Puccini has given us anything markedly new, and yet he has said a good many old things in a new way, and his score abounds with orchestral quips and oddities, pictorially characteristic, orchestrally effective, and dramatically descriptive and appropriate."

Henry Finck, writing in the *Evening Post*, found *Il Tabarro* to be the most interesting of the three operas from a musical point of view, but the audience and most of the critics agreed that the most successful of the operas was *Gianni Schicchi*. "This comedy is so uproariously funny," commented Henry Krehbiel of the *Tribune*, "the music so full of life, humor, and ingenious devices . . . it was received with uproarious delight, signs of appreciation not waiting till the closing of the curtain." Writing in the *Times*, James Gibbons Huneker found little to praise except for Puccini's little comic opera. "The gaiety is irresistible," he wrote, "and the music as frothing and exhilarating as champagne." Huneker's reaction to *Il Tabarro* can be best described as lukewarm, while his opinion of *Suor Angelica* was decidedly negative. He found it "sugary . . . mock-Maeterlinck . . . mock-turtle mysticism . . . and all insincere," noting that there was but one role "which was played with histrionic beauty by Geraldine Farrar, who, luckily, was in better voice than usual."

Many of the New York critics pointed out a change in the composer's style and his use of what they referred to as "Debussyian harmonies," especially in *Il Tabarro* and *Suor Angelica*, and for this reason it is relevant to quote from a letter that Puccini wrote the previous April, shortly after the French composer's death. The letter was sent to a journalist on the *Giornale d'Italia*, and it read in part:

> . . . When today I hear people speak of Debussyism as if it were a system to follow or not to follow, I should like to tell these young musicians of the doubts which, as I can attest from my personal

knowledge, assailed the great artist in his later years. His harmonic procedures which, when they were first made known, appeared so surprising and full of a new beauty, became less and less so in the course of time, until ultimately they surprised no one. Even to the composer himself they appeared to represent a restricted field of experiment, and, I repeat, I know how much he attempted, in vain, to escape from this field. A fervent admirer of Debussy, I was anxiously awaiting to see how Debussy himself proposed to revolt against Debussyism. Now the great artist is dead, and we cannot know the manner, possibly very beneficial, in which he would have carried out this revolt.

While the *Trittico* was having its official world première in New York, Puccini busied himself with preparations for its first European presentation, to take place at Rome's Teatro Costanzi on January 11, 1919. For him this was the real première, the first performance which would benefit by his supervision and careful attention. He worked meticulously on every aspect of the production, paying special attention to the sets, which he discussed at length with the designer Galileo Chini, and to the stage effects, which he believed were of special importance to his three short operas.

Several weeks before the performance, he traveled to Rome to work with the singers: he was especially happy that Gilda Dalla Rizza would sing not only the role of Suor Angelica, but also that of Lauretta in *Gianni Schicchi*, and that the three operas would be conducted by Marinuzzi. Always anxious before any important performance of one of his operas, he was especially nervous this time, making minor revisions on the operas during rehearsals and even, reportedly, asking Ottorino Respighi to rework a few pages of *Il Tabarro* which didn't please him.

The occasion, Italy's first gala musical event since the end of the war, was an appropriately festive one, attended by the king and queen, the Duchess of Aosta, and other members of the royal family. The audience responded rather coolly to *Il Tabarro*, showed more enthusiasm for *Suor Angelica*, but, as in New York, reserved most of its enthusiasm for *Gianni Schicchi*, which was wildly cheered. The press, for the most part, mirrored the audience's reaction. Sebastiano A. Luciani, writing in *Il Tempo*, felt that *Il Tabarro* was a failure, *Suor Angelica* contained "more elements for a lasting success, though it adds little to Puccini's fame," but that *Gianni Schicchi* was "a little masterpiece." Most of the other critics concurred, with the reviewer for *Corriere della Sera* summing up their opinions by stating that "only *Gianni Schicchi* is alive in all respects," and was "an almost perfect opera." Perhaps carried away by the excitement of hearing his operas sung for the first time, the composer joyfully cabled Gatti-Casazza in New York that all three operas had achieved a magnificent success.

With the *Trittico* launched in Italy, Puccini's thoughts began to turn to

London, where he hoped his operas would be performed in the late spring. This would give him the opportunity to visit the British capital for the first time since the war, and he eagerly looked forward to it. There was one problem, however, which very nearly prevented him from making the trip: he had learned that Toscanini was about to be engaged by Covent Garden to conduct the three operas. He was furious. The two men had reconciled after their political quarrels, but Puccini had learned that the conductor had walked out of a performance of *Il Tabarro*, loudly proclaiming that he did not like the opera at all. This, from the composer's point of view, ruled him out as a conductor for his short operas—or, for the moment, for any of his operas. He vented his anger in a letter to Sybil of March 16, 1919: "I protested to Ricordi's because I don't want that *pig* of a Toscanini; he has said all sorts of nasty things about my operas and has tried to inspire certain journalists to run them down too. . . . I won't have this *God*. He's no use to me—and I say, as I have already said, that when an orchestral conductor thinks poorly of the operas he has to conduct, he can't interpret them properly. . . ."

In this same letter, Puccini mentioned rather casually that Tito Ricordi had been forced to resign from the publishing house. This was, apparently, not unexpected. The firm had not been doing well, and Tito had spent too much money in trying to promote musicians, including Zandonai, who did not meet with public favor. For sentimental reasons only, Puccini was sorry about Tito's forced resignation, but the firm would now be run by Valcarenghi and Clausetti, both closely attached to the composer, though the latter was known to be an intimate friend of the temporarily out-of-favor Toscanini.

A few days later, Puccini was able to relax. It was announced that Toscanini would not be coming to London; according to the papers the cause was his inability to reach an agreement with the management of Covent Garden, but the composer felt the real reason was the conductor's fears that Puccini might cause a scandal if he did come.

This, however, left *Il Trittico* without a conductor. Puccini wanted Thomas Beecham to conduct his operas, but he was ruled out by the directors of the opera house. The composer then suggested Ettore Panizza, who was unavailable. No one wanted Mugnone, who was available. There was considerable discussion over who would sing in the three operas, and finally the new production was postponed until the following season. London's opera house had been closed during the war, and the management felt that there was insufficient time to organize any new productions at all for the first postwar season. Instead, Covent Garden reopened on May 12, with an old favorite, *La Bohème*, starring Nellie Melba, in the presence of the royal family, an occasion, in the words of the *Times*, "to revive former glories as closely as possible, to carry us back in memory a dozen years or more to the time when Puccini first became the ruling divinity of the Royal Opera House."

In spite of the fact that there was no longer any official reason for the trip, Puccini's desire to revisit London was such that he traveled there in late June — largely to see Sybil and to try to make arrangements for a British production of *La Rondine*. In his volume of letters written by the composer to Sybil, Vincent Seligman wrote of this visit:

> He seemed to have changed but little during the long interval since we had seen him last; his hair had begun to turn white, but it was as abundant as ever; his movements were perhaps a little slower and more measured, but the coming of old age over which he continually laments in his letters was with him a very gradual and almost imperceptible process, and no one would have guessed that he had turned sixty. . . .
>
> Above all, he had retained that simple boyish outlook on life, that keen appreciation and enjoyment of its "little things" which never deserted him. Back in his beloved London, he was exactly like a schoolboy on the first few days after term; he must go everywhere and see everything — and everything that he saw delighted him. . . .

The composer spent little time in Covent Garden — he was like a liberated prisoner, re-experiencing the joys of his prewar visits — but he did go to the theatre several times, even including a visit to London's biggest hit, *Chu Chin Chow*, which did not much impress him, and an evening watching the Diaghilev ballet. Far more satisfactory were his shopping expeditions, and Vincent Seligman wrote:

> His wardrobe had become sadly depleted during the past five years, and had to be restocked from top to bottom. My mother calculated that to walk from one end of Bond Street to the other took nearly two hours, for there was scarcely a shop window that did not retain an excellent print of his nose. I remember on one occasion accompanying them to my hosier in search of ties which, as he admitted, were a special weakness of his. By a bit of sheer bad luck his eye chanced to rest on a large pile of them tastefully assembled in a corner of the shop. I say bad luck, because these were not just ordinary ties; before I had had time to intervene, Puccini had enrolled himself an honorary member of the Brigade of Guards, the Old Etonian and Old Harrovian Clubs, and the Rifle Brigade. He was on the point of joining the Royal Artillery, when I emitted a shocked protest; those ties, I said, were not for him. . . .

He shopped for Elvira, too, buying her fabrics and handkerchiefs, but he soon became bored. He had several meetings with Thomas Beecham and other important musical figures, but all these meetings concerned the next year's plans — and he was anxious to see the operas he had composed during the war produced as quickly as possible.

The London première of *Il Trittico* finally took place a year later, on June 18, 1920, and Puccini's stay in the capital to supervise rehearsals provided him with ample confirmation of his enormous popularity in England. Not that he had need of any such confirmations: Puccini's operas led the roster of major opera houses throughout the world — during the season ending in June 1919, New York's Metropolitan had performed his works more often than those of any other composer (thirty times that season, compared with twenty-two performances of Verdi's operas); the Opéra-Comique in Paris had in 1919 given the two hundredth performance of *Butterfly*; and there were similar reports from all over the world, confirmed by the enormous royalties the composer was collecting. Nonetheless, nowhere else, with the possible exception of Vienna, was the composer as idolized as he was in the British capital, and his stay there in 1920 was proof that his popularity had not faded during the war years. "My operas support the theatre here," he wrote Guido Vandini upon his arrival in London — a reasonable statement in view of the fact that not only was Covent Garden giving four of his earlier operas, in addition to the *Trittico*, but that two other theatres, the Lyceum in London and the Surrey at Fairbain-Miln were presenting *Butterfly* at the same time. To another friend, Gioacchino Mazzini, he wrote that he was literally in his kingdom — "they call me *The King of Melody*," he reported.

The composer was joined by Forzano, and the two of them worked diligently at the rehearsals; John Barbirolli, then a young cellist in the Covent Garden orchestra and later an outstanding interpreter of Puccini's operas, noted that the composer appeared one day in an Old Etonian tie — wearing other English school ties on other occasions. Once again, Puccini scrutinized every detail of the production, but this time he erred in insisting that the set for *Suor Angelica* reproduce exactly the cloisters of the convent at Vicopelago where he had often visited his sister, since in this way the stage action was all but invisible to a considerable part of the audience.

In spite of his joy at being in London and in again supervising the production of his operas, Puccini seemed somehow tired and anxious as the première approached. Thomas Burke spied him walking aimlessly by Golden Square, "a slim, sad, detached figure. . . . A graceful carriage, hat on one side of the head, a bored air, and in the eyes that expression of grievous amusement which a child wears when it knows that something funny is going on and doesn't quite understand." Writing in the *London Mercury*, Burke said, "I watched him as he turned the corner, and I wanted to overtake him and tell him that everything was all right."

The Seligmans, too, noted that the composer was even more worried than usual at the opening night of the *Trittico*. Nonetheless, as the audience's enthusiasm grew, he began to relax and enjoy himself to such an extent that he seemed hardly to notice the tepid response to *Il Tabarro* and the very weak response to *Suor Angelica*—once again, almost all of the cheers were reserved for *Gianni Schicchi*, which delighted the public.

The following morning the *Times* summarized both the joys and the sorrows of the occasion. It explained the "success" of the three operas by stating that "they could hardly be anything but a success at the present moment, when their composer is so much the darling of the opera-going public that half, at least, of the present season has been devoted to the repetition of his earlier works."

In expressing serious doubts about the future of these three short operas, the *Times* critic noted the often forgotten fact that "the latest of his successes is sixteen years old," but the article ended on a happy note. "But what mattered most to last night's audience was that Signor Puccini was present and could be called to the stage at the end of each opera as often as the audience wished. They took full advantage of this opportunity, as well they might, for what would Covent Garden be without Puccini? It was a unique chance to offer him the personal tribute of thanks."

Puccini, again apparently overwhelmed by the occasion, left London unaware or unwilling to acknowledge that two of his three operas had failed, but after returning home he learned that *Suor Angelica* had been withdrawn after only two performances. The excuse was that the soprano had taken ill and that no replacement could be found, but he soon realized that his opera about the tragic nun—his favorite of the three works—had not taken hold with the public. He lamented the fact that it was becoming, as he himself said, a "Cinderella," but in spite of his pleas to the management of Covent Garden and to his publisher, the opera was not restored, and his *Trittico*, for many performances, became a diptych; and still later, only *Gianni Schicchi* survived, not only in London, but in many theatres where the *Trittico* was presented.

In October of 1920, there was a second homecoming for the composer—this time in his beloved Vienna, where he traveled with Elvira and Tonio for the first performances of both *La Rondine* and the *Trittico*. As an enemy alien, the composer had not been able to travel to Austria for several years, and he was delighted that the Viennese again took him to their hearts. *Rondine* was greeted with indifference at its première at the Volksoper, but the composer blamed the production for this failure; the *Trittico*, on the other hand, was a great success at the more important Staatsoper. Puccini had convinced Jeritza, at the time his favorite performer ("perhaps the most original artiste I have ever known," he wrote Sybil), to alter her schedule in order to sing the soprano role in *Il Tabarro*, and he worked endless hours with her at the piano to ensure what he felt would be a magnificent performance. He was delighted, too, with the singing of Lotte Lehmann, who assumed the title role in *Suor Angelica*. He felt certain that if the directors of Covent

Garden used the services of these two singers, his two short operas would not suffer from the neglect that he began to realize was their fate in London.

During the first postwar trip to the Austrian capital, Puccini especially enjoyed making the acquaintance of Franz Lehár, who soon became a good friend. Their meeting was described by Anton Lehár, the nephew of the composer:

> From his period of service at Pola, Franz spoke pretty good Italian. I spoke a little of it, too, Puccini spoke hardly any German. But there was no problem of communication, for already during the meal the two masters were conversing almost exclusively by quoting alternately from their works. Singing softly, they indicated the melodies. Then they both sat at the piano and played: Puccini with the right hand, Lehár with the left. The most wonderful harmonies sounded forth, Puccinisms and Lehárisms, one surpassing another in sound effects and original turns of phrase. Lehár took the opportunity to tell Puccini about his own ambition to write a tragic opera. The *maestro* shook his head. He referred to his own rather disappointing operetta experiences, and said, "*Chi vuol far l'altrui mestiere, fa la zuppa nel paniere.*" (Or, "Cobbler stick to your last.")

Following this meeting, the two musicians exchanged warm letters. Puccini thanked his new friend for the good times spent in "enchanting Vienna, the town where music vibrates in the souls of all people, where even material things have a rhythmical life," and Lehár responded that their friendship was based "on the complete harmony of our musical feeling, on mutual understanding of all that each of us wanted to express—and had to express—in music."

After a round of receptions and parties in his honor, the composer returned home, determined once again to revise *La Rondine*, which he hoped would be given in Vienna again the following year at the Staatsoper, rather than at the Volksoper.

During this period, in addition to his travels to London and to Vienna, Puccini, as always, closely followed new productions of his operas, those written during the war, wherever they were performed. He professed great affection for these latest works, but it could not have escaped his notice that they were not as enthusiastically received as his earlier operas had been. It was true, as the London *Times* critic had observed, that his greatest triumphs had taken place many years before, and that no recent opera of his had remained a permanent part of the repertory of any major opera company.

In these postwar years, then, the composer had to face the challenge of duplicating his early successes, while at the same time not imitating them. More than ever, he felt the need to strike out in new directions, to write a wholly original opera.

There had been many changes in Puccini's life during the last few years. His personal life had become more serene. There were no more Corinnas or Josephines, and he and Elvira rediscovered the warmth and compatibility that had once existed between them. Tonio, too, seemed to have settled down, and the battles with the firm of Ricordi had come to an end, with the departure of Tito. This newfound peace which pervaded the composer's personal life—the ideal climate in which to write what he hoped would be his masterpiece—was, however, disturbed by the vast changes that were shaking the foundation of Italian society in the early postwar years. It was these changes that, not long after the war, made the composer decide to make a major move—from his once-adored home in Torre del Lago to nearby Viareggio. This meant a break with the past, and a painful one, but he felt he had no choice.

"Here at Torre it is dull and almost unpleasant," he wrote to Adami on March 30, 1921, after he had already made his decision. "Everything has its day, even Torre del Lago. The place has lost all its cachet. The morning siren is now supreme. It is disgusting!" The siren was that of a newly constructed peat factory, built not far from the Puccini villa on the shores of Lake Massaciuccoli. It was not merely the noise of the piercing siren, nor the foul odors that came from the factory that upset Puccini; the mere presence of any factory changed the character of his once peaceful, isolated village.

This very isolation, and the vulnerability that it brought with it, was apparently another reason for the composer's move. Dante del Fiorentino, in his memoir of Puccini, reported crossing the lake with him in his motorboat one day, when they were approached by a fisherman, who shook his fist at the composer and shouted, "It's yours now, soon it will be our turn." Del Fiorentino noticed the lines of the composer's face deepen, and he noted an intense sadness in the composer's eyes. When they returned home, Puccini was bitter. "There's a new spirit strangling Italy," Del Fiorentino reported him saying. "There is a moral sickness spreading through the world, and it has even come to our peaceful Tuscany. I have never intentionally done anyone any harm. I've tried to make people happy. Then why should that man hate me? There was hatred in his voice and in his face. . . ."

That "moral sickness" was, for Puccini, the social unrest that had spread through the country since the end of the war. There were strikes and riots, and the threat of socialist revolution was everpresent. In July of 1919, on his return from London, he had written of it to Sybil: "I got back to Pisa at four o'clock; it was raining and there was a strike on, which was half a revolution, on account of the high cost of living." He ended that same letter by writing, "I'm just off to Viareggio in the car; I hope they won't take it away from me, because there are riots there owing to the high cost of living, and it appears that it's half Bolshevik. . . ."

A year later, he even considered leaving Italy altogether, to settle in Vienna or in London, and he wrote Sybil from Torre del Lago on July 1, 1920:

> I am so sad here, so very sad—how different the life is from London! Italy is really in a bad way . . . and I can't stand Torre much more. I wouldn't mind leaving Italy either—certainly if things don't improve I shall have to come to a decision of one sort or another—but it's going to be difficult for me, who am already an old man, to see good order restored in my country. What a contrast I find here with the orderliness and prosperity of London! There one really feels the heartbeats of a great country, whereas with us it's a disaster. . . .

Exile was not, of course, a practical solution, yet Puccini, the wealthy celebrity of his little village, would undoubtedly feel more secure, in times of social unrest, in the larger, cosmopolitan town of Viareggio, whose mild winter climate made it a popular holiday spot for vacationers from all over Europe. Today a noisy, crowded seaside resort, in Puccini's times Viareggio was not without its charms. Along the sea, the spacious beaches were lined with small multicolored wooden cabins, while the inner town retained the features characteristic of a fishing village. The composer had bought a piece of choice land there—originally he had planned to build a house which he could share with Josephine—and in 1919 he began construction of a new and luxurious villa, to replace his home in Torre del Lago.

The two-story red brick villa was set in the midst of a spacious garden of pine trees, and Puccini followed the building assiduously. He liked to call it his "California bungalow," but if it was that it was California with a distinctly Oriental touch. Japanese lanterns hung from the porches and from the larger pine trees, and the design of the main gate gave the whole a pagodalike effect. In one corner of the property stood a small, round grass-roofed house—another hint of the East.

The main house itself was richly and rather heavily furnished, and the composer worked in an enormous studio, which contained a piano, several tables (always covered with sheets of music paper), two leather armchairs, a large sofa, and a fireplace—on the mantle were several stuffed birds, a reminder of his favorite pastime. The walls were covered with paintings, and much in evidence were a letter signed by Wagner in 1861 and a highly prized letter which had been sent from the Edison Laboratories of Orange, New Jersey. The latter read: "Men die and governments change, but the songs of *La Bohème* will live forever." This letter was signed "Thomas A. Edison, September 1920."

At the end of 1921, the Puccinis moved into their new home. Delighted with the many new electrical gadgets with which he had filled the villa, the composer hoped that in time it might acquire the warmth and friendly atmosphere of his former home. Outside of the home, too, he made efforts to re-create and imitate his past, and he founded and became first president of the Gianni Schicchi Club, whose motto was "Live and let live" and whose rules included the absolute prohibition of any talk of politics or other "melancholy" subjects. Puccini became involved with a new circle of friends — writers and artists and musicians — in Viareggio, and soon became a familiar and well-liked figure in his new hometown. It was there, in the mock-Oriental splendor of his new villa, and surrounded by his new circle of friends, that he would write what was destined to be his last opera.

Turandot

When not busying himself with the lauching of his *Trittico*, Puccini had spent most of the early part of the postwar period working with Adami on revisions of *La Rondine*, which he stubbornly insisted contained his best music. Though he feared that the results might "taste like warmed-up soup," he persevered — though to no avail, since his swallow never managed to take wing. At the same time, he began the crucial search for a new libretto, but this time, surprisingly, his quest was neither a long nor a tortuous one.

In the beginning of this quest, he understandably turned to Forzano, with whom he had worked so harmoniously on two of his three one-act operas. The dramatist at first suggested a historical subject, but Puccini quickly vetoed the idea. He was more eager than ever to begin work, but he was decidedly not interested in heavy, tearful subjects. No doubt encouraged by the success of *Gianni Schicchi*, he told Forzano that he wanted something gay and light, something amusing that would not cause him or his audience too much trouble or thought. However, he was in a hurry and he wrote to his librettist, "I feel the proper spirit coursing through my veins, and I cherish now, and tomorrow and after that, the idea of an opera that will uncork the fountain of a spring that I feel pressing inside of me. . . ."

Forzano's next suggestion was a play suggested by the character of Christopher Sly, the drunken tinker who appears in the Induction to *The Taming of the Shrew*, and for whose pleasure the play is performed. If a few lines of Dante could inspire an opera, why not a few pages of Shakespeare? Forzano was working on such a play himself, and he felt that his own work might

255

serve as the basis for an operatic adaptation. Puccini was intrigued, and after several discussions with the author he began to think of *Sly* as an opera. He wasn't convinced, however; and though he wrote Sybil on July 29, 1919, that he soon hoped to have Forzano's comedy to work on, he suggested to the librettist that they might collaborate on an opera set in the hills around Lucca, a little story peopled by children, fairies, and elves. . . . Perhaps, he felt, there might be an old lady, seated by a fireplace, narrating a series of tales suggested by the legends and customs of the region.

This whimsical idea apparently did not appeal to Forzano, who persisted in his work on *Christopher Sly*. For more than a year, the composer vacillated. In July 1920, he wrote Sybil that it was no good and that both he and Forzano were unhappy about it. Only a few weeks later he decided that he would reconsider the project once the prose play had been produced in the theatre, but on September 25 he gave up all hope and wrote to Carlo Paladini, his old friend from Lucca, that "Forzano prepared a dish that was too sumptuous, and it was obvious to me from the beginning that it was indigestible."

By that time, Puccini had already chosen the subject for his new opera, the one on which he would spend the remaining years of his life. It had been offered to him less than a year after the première of the *Trittico* by Renato Simoni, a distinguished literary figure, whom the composer had known for several years. Simoni, born in 1875, was in his own right of far greater importance in Italy's intellectual circles than any of the librettists with whom Puccini had worked since the days of Giacosa. He had, in fact, succeeded Giacosa as the editor of *La Lettura*, had worked for several years as a correspondent and drama critic for the *Corriere della Sera*, and had made a name for himself as a historian of the theatre. In addition, he was a playwright of some distinction and had had operatic experience while writing the libretto for Giordano's *Madame Sans-Gêne*, which had been successfully produced in 1915.

Following the end of the war, Simoni and the composer met frequently at Bagni di Lucca, a small but popular summer resort in the mountains behind Lucca. During the summer of 1919, Puccini asked Simoni if he could look for a subject which, with the aid of Adami, he might turn into a suitable libretto. The composer himself suggested that it might be based on a theatrical adaptation of *Oliver Twist*, which he had recently seen in London. Simoni and Adami tried their hand at it—the opera would be called, inexplicably, *Fanny*—but they soon gave up. It was then that Simoni came up with another idea, one based on his own experiences as a journalist in the Far East and as the author of a play based on the life of the eighteenth-century Venetian playwright Carlo Gozzi. That idea was an adaptation of a Gozzi play called *Turandot*, and the idea appealed to the composer at once.

Turandot, written in 1761, had been a popular favorite in Italy and throughout the continent for many years. Based on a French version of a

Chinese fable from *A Thousand and One Nights,* it told of the attempt by Calaf, an exiled prince, to win the hand of the cruel, icy-hearted Princess Turandot, who required that each of her many suitors answer three riddles before taking her as a bride. Suitor after suitor had failed, and as a result each was mercilessly beheaded. The bold Calaf, however, overwhelmed by her beauty, accepts the challenge and wins, is denied his prize, and then wins again through the power of love.

Puccini was certainly familiar with the play, not only because of its extraordinary popularity, but because it had served as the basis for the one opera written by his old teacher Bazzini, as well as for the 1917 opera written by Ferruccio Busoni. He reached his final decision, however, after reading an Italian translation of Frederich Schiller's German adaptation of the Gozzi play, which Simoni had given him.

The play certainly seemed to offer Puccini ample opportunity to break his old pattern and express himself in a wholly original manner. *Turandot,* set in Peking, was a pageant, a spectacle; it called for huge crowd scenes and large choruses, neither of which had been a part of any of the composer's previous, more intimate operas. Its heroine was diametrically opposed to the typical Puccini heroine. Far from sweet or pathetic, she was a cruel, heartless tyrant, who scorned love and fought against it.

On March 18, 1920, soon after reading the copy of the play that Simoni had given him, Puccini wrote that he believed that it was time to stop considering other projects and to concentrate on the Gozzi play. He already had suggestions as to how the long, five-act play might be converted into an opera:

> We should simplify it as far as the number of acts is concerned, and we should strive to make it slim and effective, and most of all, to exalt Turandot's loving passion which has for so long been stifled under the ashes of her immense pride. . . . Turandot as seen through a modern mentality: yours, Adami's, and mine. . . .

The composer's enthusiasm grew and shortly afterward he wrote to his other librettist, Adami, to say that he was getting some old Chinese music and drawings of different instruments that they could use on the stage. "At the same time," he added, "you two Venetians must give an interesting and varied form to that relative of yours, Gozzi. Don't talk about it too much, but if you succeed (and you must) you will see what a beautiful and original work it will be and how fascinating (and this latter is essential). Your imagination, combined with all those rich fantasies of the old author, must inevitably lead you to something great and good!"

The composer's creative imagination was fired by his new project. He urged his librettists to prepare a detailed outline and not to rely too heavily on the original play, which should serve as no more than a rough basis for the opera. He was eager to get started, and he quickly grew impatient, not only for the outline but for the completed first act—if not for the whole libretto. He wrote emotionally to Adami:

> If I touch the piano my hands become covered with dust. My desk is piled high with letters—there isn't a trace of music. Music? Useless if I have no libretto. I have the great weakness of being able to write only when my puppet executioners are moving on the scene. If only I could be a purely symphonic writer! I should then at least cheat time . . . and my public. But that was not for me. I was born so many years ago—oh, so many, too many, almost a century . . . and Almighty God touched me with His little finger and said: "Write for the theatre—only for the theatre." And I have obeyed the supreme command. Had He marked me out for some other task perhaps I should not be, as now without material. I get such nice encouraging letters, but if, instead of these, one act were to arrive of our glittering Princess, don't you think it would be better? You would give me back my serenity and my confidence, and the dust would not settle on my piano any more, so much banging would I do, and my desk would have its brave array of scoring sheets again. . . . I need not only the first act, but the third also, since then the second act would have been completed.

Puccini could not, in all fairness, complain that his librettists were slow— by July 18, 1920, he had enough material on hand to offer specific criticisms of not only the first act but of the second and third as well. "We have our canvas," he wrote Adami, "and an original and perhaps unique work. But it needs some alterations, which we shall devise when we meet to discuss it." A meeting was arranged for Bagni di Lucca in late July, but in spite of the composer's enthusiasm, he still had some doubts. He wrote to Carlo Paladini that he had a "vague" hope that *Turandot* might work out, he wrote Sybil in London that he would "perhaps" do "an old Chinese play, *Turandot*," and he sent a copy of the play to the young Maria Bianca Ginori-Lisci, asking her opinion of the project. (She liked it.)

These doubts, apparently, were not revealed to Simoni and Adami when the two librettists met with the composer at Bagni di Lucca, and their meeting, which lasted for two days, was a fruitful one. The three men worked closely together and had a chance to hear the sounds of Chinese musical instruments at the nearby villa of the Baron Fassini-Camossi, a noted collector of Oriental objects and an acquaintance of Puccini's. When the librettists left, they promised to begin work at once on the versification of the first act, so that the composer might quickly start setting the libretto to music.

Puccini stayed behind at Bagni di Lucca to study Chinese music which had been sent to him from London, but—and surely Adami and Simoni were unaware of this—he was still not completely certain that he would go on with *Turandot*. On August 15, he wrote Paladini that he was awaiting the first act, but he had still not made up his mind. "I will see how this verse version comes out," he wrote. "I am as careful and scrupulous as ever; nobody can fool a Lucchese." On the same day he wrote to Riccardo Schnabl-Rossi that he would see if the originality which had permeated the rough scenario would be maintained in the finished version before reaching a final decision.

In the meantime, he thought of little but *Turandot*—the hesitancy he expressed was merely a reflection of those doubts that had always afflicted him when he embarked on a new opera—and at the end of August, he referred, for the first time, in a letter to Simoni to the introduction of a new character, one not in Gozzi's play; this was to be the innocent, young Liù, a typically Puccinian heroine, deeply but hopelessly in love with the hero.

His moods changed rapidly and unpredictably. At the end of September, he was growing impatient again, and he was ready to war with his librettists, as in the old days. He wrote an irritated letter to Paladini from Torre del Lago, complaining that they were abandoning him and that he was going crazy without work. At the same time, he implored his poets, "Don't go to sleep, I am tired of idleness."

Shortly afterward, the composer left for Vienna and the première of *Rondine* and the *Trittico*. In spite of the hero's welcome he had been accorded in the Austrian capital, he returned home worried about his ability to complete his new opera, and he expressed his fears in a letter written to Adami on November 10, 1920, from Torre del Lago:

> I am afraid that *Turandot* will never be finished. It is impossible to work like this. When the fever abates it ends by disappearing, and without fever there is no creation; because emotional art is a kind of malady, an exceptional state of mind, overexcitation of every fiber and every atom of one's being, and so on ad aeternum. . . . [The] libretto is nothing to trifle with. It is not a question of giving life that will endure to a thing which must be alive before it can be born, and so on till we make a masterpiece. Shall I have the strength to second you? Who can tell? Shall I be tired, discouraged, weighed down by years and spiritual torment, and by my never-ceasing discontent? Who can tell? Work as if you were working for a young man of thirty, and I shall do my best; and if I do not succeed it will be my fault!

In the middle of December, Puccini traveled to his recently acquired house, the Torre della Tagliata, near Orbetello in the wild coastal region south of Pisa known as the Maremma. He had chosen the spot for the excellent hunting facilities it offered and for the isolation it would allow him for his work, but he was cold, lonely, and miserable there as he awaited the promised arrival of Adami and the completed version of the first act of *Turandot*. After the librettist had settled in and the composer had had a chance to study that first act, he was both pleased and disappointed; pleased because he had something concrete to work with, but disappointed because the libretto did not live up to his expectations. He expressed his criticisms and suggestions to his librettists diplomatically—he was desperate to get on with his work and did not want to frighten off his writers—but he did his best to convince Adami that the act had to be shortened and condensed in order to make it move more quickly and effectively. However, he was more outspoken in a letter to Schnabl-Rossi, in which he confided his fears that he would never have a satisfactory libretto, and in his Christmas letter to Sybil, he wrote: "Turandot? Adami has brought me a first act which won't do—I'm very much afraid I shan't have the libretto as I want it. . . ."

Puccini left Torre della Tagliata at the end of 1920, discouraged about the prospects for his new opera and thoroughly fed up with his new house—he had struggled hard to buy the house and was already eager to sell it. Once out of the gloomy setting, however, he had a complete change of heart concerning his opera. On January 15, 1921, by which time the librettists had presumably presented their revisions for the first act, he was filled with optimism, and he wrote Sybil that "at last I've got a fine first act." He continued to write her cheerful reports from Milan, where he was conferring with Simoni and Adami, assuring her that the libretto would be unusually beautiful and, above all, strikingly original. He wrote Schnabl-Rossi, too, that the poets had worked well, and that the result would be unique, a libretto "full of color, surprises, and emotions."

In late March Puccini was happier and more certain of the opera than ever. He was anxiously awaiting the second act and urged his poets to begin work at once on the third. He wrote Simoni that he had never cared so much for a work as he did for *Turandot* and added that he felt it unnecessary to ask the librettist to "work with fervor" since he already knew of his love for "our Princess."

Such was his excitement and his passion for work that even a slight delay in the arrival of the libretto upset him. "Simoni and Adami are not producing well," he wrote Paladini in April. Nonetheless, by the beginning of May Puccini had started on the composition of the first act. As usual, he complained to Sybil of the difficulties involved and of the infirmities of old age, but he was sufficiently sure of his work to write to Gilda Dalla Rizza that the role of Liù would be ideally suited to her.

The composer was enjoying and was stimulated by his work, and his only problem at the time was loneliness and a need to discuss his problems. He was pleased with his team of librettists and with *Turandot*, but he missed the almost daily give and take, and even the angry quarrels, that had marked his relationship with Giacosa and Illica. He needed the last two acts, but, he wrote Adami in June, "I also need to feel myself loved a little and, like a faithful dog, to wag my tail. . . . As far as you two are concerned, I have a long face and my tail is drooping. . . . But it is the *Princess* who needs you. For her sake at least give me a sign that I am not yet a bit of old iron fit to be flung on the scrap heap." This need for companionship was acute, and on June 20, he again made a plea to Adami. "I am stranded. I need encouragement from someone who understands me," he wrote. "Why don't you come here for a few days? I would like you to listen to what I've done and say whether I should tear it up or keep it. Who knows? Sometimes I think it's good, sometimes not. I am at the riddles, and I'm not making progress. I've been very low for two days. This evening I'm going to Viareggio for dinner. It will be helpful, if not as a distraction, at least as a break from the eternal monotony of this now unbearable Torre del Lago."

In spite of his feelings of isolation, Puccini finished his work on the first act during the summer of 1921; the librettists, too, went ahead, and completed the libretto for Act Two. They were all pleased with the results. Adami reported to Carlo Clausetti that he was profoundly impressed with Puccini's score, and the composer wrote Simoni that, in spite of some minor reservations, he thought the second-act libretto was excellent. These few reservations, however, loomed far larger in September, when the composer unexpectedly suggested that the projected three-act opera be reduced to two acts. On September 13, he wrote to Simoni:

> I am sad and discouraged. I think of *Turandot*. It is because of *Turandot* that I feel like a lost soul. That second act! I cannot find a way out, perhaps I am tormented because of a fixed idea that I have: that is, perhaps *Turandot* should have only two acts, what do you think? . . . Condense some incidents, eliminate others, to reach the final scene in which love explodes. I don't know what to advise as the proper structure, but I feel that two more acts is too much. *Turandot* in two great acts! Why not? It's all a matter of finding the right invention for the finale. Should we do what is done in *Parsifal*, with a change of scenery in the third act, finding ourselves in a Chinese Holy Grail? Full of pink flowers and full of love? Think, think, think about it, and tell Adami. You will certainly find something, and all will be well. I am almost convinced that three acts for *Turandot* are too many.

Puccini's suggestion, reminiscent of the error in judgment he had made when insisting that *Butterfly* be presented in only two acts, was not heeded by Simoni and Adami. The composer grew frantic, and little more than a week later he wrote Adami that a personal meeting with him and Simoni was urgently needed, that the opera—about which he had but a short time ago been so optimistic—was "absolutely impossible, all wrong," and that it lacked the "pulse of life." At the same time he wrote Sybil that he feared the opera might soon have to be put aside.

His mood did not quickly improve. The following month, while confessing to Adami that his life was a torture due to his disappointment with the new opera, he wrote Sybil that "*Turandot* languishes. I haven't got the second act as I want it yet, and I don't feel myself capable any more of composing music. . . ."

His despair increased in November 1921, when he attended a performance of the *Trittico* in Bologna; he hated all three operas, which seemed to him "as long as a transatlantic cable." Not only was he uncertain about his new opera; now he even doubted the validity of work done in the past.

Simoni and Adami, too, unaccustomed to the composer's changing moods, were unhappy, and they ignored his repeated requests for a meeting and seemed indifferent to his pleas for a reconsideration of the entire scheme for the last two acts. Unable to carry on a dialogue with his librettists—and remembering how useful these dialogues had been in the past—Puccini was frustrated and hurt. Accused of losing interest in the entire project, he was put on the defensive, and he found himself in the uncharacteristic position of having to beg for understanding from his collaborators, to whom he was forced to write lengthy, almost apologetic letters. On November 9, he wrote to Simoni:

> What can I make of your silence? Did I perhaps offend you by telling you of my doubts concerning the second act of *Turandot*? You are good and you understand and also respect me; you can also take the things my troubled soul tells you even though you might not approve of them; but why don't you tell me clearly what you think? . . .
>
> I suffer from your silence. Adami, too, has not been in touch with me. Have I perhaps committed a serious crime? . . . Write me, then, and if you see Adami tell him that he has in me a good friend, who is awaiting a good word from him.

Two days later, he clarified his position in a letter to Adami, from whom he had just heard:

> Your letter saddens me. Do you think I am doing this because I have lost interest in the subject? No, by God! But I think that with a more convincing and effective second act the ship can enter the port.
>
> I feel that this act as it stands does not convince me, nor can it convince the listener. There are certain fixed laws in the theatre: a

work must interest, surprise, stir, or move to laughter. Our act must interest and surprise.

Put Gozzi aside for a while, and work with your own logic and imagination. Who knows, perhaps you can give it another, more daring structure. On my own, I can't find the solution. But if you work at it willingly, I think something good can result. I am the one who should least of all want to give up. I have already set one act to music, and, good or bad, it is there. So don't tell me that you see *Turandot* disappearing! . . . You must have received my letter from Torre del Lago in which I spoke of the duet and also came back to the idea of one single, tight last act. I still feel this way, though it is said that two acts are not enough for an evening at the opera. What does it matter if in this way the opera succeeds in becoming more convincing? . . .

In spite of these letters to his librettists, Puccini once again suspected that *Turandot* was doomed, and, without their knowledge, he began to urge Forzano to help find a new subject on which to collaborate. Forzano came up with an idea, a work referred to as *The Chinese Play* (Sybil suggested that Puccini use the music already written for *Turandot* for this new opera), but the composer realized that it was already too late to abandon a work he instinctively felt could succeed. Besides, Simoni and Adami had changed their attitude, a change which Puccini explained to Sybil in a letter written from his new home in Viareggio on December 23, 1921:

I wasn't satisfied with this libretto and I said so; the papers published the news of my disagreement with the Poets, who were simply furious. And now they've recognized how wrong they were and are going to work enthusiastically along the lines of my suggestions — And we'll see — certainly, as I see the opera, it's a very beautiful thing — but shall I be able to do it, and shall I be able to do it well? I'm a little doubtful because it is the type of opera that terrifies me; I should have preferred something of a different kind. . . .

This marked a return to a normal state, the composer doubting his own ability rather than the intrinsic worth of the project itself, but he was obviously near exhaustion when, in early 1922, he left Viareggio for Milan, where he hoped to be presented with new material by his librettists. He felt hurried and wanted to get on with his work, to get it over with, and he wrote Simoni desperately, "When will this work of ours come to an end? Either when I will be old and decrepit, or dead."

Nonetheless, he went ahead as best he could. The plan to convert *Turandot* into a two-act opera had, wisely, been abandoned — in spite of the composer's report that the librettists were following his suggestions — and he eagerly awaited the text for the third act. He cajoled Simoni and Adami to complete it quickly, but he did so gently and with humor—gone was the angry impatience that he had displayed with Giacosa and Illica many years before. In the meantime, he busied himself with the orchestration of the first act, and by late March he had already started work on the first scene of act two, that sung entirely by the Mask figures, Ping, Pang, and Pong.

This was a difficult scene, requiring a marked departure from his usual style, and he suspected that his librettists' delay in sending him more material was caused by their lack of faith in his ability to successfully conclude what was already on hand. He admitted to Adami, in a letter of May 2, that he was indeed passing through a crisis with regard to his music, but he assured him that he was continuing with the orchestration of *Turandot* and that he felt it was going well.

In the early summer, the librettists had finished their version of the third act. Puccini found much of it satisfactory, but he believed that many cuts would have to be made—he was still concerned with tightening the opera for dramatic effect—and that the final duet, sung by Turandot and Calaf, would have to be redone.

Before settling down to work again, however, the composer decided to take a badly needed vacation—the stress of his work on *Turandot* had taken its toll—and on August 20, accompanied by Tonio and several friends (they were packed tightly in two cars), he set off on an extended trip through northern Europe. The itinerary included Innsbruck, Munich, Frankfurt, and Cologne, as well as most of Holland and Switzerland. Puccini was relaxed and in excellent spirits throughout the entire trip. He was also, it was reported, uncharacteristically generous in handing out large tips to waitresses wherever the group went—although, as if ashamed of this generosity, these tips were always slipped into the recipients' hands and not left on the plates as was customary. Away from the pressures of his new opera—and it was in every way a new opera for Puccini, since its composition and orchestration presented him with problems he had never faced before—he was able to rediscover and delight in the pleasures of leisurely travel and easy companionship.

The composer's high spirits ended as soon as he returned to his home in Viareggio. In early October 1922, his sister Iginia died in the convent at Vicopelago, and with her death his thoughts again turned to his own mortality. "Poor little nun, she died with my name on her lips," he wrote Schnabl-Rossi. "Thus the Puccinis depart, little by little. It is very sad to witness the death of those we love, and those who remain await the great journey, which is, perhaps, less terrible than we think." Old age and death, of course, had been a preoccupation of his for many years, and his fears were such that he seriously looked into the possibilities of rejuvenation treatments following the end of the war. (They were ruled out because of his diabetic condition.) Now, however, when in his mid-sixties, the reality of death was inescapable, and he was constantly aware of it as those with whom he had once been associated passed away. Boito had died in 1918, Leoncavallo and Carignani and Fontana, his first librettist, in 1919, and Caruso in 1921. In addition, at the time he learned of his sister's death, he was also informed of the passing of his one-time Viennese publisher Eisenschütz. The latter had been neither a close nor an old friend, but he had been part of the composer's past.

Happily, at the end of 1922, there was a more joyful reminder of the composer's early years, one brought about following Puccini's latest reconciliation with Toscanini. The two men had been estranged since, in 1919, the conductor had been outspoken in his disapproval of *Il Tabarro*. From that time on, the composer's attitude had been, to say the least, an ambivalent one. While in 1919 he had threatened to stay away from the London première of the *Trittico* if Toscanini conducted, in 1921, he was desperately anxious that the man he had called a "pig" conduct the same operas at La Scala. On July 4 of that year, he wrote to Carlo Clausetti: ". . . As far as the conductor is concerned, I am firmly convinced that if the opera is not conducted by Toscanini, it will be damaging to me, not only materially (that is, as far as the performance is concerned) but morally as well. I know Milan (see *Butterfly*) and I cannot forget it. Without Toscanini, the opera would seem inferior. See if you can find a way of making 'peace' between him and me. I do not harbor profound resentments, and this is partly due to my nature. You yourself might want to give it a try. . . ."

Puccini suggested possible peacemakers — Renato Simoni, or Luigi Albertini, editor of the *Corriere della Sera* — but to no avail. Within a few days, he wrote to Riccardo Schnabl-Rossi that Ettore Panizza would conduct his operas at La Scala. "Toscanini will only conduct *Falstaff* and works he already knows — I've been told — and I think the reason is not to conduct my works. He is really a bad man . . . perfidious — heartless, and I believe without the soul of an artist, because those who have that soul are not so full of wickedness, and I think also of jealousy. I really don't give a damn, but it bothers me for the Milanesi, because my opera is not shown at its best for the public, more or less intelligent, with another conductor."

A month later, Puccini was still upset, writing to Simoni that "I have a thorn: that Toscanini who persists in being my enemy. And why? Who knows! I would of course like peace, but he wants to maintain the hostilities."

Given the fact that the conductor's only hostile act was a refusal to conduct an opera that was not to his liking — and that was not highly esteemed by many people — the composer's feelings were certainly unreasonable. He and Toscanini had been friends for many years; Toscanini had brought to life many of Puccini's operas as no other conductor had, and yet the composer found it almost impossible to forgive him for rejecting one of his works.

Sometime, and somehow, in 1922, the two men made up. Toscanini announced his intentions of mounting a new production of *Manon Lescaut* for the following fall at La Scala, and before it, he joined the composer at Viareggio to restudy the score. Harmony reigned, past grievances were set aside, and in December, when Puccini attended rehearsals of the new production in Milan, he was overjoyed. On December 26, the day of the first performance, he wrote to Schnabl-Rossi:

> Tonight *Manon*, a great *Manon*, and if the public is not roused, it means that we are living on Saturn rather than on Earth. I assure you that Toscanini is a real miracle of feeling, of refinement, of sensitivity, of balance. What pleasure I felt at the rehearsals. Never, never have I so enjoyed listening to my music.

The performance was a superb one, and following the third act Puccini spontaneously embraced the conductor. The public obviously shared the composer's enthusiasm; the opera was performed for a total of seventeen times that season. It was such an extraordinarily fresh experience that the reviewer for the *Corriere della Sera* was convinced that substantial revisions had been made in the score in preparation for the new Scala production. In answer to this charge Puccini wrote a letter to the editor of the newspaper the day after the opening:

> Your music critic states that I have retouched the instrumentation of *Manon*. "In the second and fourth acts especially there are many retouches, and others are evident even in the first act."
> Actually, this is a matter of some slight modifications in coloring, but the score as printed by Ricordi shows that I have not changed the instrumentation. My *Manon* is the same as it was 30 years ago, only that it has been conducted by Arturo Toscanini, which means in a way which provides the composer with the greater and uncommon joy of seeing his music illuminated by those lights which at the time of composition he had seen and dreamed of and then had not seen again. For too long in Italy we have been accustomed to giving so-called repertory works, those which resist time and unfaithful performances, in an indecent fashion. An orchestra rehearsal, none for the stage, and off we go, carrying all the foul rubbish with which little by little the abuses and bad habits of conductors and singers have encrusted the work.
> When Arturo Toscanini, with the faith and love which ignite the fires of his marvelous art, takes his scalpel and cuts away all the ugliness and brings the work back to its natural state, revealing the composer's true intentions to the public, the old work seems new to the public, and it seems changed. No, it is simply the same work brought to life by the greatest re-creator the musical world boasts. . . .

What he has accomplished at La Scala is marvelous. I travel from theatre to theatre all over the world, and I see and study what is being done elsewhere. I think it's now time to say that what is done at La Scala today is not done in any other theatre. Toscanini has not only been an organizer; he has created an institution which is the pride of Italian art; for all he has done, he has done out of his love for the opera of Italian artists.

Last year the stage direction of the operas was put in the hands of foreigners, and it was believed that they were essential. I wanted my operas to be directed by my collaborator, Giovacchino Forzano. Toscanini saw him at work, and knowing men as he does, he wanted to have him do the direction this year, and Forzano has shown how, here in Italy, direction, as concerns the movement of masses and fineness of details, can surpass — in agility and genius — what is done in foreign countries. . . . This nucleus of energy, guided and brought to life by Toscanini, brings results because of which, as happened last night, *Manon* seems to be a new opera, so much so that even I felt 30 years younger. . . .

On the night of February 1, 1923, a gala performance of *Manon Lescaut* was given at La Scala in celebration of the youthful opera's thirtieth anniversary. Following the performance, which had been marvelously sung especially by Scala's reigning tenor, Aureliano Pertile, a banquet, attended by almost 500 people, was held in the composer's honor. There were speeches and gifts — among the latter, a large silver tray from Toscanini. For Puccini, it was a deeply moving occasion, though it was also a reminder that it had been very many years since one of his operas had enjoyed the tremendous success of his earlier works.

The following day, the grateful composer wrote to Toscanini that he had given him the greatest satisfaction of his life, and he wrote to Schnabl-Rossi, "It is your duty to hear it — believe me, never has an opera been performed in such a way. . . . All in all, a true miracle."

There were further nostalgic, emotional occasions for Puccini in 1923 — above all, a small "festival" of his operas in Vienna, featuring an outstanding performance of *Manon Lescaut* with Jeritza — but it was his future which concerned the composer most, and his future depended on the success or failure of *Turandot*.

"... in the Hands
of the Doctors and of God"

In early 1923, the end of *Turandot* was not yet in sight. The first act had been completed, but neither the second nor the third act satisfied the composer, and he even considered again — only briefly — combining them into one big act. Most important, he had not begun to face the problem of the third-act duet between Turandot and Calaf and the finale that followed it. "This must reach the greatest possible heights of fantasy," he had written to Adami in late 1922. "In this *great duet*, Turandot's ice gradually melts away, and the scene, which could be an enclosed spot, is slowly transformed into a large space, filled with flowers and marble decorations, fantastic in appearance, where the mob, the Emperor, the court, and all the ceremonial pomp prepare to greet Turandot's cry of love." In the same letter, he expressed concern about the role of Liù, the gentle slave, in the last act. "I think Liù must be sacrificed through suffering," he wrote, "but I don't think this can be developed — unless we have her die under torture. And why not? This death can be an element in the softening of the Princess' heart." Liù, however, was not the real problem; she was a familiar Puccini heroine, and he was able to make her a convincing, pathetic character without undue difficulty. It was the majestic duet to be sung by two strong-willed, heroic figures that plagued him then and would continue to do so.

In the spring of 1923, the finished libretto for the second act arrived, and Puccini, pleased with it, began to set it to music. His poets were working hard, and on March 6, they sent on a part of the third act. This time, the composer was not satisfied. He worried not only about the libretto, but also about himself and his inability to work the way he wanted to. "Maybe," he wondered in a letter to Adami, "or even without the maybe, I am no longer any good. . . . I don't want to say *muoio disperato*, but I am almost at that point." He worried that he might never be capable of finishing the opera. "I am a poor, very unhappy man, discouraged, old, useless, and disheartened," he concluded. "What can I do? I don't know. I'll go to sleep so that I won't think and torture myself."

The composer seemed blocked by the new challenges the opera presented to him, especially, at that time, by the scene which opened the second act, that of the three Masks, Ping, Pang, and Pong, who comment ironically on the state of China and on the action of the drama. This scene called for a mentality and for musical elements entirely new to the composer, and even when he had completed his work on the rest of the second act, he was still dissatisfied with his treatment of "Ping and Co.," as he called them.

He explained his problems and his apparent inactivity to a journalist, Federico Candida, in the winter of 1923. "This time I am going ahead with unusual deliberation, dealing with a kind of work that is completely new to me, new as a subject, and new, perhaps, as an esthetic-musical research. It is a complex opera, wrapped in a varied and multi-faceted cloth of poetry, and for that reason what seems to be my present state of inertia, since it is filled with creative activity, should not come as a surprise."

In the course of the same interview, he explained the role of the three Masks—Gozzi's Venetian Masks whom he had transformed into members of the Chinese court: "There is a semicomic element in *Turandot*. Instead of our usual Masks, I have introduced Chinese Masks. This exoticism will also serve to justify a task I assign to these three figures. In the opera, they represent good sense. They seem to say to the Prince, 'Why do you insist upon wanting to marry that woman? There are so many women in the world. . . .' "

Puccini's self-confidence was restored by May, when he received what he felt was a highly satisfactory version of the third act from his librettists, and he worked on it steadily, if not energetically. His life in Viareggio was a calm one. His home was comfortable, and, more important, both he and Elvira had mellowed and had once again learned to enjoy one another's company. The composer wrote amusingly of his new way of life to Adami. "Elvira and I are here, the two *ancêtres*, like two old family portraits, frowning from time to time at the cobwebs that tickle us. We sleep, eat, read the *Corriere*, and with a few notes in the evening, the old maestro makes ends meet."

Throughout the summer and fall, Puccini worked peacefully on the last act of the opera, and he was gratified at the results. However, he was still paralyzed when faced with the composition of the final duet. He blamed his librettists and the verses that they had sent him. By the end of 1923, he had rejected four versions, none of which inspired him to reach the heights he felt were required to complete his opera.

During the first few months of 1924, he continued to work on the rest of the opera, and on March 25, he was able to write to Simoni in Milan that he had completed the orchestration of the entire score—except for the final duet. Once again he complained of the material that had been sent him— "Your duet has good things in it but it is not varied enough and lacks movement," he wrote—but in spite of the fact that he was revising it with the aid of Adami, it was becoming clear that, at this crucial point, the composer's own inspiration was failing him. "I have put all my soul in this opera," he told Simoni, yet that was, apparently, not enough to permit him to carry the opera to its conclusion.

Though he busied himself making minor revisions of *Turandot* and started to make detailed suggestions for the sets and costumes of the first production (which he and Clausetti felt should be given at La Scala), Puccini was for the moment without work and bored. To break his routine, on April 1 he traveled to Florence to hear a performance in the Palazzo Pitti of Arnold Schoenberg's *Pierrot Lunaire*, conducted by the composer, who was in the midst of a concert tour of Italian cities. Puccini's interest in and curiosity about modern music had never flagged. He had long been criticized for his own "old-fashioned" operas, yet even Alfredo Casella, an outspoken champion of modern music, had admiringly noted that Puccini "was an attentive and acute observer of the contemporary musical phenomenon and his knowledge of it was exhaustive and up to date." Though certainly not eager to imitate what his younger colleagues were writing (just before attending the Schoenberg concert, he had written to Clausetti that atonal music was acceptable in a concert only because afterward Beethoven and other traditionalists could come to the rescue), Puccini never missed an opportunity to hear performances of contemporary music. Certainly this trip to Florence had a special meaning for him at a time when he was struggling to finish what he expected to be the most musically advanced of all of his operas.

Puccini followed the performance of Schoenberg's then-controversial piece attentively. Most of the audience, however, did not, and at its conclusion the Viennese composer was greeted by a loud chorus of boos and catcalls. Luigi Dallapiccola, then a young student at the Florence conservatory, remarked that none of the distinguished professors at the conservatory nor any musicians in the audience took the trouble to pay his or her respects to the composer at the end of the evening. He noted but one exception, Puccini, who went backstage to congratulate Schoenberg and spent a considerable amount of time discussing the new work with him. A few years later, Schoenberg wrote appreciatively, "I take it to have been the expert judges, not the art-lovers, who received my *Pierrot Lunaire* with such hostility when I performed it in Italy. I was indeed honored that Puccini, not an expert judge, but a practical expert, made a six-hour journey to hear my work, and afterward said some very friendly things to me. That was good, strange though my music may have remained to him." Schoenberg never forgot Puccini nor his music, and always mentioned him when speaking of those who, in the years before World War I, participated most actively in the constitution of a new harmonic language.

Puccini respected, even if he did not fully understand or enjoy, Schoenberg's music, as he respected the efforts of any serious contemporary musician. He felt, too, that his own new opera would be a departure, in keeping with the period in which it was being written, and in the spring of 1924, while on a visit to Monte Carlo, he wrote Adami, "Hour by hour and minute by minute I think of Turandot, and all the music I have written up to now seems to me a joke. Can this be a good sign? I think so." Yet, that spring, Puccini was still unable to write the duet which would bring his opera to a close. His moods alternated between optimism and despair. At the end of March, he wrote to Sybil, "I'm at work on the duet; it's difficult, but I shall end by doing it and I hope it will give satisfaction—and then the opera (if God wills) will be finished." On May 18, he wrote Angiolino Magrini, a close friend from the time he moved to Viareggio, that he didn't seem to be able to work, that he wanted to finish his work quickly but couldn't manage to get to it. He expressed the same feelings to Sybil one week later, writing, "I've done no more work; Turandot lies here, unfinished. But I will finish it—only just at present I've got no desire to work."

Convinced that he would somehow finish his opera, the composer continued to give thought to its première, which he hoped would be held at La Scala the following autumn. Central to these plans was Toscanini, who he hoped would agree to conduct the first performance. Not only did Puccini have enormous faith in the conductor's ability to bring his operas to life, but the conductor's prestige at La Scala was so great at that time that his absence from the podium automatically diminished the importance of any Scala performance.

Puccini had every reason to believe that Toscanini would be willing to conduct the new opera, until the spring of 1924, when what appears to have been a misunderstanding threatened to make this an impossibility. At the end of April, the composer traveled to Milan to hear the first performance of Boito's Nerone, which its composer had left unfinished at his death in 1918 and which had been completed by Vincenzo Tommasini and Toscanini. Conducted by the latter, it was to have its première on May 1 at La Scala, and it was Puccini's intention to attend the public dress rehearsal which preceded the opening. When he appeared at the theatre, however, the entrance to the auditorium was barred to him—on the orders of Toscanini, he was told, presumably because of rumors that Puccini had spoken badly of Boito's opera. It was a terrible blow; the composer was bitterly hurt at this exclusion; and it signaled still another break in the relationship between the two men.

The June issue of the magazine Il Pianoforte was dedicated to the achievements of Toscanini, and Puccini's contribution (probably written before the *Nerone* incident) was a short tribute to the conductor in which he wrote that "the fondest and most luminous memories of my life as an artist are fraternally linked to the name of Arturo Toscanini." Puccini was right: the two men had shared some of the most glorious moments in the history of Italian opera—from the première of *Bohème* in 1896 to the rebirth of *Manon* in 1922—and this was undoubtedly one reason he wanted to heal this latest break with the conductor. Another, and less sentimental, reason was that the composer was desperately anxious to remain on good terms with Toscanini for the sake of *Turandot*.

It was not until August 4, however, that Puccini had recovered sufficiently to be able to take the first step toward a reconciliation. On that day, he wrote his old friend a long emotional letter, in which he hoped to clear up the misunderstanding. He spoke of the damage he had suffered by being excluded from the final rehearsal of *Nerone*, which he had wanted so badly to hear, and of his bitterness at the time of his departure, an unwelcomed guest, from Milan, a bitterness that remained with him several months after his return to Viareggio. He blamed a "mysterious and malicious force" for coming between them and accused a troublemaker of deliberately spreading the false rumors of an unfavorable judgment he had made of Boito's last opera. "You can understand," he wrote, "that it is painful for a man like me, who has worked not ingloriously all his life, for a man whose name is still alive and unconquered in the world, and who, because of his age, should have the right to some respect, to see himself treated in his native land in this way, and by the best people! Yes, it is really disheartening and unfair, and I can't tell you how saddened my heart is because of it. You would do me a great favor if, appreciating the feeling of loyal friendship which has moved me to write you, you would answer me. . . . If we could see each other, it would be even better."

Toscanini was not quick to answer, and two weeks later, in a letter to Schnabl-Rossi, the composer complained of an "undeclared war with Toscanini." The war, however, soon came to an end, and in early September the conductor traveled to Viareggio to see Puccini. What was to be their final quarrel was over, and the composer wrote to Schnabl-Rossi on September 7: "Toscanini has just left, and all the clouds have disappeared. I am very, very happy. I am certain that in his hands *Turandot* will have the ideal execution. This will be in April, which means I have all the time I want to finish the little that remains to be done. I showed and played for him some selections, and I think he was very pleased. So, the unpleasant situation has ended."

Puccini did not have all the time he wanted to finish the little that remained. The final duet was still to be written, and the composer once again stressed its importance to the whole opera, whose success he believed depended upon it, when he wrote to Adami in September, asking for changes in the text. "It has to be a great duet," he declared. "These two beings, almost removed from the world, are brought back to earth by love, and this love at the end will have to envelop all those on stage in a great orchestral peroration. . . ."

In October, the librettists finally submitted a version of the duet that was satisfactory to the composer; but it was too late, for Puccini was already a very sick man, so sick that it is possible to blame most of the creative impotence that had recently hampered him on the disease that was consuming him.

Since the beginning of 1924, the composer had complained of a persistent cough and sore throat, but he minimized the importance of these symptoms, which he blamed on his life-long habit of smoking several packs of cigarettes a day. By June he was sufficiently concerned, if not worried, to go to Salsomaggiore to take a "cure." There was no marked improvement after this visit, but he was assured that the condition, which was causing him increasing discomfort, would pass in time.

By summer, the condition had not passed, and on August 17, the composer wrote to Schnabl-Rossi that he had seen four specialists, each of whom proposed a different treatment. "In the meantime," he wrote, "I am not well, and there are no signs of my getting better." Tragically, at a time when he was desperately trying to finish his opera, he remarked that this illness was even destroying his interest in his own music and he asked Schnabl-Rossi if he could suggest any specialists in Germany or Switzerland whom he might consult. During the latter part of August, several of Puccini's friends — among them Sybil, who had come to visit — noticed that the composer was not looking as robustly healthy as usual, but only Sybil sensed that his condition might be a serious one, and she confided her fears only to Tonio.

By October, the pain in Puccini's throat was so great that he traveled to Florence to consult a noted throat specialist, who informed him that he had a papilloma, a tumor, situated under the epiglottis. Puccini seemed not to realize the potential seriousness of the condition, but Tonio, on learning of his father's visit to the doctor, was concerned and, without the composer's knowledge, contacted the specialist, who told him that Puccini was suffering from cancer of the throat, and that the situation was hopeless.

Tonio, horrified, refused to take the doctor's word, and several more specialists were called in to examine the composer. The doctors all confirmed the diagnosis, but they held out hope of recovery if the illness were treated as quickly as possible by x-ray; only two hospitals in Europe had the proper equipment, and it was decided that arrangements should be made for Puccini to be treated by the well-known Dr. Ledoux at the Institut de la Couronne in Brussels.

The composer had still not been informed of the seriousness of his illness, and he was led to believe that his condition would improve if the tumor were removed as quickly as possible. In spite of these assurances, he was uneasy, and on October 22 he wrote to Adami: "Will I be operated on, or will I be treated? Or will I be condemned to death? I can't go on any longer this way. And there is *Turandot*. . . ." Nonetheless, he remained fundamentally optimistic about the outcome of whatever treatment he had to undergo. In this letter to Adami and also in a letter to Schnabl-Rossi, he wondered when his opera would be finished and not if it would be finished.

When Puccini, accompanied by Tonio — Elvira had a severe bronchitis and remained at home under Fosca's care — left for Brussels on November 4, he took with him thirty-six pages of notes for the final duet and the finale of *Turandot*. He planned to work on them while undergoing the treatments for his illness.

Upon his arrival in Belgium, the composer was examined by members of the hospital staff and was informed that after a week or ten days of external treatment, internal surgery would be performed. "I am in the hands of the doctors and of God," he wrote Angiolino Magrini in Viareggio. During the period of these external applications of radium, he was allowed to leave the hospital; one evening, he was able to attend, unnoticed, a performance of *Madama Butterfly* at the Théâtre de la Monnaie. However, his spirits were low, and on November 12 Tonio wrote Clausetti that his father was often depressed. After receiving this letter, the publisher left for Brussels. Elvira was still too ill to be moved, but Fosca hoped that within a few days she might be able to accompany her mother to the Belgian capital.

After the start of the external treatment, Puccini wrote to Magrini that there had been little change, though he was feeling somewhat better. "This morning, I went out for lunch," he told his hunting companion, "and passing by a market I saw a number of woodcocks. What a pity! None for me! Even if I am cured, I can't come to the Maremma because of that blessed opera. After that, I don't know what I'll do, but for now the main thing is to be cured, and that is what we're trying to do."

Shortly afterward, he sent another letter to Magrini, saying:

> . . . I am on the cross like Jesus. I have a collar which is a kind of torture. For the time being, the treatment is external, later crystal pins in my neck and a hole to breathe through, this too in my neck. Don't mention this to Elvira or to anyone else. This hole, and a tube made of either rubber or silver — I don't know yet — terrifies me. They say that I won't suffer at all and that I must do it for eight days, so that the part that has to heal will not be disturbed. Breathing the usual way would irritate it. So, I will have to breathe through the tube. My God, what a horror. I remember an uncle of Tabarracci who had to use a tube all his life. I, after eight days, will again breathe through my mouth. What a business! May God help me. It's a long treatment — six weeks — and a terrible one. However, they

assure me I will be cured. I am a bit skeptical, and my soul is ready for anything. I think of my loved ones, of poor Elvira. Since the day of my departure, my disease has worsened. I spit mouthfuls of black blood in the morning. But the doctor says that is nothing and that I must be calm because the cure has begun. We shall see, dear Angiolino.

On Saturday, November 22, Tonio sent a telegram to Magrini informing him that the surgery was to take place on Monday and asking him to come to Brussels if possible. Magrini left Viareggio at once for the Belgian capital, and he was joined there by Toscanini's wife and by Fosca; Elvira, not fully aware of the seriousness of her husband's condition, remained behind in Milan, still too weakened by her illness to undertake a long journey.

The operation, which involved surrounding the growth with seven platinum needles, lasted almost four hours, and following it the composer was in great pain. Unable to speak, he could communicate only by means of almost illegible notes which he scribbled on a pad kept on the side of his bed. At one point, he wrote, "I seem to have bayonets in my throat; they have massacred me." In spite of their patient's pain and his weakened condition, the doctors' reports were encouraging; the tumor had been destroyed, and they were certain of Puccini's eventual recovery. Tonio and Fosca, who took turns staying by his bedside day and night, were optimistic, as was Clausetti, who wrote to Adami four days after the operation:

I am writing you on my behalf as well as on the behalf of Tonio and Fosca. I can summarize all the news for you with these words: *Things are going better than anyone could have hoped. The doctors are now saying without any hesitation that Puccini will certainly be saved.*

You must understand that no doctor would dare to speak in this way unless he were absolutely certain of being right. Dr. Ledoux, moreover, is not a person given to optimism; on the contrary, he is by nature rather rigid and reserved. During the days preceding the operation, his answers to the questions asked by the directors of the Théâtre de la Monnaie were a cause for concern, but yesterday he spontaneously told them:

Puccini en sortira.

There have been no complications in the four days that have followed the operation, there is no longer any fear that they might arise. The heart is in perfect condition, and the lungs and bronchial tubes are functioning normally. Now the entire job has been assumed by the radium, which will be his miraculous salvation. We must really speak of a true and authentic miracle of science in this case, and without the valiant doctors of Brussels, our poor and illustrious friend would have had no hope of being cured.

As I write, he is sleeping quietly. At times he is a little nervous and anxious, but that almost pleases us for it demonstrates the return of his vitality.

We now have to be calm and patient, because the treatment and convalescence will undoubtedly take a very long time, but we are all happy to wait, now that his recovery is assured.

On Sunday, Dr. Ledoux will remove the needles, and thus the first—and hardest—phase of the treatment will come to an end. . . .

On the morning of November 28, Puccini's condition was so improved that his relieved family and friends allowed themselves the luxury of lunching together in a hotel near the hospital. Later that day, a telegram arrived from Elvira, expressing her joy at the good news, but at the same time, the composer suddenly took a turn for the worse. The treatment was succeeding, but the strain on his system caused his heart to weaken. The needles were immediately removed from his throat, but the damage had been done. After a night of agony, Puccini died at 11:30 on the morning of November 29, 1924. Toscanini, in Milan, was notified at once, and he rushed to the Puccini apartment on the via Verdi to break the tragic news to the griefstricken Elvira.

Little more than a month before the composer's death, the New York Times had speculated on who might be regarded as the "greatest of Europeans." Discarding Einstein, Marconi, and Curie, the newspaper concluded that "for sheer popularity combined with a high degree of merit, the most famous European today is Puccini. . . ." Appropriately, the enormously popular composer who had been for many years welcomed as a hero wherever he went, was given a hero's farewell. On the morning of December 1, crowds of mourners lined the streets of Brussels as his coffin, covered with an Italian flag and surrounded by wreaths sent by King Victor Emmanuel, the king and queen of Belgium, and other notable figures from all walks of life, was taken to the Church of Ste. Marie where a solemn service was performed. After the ceremony, the procession continued on to the Gare du Nord, where the coffin remained until evening when it was placed on a train to Italy.

On the morning of December 3, official funeral rites were observed in Milan's imposing Cathedral. Toscanini, heartbroken and near collapse, conducted the funeral march from Edgar, and, in spite of heavy rains, the route from the Cathedral to the cemetery was lined with mourners—along the way, the hearse stopped for a few moments in front of La Scala. Puccini was buried, temporarily, in the Toscanini family plot. Two years later, on November 29, 1926, the coffin was transported to Torre del Lago, where, after a simple ceremony in the village's only church, it was carried to the composer's final resting place, a small chapel in the villa that had been his home for so many years.

On April 25, 1926, *Turandot*, the opera Puccini never finished, was given its first performance at La Scala, with Toscanini conducting. Following the composer's death, Franco Alfano, a diligent if undistinguished musician, was given the task of completing the opera, based on the thirty-six pages of notes that Puccini had left behind. On the evening of the première, Toscanini stopped the performance after the death of Liù. Choked with emotion, he turned to the audience and quietly announced that it was at this point that the composer had left his opera unfinished. For a few long moments, the audience was silent. The silence was broken by a shout of "Viva Puccini" from the balcony, which was followed by one of the most moving ovations in the history of La Scala.

Puccini left no successor; his death meant the end of a glorious era of Italian opera. His music is as alive today as it was when it was first written, and his critics, who predicted that his unprecedented success was ephemeral, have been proven wrong by the immense pleasure his works have continued to give to music lovers wherever opera is heard. It would be wrong to place him among the greatest of composers, but it is also unfair to minimize his considerable gifts. Perhaps the most fitting epitaph would be the words of Ernest Newman, who wrote:

No artist, of course, ever achieves such popularity, and such enduring popularity, among art lovers of all kinds without there being excellent reasons for it. Puccini's genius is a very limited one, but he has always made the very most of it. His operas are to some extent a mere bundle of tricks: but no one else has ever performed the same tricks nearly as well.

Bibliography

Adami, Giuseppe, ed. *Giacomo Puccini: Epistolario*. Milan: Mondadori, 1928.

———. *Puccini*. Milan: Fratelli Treves, 1935.

———. *Giulio Ricordi e i suoi musicisti*. Milan: Fratelli Treves, 1933.

Aldrich, Richard. *Concert Life in New York (1902-1923)*. New York: Putnam, 1941.

Amy, Dominique. *Giacomo Puccini*. Paris: Seghers, 1970.

Ashbrook, William. *The Operas of Puccini*. New York: Oxford University Press, 1968.

Barblan, Guglielmo. *Toscanini e la Scala*. Milan: Edizioni della Scala, 1972.

Beecham, Sir Thomas. *A Mingled Chime*. London: Hutchinson, 1944.

Bonaccorsi, Alfredo. *Giacomo Puccini e i suoi antenati musicali*. Milan: Curci, 1950.

Bragaglia, Leonardo. *Personaggi ed interpreti del teatro di Puccini*. Rome: Trevi, 1977.

Brockway, Wallace, and Weinstock, Herbert. *The Opera*. New York: Simon and Schuster, 1941.

Carelli, Augusto. *Emma Carelli: Trent'anni di vita del teatro lirico*. Rome: Maglione, 1932.

Carner, Mosco. *Puccini*. London: Duckworth, 1974.

Casella, Alfredo. *I segreti della giara*. Florence: Sansoni, 1941.

Casini, Claudio. *Giacomo Puccini*. Turin: UTET, 1978.

Cortopassi, Rinaldo. *Paesaggio Pucciniano*. Pisa: Vallerini, 1926.

———. *Il dramma di Alfredo Catalani.* Florence: La Voce, 1954.

Critica Pucciniana. Lucca: Provincia di Lucca, 1976.

D'Ambra, Lucio. *Vite di musicisti italiani.* Rome: Colombo, 1940.

Damerini, A. *Amilcare Ponchielli.* Turin: Arione, 1939.

D'Amico, Fedele. *I casi della musica.* Milan: Il Saggiatore, 1962.

———, and Paumgartner, Rosanna, ed. *La Lezione di Toscanini.* Florence: Vallecchi, 1970.

Del Fiorentino, Dante. *Immortal Bohemian: An Intimate Memoir of Giacomo Puccini.* New York: Prentice-Hall, 1952.

Dry, Wakeling. *Giacomo Puccini.* London: John Lane, The Bodley Head, 1906.

Eames, Emma. *Some Memories and Reflections.* New York: Arno Press, 1977.

Eaton, Quaintance. *Opera Caravan.* New York: Farrar, Straus and Cudahy, 1957.

Fraccaroli, Arnaldo. *Celebrità e quasi.* Milan: Sonzogno, 1923.

———. *La vita di Giacomo Puccini.* Milan: Ricordi, 1925.

Forzano, Giovacchino. *Come li ho conosciuti.* Turin: ERI, 1957.

Galli, Nori Andreini. *Puccini e la sua terra.* Lucca: Maria Pacini Fazzi, 1974.

Gara, Eugenio, ed. *Carteggi Pucciniani.* Milan: Ricordi, 1958.

Gatti, Carlo. *Catalani.* Milan: Garzanti, 1953.

———. *Puccini in un gruppo di lettere inedite a un amico.* Milan: Ente Autonomo Teatro della Scala, 1944.

Gatti-Casazza, Giulio. *Memories of the Opera.* New York: Vienna House, 1973.

Gauthier, André. *Puccini.* Paris: Editions du Seuil, 1961.

Georges-Michel, Michel. *Un demi-siècle de gloires théâtrales.* Paris: André Bonne, 1950.

Giovannetti, Gustavo. *Giacomo Puccini nei ricordi di un musicista lucchese.* Lucca: Baroni, 1958.

Grout, Donald Jay. *A Short History of Opera.* New York: Columbia University Press, 1947.

Grun, Bernard. *Gold and Silver: The Life and Times of Franz Lehár.* London: W.H. Allen, 1970.

Hetherington, John. *Melba.* New York: Farrar, Straus and Giroux, 1968.

Homer, Anne. *Louise Homer and the Golden Age of Opera.* New York: William Morrow, 1974.

Homer, Sidney. *My Wife and I: The Story of Louise and Sidney Homer.* New York: Macmillan, 1939.

Hopkinson, Cecil. *Bibliography of the Works of Giacomo Puccini.* New York: Broude Brothers, 1968.

Hughes, Spike. *Famous Puccini Operas.* New York: Dover, 1972.

Jeri, Alfredo. *Mascagni*. Milan: Garzanti, 1940.

Kennedy, Michael. *Barbirolli*. London: McGibbon and Kee, 1971.

Klein, Hermann. *The Golden Age of Opera*. London: Routledge, 1933.

———. *Thirty Years of Musical Life in London, 1870–1900*. London: William Heinemann, 1903.

Kolodin, Irving. *The Metropolitan Opera, 1883–1939*. New York: Oxford University Press, 1940.

———. *The Opera Omnibus*. New York: E. P. Dutton, 1976.

Lang, Paul Henry. *Critic at the Opera*. New York: W. W. Norton, 1971.

Lauri-Volpi, Giacomo. *Voci parallele*. Milan: Garzanti, 1955.

Leibowitz, René. *Histoire de l'opéra*. Paris: Buchet-Chastel, 1957.

Lesure, François, ed. *Debussy on Music*. New York: Alfred A. Knopf, 1977.

Lockspeiser, Edward. *Debussy: His Life and Mind*. London: Cassell, 1965.

Loewenberg, Alfred. *Annals of Opera*. Totowa, New Jersey: Rowman and Littlefield, 1978.

Lombardi, Ivano. *Puccini, ancora da scoprire*. Lucca: Lucensium Civitas, 1976.

Magri, Giorgio. *Puccini e le sue rime*. Milan: Borletti, 1974.

Marabini, Claudio. *I bei giorni*. Milan: Rizzoli, 1971.

Marchetti, Arnaldo, ed. *Puccini com'era*. Milan: Curci, 1973.

Marchetti, Leopoldo, ed. *Puccini nelle immagini*. Milan: Garzanti, 1949.

Marek, George R. *Puccini: A Biography*. New York: Simon and Schuster, 1951.

———. *Toscanini*. New York: Atheneum, 1975.

Marotti, Guido, and Pagni, Ferruccio. *Giacomo Puccini Intimo*. Florence: Vallecchi, 1926.

Mascagni, Emi. *S'inginocchi la più piccina*. Milan: Fratelli Treves, 1936.

Melba, Nellie. *Melodies and Reflections*. London: Butterworth, 1925.

Monaldi, Gino. *Giacomo Puccini e la sua opera*. Rome: Mantegazza, 1924.

Monnosi, Antonio. *Puccini a tu per tu*. Pisa: Giardini, 1970.

Morini, Mario. *Pietro Mascagni*. Milan: Sonzogno, 1964.

Nardi, Piero. *Vita di Arrigo Boito*. Verona: Mondadori, 1944.

———. *Vita e tempo di Giuseppe Giacosa*. Milan: Mondadori, 1949.

Newman, Ernest. *Great Operas*. New York: Vintage Books, 1958.

Ojetti, Ugo. *Cose viste*. Milan: Fratteli Treves. 1935.

Paladini, Carlo. *Giacomo Puccini*. Florence: Vallecchi, 1961.

Panichelli, Padre. *Il "pretino" di Giacomo Puccini racconta*. Pisa: Nistri-Lischi, 1939.

Pascoli, Giovanni. *Lettere ad Alfredo Caselli*. Edited by Felice Del Beccaro. Milan: Mondadori, 1968.

———. *Lettere agli amici lucchesi*. Edited by Felice Del Beccaro. Florence: Le Monnier, 1960.

Pintorno, Giuseppe, ed. *Puccini: 276 lettere inedite.* Milan: Nuove edizioni, 1974.

Pinzauti, Leonardo. *Puccini, una vita.* Florence: Vallecchi, 1974.

Pizzetti, Ildebrando. *Musicisti contemporanei.* Milan: Treves, 1914.

Pleasants, Henry. *The Great Singers.* New York: Simon and Schuster, 1966.

Prawy, Marcel. *The Vienna Opera.* New York: Praeger, 1970.

Puccioni, Mario. *Cacce e cacciatori di Toscana.* Florence: Vallecchi, 1934.

Reich, Willi. *Schoenberg: a Critical Biography.* New York: Praeger, 1971.

Re Riccardi, Adolfo. *I segreti degli autori.* Milan: Edizioni "Corbaccio," 1928.

Respighi, Elsa. *Ottorino Respighi.* Milan: Ricordi, 1954.

Restagno, Enzo, ed. *La Fanciulla del West.* Turin: UTET, 1974.

Ricci, Luigi. *Puccini interprete di se stesso.* Milan: Ricordi, 1954.

Rosenthal, Harold. *Two Centuries of Opera at Covent Garden.* New York: Putnam, 1958.

Sacchi, Filippo. *Toscanini.* Milan: Mondadori, 1951.

Sachs, Harvey. *Toscanini.* Philadelphia and New York: J. B. Lippincott, 1978.

Sartori, Claudio. *Puccini.* 4th ed. rev. Milan: Edizioni Accademia, 1978.

———, ed. *Symposium 2,* Milan: Ricordi, 1959.

Schonberg, Harold C. *Lives of the Great Composers.* New York: W. W. Norton, 1970.

Seligman, Vincent. *Puccini Among Friends.* London: Macmillan, 1938.

Seltsam, William. *Metropolitan Opera Annals.* New York: Wilson, 1947.

Shaw, George Bernard. *Music in London, 1890-94.* Vol. III. London: Constable, 1931.

Siciliani, Enzo. *Puccini.* Milan: Rizzoli, 1976.

Simoni, Renato. *Le fantasie del nobiluomo Vidal.* Florence: Sansoni, 1953.

Slonimsky, Nicolas. *Music Since 1900.* New York: W. W. Norton, 1937.

Specht, Richard. *Giacomo Puccini: The Man, His Life, His Work.* London: J. M. Dent, 1933.

Stanislavski, Constantin, and Rumyantsev, Pavel. *Stanislavski on Opera.* New York: Theatre Arts Books, 1975.

Tarozzi, Giuseppe. *Non muore la musica.* Milan: SugarCo, 1977.

———. *Puccini: la fine del bel canto.* Milan: Bompiani, 1972.

Titone, A. *Vissi d'arte: Puccini e il disfacimento del melodramma.* Milan: Feltrinelli, 1972.

Torrefranca, Fausto. *Giacomo Puccini e l'opera internazionale.* Turin: Fratelli Bocca, 1912.

Weaver, William. *Puccini: the Man and His Music.* New York: E. P. Dutton, 1977.

Winter, William. *The Life of David Belasco.* New York: Moffat, Yard, 1918.

Author's Note

Unless otherwise noted, the letters cited at length in this biography have been drawn from the volumes included in this bibliography. The sources for these, together with the numbers of the pages on which they appear, are as follows:

Adami, Giuseppe, ed. *Giacomo Puccini: Epistolario:* 54, 230, 257, 258, 259, 262(2)

Barblan, Guglielmo. *Toscanini e la Scala:* 266(2)

Del Fiorentino, Dante. *Immortal Bohemian:* 24, 34

Fraccaroli, Arnaldo. *La vita di Giacomo Puccini:* 240, 242

Gara, Eugenio, ed. *Carteggi Pucciniani:* 25, 27, 34(1), 38, 39, 41, 57, 63, 81, 83(2), 83(3), 84, 85, 87, 88(3), 90(1), 92, 93, 95, 107, 111, 112, 117, 119, 132, 159, 181, 211, 236, 261, 262(1), 266(1), 274, 275

Marchetti, Arnaldo, ed. *Puccini com'era:* 31, 32, 143, 153, 186, 193, 197

Marek, George R. *Puccini: A Biography:* 50, 61, 82, 88(1), 88(2), 89, 91, 150, 165, 166, 198, 199, 205, 207, 218

Nardi, Piero. *Vita e tempo di Giuseppe Giacosa:* 83(1), 140

Pintorno, Giuseppe, ed. *Puccini: 276 lettere inedite:* 90(2)

Sartori, Claudio. *Puccini:* 154, 158, 160, 233

Seligman, Vincent. *Puccini Among Friends:* 183, 191, 192, 194, 196, 216, 221, 222, 234, 235, 253, 262

The letter on page 192 is from the unpublished correspondence between Puccini and Alfredo Caselli.

My wife and I are responsible for all translations in this biography, with the exception of certain letters published in the volumes by Del Fiorentino, Marek, and Seligman, for which the originals were not available.

Index

287